Dating
.com

A guide to dating
in the 21st century

Paul Fox

First paperback edition printed 2014 in the United Kingdom
Published by Chatsworth Wade Publishing
Croft House
5 Walker Street
Glossop
Derbyshire
SK13 2DH

A catalogue record for this book is available from the British Library.

ISBN: 978-0-9928152-0-2

Published by Chatsworth Wade as above.

If you would like to contact Paul please go to www.paulfoxwriter.co.uk

Printed in Great Britain and available in digital format.

Acknowledgments

I would like to thank everyone who has made this book a reality especially my partner Jo who has endured endless re-writes, tantrums (and tiaras!). I am so glad I went to Stockport.

As a narrating author I am wholly indebted to my patient scribes, Anne Wilkie, Ali Thomas Perry and Chloe Osborne and to Dinah Balsilllie for her valuable insights and corrections.

Picturesmith Photography's (www.picturesmithphotography.co.uk) David Smith has worked tirelessly (and been sorely professionally tested) in managing to take a decent photo that won't scare the horses.

A heartfelt thank you to Dean Fetzer at GunBoss Books, (www.gunboss.com) who pulled out all the stops to perform copy editing, formatting of the manuscript and preparation for printing, not to mention invaluable technical help when needed.

May I express my sincere thanks and appreciation to Tom, Emma, Becky, Helen, Sarah and Martin at Fig Creative Services Ltd, Glossop (www.figcreative.co.uk), my hardworking and talented marketing partners.

Finally, this is a work of fiction. I'm not Simon but I admit I am a huge fan of Elton John & the Eurovision Song Contest. The places are real but the people are not although everything that happens to Simon happened to somebody.

I have tried to make this a readable and entertaining fact-based account of one man's journey through todays dating landscape. I have deliberately tried not to make fun of anyone.

I hope you enjoy reading my book.

Paul Fox

Single Again

"Well I hope they get that damn lift fixed soon," said Rick grunting as he backed into the flat with the computer.

I'd managed to wedge the front door open wide enough to admit Rick and his burden, and he was right, the lift was a bind. The management company had assured me it would be repaired by Monday. It was now Friday.

Rick gently lowered the large box onto the floor of the hallway of my new flat which smelt chemically clean with fresh paint. He put his hands on his hips and straightened up.

"I'll show you around," Rick said nothing and followed me from the hallway into the lounge and kitchen area.

It was an unusual flat. The estate agent had described it as 'fashionably quirky.' The top floor of a three-storey block, it had an internal upper level and built into the eaves was a bedroom with an en suite bathroom. This small mezzanine, jutting out over the lounge and kitchen and described in the particulars as a 'minstrel gallery' was the feature that had most appealed to me. Rick was unimpressed. "Hmm," he said, "weird, like you. Where do you want the PC set up then?"

"Up there," I pointed to the mezzanine.

"Humph, how am I supposed to get up there, rope ladder?" he grumbled.

"No. There are stairs, believe it or not! Back out into the hallway I pointed to another door, behind which was the spiral stairway. I thought he might at least be impressed with that. Looking at the large box he said simply, "Well, give me a hand then."

The two of us manhandled the box up the stairs and on reaching the small landing performed a three-point soft-shoe shuffle making a right turn onto the mezzanine.

I'd already parked a new computer chair and unpacked files, books and magazines there. From the upper level, the mezzanine was beginning to look less like a stylish gallery, than an untidy wide shelf. Barry, a mutual friend had been round and assembled an IKEA desk for me. Knowing I'm useless at DIY he'd taken pity on me when he'd seen me using the boxed flat pack cardboard coffin, still sealed and containing the desk's many parts,

1

as a makeshift low level "coffee table". Rick began levering the computer tower from its collars of polystyrene packaging.

"Now can I help?" I asked enthusiastically.

"Yes," said Rick emphatically.

"Right, what needs doing?"

"Make me a cup of coffee, white with two sugars. Then go away and leave me to it."

Relieved at this sensible division of labour, I returned to the kitchen and flicked on my shiny new chrome kettle. As I waited for it to boil, I wondered how I found myself in this situation. Single after nearly 25 years. There'd been many happy times and after the first three years of marriage, Katherine and I'd shared them with our two children, Daniel and Victoria. If anyone had told me, even just a couple of years ago, that my marriage wouldn't last and I'd end up writing about dating in middle age, I wouldn't have believed them.

I was trying to keep calm and focus on the day ahead not the one after, let alone the big vacancy – the future. I felt queasy and unsettled, as if I was on the edge of a cliff in choppy crosswinds at a point of free fall. My stomach churned constantly. I couldn't see how things were going to work out. I wasn't sleeping properly, was drinking too much, eating a fair amount of rubbish and felt too distracted to get much work done. Don't get me wrong, I was the one who'd decided to leave the marriage, so I didn't deserve much sympathy and I was fortunate in having friends who were rallying round. The flat was the start of my renaissance. It marked a final step away from married life, being an in-house husband and Dad. But despite being littered with familiar stuff, the place felt alien. Living alone was proving harder than I'd imagined. I'd only been here a few days but I was aware that I was starting to panic about being alone. A single man.

As I poured coffee into two mismatched mugs, I thought about my game plan for the computer's first task. Its maiden voyage following launch would be to surf the net and find me a date. Sod the wasteland of cardboard boxes, unpacked clothes, shoes, prints, bedding, CDs/DVDs, LPs, kitchen paraphernalia. They and the outstanding work assignments could wait. I'd heard about internet dating of course - been intrigued by personal newspaper ads in the past and recently, like everyone who owns a TV, seen dating agencies advertising on TV. I'd met a few people who'd tried it. Working alone from home was going to make it tough to meet someone. Internet dating seemed an obvious means to find myself a girlfriend. At least to try meeting someone. And I so wanted to meet someone.

Struggling up the spiral staircase with two overfilled cups of coffee was a challenge and I arrived feeling a bit dizzy, breathing heavily and sloshed coffee over Rick's jeans, he yelped and swore – he knows I'm clumsy. The barely visible floor was a chaos of bubble wrap, cardboard and wires. Occasionally, Rick would look up and mutter something profane, but things were beginning to take shape and while the coffee was still hot, he pressed a button on the computer tower and the unit whirred into life.

We clinked cups, said "Cheers!" and I slapped him on the back. The contents of half-drained cup landed on his socks and seeped into his shoes.

He looked up at me ruefully and swore again. Then glancing at his watch, he gingerly placed his coffee cup on the floor, wiped his shoes with a wad of bubble wrap which was a mistake and announced, "I must get back to work," He sounded unnaturally relieved at the prospect.

"Thanks so much Rick, I'll see you tonight for fish and chips?" I was grateful for his efforts.

"Yeah, that's fine Simon."

"I really appreciate you coming over and setting the computer up. You know how hopeless I am," I offered this last observation lamely, wincing as his shoes squeaked, leaking coffee over the lobby's straw coloured carpet as he strode towards the door. 'There goes my deposit' I thought.

He looked down at his feet. Then back at me. "Simon," he said wearily from the door, "I've known you for thirty years, I should know how hopeless you are. I'll see you tonight." He raised a hand in farewell and turned towards the lift, stalled, remembered he and the lift were headed nowhere together, swore and retraced his steps leaving a confused trail of mud-brown footprints as he headed for the stairs muttering darkly once again under his breath.

Closing the front door of the flat behind him with a sigh I realised that this was finally it. I was conscious of a missed heartbeat. I had no other visits from friends offering help to look forward to. The novelty of being the "detached-friend-in-need" was over.

I'd signed the lease for twelve months; bought a flat screen television, bed linen, basic furniture and a complete set of cutlery. I'd done my first shop as a single man – food and drink for one. The fridge was satisfyingly stocked with pomegranate juice; wine, designer beer, tiny pork pies, cheddar crackers, "squirty" cheese in a tube. I'd supplemented these essentials with half a dozen M&S ready meals. Having an ambiguous relationship with vegetables – I'd bought an avocado, a lime and some tomatoes. The freezer section had a single drawer, occupied by a pack of twelve fish fingers and a tub of Ben & Jerry's Ice Cream. Frozen anti-depressants!

I was on my own. The silence was deafening. I switched on the television, a habit I'd got into in just three days of occupying the flat. It occurred to me I could now get ill and possibly even die alone; that none of my movements, thoughts, worries or feelings, let alone my health mattered to anyone that mattered to me now – at least to a wife, lover, girlfriend or partner. I checked myself. I was being pathetic. I still had my wonderful if semi-detached family and I had my friends.

Seated, I typed "dating" into Google. A quick click on different sites revealed that the process of simply registering was going to take ages. Was this such a good idea? I was separated but still married. Katherine and I had the painful financial bit to do yet and here I was, poised to seek another possibly meaningful relationship. Maybe I should be Googling "psychiatrist" or "shrink" instead of "dating".

There were a bewildering number of sites. Where should I begin? I spent half an hour touring for suitable looking dating options but then felt light headed. I was famished. It was nearly 6pm and I hadn't eaten since breakfast. I decided to postpone research until after I'd eaten fish and chips with the boys. I checked my emails, sent a few, moved a couple of boxes around and cleared the space about the desk in preparation for settling down to some serious "work" later.

At 6.30pm I changed into my fish and chip shop outfit, jeans and a rugby shirt. As I walked the short distance from the flat across the car park and into the precinct to meet Rick and Barry, I reflected on my friends and how glad I was to have them around, especially now. I had known Rick and Barry for years. Rick was right – it probably was as many as thirty.

We were close, though I couldn't fathom why really. Rick and I have little in common. He likes football, I loathe it. I like Elton John, he likes Status Quo. I like shopping, vintage TV and the Eurovision Song contest, Rick shops for clothes once a decade (whether he needs them or not) loathes retro repeats on TV – he thinks he should get a rebate on his licence fee for these.

He finds Eurovision a sad joke. And Barry? Barry is everything I'm not. His is the "voice of reason". Calm, considered, sensible and unfailingly dependable, with a laconic sense of humour. Though we don't share temperaments we do share a passion for motorbikes. And as a touring bike, I particularly admired his latest acquisition, a Honda Goldwing.

The three of us were seated in what has to be one of the best fish and chip shops in England, the FishnChickn. It might sound unpromising and it's one of a chain but trust me, the food's great. It serves consistently fabulous fresh tasting fish and their meat and chicken pies are good too according to Rick and Barry who know about these things. The restaurant near the flat is a local treasure. It's a pleasant place, spotlessly clean and the staff are friendly and efficient. They've put up with me, Barry and Rick for years, yet somehow they still manage to be patient, professional and enjoy a joke.

The conversation got round to how I was spending my time and the boys asked whether I'd managed to get a date yet. Rick had told Barry I was going internet dating and he knew the PC was installed. The boys were sceptical about my plans. They'd already told me not to rush into another relationship, to take time to settle into my new life and be cautious. They also knew that I was keen to prove to them that I wasn't going to be single for long and they'd made it plain that if I had to get involved with someone to make it casual, approach some suitably attractive lady at the gym I was a member of, at my agent's office or perhaps a motor industry launch.

I am a freelance journalist and work from home writing articles for motor magazines and industry clients. I've an agent in London but it's not an office environment I spend time in. I only drift up occasionally, usually when a problem needs sorting out. I was hoping that finding a date wouldn't be too difficult.

I was quietly confident. Although the wrong side of 45 I was buoyed up by the fact that statistically there are a lot of 40-something plus single women – substantially more than men. Something to do with the post-war birth rate and male mortality.

Though not nearly as fit as I used to be, despite having joined a gym, friends still said that I scrubbed up well. I still had my own hair – unlike Elton John, though mine was greying fast and, whilst I didn't have Elton's bank balance, I wasn't that badly off. I was worried about the future of my finances but James, my solicitor, had explained that the divorce shouldn't be devastating financially. Barry was speaking. I really should listen to his voice of reason more often.

"So, how are you getting on then Simon, settling into the flat okay?" he said conversationally.

"Yes, thanks to you and to Rick who installed the computer earlier. I've filled the fridge and worked out how to use the washing machine."

At home I liked ironing. Katherine sorted out the washing and I did the ironing. It worked well. Well, it worked till she developed a passion for pleated skirts and the kids wore eye-wateringly expensive T shirts with logos that melted and ruined my Trusty Tefal, not to mention my bank balance as I replaced their imaginatively priced cotton t-shirts with trendy labelled gear from shops aimed at teenagers with trust monies or loaded indulgent parents.

"My life's still mainly in boxes, but they can wait. All I really need to do is find a girlfriend."

"You've plenty of time to do that," Barry and Rick spoke in perfect unison. It was as if they'd rehearsed this response, which looking back, I think they probably had.

The conversation ambled along a familiar path, from the present and an exchange of news and gossip into our inglorious past, the usual subjects – motorbikes and cars, what rubbish music there was round was around at the moment and why I (still) liked Elton John, how badly the country was being run… They're the same topics of conversation that date back to 1971 only with name and model changes. My fondness for Elton John (musically speaking) has been a constant source of amusement to the boys who take indecent pleasure in baiting me about his music on the thinnest of pretexts.

As we've grown older I recognise that they've come to appreciate Elton's genius too though they have to pretend not to. I pretend I don't know this and the game goes on. It's hard to believe that when we first discussed politics as teenagers Ted Heath was Prime Minister. We thought he was rubbish. Kenny Everett presented programmes on Radio 1 and John Peel's "Top Gear" slot (nothing to do with motors) was a fixture. We sat glued to *Top of The Pops* at 7.30pm on a Thursday and in those innocent days we just thought Jimmy Saville was odd. Rick and I wore loons, Barry was welded to his transistor radio listening to *Sports Report* and I raved to anyone who'd listen about Marc Bolan's single 'Get it On' and his appearance on *Top of The Pops* with Elton guesting on piano.

We each rode motorbikes. As for looks - even back then I used to worry about my dress sense. At least, I was 6-foot tall thanks to my platform shoes (I hope they come back into fashion). The seventies is often quoted as the decade that time forgot but I retain a secret longing to wear my crushed velvet bell bottom trousers in public again. I'd have to breathe in hard to do them up. Even back in the seventies Barry was the sensible one. He was the first of the three of us to be married – and stay married, the first of us to buy a house and still is the only one of the three of us to still regularly ride a motorbike. Rick on the other hand had been married twice. His marriage failures were a mystery. We didn't ask for details about them and he'd never discussed the problems he'd encountered. Whatever they were, he was on good terms with both his exes and seemed genuinely contented on his own. There was an unspoken acceptance that whilst I needed someone, he didn't. As the conversation continued, my mind began wander. Rick and Barry's mouths were moving, but I wasn't listening; I was musing over the websites I'd uncovered earlier. I so wanted a companion. I felt dislocated living alone and though it had only been days since I'd truly been on my own, the reality was of course that Katherine and I had spent many months being "alone" and lonely together. I wanted someone to talk to, eat and sleep with, take to the theatre or cinema, stay in and watch TV and DVDs with, shop, text, treat, simply be with. It was clearly possible. The scant time I'd spent checking the internet that afternoon confirmed this.

For in that brief thirty or so minutes, I'd discovered dating and introduction sites not only in the UK but originating from a host of nations. Recklessly pursuing a pop-up on screen I'd found myself on a Russian dating site. One of many sites from the former Soviet Union it turned out.

Why are Russian brides so popular? If you don't believe me, type "Russian dating" into Google; it seems being a mail order bride in Russia is a career choice. I'm neither exaggerating, being disparaging or unkind.

There is a vast singles industry in Russia devoted to seeking not just friendship "with a view to..." but openly and expressly, marital relations with European men. There are a considerable number of Russian dating tours organised by UK based associates of these sites.

'Imagine the horror of it,' I thought. Planeloads of men arriving in Vladivostok taken by coach on dedicated organised tours to find marriageable Russian girls. Imagine the pressure?

It didn't appeal so I didn't register, but just browsing on these sites I found myself inundated with virus threatening pop-ups and requests for my email address. Not just from girls or sites in Russia, but from single girls seeking partners in Latin America, Eastern Europe, Asia and India. And of course amongst the pop-ups, there were lots of girls wanting sex "in your area tonight".

Rick and Barry were now hotly debating the merits of the Ram Air Suzuki 250 and comparing it with the Yamaha RD250. I drifted back to Russian dating. The choice is very comprehensive. Do you want your new Russian mail order bride to be 41 or 42 and a half? Do you want her to have previously been married? With or without children? What size would you like her to be? English size eight, ten, twelve, fourteen, sixteen or larger, curvy, boy shaped, size zero? Would you like her hair to be short or longer? The variety and combination of 'options' was bewildering and it's difficult to believe that any man would have such specific requirements of a new partner. Maybe other men are fussier than me.

I became aware of Rick pointing a chip at me from the end of his fork. "You had a coffin tanked Yamaha didn't you?" he said.

"What?" I said. "Um, yes, what?"

"You weren't listening to what we were saying were you?" he pointed out unnecessarily.

"Err, yes I was," I said in a high-pitched voice.

"I know what this is about," said Rick, "you want to get back to the flat as quick as you can so you can sign up on some dodgy internet dating site."

"That is just not true!" I said, the pitch of my voice rising to soprano. Even I thought I sounded like Robin Gibb used to. They knew I did.

"Well, it is, isn't it? You can't wait to get back there and click away with your credit card so you can tell us next week you've got a date," Barry was nodding and looking mock stern.

"Well, I'm shocked!" I protested. I heard myself and knew I sounded utterly unconvincing. "Nothing was further from my mind. I'm just here enjoying fish and chips with my two oldest friends and err… " the squeak in my voice was extinguished as I ran out of words.

"And what?" demanded Rick.

"And, well… " Barry came to my aid.

"Shall we get the bill?

I'd forgotten that trying to lie to my friends or anyone else for that matter was very difficult. For a reason I can't fathom, my voice climbs an octave or two when I do. The bigger the lie, the higher the pitch. Everybody notices it.

I was once in the Royal Air Force. I wasn't a pilot and worked mostly in PR, education and recruit training. There was a surveillance unit and I was keen to pursue this briefly during my career in the force. I think they must have realised that training me to me be a spy or for combat would be pointless because if I fell into enemy hands it wouldn't take long before any inquisitors worked out how to crack my defences. Ask a question: wait for the shrill piping reply. Result. When it comes to parting we always follow the same ritual. Goodbyes are accompanied by handshakes and backslapping.

"Thanks for sorting the computer out Rick, I really appreciate it." Slap on the back.

"Barry, great to see you," said Rick to Barry as he climbed onto his gleaming Goldwing. "Goodbye."

"Mind how you go on the bike," I said, shaking his leather-gloved hand.

"Will do mate," he replied as he pulled on his crash helmet. "Mind how you go on those dating sites, won't you?" He twisted the accelerator and disappeared from sight leaving Rick to walk to his car and me with a short walk back to the flat, determined to more than just browse. I was going to do some proper research, perhaps register with an agency. I was eager to make progress.

I bounded up the spiral staircase and switched on the computer. The mezzanine was still a mess and I embarked on a quick sweep. A lot of the boxes nearby contained books and I began to empty them and stack these neatly on the shelves above my desk. By chance, the first box I started to unpack contained *Memoirs of a Geisha* and the sequels I'd read a few years ago. You may have read the books and seen the film made of the first in the series. Quite why I'd found the notion of geishas so fascinating, I don't know. Reading the books had sparked an interest I still have. I am by nature a bit of a romantic I suppose and whilst I'd enjoyed the plots of the books, I'd found the descriptions of Japanese culture and traditions fascinating. Japan is a truly foreign land and I was profoundly captivated by the idea of geishas. If an inhabitant of Mars arrived here, I reckon I'd have more in common with the alien than I would a geisha. So why the attraction? I filled the bookshelf and sat down and typed into Google, "Japanese Dating."

Looking back I don't know why I did this rather than search at the outset for a site with a local postcode of opportunities. The screen was filled with a list of Japanese dating sites. I clicked on the first, "Japanese Destiny." A form appeared on the screen which I filled in. This was seeking basic information, my name and email address. Then I clicked "send". A message arrived, almost instantaneously explaining that I should complete a detailed profile. After this there would be a telephone interview at a convenient time and I was invited to indicate three time slots for this.

I later came to appreciate that this was an entirely appropriate way for a well organised and professionally managed dating agency to operate. If you register with a site or agency and give personal details, including possibly information about your occupation, earnings or income, there should be scope for a decent dating agency to ascertain if you are who you say you are, and that your age, profession, status and arguably other details provided upon request are accurate. At the very least there should be some basic checks. Of course such scrutiny should apply equally stringently to women as well as men seeking introductions. On my initial excursion into the Oriental site however, none of this entered my head. I thought if I joined and applied, paid the registration fee and was patient, then a geisha living in Essex would simply arrive. Yes, I live in Essex. I am "neo-trendy" according to my kids. I worked on the lengthy form to complete my profile and sent it.

I had by now embarked on an illusionary exotic frolic: I could take my Geisha out – down the fish and chip shop with the guys, with all her gear on. She could do the Tea Ceremony; play the guitar thing that sounded like a cat being strangled, I could gaze at her – it would make evenings at the gym so much more interesting if she accompanied me there. The guys would make puerile jokes about her "Nipponing" in, my "having a yen for her", etc. It would be just like the book – well not quite like the book.

But wouldn't it be great? I could say things like, "Have you met my Japanese girlfriend?" I could enjoy sushi, homemade perhaps, go on holiday, even ski in Japan, and perhaps get a discount on a Toyota.

"Candice" from Japanese Destiny was scheduled to call me the next day at 10.30am. She was from the agency's London office and I had received a pleasant email from her introducing herself. She'd written that she was confident that there were lots of Japanese women who were living in the UK who would want to meet me. Sure enough at exactly 10.30am whilst I was staring at the phone (which tragically I had begun to do), it rang.

"Can I speak to Simon?" said a clipped American accent.

"Speaking."

"Hi, it's Candice from *Japanese Destiny* I would just like to run through some of the details you have supplied in your email and completed questionnaire." Candice had a sing-song cadence to her voice. It rose at the end of each sentence as though she was asking a question. In fact it became quickly apparent that Candice was always asking a question.

"Well, shuuurre," I replied instinctively reflecting her American accent then feeling ridiculous and checking myself. "Well yes of course, sure, well yes." I knew I sounded flustered. I was. Candice on the other hand sounded coolly professional, not unfriendly but confident and forthright.

"Can you state your full name, address and tell me how long have you lived at your address?" I took a deep breath.

"Simon... Leonard... Taylor. I concentrated hard to recall my new address and post code. Pause. Then, in response to her query regarding my occupation of the apartment.

"A week." The truth – three days didn't seem appropriate somehow.

"A week?" she said. "Is that ALL?" I mumbled something about moving out of the marital home.

"So you're not actually divorced as you said in your email?"

"Err... no, I am not actually divorced, but I will be."

"Hmmm," I sensed concern in Candice's sharpening tone. "So when will you actually be divorced?" she asked, rather curtly, I felt.

The conversation toed and fro'd on this point. Why was this so important? I was single and living alone. I was separated from my wife and divorce proceedings were under way. What more did she want? A letter from my solicitor? I could envisage Candice putting a red line under "divorce" and adding in red pen, and capitals, "Only in his present accommodation one week!" I could tell she was unimpressed.

"Well Simon, tell me a little about yourself." Candice had recovered herself.

I took a deep breath. "I'm a writer

"Oh," said Candice. "Have I read anything of yours?

"Probably not," I conceded.

"Well… " I hesitated, "not yet."

I laughed, nervously, going on to explain the nature of my writing. That it was commercial. She might conceivably have read my last article in the latest edition of Alfa Romeo magazine but it seemed unlikely. Candice didn't laugh or pass any comment. She asked more questions. After a while I began to tire of the volley of enquiries. They began to feel intrusive. She wanted to know precisely what my gross annual income was, whether I was a standard or higher rate tax payer, about capital and shares, pension provision, debts, what car I drove, if I owned it outright or whether it was on contract or hire purchase, my children, my parents and their home, how I spent my leisure time. The emphasis was unashamedly on net worth. But it was her final interrogatory, about leisure pursuits, which was of more obvious relevance surely than material assets that really bothered me. What was I to answer? I didn't think my current habits of hanging out with the guys, eating fish and chips, arguing about music and drifting down to the gym sounded that impressive. So, I launched into a monologue about theatre-going in the West

End, enjoying live music, reading, travelling, keeping fit and socializing. It wasn't actually a series of lies, I told myself, because under "normal" circumstances and in a happily functioning relationship, this would have been more or less a true account of an achievable and desirable shared itinerary. It definitely sounded more acceptable than the present extent of my more mundane "leisure" pursuits. I must have cleared that hurdle as Candice moved on, without comment and spat out her next question.

"As you know Simon, we are an agency for gentlemen wishing to meet Japanese ladies, Japanese professional ladies. Can I ask why you want to meet a Japanese lady?" The question hovered in the air. Then the air became increasingly leaden with the weight of it as I realised I didn't actually have an answer. Not one that would satisfy Candice anyhow.

"Simon. Are you still there?" I was staring into space, then turned to gaze helplessly at the collection of Geisha novels gracing the bookshelf. It was these that had triggered my Japanese dating enquiry in the first place. There was complete silence.

"Have you ever been to Japan?" she asked eventually.

"Err... no," I answered

"Well, what is it that you want from us?" I launched into a banal, semi-joking slightly hysterical discourse about Japanese women and how much I'd enjoyed reading *Memoirs of a Geisha* and the remaining books in the series. How the culture fascinated me. Surely, wanting to meet a Japanese woman was enough to register? Apparently not – Candice was clearly less than satisfied now. Indeed she was struggling to remain civil. "Do you actually know anything about Japanese culture Simon?" she asked frostily.

I thought about repeating that I had read all the books. In truth, what did I actually know about Japanese culture? The clichés obviously. The eating of raw fish, fat blokes wearing tea towels fighting in a ring and a manufacturing industry producing fantastically reliable but incredibly dull cars and the tradition of geishas. There is evidently a vast amount to the culture of this strange land but seriously, Candice, what more would a genuinely open minded, financially secure, sane, single British guy of good character need to know about the country and its traditions to qualify for a date? (Don't write in.) I am still fascinated by Japan and would love to visit, experience for myself its other-worldliness and find out what all the fuss is about. As I grow older, I find I am even beginning to like the cars! Before I knew it Candice was making her excuses. Not very good ones.

She ended with: "Well Simon, I will see if anyone here on our books might meet your specific requirements."

'Strange,' I thought. I hadn't mentioned any requirements, though perhaps she simply meant someone female, agreeable and Japanese who I could take to the gym and fish and chip shop. She never called back. I wondered if any man in the UK had ever met a Japanese lady through Candice and her steely gatekeeping. If you have, please do let me know and both of you can educate me about Japan.

Bruised by my admittedly inane foray into the foothills of Japanese dating and with Candice's interrogation still ringing in my ears, I decided to opt for something safer that I already knew a little about. *Friends Reunited* has been a phenomenally successful internet networking site, so I decided to sign up to their dedicated internet dating forum. I had registered on *Friends Reunited* years before, traced and been in touch with some old friends from school and College and even tried to contact my first ever "girlfriend" Georgina Grey, from our Primary School days.

I don't know if I was unusual, being impressed with a member of the opposite sex at such a young age. We had been together on our first school trip abroad, to Ostend in Belgium. My newly purchased junior Kodak camera had filled up with photos of the lovely Georgina Grey and I remember worrying on the way home about how I was going to explain the absence of any photos of Belgium when they were processed.

I can also recall working on our first project together. We had been given the task of making a papier-mâché model of the soon-to-be invested Prince of Wales.

As we prepared our model, our teacher, who discomfortingly had gone to school with my mother and who, whenever I erred gave me a warning "I will of course tell your mother" look, decided that our Prince Charles did not look quite, well, manly enough.

The pink paint we'd used for his face made him blush too rosily and his chin was smooth and bore no hair. Our teacher was critical. So Georgina and I were given the task of "sexing up" Prince Charles. We mixed together brown and white paint, dotting stubble on his chin and upper lip. I thought it was too much and turning to Georgina, said, "Doesn't he look a bit too hairy now?"

She said something then that has always stayed with me. "He looks like a beast. My mother says all men are beasts."

I didn't know what to say. We were only very young. It was long before the days of early years sex education, but I wondered what had prompted her mother to give her such dreadful advice. What had happened to her? Would I become a beast? I hoped not.

As Georgina has never replied to my request on Friends Reunited, I still don't know. I wanted to know what had happened to her. Does she believe, like her mother that all men are beasts? Our relationship as kids took place long before the days of the internet. I am sure there was a tale to tell. I shall probably never know.

Whilst reflecting on Georgina, I had managed to log onto the "Friends Reunited" site. The first thing to do was to provide basic information. I recalled this from the Japanese site and busily worked away. Then came the difficult part. What to say about myself. I was stumped.

I may be a writer by trade but I write about cars for a living. What should I write? I had a go at drafting an introduction. "Forty-seven year old divorced writer seeks girlfriend urgently."

I re-read it and knew I couldn't submit it. Whilst technically accurate, it was boring, worse – it was desperate! I tried once more... "Hello girls, thanks for stopping by my site, I am Simon, divorced, living in Essex. If you would like to meet up please send me a message." On reflection I couldn't have that either. It sounded lame, pervy – even more desperate. The cursor on the computer was blinking rapidly, as if it was laughing at me. 'No,' I thought, 'no sane woman's going to reply to that and anyway, who says "Hello girls" anymore?' Bruce Forsyth?

I finally settled on, "Hello, I am Simon. I am a divorced writer in my late forties living in rural Essex. My interests are cars, going to the gym, reading, travel and going to the theatre. If you would like to know more, please contact me."

I knew it was dull but by this stage I was losing the will to live an internet life. At least I felt comfortable with it. Then the site asked for a photo.

A quick trawl of my database photos transferred from the family Boxdrop album contained nothing acceptable There were plenty of me and the children of course; one of me on a coach going to France. Drunk on a coach going to France! Definitely not. Another of me in a dinner suit, looking like a waiter – nothing wrong with that if I found a woman fancying going out with a waiter. Some showing me twenty, fifteen, even ten years ago, but I wasn't that man any more. Few if any of the photos I had custody of were recent and there wasn't a single one that I thought I looked good or even okay in.

I needed a new photo. After all, the site repeatedly advised that I should upload "an up to date" photo. It was nearly midnight and I decided to get some sleep and sort in out in the morning by asking Rick to help.

I called him early. "Rick, where are you?"

"I've just finished seeing a customer in Town, why?"

"I need a photo."

"Of what?" said Rick.

"Me."

"Well, I haven't got any."

"I know that. I want you to come round and take a photo of me."

"What, so you can go internet dating?"

"No," I piped "I need to renew my passport."

"So, you just need to go in one of those booth things."

Damn, I hadn't thought of that. I really must get better at lying.

"Yes but I haven't really got the time, so could you pop in and take a quick photo and upload it to my computer?"

"Are you going internet dating?"

"No." I focused intently on lowering my voice. I took a long breath, lengthened my neck and dropped my shoulders.

"Are you going internet dating?" repeated Rick. Louder this time and more insistently.

"No," voice rising...

"I'm on my way," said Rick, "but you are going internet dating aren't you?"

"Yes, okay!" I yelled, angry now. "I'm going internet dating and I need an up to date photo. Happy now?"

Ten minutes later the buzzer went on the intercom. It was Rick. "Your photographer, sir."

"Come up please." I gave a long push on the release button and seconds later heard the recently repaired lift clanking away. Then it stopped. Then it started. Bloody lift. I put the kettle on, but Rick, who'd been stuck in the temperamental lift for several minutes was wheezing, in a bad mood and anxious to get the job done and get going. He snapped a couple of portrait shots on his smart phone, emailed them to me and made a sharp exit heading for the stairs.

"See you Friday," he said. I started to explain that I was really only just looking at internet dating; I didn't have definite plans to take it further. I was conscious my voice sounded thin, rising as it trailed away.

"Yeah, right," said Rick smirking. "See you Friday."

I uploaded a photo that didn't make me look too bad, input my credit card details and got an email back immediately to say that my application was being approved by the site administrator and I would be emailed once I was ready to go live on the site. How long would this take I wondered?

From my Japanese agency cross-examination I assumed that there was an army of staff policing applications, performing credit card and security checks, disclosure and debarring service checks, checks that I was divorced, really me, etc.

Surely it couldn't be this easy to sign up? An email came back more or less instantly however and welcomed me to the *Friends Reunited* dating site, as "approved".

Not wishing to be too eager but conscious that I had to have something positive to tell the guys on Friday and to demonstrate some small measure of success, I logged on. Seconds later the screen was filled with dozens of forty-something women living within a twenty mile radius of my home. I couldn't believe there was so many, nor so many living near me. Divorce isn't exactly exclusive but I was stunned at the opportunities the site opened up.

I quickly scanned through the photos. Now I know that you're not supposed to do this immediately or probably at all if exercising good manners, before considering individual profile narratives, but I did. I came across a photo of an attractive fair-haired woman. To my delight I found she lived near Chelmsford. The photograph was indistinct and not particularly large. About twice the size of postage stamp and I couldn't make it expand. There were another two photographs but in being uploaded their quality had been affected. They were black and white images which I know are considered fashionable currently, but they were rather blurred. She was good looking though. Large dark eyes and a full mouth. She had a lovely smile. She seemed suitable: the right age, 45 years old, "sociable", evidently attractive, local, similar interests. I decided to send her a message. What to say? "Hello, I live near you, do you fancy a date?" (Too direct). "Hello, I am Simon, I live near you." (She'd know that from the site). I didn't know what to say – everything seemed hackneyed, boring or a bit desperate.

I finally settled on, "Hello, I am Simon and I'm new to this site. As you can see, I live nearby. You seem very nice"

"Nice"! Christ, every English teacher who'd ever taught me would be disgusted at the use of such a lazy, lard-like word! It's the first thing I ever learned about writing stories as a kid. "Nice" is a nasty word.

But I was tired, was lost for a more imaginative adjective and couldn't improve on it. It did sound banal though. I decided I should change it – damn, too late… there, I'd done it, pressed "send". Not only had I signed up to an internet dating site, but I had found someone and sent her a message.

Not a classic, but it was sent. I'd have to polish my introductions. The boys at the fish and chip shop and indeed the staff too (fully aware of my plight thanks to the boys) would be agog at my success and tenacity.

An email arrived directly. "You have email" drawled Joanna Lumley. Sultry spoken Joanna is programmed to announce mail on my server. I love living with her. Heart pounding, I opened the message "Hello Simon, this is Stephanie. Thank you very much for your message. I see that you are new to the site, tell me a bit about yourself."

I couldn't believe my luck. I wrote back telling her about being separated, getting divorced, moving into the flat, getting my life back on track. An honest and detailed account tumbling over the keys. Her replies to my emails winged back thick and fast; back and forth we went, a dancing dialogue to the beat of tapping keys. I was thrilled at the simplicity of it and how easily the conversation flowed. We seemed well suited as correspondents; our emails were seamless and interesting. She seemed ideal.

'How easy is this?' I thought.

That Friday, as the boys gathered at the fish and chip shop and we had the usual crass jokes with our usual tolerant waitress about large portions etc. I was feeling quietly smug.

"Well Simon," said Rick, nudging Barry. "Did you get your passport then?"

I gave him a withering look, and then smiled broadly – I just couldn't help it.

"Actually," I said, trying to sound casual, dramatic pause for maximum effect. "I have a date!" And I had. I'd plucked up courage and asked Stephanie for a date. She had said "Yes" immediately. How cool was that? Neither of them believed me.

"Yes I have, I have a date. We've exchanged a lot of emails. I've even spoken to her to arrange the date."

"Who is she?" said Rick suspiciously.

"Well, she is a real girl, lives along the road and I am meeting her tomorrow evening at the "Riverside Restaurant.""

Barry piped up, "What do you know about her?"

"She is in administration."

"What does she look like?" said Rick.

"Very nice," I said.

"Is she blonde, brunette, ginger?" I didn't actually know this but my impression was that she was fair. Probably ash blonde.

"I don't really know for certain, but she is attractive," I offered.

I was bombarded with questions. Was she short? Tall? Fat? Thin? Divorced? With kids? Without?

I began to feel increasingly under siege and flat. I thought I'd done okay, had mastered the information superhighway and organised a date with a lady who seemed compatible for the following night. I felt certain it was going to be a lovely occasion and I couldn't wait to arrive at the restaurant to meet her. The boys' reactions however left me feeling deflated. I rallied, lifted my shoulders and raised my head. I wasn't going to let them spoil things.

Saturday morning arrived. I felt excited. I had a date! Then I began to panic. What should I wear? Should I wear a tie, or no tie, suit, blazer? What do you wear on a first date with someone from the internet? The last time I had been on a first date was in 1978. Even if I found my crushed velvet flairs and platform shoes I wouldn't get into them. I decided to do what I habitually do in this situation. Get everything out of my wardrobe, put on an Elton John CD and try things on. Not all at once of course. I could go for a retro James Dean look – white T-shirt, jeans, leather jacket. Then I remembered that the Riverside had a dress code so that made things easier.

Late that afternoon, having done some work and several loads of washing, I showered and shaved. Another dilemma – what aftershave to wear? I might wear something she didn't like and aftershave that repelled. I decided to get some advice – after all, lots of my friends were married to girls – I'd phone them. I rang and texted a couple of friends, Jen and Karen. I think I really just wanted to talk about my date but it was a good excuse to catch up with them. I did ask about dress and aftershave though.

Their advice was unanimous. Wear what you feel comfortable in; be yourself; use your favourite aftershave. I finally settled on a navy blue suit, white shirt with double cuffs, silver cufflinks and my favourite navy and grey Gucci tie. I splashed on some classic Chanel aftershave. I'd had the car washed specially and as I drove to the Riverside my heart and spirits were soaring. It was going to be a wonderful evening. A text from Stephanie confirmed this.

"Hello Simon," it said, "I am very much looking forward to a lovely evening and meeting you in the foyer of the Riverside. Stephanie x." I fired one back, "So looking forward to meeting you. Already on my way, Simon xx."

I parked at the Riverside, a restaurant I had been to on a number of other occasions with business associates at lunchtime for meetings. It was conspicuously different this evening. There were candles on the tables and softer lighting, the staff were dressed more formally and in place of wooden testers, there were crisp white tablecloths. In all, a more intimate atmosphere. I hung about in the foyer trying not to look obvious though since the staff all knew me, trying to appear inconspicuous was pointless.

"Hello Simon," said Madeleine at reception. "Don't normally see you in the evening."

"I am on a date," I said lightly.

"How lovely, we shall make sure we find you an extra special table," she said, touching my arm affectionately. "Good luck, I hope it goes well."

"Thank you so much."

Clive, a pleasant waiter I knew came over to greet me. "Hello Simon, I saw your reservation." Clive's one of those discreet servers who know what diners want, when they want it and doesn't bother them in between times. I was glad he was working that evening.

"I'm on a date," I volunteered.

"That's marvellous. I'll do all I can to make sure you have a memorable evening."

She was late: it was now 7.35pm. I drifted into the restaurant then back to the foyer. I was going to send her a text. Perhaps she was lost, had had an accident, or had decided not to come after all? As I was reaching for my phone I became aware of a figure approaching me. Out of the gloom of the car park, the figure came and stood in front of me. It was a lady with honey blonde hair, heavily made up and wearing rimless spectacles. These magnified her eyes which were outlined with black eyeliner and dark eye shadow.

"Excuse me," she said.

I thought she wanted to know the time. Then I thought she had perhaps mistaken me for the Maitre'D. I thought her husband was probably parking the car. To be honest, I was rather irritated at the distraction as I was in the process of composing a text to Stephanie. I checked myself; I was being thoughtless and rude.

"Yes," I said. "I am sorry, can I help?" Her face lit up. She smiled at me. "I think you can," She had obviously mistaken me for staff.

"I'm sorry," I said, "I don't work here, I am actually on a date."

"I am sure you are," she said. "You are Simon aren't you?"

She knew my name? How?

It was one of those moments when the world goes wobbly, shaking on its axis as if its molten stomach is churning. Who was this lady and how did she know my name? Perhaps she was Stephanie's Mum? With a message for me?

"Yes, I am Simon," I stuttered, "Who are you?" She laughed.

"I am Stephanie," she spoke, in a broad Cockney accent. If this were a cartoon film, my jaw would have dropped to the floor. Stephanie had to be in her mid to late 60s!

I think I may actually have gaped at her – I recall being stunned. How could this be Stephanie? Neither of us spoke. I attempted to, but nothing came out. I wanted to say "But you were lovely – you are not in your mid 40s!" But I didn't.

Though every fibre of my being was inclined to tell her the truth, this being "You are clearly not the lady in the photos; possibly the black and white, but that must have been taken in the 1970s and you have deceived me!" I realised that to do this would have been cruel and unnecessary. There was a fleeting moment when I could see fear in her eyes; she was afraid I might say something rude or hurtful. Several anxious seconds ticked by and I knew that I was going to have to say something.

"Shall we go in to dinner?"

As I drove home that night I was trying to feel cross and injured – the one cheated.

But what had really happened? In truth, I'd enjoyed a pleasant evening, though not the one I had anticipated. Stephanie was intelligent, warm and witty. She told me about her abusive marriage and how she had plucked up the courage to leave her husband, she spoke of her children, friends and of her determination to meet a suitable man. She spent a lot of time on dating sites and had spent money she could ill-afford on agency subscriptions.

She had a stock of stories to tell about her encounters as a result of this. Some funny, others not. She had clearly once been very attractive and was still good looking. A well preserved 67 year old she told me candidly that she lied about her age to meet men. She explained that when she had first begun seeking to meet men on the internet and given her true age, she'd had no success at all. Men in their 60s and 70s she'd identified as potential companions were seeking to meet women in their 40s and 50s and wouldn't consider her. She had resorted to lying about her age and apologised for the deception.

The awkwardness returned as we said goodbye in the car park. I said something deliberately formal like, "Thank you for a lovely evening," intending to signal that we would not be meeting again and then there was a pause, silence. She lifted a finger to my lips and said sweetly

"I know we won't see one another again but thank you for a wonderful evening." She kissed me on the cheek and was gone. I realised that her response might mean she hadn't actually found me appealing; it could have been a genuinely mutual decision and I was humbled. Perhaps I was too old or boring for Stephanie! I didn't think this was the position but who knows?

My first internet date hadn't met my expectations and I knew the boys would treat it as having ended in embarrassment and failure. What should I tell them next Friday at the fishnChickn? Feeling frustrated and mildly aggrieved, I cranked up Elton on the CD player; his voice filled the car "It's a little bit funny..."

'Too right,' I thought, 'The soundtrack to my life!'

Coffee & Cake

Life had developed a new pace and there was a fresh order to things. I went to bed alone and woke up alone. The marital/family hustle of getting children to school and college was a ritual I missed. Sharing a home with other human beings was another routinely comfortable habit I missed. The flat was so quiet. When I awoke now I'd immediately switch on the computer, drift downstairs and put the TV on. I was developing an addiction to breakfast TV. I don't know what it was about it but I felt compelled to watch it – channel surfing between BBC1, ITV and Sky News. I normally ended up watching the channel whose presenters had the longest legs and shortest skirts whilst drinking a cup of tea before getting washed and dressed. My habit of leaving the TV on low as background "white noise" whilst I was in the flat and working felt comforting. I felt less alone somehow.

As I was watching breakfast TV one morning, I heard the computer firing up on the upper level. It was Joanna announcing in her seductive low drawl. "You have email."

Subscribers to the dating site I'd joined receive an email when anyone seeking contact sent a message. This saves logging onto the site separately. "Jane" had sent me an email.

I was delighted and opened it with anticipation.

"Hello Simon, I read your profile and you sound very interesting. Please tell me more about yourself, best wishes, Jane," and a kiss! A photo (colour, recent?) Of a sweet faced blonde 40-someone.

I replied immediately of course. "Thanks Jane for your email…" I rattled off something hasty about being separated, divorcing, 47 years old, a writer, basic potted biographical stuff. The more I wrote my "auto bio" narratives, the easier it was becoming. I wondered if I should create a template.

The following day I found myself sitting in a cafe in Maldon waiting for Jane to arrive. Though I'd only just signed up for internet dating even I could tell this was a highly unusual scenario. I'd met Stephanie after we'd exchanged half a dozen or more emails and we'd chatted on the phone and arranged to meet. Since then I'd had several email "conversations" with other women on the site, writing about films and books, food and holidays we liked. None of them wanted to move on to making arrangements for a date this quickly though. I knew that this was normal and that most women like to spend time developing a dialogue, then speaking on the phone, with third base being the meeting. Jane was different. She wanted to meet up immediately. Nothing wrong in that, I thought. She had suggested the cafe, about nine miles from my flat and near the Blackwater Estuary.

Jane said she would be arriving in a blue BMW. As I sipped my cappuccino, worrying that this was a mistake because of the froth, I scanned the cafe's car park – couldn't see any blue BMW's. Then on cue, a royal blue BMW estate car swung into it. 'Could it be her?' I thought. It was. She stepped out of the car and came into the café. I stood, smiled and she introduced herself.

She was happily just like her photo – blonde, slim, wearing large "Posh Spice" style sunglasses, which hid her eyes. She wore a short blazer type jacket, white shirt and jeans. She said that she recognised me from my profile photo and the description I had given of what I would be wearing. Dark grey jacket, pale blue shirt, navy jumper, beige Chinos. It had taken me a while to dress. I was hugely relieved that Jane was the image of her online photo. She was good looking with a wide smile and perfect teeth. When she eventually removed her sunglasses, I could see she had green eyes. She was wearing a fragrance that I thought I recognised as *Shalimar,* a perfume I'd bought Katherine a couple of Christmases ago. I asked her about it and was right. She seemed impressed with this.

We got on well. She asked about my work. I explained that before writing for car magazines and industry clients, I'd worked in financial services and before that in the RAF. It turned out her ex-husband had served in the Air Force so she knew all about force "speak", had attended many official functions at venues I'd been to and had stayed at the Forces Club in London at Piccadilly, a favourite haunt of mine.

Soon our coffee cups were drained and I wished we could have been enjoying lunch or even dinner. Why wasn't this a dinner date? Why had I just opted for coffee? How weak-kneed was coffee? I could have kicked myself. Who goes for coffee on a first date? I found later that in fact lots of internet hopefuls do. Coffee and lunch are more popular occasions than dinner amongst the online dating fraternity.

I did notice Jane glancing at her watch a few times. Was I boring her? Perhaps she didn't fancy me? Maybe the boot was on the other foot now and she was just being polite? Far too soon our date was over and she was on her feet. "Well," she said. Oh no, my heart sank. This was it – "goodbye."

"I was wondering if we could meet for dinner," I blurted out.

"I would love to," she said.

'Wow!' I thought. "What!" I actually said, surprised at the immediacy and enthusiasm of her reply. "I mean, when?" Then she corrected herself and said, "Well lunch, let's do lunch. That would be easier to arrange this week. I have a young child." We settled on lunch two days later. As I stepped into my grey Alfa I was elated.

'You've cracked this,' I thought to myself.

She was intelligent, good company, funny, looked great. I had a charming text message from her later, saying how much she had enjoyed coffee and was looking forward to lunch. The guys at the fish and chip shop wouldn't believe this. The next morning I started to get anxious about what I was going to wear – again. What do you wear to a lunch date? Same as for coffee? Depends on where we go I thought. Where should we go? In a further text message Jane pointed out that she wouldn't be able to stay for more than a couple of hours and somewhere local would be good. She was going to come to my hometown as she was going to be nearby during the morning in any event. Back to what to wear – and again where to go? We would have to go out as I hadn't shopped for nearly a week and I anticipated that Jane probably wasn't the sort of woman who would be elated at being offered a fish finger doorstep sandwich. Even my individual a la carte version – "au gratin" with a choice of "squirty" or cheddar cheese probably wouldn't appeal to her. I had time to shop for supplies but I doubted she would come to my flat anyway. So, that morning whilst trying to write, I was distracted by trying to decide where we should go.

Now I realise that making an effort to plan a lunch date might sound fussy and unnecessarily time consuming as lunch just doesn't sound that romantic, but I have discovered over time that some of the best dates happen at lunchtime. There is a dating agency called "Only Lunch" dedicated to arranging these. After all, as with coffee dates, you're not investing in dinner which takes time, trouble and involves expense, just lunch. If it works out, you can take it further and go for dinner. If not you don't have to see one another again. Little time has been "wasted" and it's not cost a great deal. Jane had been adamant she had limited time so I decided to book the restaurant attached to my local gym. It's not the most intimate setting, but it is smart; comfortable and newly refurbished and has a relaxed informal and quiet area with sofas as well as a contemporary light dining room. It's got a modern bistro feel. The food was highly regarded and freshly cooked, not crankily healthy. They offered light lunches and trademark specials, all tried and delicious. The measure of its success was that plenty of gym members and their guests ate at the place in the evening. The alternative was a pub and, though there are many close by, I couldn't think of one that was suitably appealing. I texted the details of the gym and my car park over to Jane and settled on wearing blue jeans, a royal blue cashmere jumper, white shirt and a blazer.

A text arrived, "Here, x" and I hurtled downstairs, the lift though officially in working order was labouring tiredly on its journeys between floors. It was still often temperamental, stopping on occasions between landings without apparent reason. I was so eager to see her. I wondered if she had spent as much time agonising about what to wear as I had. I think it is a common fallacy to assume that men don't worry about what to wear, what to say, etc. I wondered if Jane would be wearing her sunglasses this time. As I stepped out of the main door of my building, Jane's car pulled into the car park. I was pleased to see that she wasn't wearing her sunglasses, though they were perched on top of her head, Jackie O style.

As she climbed out of the car I felt a glow of pleasure. She was wearing a champagne coloured dress, a wrap around her shoulders against the autumn chill and flesh coloured tights. I wondered if they were stockings. Her shoes were nude coloured with very high heels, "stilts". Her blonde hair was swept back behind her ears and she carried an expensive looking bag over one arm. She looked very striking. She seemed happy to see me and smiled warmly. There was a slightly awkward moment when she looked at her watch and confirmed that she was short of time again but I assured her the restaurant was close and we hurried across the car park to the gym, a few doors away from the fishnChickn. I'd told the staff I was on my first "second" date and they had placed a rose on the table. To say it went well would be an understatement. We were very relaxed together. She was so easy to be with, the conversation had no fault lines and Jane was amusing and apparently amused by me. I recall us both laughing and smiling throughout the meal. It felt wonderful to be with her.

She spoke of her marriage briefly. I learned she worked part-time in a business she had established with a friend. She had a young child, a daughter. Although I wanted to know more I sensed that asking too many openly direct questions might seem intrusive at this stage; so we talked of neutral events, books, films, holidays. We were two single people, enjoying one another's company over lunch. A couple of large glasses of house Sauvignon Blanc were going down well and I was enjoying myself.

Our conversation wasn't remotely flirtatious although I noticed that Jane was quite tactile. She touched me a couple of times on my arm, stroked my jumper and asked if it was cashmere. She seemed genuinely interested in me and to be enjoying herself. She did however keep glancing at her watch. The service was efficient and soon we were onto coffee. At least, we ordered it. Then Jane decided she had to go.

I replayed the last few items of conversation in my head and wondered if I had put my foot in it and said something that had upset her. I thought how it would be just typical of me to do this. I walked to the bar, cancelled the coffees and paid the bill. Jane was on her feet at our table. She put her sunglasses on her head, threw her wrap around her and headed for the door. I was certain now that I had upset her, said something indiscreet, but she resumed our conversation as we left telling me that she had remembered seeing the flats where I now lived being built. I was relieved. Perhaps I hadn't upset her after all and she was just genuinely tight for time. We had been at the restaurant for quite a while after all and time had evaporated.

Arriving at her car, adopting my best "Hugh Grant" voice I told her it had been lovely to share lunch and that I would very much like to see her again. There was an uncomfortable silent moment. We looked at one another. Should I shake her hand, peck her on the cheek or just walk away? The decision was taken out of my hands when Jane leant towards me and kissed me fully on the lips. She looked at me openly and said

"You know, I think I will have that coffee after all."

You've probably gathered I'm not that quick on the uptake and a little shy. I stepped back from her and took her hand to head back to the gym.

"Oh no," she said, stopping on the pavement. "I thought you might like to show me your new flat."

Moments later we were in the lift and on our way to the third floor. I prayed the bloody thing wouldn't stick between landings. My anxiety returned. Had I any coffee in? If I did it was probably only instant. Why hadn't I appreciated that this attractive 40-something divorcee might want coffee? I should have bought some freshly ground stuff. I like coffee, I like buying it when I remember to and was amused by that series of ads for Gold Blend some years ago featuring the couple played by Anthony Head and Sharon Maugham, who lived in separate flats in the same apartment building. Remember them? The storyline left the audience in suspense as to whether they might get it together. Would they? Wouldn't they? It was crass stuff really and the couple were annoyingly smug and irritating but I recall it was a popular series of ads and made compelling viewing for many.

'Blast,' I thought returning to real-time. I was certain I only had Instant coffee in. In the mercifully uneventful thirty-second ride in the lift I was fretting about the state I'd left the flat in. I knew there were newspapers spread all over the lounge, the computer would be whirring away on the mezzanine floor, and the flat would be like an unmade bed throughout. Oh God! Jane was talking about her house and the plans she had for it. Regrettably she seemed genuinely interested in seeing the interior of the flat and where I lived. If only I'd known this might happen. I explained that it was a bachelor pad and I wasn't naturally tidy to prepare her. She just laughed.

Once inside the flat, I switched the kettle on and left Jane in the lounge after scooping up the papers and stuffing them under the sofa. I found my best cups and saucers dismissing the eclectic collection of mugs I'd "rehomed" as unsuitable for the occasion. I politely enquired if Jane took sugar, milk – "just milk" – of course. Do any women take sugar these days? She asked about the upstairs after an inspection of the ground floor and I explained that the main bedroom was up on the mezzanine where my "office" was. She expressed surprise at this "unusual" arrangement as she put it. I laughed and said I would give her a guided tour. She didn't reply.

I used the downstairs loo as the kettle boiled and after washing my hands, I stepped into the kitchen and began preparing the coffee, at speed, working on Jane's time scale now. It struck me that she must genuinely like me. She was evidently an extremely busy lady yet here she was, spending precious time with me. I stepped into the lounge with the coffee. No Jane! When I had left her she was sitting on the edge of the sofa. It wasn't a large flat. I could see almost everywhere at once.

"Jane?" I said. In my perplexed state I even looked behind the sofa. Stupid! What on earth was I thinking of? She was a grown woman. She wouldn't fit behind the sofa. I put the coffee cups down on a side table and headed into the hallway. She must have decided that the prospect of my instant coffee was so unappealing that she'd leave. Or perhaps she'd had second thoughts and didn't like me after all. There was no sign of her in the hallway, or in the downstairs toilet. Then I noticed her handbag, cardigan and sunglasses on the arm of the sofa.

"Jane!" I called and went over to the stairs.

"I'm up here," she replied.

I relaxed. She had obviously needed the bathroom whilst I was using the downstairs loo. As I got to the top of the stairs, passing the mezzanine office on my right and my bedroom to the left, I saw her. I retraced the couple of steps to my bedroom and nearly passed out. Jane was sitting on the end of my bed facing me. She was wearing her shoes, stockings with lace tops, a cappuccino coloured bra and knickers with cream lace trim – and nothing else.

She smiled, and said, "I've made a start."

I was stunned. I didn't know what to think. She looked lovely. Guerlain's *Shalimar* hung heavily in the air. Seconds later we were writhing about on the bed. I was trying to get my jeans off and my jumper over my head at the same time.

I recall saying something like, "Are you sure you want to do this?" praying she would say "yes".

It was fantastic. I hadn't had sex for a long while. Jane took me in her mouth, it was sensational. I am probably the one man on the planet who cannot climax through oral sex but that didn't matter – I still love it and it's glorious foreplay. In an instant Jane's cappuccino coloured underwear was on the floor and she was on top of me. What a lunchtime!

Just as I thought I couldn't experience anything more wonderful that day something extraordinary happened. We had changed positions, Jane was kneeling on the bed and I was taking her from behind, which gave me a good opportunity to check out her bottom – magnificent, full and dimpled. She was very clear what she wanted and let me know in no uncertain terms that she was about to come. I thrust deeper into her – she was silent – then let out the loudest and longest moan I have ever heard. It was extraordinary, "Oooooooooh," and as she exhaled, I thought it was all over. She however took another breath and started on a second endless "Oooooooooh."

If you have seen *Porkies* you will know what I mean. Jane's vocal appreciation was like the rendition in the film. If you've not seen it, consider an endlessly sustained high-pitched lowing from a cow during calving. I hoped she wasn't in pain and tried to check but I was on the point of climaxing myself, and I didn't know whether to hold back. I was trying to decide if Jane had actually climaxed or if she was still building up to it. Over lunch we hadn't discussed this… "Jane, what do you do when you come?" didn't seem to follow naturally from "So Jane what's your favourite film?" The noise was unbelievable. I couldn't hold on – I came, deep inside her.

We lay on the bed together and I don't know why, but I felt shy. I didn't know quite what to say. "Thank you very much" seemed formal and ridiculous. "That was very nice" – trite! What do you say when you have had such glorious unexpected sex?

Jane touched my hand and simply said, "That was wonderful Simon."

She still had on her watch and stockings and shoes. She glanced at her watch and said, "I must go now." She threw herself into the bathroom, came running out a moment later, pulled on her knickers, and bra. I helped her find her dress.

Women do up bras differently don't them? If you are a girl and reading this, how do you do yours up? Jane held the cups up on her back, did the bra up in front of her, whizzed it round, put her boobs in the cups then put her arms through the shoulder straps. Is that normal? I'd not seen a girl do that before. It was entertaining. I have come to the conclusion that bras are a mystery and most men have a nightmare undoing or doing them up – certainly in haste! After Jane had manoeuvred herself into hers I zipped up her dress and she proceeded to beat an almost indecent retreat. She gathered up her things from the lounge, threw her top around her, grabbed her sunglasses and was gone.

I was ecstatic, I punched the air. I phoned everybody of course – not gentlemanly – but I had to tell the boys and Friday was too far away. I had to tell them that not only had I seen Jane for lunch, but the deed had been done and it was glorious, and that she wore stockings.

Rick laughed, said, "Good on you!"

I said I was hoping obviously to see her again and might not make Friday fish and chips – that as I was now obviously in a relationship they might need to cut me some slack. She had left less than half an hour before, but I had convinced myself she would want to see me again.

Then Barry was on the phone. And after telling him the news he enquired, "Did you use a condom?" I didn't answer at first. I was shocked, I am truly ashamed to say that this hadn't even entered my head. I'd bought condoms when I was single, used them occasionally but they often remained unopened. I know I am going to get letters about this but I had had a vasectomy some years before, had never had any hint of an STD, not even thrush which I know lots of married couples can have without the involvement of a third party. To my knowledge I'd never had a girlfriend with any problems or admitted history of infections of that or any other type. Looking back, my only poor defence is that as a man in his late 40s, protection from STDs or impregnating a partner weren't really on my radar. The AIDS "pandemic" of the 1980s/90s had by-passed me as a married man. I hadn't planned to have sex with Jane. It never occurred to me that we would on this occasion. I was now however very concerned. Looking back, our actions were plainly reckless. Jane didn't ask if I had

had a vasectomy or whether I was using a condom and I did not enquire if she was on the pill. Our encounter had been fabulous though. I await the postman with letters of disapproval.

My friends would say I wear my heart on my sleeve and they can judge my moods easily. The condom issue was still on my mind because I was getting texts from the boys enquiring whether I was starting to "itch" yet, had I any nasty rashes? Was I feeling okay?

Another read: "Have you seen the doctor yet?"

And later still, horrifically: "Has it dropped off then?"

They were meant to amuse but revealed an odd tangent. My male friends assumed that if there was to be any contact with STDs it would be Jane passing it on to me, not the other way around! Thank God the potential for me to be a new father hadn't occurred to them. I consoled myself with the thought that I was sure we were both safe and that Jane and I were now in a relationship anyway so it would be resolved.

As it was late Autumn I began to muse about things. Would we be spending Christmas together? When would I meet Jane's daughter? When should she meet my children? Would the neighbours get used to the noise from my bedroom? Of course, being me I was overlooking one unpalatable fact. Apart from a text saying, "Thank you for lunch! Jane x," it had been three days since I had heard from her.

I had been texting her asking about her days; work; was she okay, "good night", "good morning", "good afternoon" – bit desperate that – no reply. I had tried of course to telephone and though it was lovely to hear her voice, the calls went straight to answerphone. I comforted myself with the notion that she was busy. After all this had been a motif in every conversation, email and text I had had from her. I had never known anyone to check their watch so often when supposedly relaxing. It must be hard to find time for a relationship when she had a child and worked part-time.

Friday – Barry, Rick, fish and chip night – me and the boys. Not surprisingly plenty of backslapping and jokes about my knob dropping off. Rick had asked to see a photo of Jane, preferably in her undies. I had asked her if I could take one but she had declined. There were photos on the website of course and I mentioned this. Barry was more circumspect. He wanted to know about Jane – where she lived, worked, how long divorced. Then the killer question: when was I seeing her again? My attempt to manoeuvre the conversation elsewhere failed dismally. Barry got it in one.

"Have you heard from her?" He asked directly.

As the remains of our meal stared us in the face, I had to tell the truth. "No, I haven't heard from her." I was dying to say that we were planning a weekend away or that I was going out with her again for a meal, that we were meeting her friends. Something that was and that sounded 'normal'. But there had been nothing and I was forced to admit this.

"Well," Rick said, "You must have been rubbish shag!" Dear old Rick. I protested and told them indignantly about the noise she had made.

"Well," said Rick, "she probably just wanted you to stop, or get it over with," He asked how long it had lasted.

"What a ridiculous question!" I said. But he persisted. "She instigated it, got undressed, took me in her mouth, we had sex more than once and it lasted several minutes."

He was unimpressed.

The euphoria of Tuesday had completely evaporated. It was Friday and the weekend was stretching endlessly ahead of me. I kept looking at my phone and this reminded me of Jane's "watchful" attention.

It was Thursday, the following week, and I was on the brink of a further admission of defeat before the jury of the boys at the fish and chip shop – when she finally made contact. The landline in the flat rang infrequently. It was about lunchtime when I answered it.

"Hi Simon," said a voice, "it's Jane."

I stood up taking off my reading glasses I was standing up, as if to attention! Why? Ridiculous, as she obviously couldn't see me. Thank God she couldn't see me!

"I am so pleased to hear from you," I gushed. Then I gushed some more: "I was so worried I hadn't heard, I thought I had done something wrong."

Jane listened then said simply

"I have just been a bit busy that's all... as usual," she laughed, "but I am passing and just wondered if I could pop in for a coffee?"

I was flabbergasted. "Yes of course," I said, then "Shall we meet at the gym?" Jane wanted to come to the flat, was that okay? She'd like a coffee!!

"Yes of course!" Gush, gush, gush.

"Great," she said, "see you in half an hour." Click went the phone.

I went into overdrive. Brushed my teeth, gargled with mouthwash, brushed my hair, splashed on aftershave, collected magazines, books and other debris from the lounge and stuffed them in the footstool.

I prised out a brand new cafetière from its box, and sliced into a glossy packet of posh Lavazza Italian coffee, strength 3 I'd bought the day after Jane's first visit to the flat. The boys would be eating their words along with their chicken, meat pie and chips. We were back on track. She had simply been busy and not able to phone. It could happen to anyone – just busy, that's all. Great... We might talk about the future, possibly about plans for Christmas, only weeks away. I wondered what Jane would be wearing; whether she would she still be sporting her trademark sunglasses.

The intercom sounded and I let her into the flat.

I was thrown. Taken aback by her clothing. She was dressed from head to toe in black. Black shiny boots with stiletto heels, thick ribbed tights, a black pencil skirt and a tightly fitting polo neck. I made a joke about the coffee, which on her previous visit we hadn't had any opportunity to drink.

She laughed. Her blonde hair was swept back into its customary ponytail. Her pillar-box red lipstick matching glossy scarlet nails was in fabulous contrast to the starkness of her outfit. I could smell *Shalimar* once more.

After a brief, slightly awkward and unnatural embrace we sat down in the lounge to drink our coffee.

"I am so glad to see you," I said and explained that I thought I had done something wrong.

"Oh you know me," she laughed, tipping her glorious head backwards. "I've just been busy, you know, with work."

I asked her to remind me what she did. "Oh, just admin," she said airily, "not nearly as exciting as being a writer."

Emboldened, I pressed a little further, and asked where she worked.

"Oh, it's close," she said and waved her perfectly manicured hand, vaguely indicating Southend, as she sipped her coffee. "Anyway, enough about me; tell me what you have been doing."

I talked of writing, going to the gym, meeting up in London with my publisher and spending time with my kids. She didn't really answer, just nodded, sipped her coffee, and glanced at her watch. My impression was that I wasn't really engaging with her and I started to feel mildly anxious. She really did seem obsessed with that watch. Was this some unusual medical issue? It was quite a decent watch – I like watches – but her jewel encrusted Tag Heuer was starting to annoy me.

"Are you okay for time?" I asked, guessing her answer.

"Well, I am a little pushed," she admitted and smiled. My slight annoyance melted instantly. She was lovely. Her sunglasses were still perched on her head. I had only seen her without these when we were having sex. When I pointed this out to her she roared with laughter. Soon we were embracing again, frantically kissing. She shrugged off her coat and it fell with a crump onto the living room floor. This time I took the initiative – "Shall we go upstairs?"

"I don't think I have time for upstairs," she said breathing heavily.

Holding her close, with her perfume filling my nostrils, I continued. We had moved over to an armchair in the lounge. She seemed to instinctively lean over the back of the armchair. Standing right behind her now and kissing the back of her neck, it was clear what she wanted me to do. I started to lift the hem of her skirt up, but as it reached her thighs, I realised it was too tight to go over Jane's shapely bottom. I reached around to the front to find the zip, not at the back or side; more fumbling – does this really annoy girls?

"Undo the buttons," she said.

There were two in a horseshoe formation – I undid them. Underneath, the polo necked jumper proved not to be a jumper after all, but a "body" which fastened between her legs with press stud "poppers". Not the sexiest item of underwear during breathlessly aroused manual removal but apparently comfortable to wear and a firm favourite with lots of girls because they give a clean, fitted outline.

Labouring to extract Jane from her "body" proved a considerable hurdle. Coming to my aid she helped me undo the studs and I pushed the "body" up her back then negotiated pulling her crocheted tights down. Jane's bottom was by now lifted high up over the back of the armchair and as I manoeuvred myself into position to take her from behind, she looked over her shoulder and said, "I have a G-string on as well Simon."

I looked and saw a sliver of black fabric. I pulled this down to the top of her boots marvelling at the complexities of the garments, given Jane's obsession with time.

I was soon taking her from behind and Jane was doing her characteristic noisy moaning thing. She was bending from the waist forwards and I was trying not to get tangled up in the debris of her clothing around her knees and boots. I moved her "body" further up her back and tried to take off her bra but without success.

I moved my hands to her breasts – her bra lifted up of its own volition. Her nipples were hard, and I rubbed one between my fingers. As before, her pleasurable response was awesome. I was certain the neighbours were going to start banging on their ceiling, my floor, if they were about. I prayed they were out.

I was still inside her when it suddenly occurred to me that this, the sex was perhaps all she had come for. I was having an enjoyable time; don't get me wrong, but maybe Jane, with her seductive perfume, delicious body and considerable but lovely clothing, just wanted sex? I knew so little about her after all.

Then the inevitable happened. At the last second before I came, I took a step forward and became caught up in the tights, skirt, body and G-string around her boots. A second step forward to compensate and I caught the back of her heel. She yelped and stood up. I tried to stand, fell back and in doing so a spurt of semen flew into the air, hung there for an instant before landing on her skirt.

We both laughed self-consciously, but then she became concerned about the state of her skirt. In the bathroom she frantically sponged the small stain, glancing at her watch. I knew what was coming. She was going.

In what seemed like a repeat indecent and unceremonious post-coital instant, she was gone. I am not going to lie, and say I felt used, abused. But I did feel that I hadn't actually "seen" her and I would have liked to have talked over a drink. We should have had the discussion about condoms!

She had promised me as she departed, that this time she would keep in touch, call sooner and that next time we met we would spend more time together.

Despite this, I was left in some turmoil, unsure how I felt; whether pleased? Anxious? Perturbed? The sex had been good, although not very relaxed and for a second time, somewhat comedic. At least I could tell the guys tomorrow I had seen her again. Was I perhaps expecting too much of dating? – Perhaps this was what it was like for everyone in my position? Later on I realised that most single people faced with Jane would probably have understood what was happening. Not me, though. Not then.

I had started to think about her outfit. As I have described, she was dressed completely in black, the theme extending to a smart black trench coat and shiny handbag. Not a fashion handbag though, more a functional bag, possibly for work? I know lots of women are big fans of bags and shoes. Jane struck me as a handbag-fashionista type of girl. Who goes to work dressed completely in black (apart from undertakers and barristers)? And thinking about it, whilst the red nails would have taken a while to paint, they were covered, on her arrival, in black gloves. The lipstick was probably speedily applied, maybe in the car or on her way up to the flat.

What did I know of her? She had brushed aside my enquiries about her work. Maybe she was a police officer? Undertaker? I was puzzled. I decided to text her.

"Hi Jane, lovely to see you, however briefly, hope I can see you again, loved your outfit. Was worried you had been to a funeral!" As soon as it left my phone I regretted sending it. I often send texts then regret doing it – it's a habit that has got me into untold trouble.

A text came back immediately: "Ha, sorry about my outfit, but yes I have been to a funeral, x."

I replied, "Gosh, I am sorry I should have asked before. Was it someone close?" I felt pretty awful. Perhaps she had called in for comfort and solace and all I had done was roger her senselessly over the back of the armchair. There was no reply or explanation from Jane and to this day I don't know if she had actually been to a funeral or not.

Friday fish and chips that week was cancelled due to illness, both Rick and Barry were unwell with flu. I decided to go shopping.

I wandered around Lakeside Shopping Centre looking at clothes and stuff I might buy the kids for Christmas and I picked up some more coffee – just in case. I hadn't properly mastered the art of living alone yet and cooking remained something of a mystery, but from the outset I had discovered Marks and Spencer and had bought prepared meals and practised a few chat up lines about food and cooking there. If you are a newly single man and have gone from living at home with your parents or from a shared flat to living with your wife, you may not necessarily know too much about cooking. I know that sounds sexist and old fashioned and there are an army of men out there who cook routinely, lovingly and with boundless enthusiasm and creativity for their wives and families. Television cookery features are hugely popular but whilst as a nation we might be entertained by Jamie, Gordon and the Hairy Bikers, the statistics reveal that their enthusiasm doesn't appear to have converted many of us from "heater uppers" into practising cooks. Anyway even if you do enjoy cooking for friends or family, it's still different doing it just for one. My solution then was to become familiar with and patronise Marks & Spencer's food hall

.I liked the choice of decent food – not only the "manual" type that involves stuffing a chicken – but ready-prepared tasty meals that only needed unwrapping or heating up. If I wasn't sure about how to cook something and needed help the staff were invariably very happy to advise. Indeed it is surprising how many women will talk about food and its preparation to a lone male in Marks and Spencer. In the US singles making friends with men/women in supermarkets is a well-known phenomenon. It's the stuff of Rom-Com film and TV, ads and even formal date opportunity gatherings. From personal experience I'd found that the staff, male and female, could be very conversational. Indeed some staff had been more willing to chat in passing about their lives than lovely Jane had disclosed on our dates. And we'd had sex – twice! Jane – ah Jane who was now fully occupying my thoughts as I stopped in front of an expensive-looking lingerie shop. I window shopped and "bought" her an imaginary Christmas present, a pink satin lace up basque with matching knickers.

Imagine my delight then when on arriving back at the car park as I left Lakeside, I spotted Jane's royal blue BMW. At least, I was fairly sure it was hers. In the back of it I noticed a child's safety seat. I knew she had a daughter of course, though as Jane was 42, I'd anticipated that the child would have been 10 years old or thereabouts. I'd had to make assumptions about Jane because she had told me so little of her life. I thought about texting her, but decided against this.

Opposite the car park was a coffee shop. I was thirsty and this was the only option readily available to treat my newly acquired proper-coffee habit. It had the added advantage of allowing me to keep Jane's car in view as I had a coffee. I wasn't sure what I was thinking of looking back. I think I wanted to see her arrive, if she did – and I thought I would just wait and see – give it a while. I could surprise her – buy her a coffee. Maybe show her the lingerie shop and buy her the basque I'd seen. I sipped my Mocha; making it last longer than necessary and having finished it, spent some time people watching. After several minutes of this however I felt conspicuous. What on earth was I doing? Becoming a stalker? Was I stalking Jane? She might be hours. This was foolish. I got up to leave.

Then my patience was rewarded. There was Jane. She was walking to her car accompanied by a tall chap in a suit. With them was a small girl, maybe four or five years old. They had bags of shopping; they were chatting; laughing, they seemed close. I felt miserable. Whilst it was theoretically possible that the man was her brother, a cousin, or possibly an uncle, in my heart I knew that she was married and apparently happily. The tall "suit" was her husband and the father of the little girl. I realised what I should have known much sooner. I was Jane's bit of "spare".

You will probably have guessed long before now, well, long before me, that Jane was interested in a dash of extra-marital sex, the occasional lunch and some flattery. Whilst I couldn't condemn her for this (I confess to having been unfaithful during my marriage) I couldn't understand why she had used a dating service for singles. There are ample sites purely for married men and women to have encounters whether sexual or otherwise – for them to engage in affairs, or simply enjoy platonic relationships. Why had she sold herself as a single girl? Was her name "Jane" at all? Did she work? Was anything she had told me true? How many other men was she seeing? I felt demoralised and stupid. How could I have been so naïve?

I made my way home to the flat. I thought of Christmas and how empty it was going to be. I decided I was going to be open with the guys at our next meeting. I had also decided I should text Jane and did so the following morning asking how she had enjoyed shopping the previous evening with her family.

In fairness to she didn't deny anything, said she would call later and then to my surprise actually did. She quizzed me on what I had seen and I told her. I was at pains to let her know I hadn't actually been stalking her. She admitted to being married and apologised for deceiving me; told me she was unhappy in her marriage, which she described as 'loveless' and that she was thinking of leaving her husband. She had been surfing dating sites out of curiosity; had decided to join one and had been intrigued by my profile so arranged to meet me. She thanked me for treating her well, said she'd genuinely enjoyed being with me and wished me all the best for the future. She was undecided what to do having a young child who it turned out was just 5 years old. She ended by saying she would be in touch when she had taken steps to resolve her marital problems and had separated. When the call ended I knew I'd never hear from her again. It would be too embarrassing. I felt overwhelmed with disappointment. I realised that I was going to have to toughen up. I had had two dates and they had both been disastrous.

Rick's reaction was incendiary. He caused something of a stir in the restaurant.

"Bitch!" he spat out, causing other diners to look around. "What an absolute fucking bitch – you should go round to her house and tell her husband what she was up to!" Barry was more pragmatic. "Can't you contact the dating agency and tell them?"

I didn't know but thought probably not. Presumably, if she was paying the agency fees then they'd be uninterested in how she was managing her private life. The earlier encounter with Stephanie who had turned out to be more than 20 years older than her claimed profile and photo suggested was an even more obvious case in point for a rigorously managed dating service. But would they actually be concerned? The guys were unimpressed with dating agency partnerships and my progress. They counselled me against further forays onto the net and dating/encounter sites and told me to concentrate on my work. Someone would turn up if I just got on with my normal life and relaxed.

Having listened to my friends' sound advice, I proceeded to take absolutely no notice. Logging on to Friends Reunited Dating, I was soon chatting to a lady from Essex who had posted a decent quality, recent photo (I asked and she confirmed this) who importantly also assured me she wasn't married and was looking for a long term relationship. Promising, I thought. "Claire" sent a recent photo to my mobile phone of herself at a local pub that we both knew. She was single, local and sent detailed interesting emails telling me about her life and work as a civil servant in the VAT office in Chelmsford. She had never been married, had just turned 40 and was keen to meet up. She described herself as being interested in antiques, particularly furniture.

I am not that interested in antiques, but I do have a passion for military history; swords carried at Waterloo; artefacts from our Civil War etc., but trying to tell one Queen Anne sideboard from another, or identify a Marie Antoinette dressing table, doesn't excite me. There is however a large antiques emporium in Battlesbridge, close to where we both lived. Claire told me she often spent her Sunday mornings there, wandering around the outdoor barns and stalls selling antiques. The range of antiques was comprehensive. There could be a military sword waiting for me, she'd written teasingly. We arranged to meet at a pub within the complex and I think I mentioned lunch, though half-heartedly, given my earlier experience. Claire said that there was a well regarded tearoom at the complex with a solid reputation for delicious homemade cakes. I was relieved. Cake seemed like a safe option.

Thinking about Marie Antoinette and her dressing tables, I am told by a friend that these can genuinely appear for sale at auction houses. How many bedrooms and dressing tables were there?

I mentioned this to Claire on the phone and we agreed to look at dressing tables, though not necessarily ones owned by the former Queen of France.

She told me that the Palace at Versailles had over 500 rooms, sumptuously furnished rooms, so theoretically she probably owned a lot of dressing tables. I doubt she sat at each one of these. I felt a Google search

Paul Fox

coming on – or was it just a desire to be as well informed as Claire and perhaps have something more to say on the subject when we met? I didn't bother with this though. I decided to let her inform me about her interest.

Claire said she would be driving her black VW Golf and when I arrived I was pleased to see her car there. She was petite and dark haired. She walked over and introduced herself. She was wearing little makeup and had a fresh and delightfully freckly complexion, grey eyes and a lovely smile. She was wearing trousers – I felt a pang of disappointment as I am a confirmed and very definite "leg" man – but this was a sensible option as we planned to walk about outside and it was a typical November day, bright but chilly.

We started to potter around the outside stalls and it was apparent that Claire was knowledgeable about antiques and a regular visitor at the Emporium. She was on first name terms with many of the stallholders with whom she was enjoying casual banter. I began to relax. Claire was pleasant and entertaining and I was learning something of antiques. She indulged me by checking out a stall that was selling military hardware and memorabilia. The stallholder was trying to sell me a ceremonial sword, which he promised faithfully, had been carried at Waterloo. Claire told him she thought he must mean Waterloo Station. She made me laugh by pulling faces at me from behind his back. Feeling chilled and agreeing that we were hungry, we headed to the Tea Rooms. I ordered tea and we each chose a cake from a glass cabinet. We decided upon a plan. We would head back into the complex, finish seeing the stalls for a while then have lunch. An hour later we were seated in the pub where we'd met. We ordered a glass of white wine each and talked. Claire was patently an organised person. I'm a little wary of such women. I don't mind them being organised, I just don't like them organising me.

As I sat down she said that she had something to ask me. I took a breath. 'What's coming?' I wondered.

Without waiting for my reply however she said out of the blue "How do you feel about Cornwall?"

It took a while for the question to sink in. "Do you mean the County of Cornwall? The Duchess of Cornwall?" Was I missing something here? Did she mean some kind of antique or source of antiques? "Cornwall as in the place?" I ventured.

"Yes," she said, "what do you think of it?"

When I worked for a financial service company we had had customers in Truro and I used to fly down via Gatwick and Plymouth. Claire told me she had been on the same flight route and asked if I liked it. I admitted I

40

did from what little I could recall of the odd family holiday there and work visit to the County.

"Why do you ask?" I said.

"Well," she said, "I am thinking of moving there – well back there actually – I moved there a few years ago, but it didn't work out. What do you think?"

I was bemused. Was I supposed to consider her moving back? Was I supposed to be included on such a slender acquaintance? She then spoke continuously about Cornwall. I thought she might be breathing through her ears at one point so breathless was her dialogue. The monologue had to have lasted fifteen minutes at least.

I sank deeply into my chair. Was she looking for someone to go with her to Cornwall? Why was she dating in Essex if she wanted so desperately to go to Cornwall? Surely, she should go there then start dating some nice Cornish man? I hesitated. Was I missing something obvious? She had previously commented that as a writer I could live anywhere.

"Why do you live in Essex?" she asked rather aggressively.

I told her that I had been born here and that my children lived near to me.

She interjected immediately and said that that was no reason to live here. My kids could surely travel to visit. "Why not make a move to Truro?"

The obsessive nature of her conversation was decidedly odd. I tried to divert the conversation elsewhere and distract Claire, but she seemed to be developing Cornwall-based Tourette's. My efforts were in vain.

By now I had drunk an entire glass of wine. The atmosphere had changed and Claire appeared petulant. Since "Cornwall-gate" had been on the agenda I had been feeling awkward and confused. We didn't stay for lunch.

I didn't offer to buy this and Claire said she was "full of cake" and didn't want lunch. The mood had patently soured and I wasn't sure why. When I suggested we leave, she readily agreed.

As we headed out into the car park she had another go and said, "So, would you be averse to a move to Cornwall?" I simply nodded.

It was bizarre! We had just met and here she was asking me to seriously consider a move to another county with her, miles away from Essex. I never saw her again. But I often wondered if she did move there. Claire, if you are reading this in Truro, I hope you found happiness and a Marie Antoinette dressing table.

"The Great Escape" – From Christmas

Rick's reaction was predictable. "Cornwall!" he exploded, "fucking Cornwall! What does she want to go to Cornwall for? Why doesn't she just go to Cornwall and find a bloke down there?"

My thoughts entirely.

Barry brushed Cornwall and Claire to one side with a timely interjection. "What are you going to do for Christmas Simon?"

"Ah... Christmas... ah, I'm not entirely sure." I was fast approaching my first single Christmas since 1978 and it didn't appeal. Katherine would be sharing Christmas with the children and her family. Arrangements had been made for me to have a Dad and kids "Christmas" on the Tuesday before 25th and since Christmas Eve and Boxing Day fell on a Thursday and Friday, there would be a long gap to fill before our agreed usual routine for family contact started again. What was I to do?

I had had offers from several friends to spend Christmas with them and their loved ones, but I was acutely aware of the obvious. That Christmas is a time for family. I have few close relatives now that my parents have died and though I remained fond of my in-laws, my separation from Katherine had affected that relationship. We would exchange cards but I had accepted they would find it a strain if I was at an all-family Christmas day. I knew that I was genuinely welcome at friends' homes, but I also knew that despite their generosity I'd still feel something of an interloper at their family celebrations and I had no wish to be the sad, single, left-over male friend. The "Uncle" that wasn't.

I returned despondently to the flat and fired up the computer, typing "singles holidays at Christmas" into the search engine. There had to be a prospect that something would come up. An option that would allow me to hold my head high as a single man at Christmas. Not home alone was my aim.

What I found was an all-inclusive package, "Christmas in Venice", departing on Christmas Eve, returning the day after Boxing Day for single travellers interested in a cultural break. The company offering the holiday, *Just You*, didn't advertise the trip as a venture aimed at singles seeking to meet someone and it wasn't offering any form of matchmaking. It is a specialist operator offering holidays worldwide designed to help people decide if organised singles holidays are for them. The hotel looked appealing, the itinerary interesting: Christmas Day and Boxing Day catered for with what was advertised as "superb food" and "seasonal excursions" in good company! I'd been to Venice before. It was a known quantity and a place I had vowed to return to. What could be better? I checked out the hotel on TripAdvisor looked at testimonials from previous customers who'd travelled on trips organised by the company, part of the Page & Moy Group, checked their profile (bonded, regulated, blah blah) and I booked.

The next day I phoned everyone. You can probably guess Rick's response...

"Venice, fucking Venice – what's in Venice that's not available in Essex?"

"I thought it would be fun," I offered. I think my friends were secretly relieved that I wasn't going to be a spare part at risk of spending Christmas with them, but it didn't stop them commenting and pouring scorn on my idea of going to Venice. 'Tough,' I determined, it was booked and I was due to be at Gatwick at 8am on Christmas Eve for the 10am flight to Marco Polo airport.

The rescheduled Christmas with the children went well. A day with my teenage children and ex-wife at our former family home. Katherine cooked turkey and all the trimmings; we swapped presents and watched National Lampoon's *Christmas Vacation*, an annual family tradition. There was no tension but it felt odd being together again for a substitute but otherwise traditional Christmas "day" in our former family home. I left the house with mixed emotions and returned to the silence of the flat.

Once there, I had a look over the confirmed booking and brochure sent by the tour company. I was starting to feel anxious. What if it was awful? What sort of people end up going on these holidays? Were we all going to be "freaks" of nature at Christmas? Sad leftovers from broken families.

I am invariably nervous about travelling on holiday and find the process of packing, leaving, arriving, ticketing and hanging about a strain. This Christmas was no exception. And I always arrive early – ridiculously early at airports. My obsessive approach to air travel used to drive Katherine mad. She would grumble that I'd fuss over leaving home with enough time at the airport "to read, if not write a bloody novel!" The night before I flew I slept badly, got up at 5am and arrived at Gatwick well before seven o'clock. Check in was closed but Gatwick was full of revellers, many presumably heading home to family and friends. Some well over the "flight limit" as they staggered about the concourse. I only truly started to relax after I'd checked-in my luggage and headed for the gate.

I scoured the area for singletons that might be fellow tour members. Funny how, when you are single, everyone else seems to be attached. Gloom descended... what was I doing? 'Oh well,' I thought 'there's no going back now.'

As my BA flight climbed into the grey skies above Gatwick that Christmas Eve, I could only imagine, with an increasing sense of foreboding, what lay ahead. A couple of glasses of complimentary Christmas Eve Champagne courtesy of BA began to take effect and I started to calm down.

Though I dislike the whole departure/arrivals pre-flight fandango, I genuinely love flying. Once on board I relax. I reserve an aisle seat if possible (so I can check out the stewardesses' legs. Yes I know it's unforgivable!). I went to the toilet twice covertly checking to see whether there were any conspicuously other singles on board. No one appeared to fit the bill. This ramped up my anxiety and I felt a measure of despair.

It wasn't long before we were making our descent to Marco Polo airport and whilst the sun glinting off the water was a good omen. I started to feel tense. Is it just me or do other people find all that baggage reclaim stuff complicated? I keep meaning to personalise my luggage since I always panic when I see twenty of "my" cases arriving on the arrivals conveyor belt.

Concentrating deeply on which carousel to go to, I located a trolley and waited for my bag. As usual I'd packed excessively in spite of only being away for three nights. I had an oversized case and had had to pay extra for it. I had reasoned that if I was going to meet a 40-something Kristen Scott Thomas look-alike, I was going to meet her in Venice. So I figured the supplement for several choices of gear was worth it. I've always liked Kristen Scott Thomas. You can more or less guarantee she will take her clothes off in a film, She has got that French/English Rose "thing" going on which I find very appealing.

I was jolted out of my reverie when I spotted the vast hulk of what I thought was a familiar "extended family size" case lumbering along the carousel. There were a lot of these on the unit. Was it/wasn't it mine though? The anxiety I felt at this point was acute – was it actually mine or some other idiot's enormous baggage? Could I grab it in time before it disappeared? Would it ricochet off someone frail as I hauled it off the carousel and break their hip or leg and involve me in an action for negligence? As I am naturally clumsy would I end up on the carousel and look totally and utterly stupid? The suspense was overwhelming.

I leapt on the case, dragged it off and was just getting my breath back and wishing I'd worked harder with the 22kg weights at the gym when a woman of a "certain age" approached. She had a much smaller case.

"Hello," she said, "are you on the singles holiday?"

'Oh my God,' I thought. She was lovely, very elegant, head of thick grey hair, immaculately made up and well spoken, but more like Kristen Scott Thomas's Mum. I thought of Stephanie. I hesitated, said "Yes." Well actually I meant to say "Yes" but what came out of my mouth was a high pitched "Yeeees".

We were immediately approached by a second lady, she looked even older. "Are you both on the singles holiday?" she asked.

I turned into Basil Fawlty. I had a ridiculous fixed rictus of a grin on my face. This was going to be hideous. I had managed to book myself onto "Oldies-in-Venice-dot-com".

I would be surrounded by elderly ladies for Christmas. They would smell of lavender and talk about artichoke rearing, the W.I and how radical it had become or "The War". In fairness, the war subject would have interested me. I enjoy war films and have seen The Great Escape so many times, I think I am in it. I always think that the next time I see it Steve McQueen will make it over that wire and escape on his Triumph – what a film!

The second lady asked me to help her retrieve her bag from the carousel.

I marched off enthusiastically muttering, "Yes dear, of course dear," cue Basil Fawlty or perhaps Uriah Heap. And there I was again playing carousel roulette, looking now for a modest tartan suitcase. I ask you, who goes to Venice with a tartan suitcase? It did make it easy to spot on the carousel however.

I had resigned myself now to having a terrible Christmas though I knew I was being boorish because both women seemed delightful and were perfectly charming. They had both by now referred to me several times as "young man" and given that I was nearer 50 than 40, things weren't all bad.

The formalities of passport control were ahead of us. I become very proper when I go through this and as I hand over my passport, proffer a 'good morning' or 'good evening' and say "thank you". It's not exactly cowardice. Immigration officers just inspire this programmed response from me although the older I become the less impressed I am by uniforms and rank.

At the other side of passport control my two new lady friends caught up with me. As is surely apparent by now I'm not that bright and whilst any "normal" person would have worked out that there'd be passengers coming from other UK destinations, probably also from abroad to join the party organised by *Just You* and travelling to our hotel, this hadn't occurred to me. There were even other flights from Heathrow that day alone arriving within minutes of mine. Then I spotted the *Just You* tour guide sign: "Christmas in Venice. THIS WAY". To my huge relief I saw a sizeable group, older and younger travellers, some chatting, others checking mobile phones or, discreetly, one another.

Whilst the formalities were being dealt with by the company representative, I noticed an attractive blonde lady who looked like a shorter version of Jerry Hall.

Still in Basil Fawlty mode, I sauntered over. "Hello there," I said. (It's amazing how pissed I had become on two glasses of Champagne.)

"Hello," she said, in a soft Irish accent.

"Ah," I said, stating the obvious, "you're Irish?"

"Yes," she said, "how did you guess?"

I can offer no advice whatsoever about chat-up lines. I don't have any that I can reveal work. Actually I don't have any at all. Though I am in my mid-ish 40s I can still become tongue tied and blank when I meet a woman. I just didn't know what to say next.

Rick would have said something casual and witty about potatoes, or the Eurovision Song Contest: Dana, Terry Wogan or even Graham Norton. Probably something inane, but at the very least it would have been an ice breaker.

I didn't have time to worry about a response though as we were interrupted, blessedly by our dedicated tour guide, a tall, smartly dressed girl called Anna-Frid: Danish, jolly and clearly capable. She announced that we'd be travelling to our hotel by water taxi and there were to be five guests in each. If we looked at the reverse side of our tickets, we would see a number for our water taxis. We were to proceed in batches of five.

Without saying a word the Irish "Jerry Hall" turned her ticket over. It read 1. Mine was 5.

"Oh well," she said, "see you again," and was gone.

The boat had aerofoils and the as the craft lifted out of the water I did a quick head count. We were about twenty-five in number. Christmas Eve and it was sunny and bright in Venice but ferociously cold. I wore a long overcoat, sunglasses and gloves. As the water spray hit the hydrofoil it turned to droplets of ice. My glasses were welded to my face. I turned up the collar of my "duvet coat" as the kids called it on the basis that it was bulky and only made an appearance when it was freezing. Maybe this wasn't going to be so bad after all? I couldn't see "Jerry Hall" but I knew she was about. The two elderly ladies were on my craft.

"Hello again young man," they said. I became their willing porter, manoeuvring tartan case, bags and overcoats. Though it was ridiculously gratifying to be called a "young" man I was hooked by their attentions nonetheless.

If you haven't been to Venice in winter – go. It is simply magical. As the city emerged from the lagoon, warm golden lights highlighted honey coloured stone and the water was spangled with brilliant slivers of light. Like shivering diamonds. Christmas Eve in Italy and Venice was fully dressed for it. My mood was lifting and soon we were tying up at the hotel.

Anna-Frid called out our names, handing out envelopes containing our room keys and issuing instructions for us to meet at 5pm for a briefing. Lunch could be taken in the dining room if we wished. Dinner would be at 7pm. Now it was free time.

I looked around for Jerry, but I couldn't see her. Both my newfound friends needed assistance getting their room keys to work and planned to eat some lunch before taking a walk and having a rest.

At the briefing I had learned that if any of us was interested in going to Midnight Mass, the iconic gold lined church in the Centre of Venice, St Marks, would already be filling up and shortly inaccessible. Unless we wished to stand outside and watch the Mass on screens we would not be able to take part in the service there. It was only 12.45pm.

Anna-Frid was keen to extol the virtues of a small catholic church around the corner from the hotel, the Madonna Dell'Orto in the old Jewish quarter near the railway station. I decided this was for me.

On our arrival at the hotel and before the group briefing I'd spoken with Anna about Mass at St. Marks and she'd explained about the problem of going before enquiring if I was Catholic. When I assented she had asked whether I might act as a coordinator for those members of the party interested in attending a service celebrating Christmas.

'Ironic,' I mused, because at school I was the worst altar boy in living memory and for decades after I resolutely ignored my faith.

It was my divorce that had led me back to Catholicism. Alone on Sundays, I'd ventured back shyly to the local parish Church slipping into the back row at the last moment before mass started. The priest there had since become a friend, the words and rituals of the Mass brought me comfort and I was now looking forward to attending Midnight Mass in Venice.

In my role as Mass coordinator Anna had asked me to circulate amongst our group after dinner, collecting the names of anyone wishing to join me in attending the Midnight service and arranging a rendezvous in the hotel foyer at 11.40pm. The next dilemma; what to do next and what to wear for dinner? Tired from lack of sleep, anxiety plus some alcohol, I opted for a nap, a short walk, a shower and dressing. Best laid plans.

I fell asleep, slept deeply, and woke at 6.30pm furious with myself for having such little time to shower and dress. I don't do "casual" confidently. I had been wearing a blazer and roll neck that day, but it was Christmas Eve after all and I felt I should change. I settled on black trousers, white shirt, black jacket with velvet collar and a red/grey coloured silk tie. I completed the ensemble with my favourite cuff links and the same *Chanel* aftershave that had wowed Jane in the flat previously. I felt a bit overdressed to be honest, but, importantly, I felt okay with what I was wearing.

Taking a deep breath I headed to the dining room where there was a whirl of people. Everything was expertly organised. I found my name on a table plan. I was on Table 3. I didn't know about Jerry Hall, but the women from the airport – "Hinge and Brackett," were on my table.

The restaurant overlooked the canal and was at a level slightly beneath but immediately to one side of the hotel's dining room. From its full-length plate glass windows, I could see gondolas decorated with scarlet and gold brocade coverlets and candle-lit lanterns floating past.

The meal was excellent, the wine decent and plentiful and after dessert had been served but before coffee arrived, I was on my feet, wandering around the tables, introducing myself and asking people to join me for the Mass at Midnight if they wished. I had a simple sales pitch, not one officially approved by the Catholic Church...

"Hello," I said, "I am Simon, Happy Christmas. I am going to Midnight Mass at the church around the corner, if you would like to join me at twenty to twelve... or burn in hell!" Delivered of course with a smile.

Jerry on Table 1 looked lovely in an emerald green dress with a black sash. She said she would come. In all, we were eight in number. We met and sat in the reception lounge talking easily whilst waiting for Anna-Frid to escort us.

The Church was an arresting building; circular, with a cool grey interior and with the ceremonial altar at its centre. It was lavishly decorated, lit with tall pillar candles and red floral displays with two tall candle lit trees on each side of the entrance doors. The service was held in Italian of course, not Latin which I might have been able to follow as a child rote-reciter of the Old Mass. I had the impression that we'd probably all drunk a fair amount during the evening given the enthusiasm with which we joined in the communal hymns and the fact that we were singing lustily in a foreign language as part of a foreign congregation. Happily "Oh Come All Ye Faithful" is an international Christmas "hit". It was a moving occasion. Jerry sat next to me.

At the conclusion of the service the priest made his way to us. I wondered if he was going to admonish us or offer choral tuition but he grinned broadly and gestured towards the sacristy indicating by miming that we should join him for a drink. Praise the Lord indeed! He spoke little English, in fact none that was intelligible. We drank several glasses of a powerfully strong liqueur, a variety of Limoncello that tasted of lemon and chocolate. Most of the congregation seemed to have joined us in the tiny sacristy and I found myself in a crush of fellow holidaymakers. Jerry was beside me. We began to talk. "Have you ever been to Ireland?" she enquired.

I had. Belfast in the 1970s, neither England nor Ireland's finest hour we agreed. My mother had been a great fan of Ireland and all things Irish from Dana, Val Doonican and the Spinners, to black and white pudding. I told her about this. She was wearing a smart camel coloured overcoat over her emerald dress. Her soft Irish accent was intoxicating and what the priest was handing out even more so. We stayed for nearly an hour and drank several celebratory glasses of liqueur and then wine before saying our goodbyes to our expansive host, Padre Ricardo and fellow italian congregants who'd been drinking with us and who generously pummeled me on the back as we left.

We walked back to the hotel. It was 3am and the streets were iced. But I felt a warm glow and ridiculously contented when Jerry whose name was Niamh (pronounced Neave) put her arm through mine. Back at the hotel the staff were still officially on duty and to our surprise given the late hour, happy to serve us. We guessed that they were probably enjoying an informal party of their own as the atmosphere was so relaxed.

We piled into an intimate bar in the lobby and feeling expansive, I ordered a bottle of Champagne and invited my fellow churchgoers to join me in a nightcap. In the small hours of Christmas Day, conversation flowed. Niamh removed her camel coat, sat beside me, glass in hand.

"So Simon," she said, in a soft Irish accent, "what's your story?"

In dating encounters this question is a common opening gambit. I know some singles can find such an enquiry at the initial stage of an encounter uncomfortable… too full on, personal and intrusive, but I had come to find it reassuring. With no chat-up lines or confidence in small talk, knowing that I could answer such a FAQ fluently and in a manner that had made other women laugh and maintain at least polite interest in me was encouraging. I suppose it's about finding comfort in ritual. We all have our own story to tell and in the retelling can polish its delivery. I still felt winded after my encounter with Jane and my self-esteem had taken a kicking. I was sitting close to Niamh as we talked; close enough to her to notice that she smelt lovely. She told me that it was *Chanel No.5*.

"Hinge and Bracket" my elderly friends were sitting with us and were engrossed in conversation.

I noticed that from our first evening together a number of the group's members seemed at sufficient ease to converse frankly about their lives. Whilst alcohol undoubtedly helped it seemed more than that. Perhaps being together as strangers at Christmas and in a foreign setting allowed guests to become expansive. Not knowing one another gave a certain freedom to our exchanges.

We had been joined by about a dozen others from our party and whilst the churchgoers amongst us were already regarded as a sub-group – "The "Holy Ones" we'd been called affectionately enough, everyone in the group appeared comfortable and appeared to be getting along well. I hope that if you are a single traveller and find yourself on such a holiday, your experience will be as positive and enjoyable as mine.

People go on singles holidays for different reasons of course. I was there principally to get away at Christmas and avoid the embarrassment as a single man of having to fend off or accept friends' invitations. It would be a bonus if I met someone. My companions had other reasons. "Hinge" had a husband in a nursing home suffering from Alzheimer's and "Bracket" had lost her husband to cancer the previous Christmas.

Another woman, Hilary, described wanting to be away from her adult children and spend time in Italy. She was glamorous, probably in her early sixties and she spoke about her adult children and family life; of being treated by her children as an accommodating baby sitter though she worked long hours in her own business and had an active social life. Since her divorce, she said, she felt that she wanted and was entitled to some time to herself and to "do her own thing" without feeling the pressure of dividing herself between family at Christmas. She was "rebelling" at being expected to care for her delightful, but active young grandchildren when she was in need of rest and relaxation.

"And you Niamh, what's your story?" I asked having delivered my "script" on finding myself single in Venice and alone at Christmas. I wanted to add, "You are so attractive; why on earth are you single?" But I restrained myself.

Niamh stared at her Champagne glass for a while, looked at me as if she was going to say something, then didn't.

I felt as though I had to ask something else and so I said "Have you ever been married?" A silly question really. I just assumed that anyone who was single in their forties had been married.

Again, Niamh didn't answer, and then she smiled and said "No, I never have been married. I got close to being married once but it didn't happen."

Fortified with Limoncello, wine, Champagne and curiosity I pressed for an explanation. "How can you be nearly married?" I laughed.

"Well, I was," said Niamh, "but it was a long time ago and it is very late."

I realised I had upset her by pressing her with my question and laughing. A clumsy alcohol-fuelled mistake, instantly regretted.

Niamh gulped the remaining dregs of her Champagne and stood up. I did too.

She picked up her bag and coat signalling that the evening was over. I felt awful that I'd caused her to become upset. I realised I shouldn't offer to escort her to her room. With Niamh's departure, the party began to break up; people stood and wished each other "Happy Christmas". As Niamh reached the lift she turned and looked back.

"See you at breakfast Simon. I am on table one," she smiled.

The hotel served breakfast until a civilised 11am and I just made it. There was the usual dilemma; what to wear on Christmas Day in Venice? The only thing on the itinerary was a walking tour of Venice, starting after lunch, if I went along. Even though it was very late I was pleased to see Niamh was still eating breakfast. There were several seats at her table.

I wished her "Good morning" and enquired if she had slept well. I'd imagined we'd all be unconscious after the amount of alcohol drunk the previous night.

"Please do join me," said Niamh.

52

I took a seat and without pausing said simply, "I am sorry that I upset you last night."

"Not at all," she said, sounding strangely like Mrs Doyle from *Father Ted*. I thought it best not to mention this. She changed the subject. "Are you going on the walking tour?" she enquired.

I'd been thinking of not bothering, but decided instantly that I was "looking forward" to be going!

"Well then, why don't you take me to lunch beforehand and I will tell you all about it?"

Christmas lunch was going to be tricky. We hadn't booked, it was Christmas Day and Italians like to eat dinner late. But lunch? Our group celebration dinner was booked for 9.30pm in the hotel.

"Well," she laughed, when I pointed out that we might have a problem booking somewhere, given the holiday. "Let's just see if we can have a glass of wine, a snack and a coffee. Whatever we can find."

I was elated. "Good idea!" I gushed.

Looking back at the holiday it was interesting to see how members of the group gravitated towards others and forged relationships. "Hinge and Brackett" having met at Marco Polo airport shared anxieties and experiences regarding absent/lost husbands. They were inseparable within twenty-four hours.

The glamorous Hilary, who was dodging childcare and onerous family responsibilities interestingly, emerged as group leader/den mother. She had a natural, gently authoritative, nurturing demeanour. With her stunning jewellery, expensive clothing and immaculate make-up, it was hard to believe she was considerably older than I had guessed and seventy in a few months.

As for the men in the group – we were in the minority and were a mixed bag. Daniel was a barrister from Guernsey. He was routinely formally dressed throughout the holiday. He was wry, sharp witted and could be hysterically funny. John from the Midlands with a broad Walsall accent was mild mannered, reserved and though he didn't say a great deal, was amiable, seemed contented in our company and was prepared to join in everything. He dressed very casually in jeans and thick jumpers during the days. I never got to know much about him though Daniel told me in a gossipy aside that he was a multi-millionaire.

Lawrence, who came from Brighton, was lively and entertaining. He ran an art gallery with his gay partner Angus who was spending Christmas with his elderly parents. Though they knew of their son's and Lawrence's relationship this wasn't openly acknowledged by them or discussed and

Paul Fox

they hadn't met Lawrence. Having acted to preserve Angus's parent's sensibilities, Lawrence and Angus had re-scheduled their "Christmas" for after Lawrence's return from Venice.

Andy was a session musician, played the guitar and lived on the Scottish borders. Also divorced he wanted to escape a Christmas at home too.

After quickly changing in my room with an eye to the weather, which remained cold but dry and bright, I hurried down to reception. Niamh was about five minutes late and came beaming along the marble corridor. She was dressed warmly, hat, gloves, the lovely camel coat she wore to Mass, expensive looking boots, and an aura of scent about her.

"Sorry I'm late," she smiled, companionably taking my arm and saying "Where are you taking me then?" We went out into the Christmas Day crowds.

We walked along arm in arm and I thought of how that's such a great thing to do. It felt reassuring that Niamh wanted my company and was happy to be in such close proximity to me. I asked her about where she was from. She'd mentioned just before Mass that she lived in South East Ireland near Waterford. We walked and talked.

Venice is a beautiful location at any time of year, except from experience, during July and August when it's oppressively hot and the City is too crowded for my liking. But to be in Venice on this crisp, glorious Christmas Day, meeting an Irish Jerry Hall look-alike and heading for what was shaping up to be an entertaining day was glorious.

Because Italians eat late, the restaurants open at 1pm weren't as full as I'd thought and we soon found a pretty restaurant off a small square. Despite the weather we opted to sit outside beneath a series of efficient patio heaters that are now everywhere in England, the heavy-duty models that sear your face off with the heat if working properly. Soon we had discarded our coats, ordered a light lunch and were toasting each other with the first of many glasses of wine.

I've already owned up to having no decent chat-up lines and as I stared across the table at the stunning Niamh, I heard myself saying something so totally crass and stupid given the conversation that had ended our evening just hours earlier that I winced as I spoke.

"So, how come a lovely woman like you is on a singles holiday?" It really did sound creepy as I uttered it. Fortunately Niamh laughed, wasn't offended.

"Well, I'm single as I said the other night. I've never been married and I probably never will be. Growing up in Ireland, I assumed I'd be married by now. I thought I'd have children, but it seems it wasn't to be." Her mood became more serious. Picking up the thread of the conversation from the previous night she continued. "In fact I was all set to be married as I said to you."

As is apparent, I have a tendency to suffer from "foot in mouth Syndrome" and I was trying not to say the wrong thing, but I wanted to know more.

"What happened?" I asked sensing at this point that being direct was the correct approach. After what seemed an age she said simply.

"I didn't turn up."

"What for, the wedding?"

She went on to explain that she'd been engaged when she was twenty one; had saved to get married, planned a wedding over several years and three years later, the church was booked, the reception was organised and a hefty deposit paid; the bridesmaids dresses chosen, fitted, ordered, were bought – all the paraphernalia of getting married was in place. Niamh went on to say she'd had some doubts about her feelings for her fiancée and wasn't sure whether she really loved him. Forty-eight hours before the wedding she tried to discuss these concerns with her mother who'd brushed them aside as "wedding nerves" She'd spoken to her fiancée about whether they should postpone the wedding and this had ignited a furious row. There were so many questions I wanted to ask.

"My goodness. When did you tell him?"

"I didn't," she said, "I just didn't turn up. At the time I should have been walking down the aisle I slipped out of the house, got on a bus, headed into Dublin and checked into a bed and breakfast."

If this were a film with a cheesy ending I imagined it could be entertaining. There would be scenes of Niamh sitting on a bus in her wedding dress, small suitcase in her hand. But it was clear that Niamh had been deeply affected by the decision not to get married and leaving it so late to run.

Apparently her fiancée had been devastated but was still willing to carry on with the relationship. More surprisingly, her mother had been the most critical and vitriolic, claiming that she would never get over the embarrassment, to say nothing of the cost and asking to know petulantly when she would get to wear her mother-of-the-bride outfit again. She must have been disappointed but her lack of support for Niamh at that time appeared heartless. There was still a distance between them and Niamh said she found it hard not to resent her mother for her reaction.

We'd only known one another for just over 24 hours and putting aside the obvious physical attraction, I felt close to her and was touched that she'd been prepared to disclose such intimate detail about her life.

She then explained that there had been other relationships after she and fiance had finally part. She ended her explanation saying, "I get quite nice boyfriends and we have a good time and then I just think 'Oh, I can't be bothered with all this again'. If you've read any of the numerous books or articles written about dating by women, you will doubtless come across a chapter entitled 'Commitment Phobia by Men', but not for the last time in this book will you hear about commitment phobia by women."

We'd drunk our way through a bottle of Prosecco and were now sipping cortados, tiny cups of coffee with almond biscuits. We wandered back to the hotel ready to join the walking tour for three o'clock. As we approached the group, Niamh took her arm out of mine. We were back in more formal group mode. The tour was a delight and we enjoyed the intelligent commentary of an informed and enthusiastic guide. I was pleased to see the hotel as we turned the final corner en route from the Rialto Bridge. We'd had an entertaining tour and learned much about Venice but I was tired and needed a rest. Our gala Christmas dinner being scheduled for 9.30pm o'clock meant there was plenty of time to unwind and prepare for what promised to be a night to remember. After a doze, I showered, watched TV, got dressed into my dinner jacket and headed for the downstairs bar and dining room.

The hotel had surpassed itself. There wasn't one, but six Christmas trees in the main dining room decorated simply with white garlands and clear lights. It was stylish and effective. Each member of our group had dressed formally for dinner. We were still sitting in our strict table order. Niamh was seated on table 1 and I was on table 3. She was wearing a full-length black satin evening dress, shoes with diamanté heels, red lipstick. Her blonde hair was piled on top of her head. The restaurant was full. Dinner was a 5-course meal. I was surprised to find that the main dish featured stuffed roast turkey with a vast array of vegetables. I was surprised that there wasn't an Italian option what was served was a traditional English Christmas dinner and the theme continued with a choice of Christmas pudding, mince pies with brandy butter. It was superb.

What a Christmas Day it had been! I felt elated but it wasn't over. After the vast meal we made our way to the hotel's waterside lounge/bar. It was well past midnight and into Boxing Day as people drifted into clusters. I sat beside Niamh and Hilary, John, Andy and Daniel joined us. We were discussing potatoes, perhaps inspired by the three varieties served with dinner.

Niamh was holding court, saying that annoyingly some English assume that potatoes are still a staple crop and valuable Irish export and that all Irish are potato experts. In mid-laugh I was alerted to "Hinge" (or was it "Bracket"?) weaving into the bar. She was giggling and obviously plastered. She sat down heavily between Niamh and myself after I grabbed a free chair and steered it towards her as she careered alarmingly in our direction. Andy had taken her arm guiding her towards it. We tried to make conversation, but got nowhere.

You know how it is when people are so drunk that they've no idea what they're saying, you've no idea what they're saying but are trying to go through the pretence of ignoring the elephant in the room, which is "You are completely drunk!"

Don't get me wrong – I'd had a fair amount to drink and so had Niamh, but we were still conscious, upright and sentient, at least to one another. "Hinge" (or was it "Bracket"?), was getting worse. She was now slumped in the chair and snoring heavily.

Niamh leaned over to me and said: "I think we'd better take her to her room."

I nodded in agreement and leant towards her and said slowly and with emphasis, "We're just off to bed now, can we give you a hand?" I'm sure Niamh caught the hopeful expression on my face. Without any embarrassment, my arm was offered and taken and after gently getting our elderly friend to stand, we were soon in the lift on either side of her.

Hinge's room (we'd established it was her) was on the same floor just further along the corridor from mine and once outside her door and after a bit of fumbling in her bag for the key, we deposited her gently on the bed. After a brief discussion about whether we should put her in the recovery position and whether she was safe to leave she seemed to rally. Recognising she was indeed fine, just very sleepy, Niamh pulled the covers over her. We left leaving a lamp switched on in her room and tiptoed out onto the corridor, heading back towards my room. 'Hmm' I mused, 'what would be the gentlemanly thing to do? Should I invite Niamh in for coffee or another drink?'

As we stepped nearer to my approaching door I decided to go for it. Niamh was holding on to my arm, laughing about "Hinge".

"Well, this is me," I said, stopping outside my room door.

"Oh really?" she said.

I turned into Hugh Grant "Err... I was wondering if err, well in fact, if you were err, not doing anything, whether...?" Niamh smiled. In fact, she threw back her head and laughed.

"Whether I'd like to come in for a drink?" she offered taking my fumbling initiative.

"Yes," I said.

"Yes please, I'd love to, Simon."

The great thing about hotel rooms, especially small ones like mine, is that the only place to sit is on the bed. What a bonus, Niamh on my bed, drinking wine that we found in the mini bar. She looked so Christmassy. I couldn't work out what was making me more drunk – was it the copious amounts of alcohol I'd consumed that day or the sheer intoxication of this wonderful woman?

Niamh reached up and pulled a slide from the back of her hair and her blonde locks tumbled to her shoulders. It seemed to me to be some form of signal and in an instant we were in each other's arms, rolling about the bed. Niamh rolled onto her back and lifted one knee into the air. I instinctively ran my hand up the outside of her leg. She was wearing stockings! They were the hold-up variety with a lacy elastic top to them – very pretty.

I started to try to slip my jacket off, planning to drop it casually on the floor, as my great hero, James Bond would in such a situation. As I stood up momentarily to finally shrug it off, I could see that Niamh, under her evening dress, was wearing vivid pink knickers. My favourite! I love girls who wear pink knickers. Taking my jacket off, however, was a mistake. Niamh had taken the opportunity to plant her feet firmly on the floor and she drained her glass in a single gulp.

"Well Simon," she said, "thank you for the drink but we both know where this is heading and I think I should go."

I switched from being James Bond to Hugh Grant again.

"Err well, if you must."

She very gently put her finger to my lips and said: "Yes, I must," then kissed me warmly and headed for the door. As she was about to step out she turned, smiled and said, "Good Night Simon. It's been a grand day and I am so glad we've met. See you at breakfast."

What a day! Getting into the rumpled bed, not that we'd made it under the covers, alas, I checked my mobile phone. I'd received messages and Christmas greetings from the children, a couple of relatives and friends. In twenty-four hours I'd gone from despair at why I'd booked this God-awful holiday to euphoria. I would like to say I fell soundly asleep... but I didn't. I was thinking about pink knickers. Niamh's pink knickers were perfect. Perfect? They were bikini style (I don't like thongs), they were bright pink, sort of Barbie pink with white lace around the legs and waist. Pink knickers are just the best. Why is that? For the answer, we have to go all the way back to 1971. If this was a film instead of a book, what follows would be the dream sequence. The picture would go all zig-zaggy...

I went to an all-boy's Catholic secondary school. I think such institutions are banned now. At least, if they're not, they should be. We were taught by elderly Priests and a few decrepit civilians. In the second term into this sea of misery sailed a new laboratory assistant.

She – yes, SHE was a vision, not unlike Niamh really, long blonde hair, petite. Her name was Mrs Pike. The school was introduced to her in an assembly, the most momentous assembly I'd ever attended. She was appointed to work alongside the new science master, Mr Pollard.

He'd come straight from university by the look of him. Much to my parents' disgust he had a beard and long hair. He looked like a *Top of the Pops* dropout they'd said disparagingly. The school building had recently undergone some improvements and a new wing had been added. There were open staircases, suspended runways and walkways. It was aptly named "The New Science Block" and it looked dramatically futuristic for 1971. Don't bother going to look for it. It's now a housing estate, along with the rest of the school.

I was thrilled to see Mrs Pike in the science block. I used to arrive especially early for the science lesson. She was wonderful.

I decided she looked like the blonde dancer, Babs, from *Pan's People*, on *Top of the Pops*. She was literally a breath of fresh air. She even spoke to us, me in particular, like we were – well – human. I'd often help her get the lab ready for lessons. After one such lesson, she came over to me and said "Thanks for helping me Simon," and touched the side of my face. Wow! I thought I was going to faint. I vowed I'd never wash my face again. I experienced a rush of blood, but not to the head. I was so besotted with her that I couldn't speak to answer. I knew that if she touched me again, I'd explode.

One stifling July afternoon I was thrilled to see that we had an un-timetabled double science lesson. But Mrs Pike was nowhere to be seen. Mr Pollard waffled on for ages about molecular structure. I was fed up, hot and bothered, but all that was about to change. The door of the lab

Paul Fox

near where I was sitting opened and in stepped Mrs Pike, an urgent air about her. Her white lab coat was gleaming in the classroom sun. I thought she looked like an angel. She waved at Mr Pollard.

"I need some help," she said. "There's been a spillage next door."

"Yes of course," he said.

I was closest to the door.

"Taylor," he said, "go and help Mrs Pike."

I was up in a flash, practically bolting toward the door. We trotted to the lab. It had tall wooden tables with matching long legged stools and was set up for an exam.

"I've spilt some mercury. One of the tubes fell off the table. Could you help me mop it up?"

I let out a squeak of "Yes, of course." The floor was wet with cleaning fluid and I was trying to keep my eyes off Mrs Pike and on the job in hand. When looking up, I noticed she had bent herself over a stool in the far corner of the room and she was cleaning a ledge about six inches from the skirting board. She was showing an awful lot of leg. I tried not to look, but I couldn't help myself.

Suddenly there was a noise like a rifle crack. Mrs Pike shrieked. The stool had given way underneath her and she was now doing a handstand against the wall – trapped between this and the table.

As I rushed across to help her up, her white lab coat descended and by the time I reached her, all I could see was a pair of glorious long legs stretching right up the wall and bright pink, closely-fitting knickers. I have never forgotten it. I helped her to her feet. I thought she'd be very annoyed, but no.

She smiled. "Well, you've seen something you shouldn't have been seeing today."

"Yes Miss," I said.

I returned to my early Boxing Day slumber. I couldn't wait for what tomorrow would bring. When I awoke bright sunlight illuminated my room and I was relieved to find that I didn't have a hangover. There were still twenty four hours of the holiday to go. My mobile had been plugged beside the bed and I glanced at it and saw that I'd received more messages from friends and family. As I scrolled through them I noticed one from my gym trainer, Melanie. Yes, not only had I joined the gym, I was taking it seriously and was having instruction from my own trainer. Her message read, "Hi Simon, Happy Xmas, hope u r enjoying Venice. Melanie X PS R u still single?"

60

I'd answered all my other texts and sent one back to her, "Venice is wonderful, met a nice Irish lady, but yes, still single. Why?"

One came back immediately saying "R u up for a blind date?"

I'd never been on a blind date so I sent one back saying "Sounds good – who with?"

"Wdnt be much of a blind date if I told u who it was with Simon. I'll sort it out 4 when u gets bck. Enjoy the rest of stay. Mel x."

The arranged seating plans had now been abandoned and I sat next to Niamh during breakfast. The only item on the itinerary today was a trip to the islands of Murano and Burano. Niamh was saying that she was interested in purchasing a chandelier for her house. 'Must be some house,' I thought. Murano glassware is highly prized and extremely expensive. As we stepped onto the water taxi, Anna-Frid was announcing that there was no organised lunch. However she could recommend a few good restaurants on the island of Murano and could phone ahead and organise reservations. Would anyone like her to do that? She looked at the group enquiringly. I was about to put my hand up when I felt Niamh's hand on my arm.

"Let's make our own arrangements," she said.

As our high-powered water taxi pulled up alongside the jetty at Burano, a handful of elderly looking gentlemen were there to help us off the boat. Anna-Frid explained that they were retired gondoliers who worked for tips helping tourists on and off the boats. Quite spontaneously our group split into two. The girls went one way and the guys the other. It was the first time it had happened.

We agreed to meet in an hour. The island on a slight acquaintance looked worth spending at least a day exploring with its lace artwork studios, Venetian mask shops, market, Church and unusual Bell Tower. An attractive island with multi coloured pastel buildings along the water's edge it seemed more Caribbean at first sight than Italian. It was the first time I had been alone with the other guys in the group. I think women imagine that when men are alone together they talk about sex or them, or both. Well I'm sorry to disappoint – we hardly ever talk about sex. As Daniel, ambled along beside me, he said.

"You seem to be getting on very well with Niamh."

I realised other people had noticed, especially as we had now started sitting together, so it seemed pointless denying it. "Yes," I said

"She's very nice, almost delicious," he said with gusto.

"So why is a high-powered barrister on a singles holiday?" I asked him. It was a bloke's way of asking "What's your story?" He explained he'd been married three times. Each wife was a "gold digging bitch". He told me he was independently wealthy so despite the ex-wives' "wrecking-ball attempts" at fleecing him, he'd managed to remain comfortably off. He flashed gold Rolex as confirmation of this status. "Do you think you will get married again? I asked. It seemed unlikely but I was trying to be polite. "No fear!" he exclaimed, unnecessarily explosively I felt.

"Can't stand bloody women, all they want is your money. Can't even be bothered with the shagging any more..."

Lawrence, who was a few steps behind us, had obviously overheard our conversation.

"Fancy batting for the other side then?" he enquired.

"No thanks," said Daniel, "I don't do pain!"

We turned back towards the landing stage where we were to meet the women.

I wasn't convinced of the accuracy of our tour guide's description of Burano as a haven for retired gondoliers. Most of these men looked pretty down at heel and were making half -hearted attempts to sell tatty tourist merchandise including fridge magnets and key rings. My daughter Vicky collects key rings so I purchased one with a sample of lace within its plastic case. Anna Frid was handing out details of restaurants she had booked for lunch on request. Our self-appointed group leader Hilary had called out as Niamh and I as we tried in vain to slip away from the rest of the group unnoticed -

"You two not joining us then?" she called. Before we could reply she threw out both her arms as if to wave us away and said "Go and have a great time," There were several shouts of "Bye, love birds", and "Remember to eat something."

I was delighted to be alone with Niamh again. I realised I hadn't minded being spotted. In fact, I felt pretty smug. I had this lovely woman to myself. Murano is livelier and more sophisticated than Burano. There was plenty to see; an abundance of charming restaurants and bars with white tablecloths and straw covered wine bottles dotted along the quayside within the adjacent harbour. "Are you hungry?" asked Niamh. It had only been a few hours since breakfast but there was something about boat travel and fresh air that had heightened my appetite. "I am a bit," I ventured.

"I'm starving," Niamh declared.

We settled on a waterside restaurant and began surveying the menu greedily. I love Italian food and so did Niamh it turned out. I was happy to see that they offered one of my favourite dishes, spinach cannelloni.

Niamh chose a risotto dish with fresh peas. We ordered two glasses of the local staple, Venetian Spritz as an aperitif – the menu described it as white wine, sparkling water and "Select", a ruby red coloured, orange tasting local liqueur. I'm not keen on sparkling alcoholic drinks unless the drink is Brut Champagne preferably Veuve Cliquot, but this was very good. We began chatting. Niamh was describing how she was proud of being Irish and we spoke for a while about people's perceptions of Ireland. It seemed trite but true she was saying that many visitors' views of Ireland seemed to be informed by stock comic characters such as Father Ted and Terry Wogan. We laughed about the Eurovision Song Contest again.

Why are Irish people considered by some to be dense or unintelligent? President Kennedy on his visit to Dublin in June 1963 commented that Ireland's influence on history has been far greater than its relative size. I knew of this visit as I have an interest in American history and particularly, JFK. I explained what I knew of the visit and about the Kennedy clan in Ireland to Niamh. She had the grace to appear interested and smiled at me "We're getting on so well Simon. I'm really glad I came on this holiday. I only booked it a week ago. I couldn't stand another Christmas at my sisters."

"How amazing," I said, "I only booked it a couple of days ago. I couldn't stand a Christmas with other people's sisters. And their children, parents, Uncles..."

"Well," she said, laughing "that's fortunate for both of us."

She held my gaze for a fraction longer and glass in hand leant towards me. I picked up my glass of frothy sparking Spritz and declared a toast "to us". We clinked glasses and then I kissed her. I'm normally rubbish at seizing the moment, but I know I judged the situation accurately. It was one of those perfectly timed intuitive instances.

And then my left thigh started to vibrate. It took me a couple of seconds to realise that it was my mobile phone, not an electric current spontaneously generated by the kiss. I had set my phone on silent as I didn't want to interrupt our meal. I ignored it.

We drank a bottle of chilled white Italian Gavi with our meal and after drinking coffee with tiny spiced biscotti wandered slowly back to the meeting point to join the rest of the group.

Hilary and Anna-Frid were in animated conversation. "Good news," announced Hilary, "we're off to see some glass blowing." Anna-Frid took over: "I did not think they would be working on Boxing Day but they are and have agreed to extend their factory opening hours so that we might visit." I was impressed with her dedicated enthusiasm and professionalism. She was a great rep.

To be honest, I wasn't thrilled at the prospect of going to a glass blowing demonstration. I mean – how difficult can it be? But an hour later I stood next to Niamh in front of a volcanically hot kiln. A tall Venetian wearing a thick leather apron introduced himself as Enzo and picked up a long steel tube. As he began opening a kiln door. I thought my eyebrows were going to crisp and drop off.

He dabbed the pole into the furnace and brought out a lump of molten glass – bright and white hot and dripping like clear honey. To my amazement, never having witnessed the process before, Enzo placed the other end of the tube in his mouth and began to blow. In thirty seconds there was an identifiable jug on the end of the pole. Producing a pair of thin bladed shears he swiftly fashioned a handle and in one movement attached it to the jug and placed it before us. I had thought glass blowing was a mechanised process, the blowing being from bellows or directional air dryers. I was impressed. The answer to the question of how difficult it could be is "Bloody difficult!"

"Wow!" I said to Niamh, "How clever is that?"

"I know," she said in her Southern Irish brogue, "they do it near us."

"They make glass in Ireland?"

"Yes!" she said indignantly. "Have you never heard of Waterford Crystal?"

We turned again to Enzo who was now fashioning a horse from another lump of cooling melted glass, using the tube to inflate and fashion the body of the animal. I turned to Niamh and said "Gosh, you've got to be good at blowing to do that."

She smiled and said "And sucking," raising one eyebrow. We both laughed.

'Well, there's always hope,' I thought.

As we sped back across the lagoon in the water taxi, Anna Frid reminded us that we had our last gala dinner that evening at 8.30pm. Dress code was black tie and we would be free to sit wherever we liked and with whomever we liked. The rest of the group turned in perfect unison and looked at us!

'I'll need some intensive sessions at the gym when I get home,' I thought. All these meals were playing havoc with my waistline, to say nothing of the booze we were all consuming.

The following day the water taxi cut through the icy waters of Venice lagoon on the way to the airport.

Boxing Day evening's gala dinner had been another great occasion and I'd thoroughly enjoyed myself. After yet another multi-course gourmet dinner we'd again headed for the bar, and a large group of us had sat talking into the early hours. Niamh had worn a stunning white and gold evening dress and looked amazing. I'd hoped of course that she'd join me in my room at the end of the night, but it wasn't to be. There had been music organised by the hotel, a small band and we'd danced into the early hours. I don't actually dance recognisably but had made an effort and 'danced' with Hinge and Brackett, individually and together! I even danced with Lawrence. I made a clumsy attempt at asking Niamh back to my room, but she turned me down.

"You know what? Half of me would really like to, but the other half says 'it's late, I'm tired and really, I should go to bed on my own'," she'd said. I didn't know whether to feel pleased or offended and comforted I with the thought that she hadn't actually said, "Go away, you're hideous."

She had kissed me deeply on the lips before she disappeared into the lift. I drank the remains of my wine and reflected for a moment, through my drunken stupor, on the holiday. It had been unexpectedly successful. I wondered if I'd ever see Niamh again. There had been no mention of keeping in touch or swapping phone numbers, e-mail addresses anything like that at all. And now departing from the hotel, in the water taxi we stuck to the ticket system devised by Anna-Frid and as on our arrival, we found ourselves in separate craft.

I caught sight of her on the landing stage at the airport, but she was engrossed in conversation with Hilary and so my default setting engaged and I braced myself, panicking about checking-in, as I always do. I looked round in the queue a couple of times to see where Niamh might be, but I couldn't spot her. As I was handing over my passport and asking for my usual aisle seat, I became aware suddenly that she was next to me. Had she jumped the queue?

"Are you checking-in for the same flight, Madam?" said the Italian check-in clerk.

"Yes I am," Niamh handed over her ticket.

I started to gush: "Oh, hi," and "How are you?" and "Well, I didn't see you at breakfast even..."

"No, I didn't catch breakfast," Niamh said.

"Would you like to sit together?" the attendant said.

I didn't answer.

Niamh spoke for me: "Yes we would." she said emphatically.

The flight back to what the pilot announced kindly were the "grey skies of England and rain in most parts," was uneventful. I was preoccupied in deciding whether and how to ask Niamh if I might see her again. Did she want to see me? She wanted to sit next to me on the plane but I didn't know if that meant anything.

We joined the queue for passport control together and I felt awkward. The conversation seemed artificial, stilted. We talked banalities, of the weather! I went through passport control after Niamh and joined her at the carousel. I explained to her how anxious I get about grabbing my luggage. It's ridiculous I know. On this occasion my anxiety was vying for superiority with embarrassment at the size of my enormous suitcase.

Niamh was travelling on to Dublin and so saying our goodbyes was fast approaching. My car was checked into one of those chauffeur services, where they pick you up from outside departures and you ring them when you land and they come and drop the car off. Seems to work quite well, although I have always been slightly nervous about what they do with the car whilst you are away. I keep meaning to make a note of the mileage on arriving at airports but somehow never actually do. I wondered if there might be time for a coffee with Niamh, but it wasn't possible.

With both our bags in tow and Niamh heading off to catch her flight to Dublin, the chauffeur service rang to say that they were waiting with my car. I turned into Hugh Grant again, well, a sound-alike. After all I don't have the floppy hair, or a famous girlfriend; in fact I didn't have any girlfriend.

"Oh well," I said, "I guess this is goodbye."

"Yes," said Niamh. "It's been wonderful. I've so enjoyed your company Simon."

There was that silence, the "shall I ask to see her again, ask for her phone number?" dilemma. I didn't know what to do. 'She could only say no' I thought. It occurred to me that the same issue might be occupying Niamh's mind. I sensed we both wanted to say things to one another, but didn't want to spoil the friendship or the time we had enjoyed. I didn't want to go too far. I hesitated. Hesitated again. Fortunately, gloriously, Niamh reached into the pocket of her camel coat and pulled out a small envelope. On the envelope was written one word. "Simon".

"Open it when you get in the car," she said. And with a long kiss and a look at her watch.

"Bejesus," she said. The first time I'd heard her come up with an Irish cliché, "I must be gone." And she was.

I was relieved to see my Alfa was in one piece. The driver handed the keys to me and soon I was on the motorway – familiar territory for me. I opened the envelope as soon as I got in the car and it contained a small card that Niamh had obviously purchased from a shop in Venice. It had a picture of the Grand Canal and Rialto Bridge on the front of it.

Inside she had written, "Hi Simon, thanks for making Christmas so wonderful. Let's keep in touch." She had included her home and e-mail addresses and both home and mobile phone numbers. It ended, simply "Niamh" and a kiss.

I punched the air, kissed the envelope and pressed the CD changer. Elton sang "I wanna kiss the bride!"

Blind Date

The days between Christmas and New Year have always seemed to me to be a bit of a no-man's land. When I lived at home with Katherine and the kids we used to call it "Twixtmas".

With no submissions to prepare till a couple of Mass-market motor manufacturers pre-launches in January, I'd felt despondent at the prospect of the solitary drift between the two holidays. But that was before settling upon my plan to sidestep Christmas in the UK.

Instead of feeling at a loose end rattling around the flat, the trip to Venice had been left me on a high, buzzing with more energy than I'd had for years. I sorted out the contents of cardboard boxes and flattened the containers; the children came round and we walked to the pub for lunch; we shopped at Lakeside and watched DVDs at the flat together.

On 28th December when I was relaxing and alone I thought about what I might do at New Year's Eve. Rick had mentioned coming over. Then I remembered. Of course, I'd got a date!

Conscious of the damage to my waistline that I had been worrying over whilst over-indulging in Venice – I can put on pounds in just days, I decided to go to the gym the next morning.

Although I didn't have a formal session booked with Melanie, I was planning to do a workout anyway. I don't know why I'd been so afraid of joining the gym. I thought the place would be full of muscle-bound hulks, strutting their pecks.

I don't like the atmosphere in men's changing-rooms and whilst I know that must sound ridiculous, I can't help it. It was another disincentive. My gym is nothing like my imagined physical perfection factory. It's friendly and the members are all shapes and sizes, ages, abilities, male and female. There are disabled and plenty of 60-plus members. Over the course of the last few months the gym had become my "local". It felt like a second living room. After showering and changing I went downstairs to have a coffee and to find Melanie.

"Hi Simon, how was Venice then?" she asked.

"Fantastic," I replied, "I couldn't believe how good it was."

"Are you still up for that date?" she enquired.

"Yes," I said. "Are going to tell me who it's with?" Melanie grinned and said teasingly.

"No, I'm not, but you'll like her, she's lovely. I'll text you her name and telephone number later today and you can have a chat to her on the phone, how's that?"

"That's fine, I'd like that," I said.

As I walked back to the flat mulling over the assignments I had coming up and the background research I could usefully put in to prepare for the write-ups I wondered whether I should really be going on a blind date. What if I managed to start a relationship with Niamh? I'd texted her once I got back home, saying how pleased I was that she'd let me have her contact details. She'd sent a simple text back saying "That's fine, no problem at all, let's speak sometime on the phone and I'll send you a test e-mail to make sure I've got your e-mail address right." Nothing more than that, simple and friendly. I was tempted to tell her about my blind date. I didn't, but of course I did tell the guys.

Fish and chips that week were off because of Christmas, but I'd contacted Rick and Barry by phone. Rick answered his phone and spoke with the worst Irish accent I've ever heard.

"Hello there, how were the festivities? Will you be going across to the old country then?"

"Don't be daft, Rick," I said, "I've only just met her. She's very nice but far away and anyway, I've some other news, I've got a blind date on Friday."

"Oh my God," he said, "who with?"

We went through the scenario. If I knew who she was; I wouldn't be on a blind date with her would I? But I did explain that Melanie was going to text me her phone number. There was a long pause, "Well, I don't know why you're bothering," he said sharply.

"Why," I said, "what's the harm in it?"

"Look, Simon, she's bound to be your trainer's designated, ugly mate, isn't she?"

"Why? Why would she be ugly?"

"Well," Rick said, "look, if she's got to get her trainer to organise dates for her, she's not exactly Miss Popular, is she?"

"I think you're being unnecessarily harsh, and anyway I've not even spoken to her yet, I thought I'd book *The Riverside Restaurant* again," I ventured. I could be the cabaret for the staff again I thought ruefully.

"Whoa!" he said, "why are you doing that? Just take her out for a drink if you must, she's bound to be awful and make sure you have some sort of get-out clause, you know a get out of jail card."

"What are you talking about, a get out of jail card?" I said.

"Well, say she is an ugly mug or somebody ancient or odd, you can call or text me then I can call you and get you out of it."

It seemed a ridiculous idea to me then but I now know (because I've been on the receiving end of them!) that a lot of people put in place "exit plans" or have means of abandoning a date they can't face fulfilling. Most dating sites recommend that clients involve a friend or use an excuse if they feel uncomfortable or misled or it seems appropriate for any other reason. I can see the point in saying you're going to call a friend to check that everything is okay with this applying to both men and women. But as a dating "newbie" it seemed unromantic and calculated. I decided I should do some work. I'd got quite a few emails. I scanned through them, ones from my agent, Julian, my bank manager, a handful of round-robin New Year jokes from friends, and two from the dating site. I resolved not to open them until after I had done some work. It would make finishing assignments in January easier if I was going to have to juggle completion dates with having a girlfriend and possibly travelling to Ireland.

My conscience was pricking me about the blind date as I felt there was unfinished romantic business between myself and Niamh. Maybe I should call Melanie and tell her I had changed my mind about the blind date. But then again, I hadn't heard from her with my date's number so I decided to delay the decision about going or not until I heard from one or other of them.

I congratulated myself on being so organised. It's pretty unlike me. I'm normally distracted by the slightest thing and finding ways of avoiding settling to work is a habit I've spent a lot of time perfecting.

Of course I couldn't resist opening the dating emails. I had done an hour and a half's work but I was too intrigued by who might be in my Inbox to do more. One email was from a woman in Coventry, a long distance, over 125 miles from where I live. She looked good. Her profile picture appeared professionally done and she had written "I know you live a long way away, but I thought you sounded very nice and I just wanted to wish you Happy Christmas."

'Lovely' I thought and sent one back. I said I liked the idea of being sent to Coventry, especially if she lived there, or something corny like that. The next wasn't a personal message but a dating site that had a personal introduction service asking whether I might consider joining. It looked an established outfit and its online blurb and brochure stressed it catered for professional clients. They would interview me, they would

Paul Fox

photograph me (oh dear, I thought) and then they would match me up with somebody "ideal".

It was quite appealing, but then I looked at the price – on special introductory offer – just £1,750!

'Maybe not this month,' I thought totting up the cost of the Venice trip.

What I've learned whilst doing research is that £1,750 isn't expensive and some agencies charge clients up to three times that amount. I've also discovered that women clients pay more than their male counterparts. If you are thinking of joining a fee paying agency ladies, my advice would be to negotiate hard on the price, especially if you're going to potentially meet somebody like me!

That evening everyone was busy so I had another night in on my own. I'd managed to *Sky Plus* a batch of missed Christmas favourites and was settling down with a glass of wine to watch my absolute favourite Christmas film – not National *Lampoon's Christmas Vacation* – but The *Great Escape*. Just at the cringe moment – where Gordon Jackson (Mr Hudson from *Upstairs Downstairs)* gets caught with Richard Attenborough on the bus… "Have a good trip," says the German officer.

"Thanks awfully old boy," replies Gordon Jackson, an escapee, in perfect English (twit!) – My phone bleeped. I had a text message. It was a new number. It simply said: "Hello Simon, I'm your blind date for Friday if you still want to turn up! I think perhaps we'd better talk first, don't you? Best wishes, Shilpa."

'Shilpa,' I thought. Maybe she's got predictive text on, maybe her name is Sharon or Sandra nothing wrong with them, after all this was Essex. But who would get their own name wrong. It would be like me typing "Simone"! I was beginning to feel slightly wary. What if Rick was right, what if this was Melanie's designated ugly mate. I'd be wasting New Year's Eve.

But then I didn't have anything else appealing on the horizon. I hadn't any plan at all. So well why not?

I texted back "Hi Shilpa, thanks ever so much for texting me. Yes, of course I'd love to meet up on Friday. What time shall we say, about 7 or 7.30? And where would you like to meet? When would it be convenient to call to confirm. Best wishes Simon."

I'd seen the warnings on the web encouraging singles on first dates to meet somewhere neutral. A safe public place. Though in a practical sense these might be regarded as applying more to women than men, I thought I'd exercise discretion. I suggested we should meet at the gym. I received

72

a reply by text immediately saying "I'm sure Melanie wouldn't introduce me to an axe murderer. Why not pick me up from my house?"

I felt a bit silly after that. "Yes of course, I'd be happy to", I texted back.

I had a reply by return saying "I'm going out now so perhaps we could talk tomorrow?"

"Yes I'd like that very much", and I got back to *The Great Escape*. Would Steve (McQueen) make it over the wire this time? I wondered what "Shilpa" would be like and what her real name was. I phoned Rick, having put the film on pause.

"She sounds awful," he said, "fancy texting you first, how forward. And where's she going now this time of night?" I looked at my watch. It was only 8.30pm.

Rick is patently not the most romantic person in the world. Though well aware of this, his relentlessly negative attitude was beginning to put me off a little. After Steve McQueen failed, yet again, to get over the wire in Switzerland on his Triumph I went to bed. 'Oh dear,' I thought, 'Friday's only the day after tomorrow. What am I going to wear?'

Arriving at the gym for my workout the next day the staff were occupied preparing for the New Year's Eve party. I managed to speak to Melanie about Shilpa. Her name wasn't Sharon, Sandra or Shirley, it was Shilpa and she was Indian. Apparently she had been divorced for six or seven years, hadn't had a relationship for a little while and was fed up with spending the weekends on her own.

"I think you'll really like her," she said. "In fact, I've been expecting you to bump into her as she's a member here too. I thought if you did you'd be bound to ask me who she was." I was sure I hadn't seen her in the gym, there were a few Indian ladies there, but no one I could particularly recall.

Rick had obviously spoken to Barry about the New Year's Eve blind date because Barry had rung and said "Why don't we get together for a quick drink? Can't do fish and chips, fed up eating, tell us about Venice, the woman you met on holiday and this mysterious blind date."

I didn't know whether to be irritated or not. If you're single, your love life is a bit of a 'free-for-all' really. In my case everyone felt entitled to comment on who I was dating, why I was dating them, how they (the boys) felt about it and what I should do. Whilst I am inclined to talk freely about my love life, my feelings and what's going on (I wouldn't be writing this book otherwise), I was starting to feel that the guy's observations were becoming intrusive and patronising. After all, what was the worst that could happen? It was a blind date but I wasn't that 'blind'. I already knew something of Shilpa, had spoken to her on the phone a couple of times now and was looking forward to spending New Year's Eve with her. I, Rick, Barry sat in the bar at the gym on the Thursday night and I was sulking. And I can sulk!

"Look Simon," said Barry, "all we're concerned about is that you just seem to be trying too hard, you're constantly worrying about meeting somebody. Why don't you just relax?"

Talking to friends and colleagues I think singletons in middle age fall into two categories. There are those that never really want to be married or in a serious relationship again and those that do. I was in the latter camp. I wasn't part of a couple and I needed the companionship, the closeness, shared love and sex with a partner.

Whilst I like and do truly value my friends, constants throughout my life, they obviously couldn't take the place of a woman and I hoped one day I might find someone to settle with and marry again. Apart from Rick and Barry I have several single, divorced male friends who are so content with their detached family lives, friends and hobbies they actively avoid cultivating relationships with women who might want more than sex or occasional contact. They have casual girlfriends but wouldn't dream of living with a woman or marrying again. For me that wouldn't do. I wanted to be in a long-term relationship again. One with a future.

As we wouldn't be seeing each other the next day, we toasted a "Happy New Year" to ourselves and the start of my first year as a singleton. I'd made a bad start at dating but things were looking up. There was tomorrow night to look forward to. *The Riverside* had managed to squeeze a table in to accommodate my late booking. Try though I might to suppress it however I couldn't tune out Rick's grim prediction of my blind date.

Ringing in my ears on that 30th December night, his parting shot had been, "Look Simon, don't get your hopes up, remember what I said, she's bound to be the gym's very own Bridget Jones."

Shilpa had mentioned that she liked books and reading, going to the gym, looking after her daughters and, well… not much else really.

"There you are," Barry had said, "bet she's a librarian or something really dull. Bet she wears glasses, so call us if you want to get out of the date, we'll come up with some plumbing emergency or something."

I had to keep reminding myself that they weren't being fatuous and mean about Shilpa for the sake of it. They were actually concerned for me and my soft heart.

I confirmed to Shilpa in the morning that I'd be picking her up at 7.30pm.

"Will you be arriving in a taxi?" She'd asked. "After all it is New Year's Eve."

Typically for me, I hadn't thought much about the detail, just blind date, nice restaurant, dinner. The fact that it was New Year's Eve and everywhere had been booked for weeks, including every taxi in Essex just hadn't crossed my mind. I started to get anxious: Should I try and book a taxi? What if she is awful? If she really is Melanie's designated ugly mate? I wondered. It would be a waste of a taxi and I'd be on my way home within fifteen minutes. After all, thanks to Rick, I'd got the "plumbing emergency" now tucked up my sleeve.

Our plan was hatched. It was simple. I just had to text "Vesuvius" to Rick and he would call saying that there'd been a flood at my flat (we'd toed and fro'd with code words for "get me out of here". My personal favourite was "Broad Sword calling Danny Boy" – from *Where Eagles Dare* but we had finally settled on "Vesuvius" for reasons I can't actually remember now except of course it came from *The Dam Busters* film). Honestly, who would fall for an emergency plumbing disaster on a blind date, especially on New Year's Eve. If you have actually had one of these you have my sympathy. After several glasses of wine we thought it was a great idea.

Over the next few hours and early on that New Year's Eve, I'd managed to convince myself that the evening was going to be a complete waste of time. I even thought of feigning illness. Why didn't I just go to the gym's party, get drunk and walk back to the flat? After all lots of nice girls go to the gym as the guys kept telling me. But I was committed now to seeing Shilpa.

My anxiety heightened. I felt totally confused. Is it like this for everybody? Does everybody worry about dating so much? The guys hadn't helped. Why couldn't I just relax? I settled on driving and at exactly 7.30pm I pulled up outside Shilpa's house. An impressive large detached place with a gated driveway, pillared entrance porch, at a guess, six or seven bedrooms. It wasn't until I parked that I noticed a sizeable conservatory and sweeping lawns. There was a gold Toyota Land cruiser on the driveway. I remember thinking that it was a serious 4-wheel drive favoured by the Taliban and the UN alike. Then 'Oh my God, what's she going to think of my flat?' I consoled myself with the notion that she was bound to be awful and so it wouldn't ever be an issue.

I pressed the buzzer outside the gates with some anticipation, mentally preparing for disappointment.

"Hi Simon," said a voice I recognised as Shilpa's. "I'll be out in five. Just hang on and I'll be with you." She sounded pleased to hear me. Maybe she didn't have many dates. Melanie had said she hadn't been in a relationship for a while.

'Stop being so negative' I told myself. Then 'Why do I do this sort of thing? Why?' I thought as I hovered outside the gates. A wrought iron side gate I hadn't noticed on arriving clanked open. And there she was.

"Hello," she said, extending a hand, "I'm Shilpa."

I couldn't speak.

I couldn't move.

I was paralysed.

Speechless.

She was absolutely stunning.

Huge oval shaped brown eyes, thick shoulder length jet-black hair that shone in the moonlight. Her hair wasn't the only thing that shone – she was wearing a silver grey dress with a close fitting bodice and a box pleat skirt, just to the knee. Despite the chill, her shoulders were bare, though she was carrying a black jacket and wearing strappy black shoes. She was slim and slightly shorter than me (blessedly). I still hadn't spoken. Could I? I just couldn't muster up Basil Fawlty or Hugh Grant or even me? She tilted her head to one side and said.

"Are you okay?"

I pretended to have a cough, I coughed and coughed, not very convincingly, then managed to mutter "Yes, I'm fine, I'm sorry I'm absolutely fine, I'm Simon, and gosh you're very, very attractive." Oh God, what a pathetic thing to say, I just don't know why I did this. She would think I was so superficial. If she thought I was a lightweight twit she had the grace not to show it.

"Thank you," she said smiling. I was aware of perfect white teeth.

"Shall we go or would you like to come in for a drink?"

"Come in for a drink?" I didn't know what to think. I didn't know what to say. I just wasn't prepared for her invitation.

"Well, um, I did book the restaurant, so shall we go?" I mumbled.

Why didn't I go in for a drink? What an idiot. I was totally useless. Looking back I think I felt overwhelmed and totally unequal to this ravishingly beautiful woman. And she was very lovely indeed. I had definitely not seen her at the gym. So much for Christmas Day, Boxing

Day and Twixtmas. New Year's Eve was looking fantastic. I opened the car door for Shilpa and she sat in it expertly – sideways onto the open car, her knees and ankles together as she sat down and spun her ankles into the well of the car, gathering her skirt as she went.

The last time I'd been to *The Riverside* was with Stephanie. I'd explained when I made the reservation that I was on a blind date.

"Not another one, Simon, surely not?" Madeleine on reception had laughed.

We arrived at our table. It wasn't ideally placed, crammed in between the toilet and the kitchen, possibly the worst location in the restaurant, but then it was New Year's Eve and I had only booked a day or so before. With hindsight I'm sure Madeleine, Clive and the rest of the staff were determined to accommodate my booking on the basis that watching a second dating disaster unfold would be a laugh. I'd managed to engage her in small talk in the car, but now, seated at our table and feeling slightly more confident I summoned up Basil Fawlty and he blurted out in a chipper manner.

"So, you're Indian then?" Shilpa took a sip of her Champagne and said "Yes, I'm Indian."

"So were you born here to Indian parents, or..."

"No," she said, "I was born in India. In Bombay. It's now called Mumbai."

Why do they change the name of cities? It drives me nuts. What was wrong with Constantinople? And Ceylon? Why Sri Lanka? Stalingrad, now Volgograd. I blundered on.

"So, why did you decide to come to England?" I must have sounded like a border official or uniform at Passport Control: "State your business in the United States."

Remember those forms they used to issue on board flights to America which had the astonishing endorsement: "Is it your intention to bring down the government of the United States during your visit?" What a stupid question! I had a friend – and this is true – who drank too many glasses of wine on board his transatlantic flight and for a laugh and in answer to that question (which should always be an unqualified "No") put "Sole purpose of visit". Immigration border control at Detroit airport didn't see the funny side and he ended up spending six hours in a police cell while he sobered up and his employers came to get him.

Fortunately Shilpa was more adept at conversation. "Well, I didn't actually decide to come to England, my parents did, I was five. It was the mid-1970s and my parents thought we'd have better prospects here in England. It's ironic now as India has a respected space programme, every insurance company in the UK has a call centre there and their health service is better than ours," she said.

She went on to explain that when her family first came from India, their relatives used to come to England to have their babies. Now they all go over there. I didn't know much about India. My grandfather had fought in Burma during World War II and commanded a Sikh regiment. I can remember him telling me tales of how brave the Sikhs were and how he'd often left wounded men at Indian villages. The locals had nothing much for themselves, but what they had they shared and every man that he left to be cared for by the Indians survived, at terrible cost should they have been discovered by the Japanese.

I was brought up at a time when it wasn't considered racist to make fun of Indians and it was acceptable to ape their perceived customs and accents. Peter Sellers grinning "Goodness, glacious me" and the show *Love thy Neighbour* with Alf Garnett were popular comedy standards. It was a different world then.

Shilpa nodded and smiled. She spoke movingly about coming to England; of a train journey that lasted weeks, crossing Europe and ending up in East London. In India she remembered living in a detached villa on its own estate and her family had an Aya, a nanny and an Ama, a cook and plenty of servants. It was warm and sunny and her family arrived in East London in October. She said she'd suffered badly with the cold and even now, nearly forty years later she still wasn't fully acclimatised to it.

She also spoke compellingly about racial harassment. She too had been on dating websites and told me that on several occasions she had experienced outright rejection, instances where once men realised she was Indian, she never heard from them again though they had already spoken for some time, emailed and enjoyed a decent dialogue. One guy had phoned up and asked conversationally, "What sort of a name's Shilpa then?"

"It's an Indian name."

"Why have you got an Indian name?" he had asked.

"Well, because I'm Indian," she'd replied. He had simply put the phone down.

She told me she had worked before having her family as a glamour model until she met her husband who didn't like her appearing scantily dressed for photo shoots. As for her marriage, she explained that she'd been married for about ten years, but it was a rocky relationship and they were ill matched. Her husband had left her suddenly for someone else. A woman he worked with. His parting shot had been that he just "couldn't stand it any longer". She didn't elaborate on this. Maybe I should have asked her what she thought he meant by this. It did occur to me to do so but I felt it inappropriate and congratulated myself on my sensitivity for once. I told her about my own relationship with Katherine and how I hadn't left for anyone else and that our marriage had just died really. We'd got through a whole bottle of Champagne and were still eating our starters. Stupid really as I was driving.

"Now, no more questions," Shilpa said. "Shall we have another bottle?"

"Yes let's, but let's see if I can get a taxi first," I replied.

The Riverside staff were helpful, they managed to arrange for a taxi to pick us up later that night after we'd eaten and walked into the nearby town centre to join in the New Year celebrations. I was given permission to leave my car at the restaurant overnight and collect it the following day. I was so engrossed in conversation I hadn't noticed that my mobile had gone off a few times, I'd put it on vibrate. Whilst I was organising the taxi with Clive I glanced at my phone, it was Rick, four missed calls and Barry as well and two texts. I quickly phoned Rick.

"Ah yes, hello there," he said in a strange, fake accent. Welsh? Geordie? "Yes, I'm sorry to say you have got a leak in your flat. I'm in the flat downstairs and err..." I was puzzled then realised that Rick must have thought I was phoning to get me out of the date.

"Listen you clot," I said, "I'm just phoning to say she is absolutely lovely."

"What?" He said. "What do you mean, what is wrong with her?"

"There's nothing wrong with her," I said. "She's absolutely lovely, she's stunningly attractive, I'm having a wonderful time and I hope you are."

There was a pause, quite a long one. "You're making this up Simon, aren't you? I bet she's a right dog,"

Through gritted teeth, trying to smile into my phone as Shilpa was now looking at me, I said, "She's really lovely."

"Is she Indian?" he said.

"Yes, she's Indian."

"Has she got a sari on?"

"No, she has not got a sari on."

"Has she got one of those dots on her forehead?"

"No, Rick, she has not got a dot on her forehead, she hasn't got a sari on and even if she did, I actually like saris."

"Bollocks," he said, "You've just made that up haven't you? Have you been out with anyone with a sari?"

"Look Rick, I'm not having this conversation now, she's absolutely lovely, I'm having a wonderful time, thank you for your concern, Happy New Year and I'll give you a ring tomorrow."

"Okay," he said grudgingly, "I'll see you tomorrow." Click.

"Taxi's all organised."

"Oh, good," she said, "It's New Year's Eve, let's paint the town red."

And, boy did we! We finished our meal at *The Riverside* and walked the short distance into town. We went into a couple of nightclubs, had drinks, walked by the river and watched the fireworks in the park. She didn't say too much more, but then it was New Year's Eve, there was a lot going on and we were on a first date. We laughed, enjoyed one another's company and for once, I relaxed and it worked. Was she going to put her arm through mine like Niamh did in Venice? Well, yes she did.

"You don't mind if we hold hands?" she said. It was so natural, so easy.

The fireworks over the park were spectacular. I don't normally like fireworks. I associate them with Bonfire Night. Why we celebrate Bonfire Night, I just don't know. Don't write in, I do know the answer, Guy Fawkes and all that. It's a hangover from being a Catholic kid when I always thought they were having a go at me personally. I thought they wanted to burn me too. I also detest Halloween. All that trick or treat nonsense – one of the worst American imports. I don't mind little kids dressing up, doing trick or treating, but feral teenagers shouting out 'trick or treat' on your doorstep and wearing ugly masks can be intimidating. 'Bah humbug' I know. I told Shilpa about this. Watching the fireworks climb into the heavens, burst into coloured puffballs and shower to earth whilst huddling together for warmth was wonderful.

Basil Fawlty spoke. "Do you have anything like this in India?

"We have New Year's Eve in India Simon. In fact I think you'll find it is New Year's Eve in India right now." she said with a wry teasing smile.

I laughed ruefully.

"And we have Diwali of course," she continued patiently.

"What's that?"

"It's the Festival of Light." Hmm, I'd noticed Diwali cards turning up in cards shops in London. "But as I left when I was five, Simon, I don't really remember much about it."

"No, really," I said, turning now into Alan Whicker. "I'd really like to know more about India." She just laughed.

"Well, it's hot. I think our taxi is waiting, it's half past one and I think we should go.

'Why does tonight have to end?' I thought. It had been a fabulous date. Our taxi driver turned out to be someone I knew. Jim. He'd picked me up from the rail station and the odd TV assignment when a studio paid for a cab into London. In fact it had often been Jim who'd turned up.

"Hi Simon," he said. "You had a good time?"

"Brilliant," I said. "You?"

"Oh yes, Simon, I absolutely love working on New Year's Eve," he said sarcastically.

We laughed and then Shilpa became rather quiet, pensive. I wondered if she was thinking of new years' past. It was only a twenty-minute journey back to the flat or her house. Those big, brown eyes looking at me, I just wondered, should I go for it, ask her back to the flat? Jim was ahead of me.

"Where we off to then people?" he said, glancing nonchalantly in the rear view mirror.

"Well, Simon," said Shilpa "where are we going?" There was a pause. I didn't know what to say. "Just head back and we'll decide," said Shilpa, coming to the rescue.

"Okay," he said. "Will do, just let me know, people."

"I've had a wonderful evening, Simon," she said. "And truly I don't want it to end. Look the Party at the gym will still be going on. Why don't we gate-crash it?"

"Brilliant idea," I said. "The gym, Jim!" We all laughed.

The New Year's Eve revels at the gym were still in full swing, but there were bouncers on the door looking officious and in need of some fun.

"You're rather late," said one, "The party started a long time ago."

"We're a bit late," I conceded.

"You're very late," he said. "Can I see your tickets please?"

"Err, well, um, don't actually have any tickets, but we are members of the gym," The bouncer looked dismissive, stared at Shilpa then shook his Massive shaven head slowly from side to side. Fortunately Ian, who owns the gym was passing and came to the door.

"Hi Simon, hi Shilpa," he said, nodding at the bouncer, who walked off.

I said, "Look, we were just out and well I know it's pretty late and we haven't any tickets, so is this okay?"

"Of course," he said. "Come on in, grab a drink, and enjoy the party."

Paul Fox

After a couple of glasses of wine we were on the dance floor. I'm a truly hopeless dancer and whilst I'm not so shy I wont try, I always end up dancing with my thumbs in the air making stepping shapes. My children refuse to let me dance. Shilpa was a natural mover, a dancing Queen and was attracting a lot of attention as she danced.

Then at about four o'clock in the morning, the DJ decided to slow it down and to the strains of 'I'm not in love' by 10CC, we had our first long, slow dance. I can do this if I really concentrate on where my feet are, or have had a lot to drink and just go with the flow making sure I can hoist a dance partner to safety if I overbalance.

"I love this record," I said.

"Hah, record!" Shilpa said. "You're showing your age!" The alcohol was beginning to go to my head, well, not exactly my head, if you know what I mean. I was feeling very amorous holding Shilpa in my arms.

"Well I guess we really should be calling the night to a close and I was wondering… " She laughed. "No Simon, I'm not coming back to your flat, but you can walk me home." Oh yes, of course, I didn't have a car. "Only one problem, Simon," she said. "I can't walk in these shoes."

"Well, you've danced all evening in them," I said.

"Yeah exactly and now they hurt. I just can't walk that far. Sorry but you're going to have to carry me."

"Okay," I said, "No problem whatsoever." At the most I thought she must have weighed about seven and a half stone. I didn't manage to carry her all the way to her place, but with Shilpa dangling her black evening shoes on one finger and still singing "Auld Lang Syne" I carried her almost to her door.

I was so relaxed and, well, drunk, I kissed her full on the mouth and she responded magnificently. "I'd love to see you again," I said.

"Well you know what you can do," she said, rather stiffly.

'Oh my God!' "Pardon?" I said.

"Well, you know what you can do," she repeated.

"Well, err, err..."

"Just ask me. Goodnight Simon and Happy New Year."

All I had to do now was walk back. I turned up the collar of my jacket and headed back to the flat, looking at my phone as I went. "Happy New Year" messages from the children, several from Rick, Barry, wanting to know how it had gone, and all at about the 12 o'clock mark. It was now almost 5am.

I was exhausted, I fell into bed thinking, 'this dating lark, it's so easy.'

82

I didn't open my eyes until ten to eleven the next morning and nursing a headache. I texted Shilpa, "Thank you so much for a wonderful New Year's Eve, it was just so special, I'd love to see you again. When are you free? Simon x". I made a cup of coffee, black and strong, switched on the TV and waited for her reply.

It didn't arrive immediately as I'd hoped. 'Perhaps she's still asleep,' I thought. I resigned myself to the fact that I wasn't going to be in a fit state to do anything that day, not even retrieve my car.

I then remembered the guys said they were going to pop over. The children were off to Lakeside.

I'd Sky plussed the Jools Holland show *Hootenanny* and I was flicking through that when the door buzzer went. 'Shit,' I thought, 'must be Rick'.

"Hi lover boy," said Rick in a wholly unconvincing Asian accent. "Is it safe to come in? She's not still up there is she?"

"Yes, it's safe to come in, just quietly please," I said, sighing and pressing the buzzer. Rick came wandering in.

"Happy New Year old boy. So it went alright did it? She wasn't a minger after all?"

"No, she wasn't. She definitely wasn't a minger, she was fantastic."

Making us two quick cups of coffee, again another strong one for me, I told him all about her.

"Is Barry joining us?" I said.

"No, too pissed. What about the Irish bird then, have you given up on her?"

Thinking of Niamh, I felt slightly uncomfortable. I don't know why – after all I didn't know how she was spending her New Year's Eve and we weren't in a relationship, let alone a committed one were we? Perhaps I shouldn't have gone on the date with Shilpa though.

"Don't be daft, Rick," I said, "She lives in a different country. I've had a New Year's text from her and a couple of emails."

"So you're not going to see her again?"

"Well, I don't know, I might do."

"So it's all Shilpa, Shilpa, Shilpa now, is it?"

"Rick you are being ridiculous, I thought she was very nice, but who knows I might never see her again."

"You're such a liar, Simon. Your voice has gone all Barry Gibb again hasn't it? I can always tell when you're lying, the truth is you can't wait to see her again and you've forgotten all about the Irish bird."

"That is not true," I squeaked.

"So you're not going to ask her out again then?"

"Who?" I said, pretending not to play this game.

"Shilpa and what's more, I bet you've already texted her haven't you?"

"No."

"You have haven't you?"

"No."

"You don't know the first thing about dating do you? There is no way you should text them immediately the day after, you should wait at least three days before you contact them. And knowing you, I bet you've texted her at least once, haven't you?"

"No, I have not," I lied.

"Show us your phone then," he said.

"No."

"You have haven't you?"

"Yes, okay, yes I have texted her." I was defeated.

"You're such a twit, Simon, now she's going to think you're desperate, but then you are I suppose aren't you?"

Rick continued in the same tedious vein for a while. I kept an eye on my phone, hoping that Shilpa would respond, but she didn't. After Rick left, I logged onto the computer. There were a few more emails wishing me "Happy New Year" and another inviting me to join the bespoke introductory service. I deleted it straight away, no point, Shilpa was fantastic, but then so was Niamh. If only she lived closer. 'Why do people go on these sites?' I thought, smugly, my recent triumph at meeting Shilpa trumping common sense. 'There are so many great women out there. It just takes a mate to broker an introduction.' With that in mind I texted Melanie. "I had a great time last night. Thanks so much for the introduction."

She sent a text back. "U r so welcome, I knew u wd like her." But there was still nothing from Shilpa.

Each of the dating sites I'd registered with as a subscribing member had automatic update services. They forwarded new member details. I don't know what happens on New Year's Day, but hundreds of people must have been visiting the dating sites and signing up given the volume of new profiles registered in Essex and the Home Counties. Presumably it's to do with people's New Year resolutions, like joining a gym and a symptom of the toll of stress at Christmas and the disintegration of relationships over the holiday period. New Year's resolutions take many forms I mused. I try and avoid the gym in January. It's full of new members in brand new trainers with new iPods, who've been to Decathlon or JD Sports and got all the gear having resolved to get fit. I see them a couple of times and then mostly never again. My dating member sites continued to bombard me throughout the day with emails about new ladies joining. Joanna Lumley was working overtime. I thought about just cancelling my memberships, but didn't. There was still nothing from Shilpa.

It was now Sunday evening and I kept looking at my phone, still no text or call from Shilpa. I looked at some of the messages on the New Year's dating site; some were amusing. One was from a woman with an evident sense of humour. Instead of describing the sort of man she would like to meet, what films she watched, books she enjoyed and what she was hoping for, etc. she had written candidly, "Hello boys, well I'm looking for a man, not a boy. Be realistic, if you're just looking for a shag, don't bother contacting me. I don't want to see pictures of your Willy but if there are any genuinely honest men out there that are looking to date a real woman, get in touch, otherwise don't bother! PS. Be realistic about the distance. I live in Brighton, if you live in Aberdeen it's probably not going to work!"

To this day I am still amazed at how many single people there are. If I look at my friends, half are still married, half are divorced. Of those who divorced, all now apart from Rick have re-married though some of these are single again. I was beginning to feel anxious and unnerved that I hadn't heard from Shilpa. Should I text again? What was the etiquette? Was Rick right? Perhaps she would think I was desperate? Perhaps she simply wanted a date for New Year's Eve. Had I imagined that it was a good date? What if she just didn't like me?

To ease my anxiety and distract myself from the phone, I decided to go online. Instantly I had a pop-up from a new dating site aimed at people who wear uniforms – in the course of their work I hasten to add though the alternative is also out there. This site catered for the armed forces, police, nurses and doctors amongst others. I wondered if I could apply after all I had been in the RAF. My uniform was still kicking about the flat somewhere. Glancing up at my bookshelf again, there were quite a few RAF themed books including the wonderful *Reach for the Sky*. I wonder what my former service mates would make of my predicament now.

When a member of the Force I used to enjoy living in the Mess, the accommodation on bases for officers. Only a handful of messes have rooms with en-suite facilities. There are washrooms, bathrooms and toilets dotted along corridors but few are marked "male" or "female". They are mainly unisex with individual cubicles and officers are expected to exercise care and discretion when in residence.

I invested in the largest dressing gown I could buy and would always take this with me to bases on postings. The girls did the same, they had even bigger dressing gowns as I recall. A polite "Good morning" was normally the only phrase uttered whilst crossing the no-man's land of the shared bathrooms. One particular Air Force base I went to though had a deck type arrangement where several rooms share a communal bathroom. It sounds primitive but normally it worked okay. Usually you'd share with people of the same sex anyway.

As I arrived at this particular base, the Flight Sergeant showing me to my quarters and said, "You're quite lucky this time, Sir, you've got a deck to yourself. I think there's somebody moving into the room next to you on Friday, but for most of the week you'll have the bathroom area to yourself."

"Thanks very much," I'd said and went about my duties for the week, abandoning my large dressing gown and bowling into the bathroom when I wanted to, like at home, until Friday.

Of course being me, even as an RAF Officer, I was pretty hopeless. One night I was staying in the Mess and as it was cold I'd worn pyjamas to bed. The next morning I crashed into the bathroom to be greeted by the sight of a female RAF Officer, wearing her uniform shirt, tie undone just round her neck, open, wearing black stockings, a white suspender belt and white knickers. She was leaning forward slightly over the sink, applying her make-up. She spun round immediately.

"Ah, good morning."

"Err, good morning," I said. "I'm sorry, I forgot that you were moving in, they didn't tell me, well they did tell, but I'd forgotten. Anyway, I'm Flight Lieutenant Taylor," I babbled away and held out my hand. She was very attractive. She immediately pulled down her shirt to cover the top of her underwear. I said something like "Um, I'll leave you to it," as I backed out of the bathroom.

A little while later I heard a knock on my door and a voice: "Bathroom's free if you'd like to use it," said my housemate.

"Oh, thanks very much," I'd replied.

I'd noticed her uniform shirt didn't have any rank braid on it. The fact that she was there meant, like myself she was an officer. I smiled to myself as I went down to breakfast and didn't think more about it. However, I've liked black stockings and white underwear since then.

After that day's flying I walked to the station headquarters. I was wearing my flying suit and what used to be called a side cap. They're wedge shaped like the caps the staff wear in McDonalds and the subject of some derision, but they do fold flat and you can easily keep them in the pocket of your flying suit, rather than worry about wearing a bulky peak cap.

As I walked past station headquarters, I noticed the attractive blonde colleague from the bathroom. She was walking towards me. I smiled broadly. She didn't return the smile but she did look at me. Then I looked at her rank braid denoting whether she was senior to me or not. She was. She was a Wing Commander and I had to salute her. I saluted "Good afternoon, Ma'am."

"Good afternoon," she said. I thought I detected a faint smile.

'Well at least I know what colour knickers you've got on.' I thought. It was funny, one of many laughs I had during my time with the Royal Air Force.

I studied my phone again – I was becoming obsessed with it really. It had a little light on it that flashed when I had a new message. I kept looking at the light. It wasn't flashing. Maybe there'd been a break in the signal and my text hadn't got through? She might be sitting at home thinking, "Well, he's not contacted me; he must think I'm unattractive, or because I'm Indian."

'This is ridiculous,' I thought, so I sent her another text. "Hi Shilpa, hope you've enjoyed New Year's Day as much as we enjoyed New Year's Eve." Yeah, I know it was corny, but it's really all I could think of. "Going to have a very early night, hope you're okay. Simon x." Sent. Nothing. Sunday evening dragged by. I switched my phone off, on again, still nothing. Then Barry phoned.

"Hi," I said. "Are you still pissed?"

"No, are you?" he said.

"I understand your date with the Indian lady went well. Hardly surprising, after all you've been a cowboy all your life, Simon." Then the question I was dreading. "Have you heard from her?"

"Err, well, no I suppose the answer to that is Barry, well when I say I haven't heard from her, what I mean is that well, in actual fact although we have communicated, or rather I've communicated, I have not."

"So you've not heard from her have you Simon?"

"No, I haven't."

"Oh well," said Barry, "maybe it's for the best, and after all you've still got the Irish bird, haven't you?"

Paul Fox

"I have not got the Irish bird as you put it. Niamh and I have been exchanging emails, but not very frequently. I believe she is on holiday in Dublin with her family and I hate to point this out, but she does actually live in Ireland. It's not going to be that easy is it? And I do wonder why you and Rick find my disastrous love life so hysterically funny, but actually I had a wonderful date with Shilpa and no, I haven't heard from her, but I'm sure I will do."

"Well see you for fish and chips on Friday then. Good luck," said Barry evenly and ending the call.

Ah, yes of course, Friday – only a few days to sort things out. Oh well, I thought. As I hadn't heard anything from my second text to Shilpa, she clearly hadn't liked me and frankly I couldn't blame her. I mean, I was useless at conversation. Who wants to know about which days of the year you don't like? I was sure I'd bored the pants off her. Then I started thinking about her pants and wished I hadn't. I wondered if she liked wearing pink knickers. Oh God, it was all getting too much. Then the phone rang. Shilpa?

"Hello," said a familiar soft Irish accent.

"Hello, Niamh," I said. "Well, gosh thanks for calling me. Happy New Year."

"Happy New Year to you," said Niamh.

"Where are you?" I said. "Your e-mail said about going to your parents in Dublin."

"Yes, I'm still in Dublin. I'm staying over for a couple of days, my Dad's not too well."

"Oh, I'm sorry to hear that," I said.

"What did you do for New Year?"

I hesitated. What should I say? I couldn't really tell the truth, but on the other hand I didn't want to lie.

"Well, I went to a party at the gym."

"Oh yes," she said, "you mentioned it. Did you have a good time?"

"Yes it was alright," I said. "You know, just the local gym, nothing special." My mind was racing with how to distract Niamh from asking more questions about my New Year's Eve.

"Tell me, do you have Fireworks Day in Ireland?" I ventured. What!

"What?" she asked, sounding puzzled.

"Fireworks, err, I was thinking about fireworks, do you have Guy Fawkes in Ireland, 5th of November, that sort of thing?" I winced. It was a stupid question.

"No Simon, no we don't. Anyway, I was wondering when you were back to work?" I breathed with relief.

"Well, you know me," I said. "I don't really work. Got a few assignments to do, but um, what about you?"

Niamh was a dentist. In Venice when talking about our work I'd explained to her that whilst I have a charming dentist, I loathe having to attend appointments. I go regularly, have everything done she recommends and yet I always need more treatment. I've had whitening, straightening, capping, filling, regular cleaning and spent thousands. Then there's the pain, root canal work being particularly unpleasant. So I was secretly disappointed when Niamh told me she was a dentist.

"Do they have dentists in Ireland?" I remember asking jokingly. She wasn't amused.

"Course we've got dentists in Ireland you bloody fool and we've running water and electric light."

"Yes, of course!" Anyway, Niamh was back at work the following day.

"Well, it's nice talking to you," she said. "And whatever you're doing, enjoy your week. Maybe we could talk next weekend, I'm pretty busy till then."

Niamh had an organised life. She had described herself as a creature of habit when we first met. Maybe all those years alone had encouraged such a tendency? Maybe I too would become like it in time. I'd only lived alone for a few months but as I've described I'd already developed established routines of my own. The computer switch-on and breakfast TV as soon as I awoke, the same food each morning (Weetabix), lunch at the gym each weekday I was working at home, watching *The One Show* faithfully each evening, fish and chips with the guys on Friday. I was becoming an institutionalised singleton myself? It was delightful talking to Niamh. Conversation was so easy with her, just naturally sociable and she did seem sincerely interested in what I'd had to say. She'd finished with "You must come over sometime and see the running water and electric light for yourself. I can even show you my surgery."

'Now that would be a thrill,' I thought. In reality, I felt sure that whatever I did with Niamh, I would enjoy myself. I still hadn't heard from Shilpa.

I'd managed to get an assignment to write about a new car – a Lexus hybrid. I'd worked for a mass circulation car magazine and my agent said that they'd like me to do a write up on the vehicle for a forthcoming eco-cars edition.

It was a decent commission. I'm not from an engineering background and don't write detailed mechanical specification reviews of cars when I prepare copy for print, but I have been a confirmed petrol head ever since I can remember and have a genuine passion for motor cars.

In particular Alfa's – they are art on wheels with their stylish lines, beautiful interiors and furniture. They have their flaws and can be unreliable but they're stunningly crafted and exude style and éclat. My style of journalism has evolved from an appreciation of the drive characteristics and experience of vehicles. I can write poetry about Alfa Romeo motor cars.

I'd genuinely loved each of the Alfa's I'd owned, particularly the 166 and GT's and had contributed several pieces to the Alfa magazine. Now I had a commission to write for Lexus. Brilliant! Dullest cars on the planet? Though I had yet to critically evaluate the car, to my mind all Lexus cars look like they've fallen out of the ugly tree and hit every branch on the way down. Why have I got such a useless agent, why can't he get me job writing about Ferraris, Spyder's. Maserati's or Bentleys? Never mind, it was money and I needed it.

A dealer was scheduled to deliver the car to me during the following week and I was to appraise it then write the article about it within two weeks. I flicked through the rest of my post despondently. A few red utility bill reminders and a letter in a posh heavy cream envelope with embossed writing. I noticed a Mercedes Benz symbol in the corner, opened it up and saw it was an invitation to the launch of a new model at the fabulous *Toll Booth Hotel* at Dedham, near Colchester.

I knew the place, a lovely hotel in a beautiful location, close to where John Constable painted *The Hay Wain*. North Essex as it blends into Suffolk along the coastline is picturesque and gentrified. It was also reasonably close.

The hotel was renowned for being elegant and expensive and would be an ideal location for a black tie dinner. There would be press and photographers in attendance. It was in four weeks and I could take a guest. I wondered if Niamh would fly over from Ireland. It would be lovely to take her and she could wear that beautiful floor length dress she had worn to the dinner on Christmas Day.

An email from Lexus stating that following my agent's instructions, they would deliver the car to my flat on Friday morning at about 8.30am was in my Inbox. They'd have a job getting it up the stairs I thought. My phone vibrated. A text. Shilpa? No, Rick.

"Have you heard from her yet?" it read.

I texted back "Piss off."

He responded with "Touchy!"

I rang him saying, "No, but I have heard from Niamh and I've been invited to a very posh do by Mercedes Benz and I can take a guest and guess what? It's NOT going to be you!"

"Well I wouldn't want to go anyway," he said, "who are you going to take? Won't be Shilpa and Niamh won't fly over from Ireland for one night will she?"

"Well she might," I retorted.

"You could take the married one, just ring her husband and see if he'll let her out for the night." I laughed at that – Jane would have made an ideal guest.

"See you for fish and chips on Friday and I'll whiz round in this new Lexus and see what you think of it."

"Well, they're crap aren't they?" he offered. For once I was inclined to agree with him.

It was Wednesday before I heard from Shilpa.

"Hi Simon, thanks for your texts. Sorry I haven't texted back but I left my phone in a friend's car and have only just retrieved it. I had a wonderful New Year's Eve. Thank you so much. Hope to see you again sometime. Shilpa x."

I was pleased I'd heard from her, but her text was pretty noncommittal. I mean, "see you sometime" didn't seem red-hot keen. Hmm, I had a few days before I had to face my weekly ordeal at the fish and chip shop. I'd even suggested we actually change venue.

"Why?" asked Rick and Barry.

"Well, we go there every week."

"Well, what's wrong with it?"

"Oh nothing wrong with it, I just thought we might like to change it. We could go to the gym."

"What so you can bump into your Indian lady perhaps?"

"Okay," I sighed, resigned, "I give in."

Oh, well, at least Shilpa had been in touch and I could let Melanie know I'd hopefully be seeing her again.

This happened sooner than I thought. The next morning when I unexpectedly bumped into Shilpa at the gym, and I do mean literally bumped into her. The gym corridor goes right, then left, then right again and on the last bend I careered into her.

"Oh gosh," I said, "I'm sorry." It was a moment before I realized it was Shilpa, she just looked so different. As I have mentioned ours is a relaxed and low-key gym. Unlike others I've heard of, members at ours don't tend to dress up to exercise. There are a few who have the latest designer trackies and trainers but Shilpa wore a simple vest top that had clearly seen better days; grey and very baggy, jogging bottoms and battered trainers. Even through her dark skin, I could see she was bright red, her hair was soaking wet with sweat. She seemed equally surprised to see me.

"I wish I hadn't bumped into you looking like this," she said.

"That's okay, it's nice to see you," I responded. I really meant it.

I thought I should seize the moment. "Well as you're here and I'm here why don't we go for coffee I mean I'm not doing anything, well I will be doing something, I'm seeing Melanie, I mean, well you're here right now..." I prattled on.

Shilpa didn't say anything, but waited patiently for this bout of verbal diarrhoea to stop, smiled and said.

"I'm definitely not having a cup of coffee like this and anyway, as you should know, I don't drink coffee."

Shilpa had declined a coffee at our dinner in favour of green tea. She clearly expected me to remember this. I thought she was going to say "you can take me out for a drink" or something, but she didn't. She simply said "Nice to see you," picked up the gym bag I'd knocked out of her hand and disappeared.

As she turned the corner I couldn't see her, but heard her call out "And watch where you're going next time!" with a laugh.

I went on into the gym hall and spotted Melanie. I was working on the ski machine and she came over, "Hi Simon, you've just missed Shilpa," she said.

"Well, I didn't actually, I collided with her downstairs." I didn't elaborate.

"I understand your date went well?"

"Well, yes," I said. "I thought it was fantastic."

"And you ended up here at the gym, dancing until all hours?"

"Yes," I said, "and I carried her home. What did she say to you?" I asked, thinking that I might get some extra information or some better insight, not realizing then that girls don't let guys know what they tell one another, especially about guys and especially about guys asking about them.

"She just said she enjoyed the date very much," she said discreetly.

"Is that it?" I said.

"Well, yes."

It was clear even to me then that even if Shilpa had discussed me Melanie was not going to reveal it. She turned her attention to my exercise regime and asked how I felt I was doing.

I told her that I felt my fitness was improving slowly and the excess weight gained over Christmas was starting to shift, but confessed I was finding exercising hard work.

I was keen for more information, but clearly wasn't going to get it from Melanie so I resisted the temptation to manoeuvre the conversation back to Shilpa and our first date. Over the next few days I tried to settle into the routine of work. On Thursday morning at 8.30 am, bang on time, the entry phone of the flat went.

"Mr Taylor?" said a crisp and efficient voice. I thought it might be Pete messing about again, but it was the man from Lexus.

"Yes," I said.

"The test drive for Lexus."

"Come on up," I said and pressed the buzzer.

I opened the front door of the flat and my Lexus visitor stepped into the hallway.

He was breathing heavily and was red faced. I didn't need to ask why. That bloody lift! My visitor was not happy. I'm not inclined to complain or be over critical, but if you're a driver, delivering a car to someone whom you want to write nice things about it, wouldn't you be friendly, or at least civil? I offered my visitor a cup of tea, asked him where he'd come from and whether he needed a lift to the statio

He said tersely, "No, Slough. No." and that was it! How he was going to get back from where I lived to Slough? Was another car and driver waiting for him? I didn't know. Perhaps he'd had a row with his girlfriend. He was in a filthy mood. He flung me the keys to the car on the kitchen worktop, I signed a release form and he was gone.

I'd been thinking about the forthcoming gala dinner and how I'd like to go. It would be a useful networking opportunity and was in a lovely hotel. I could dust my dinner jacket off and enjoy a night out and dinner with a companion. But who? I decided to run through my options. In an attempt to organise my thoughts I found a pen, some paper and wrote a heading "Mercedes Do – who to take?" My options were then:

1. Ring Niamh and ask her to come over and be my guest.
2. Ask Shilpa.
3. Ask Jane's husband if I could take her.

It wasn't looking that good. Though I hated to admit that Rick was right, it looked unlikely that Niamh would fly over from Ireland for an industry dinner. And where would she stay? Hopefully with me and hopefully she'd wear her pink knickers! But she might expect to stay in a hotel. Perhaps we could stay at *The Toll Booth Hotel*. I should check it out. Shilpa was the obvious choice but rather elusive and aloof – and Jane? I'd had no contact with her since our phone conversation months ago now. I wasn't surprised.

I was getting a tension headache thinking about it and to divert myself, I went to look at the Lexus. Plodding down the stairs I determined that I really had to get into work mode. Lexus wanted the car back in a week; less than a week in fact. I was going to have to write a full user analysis article for the client magazine by the end of the following week. By the time I arrived on the ground floor, tapping the silent, dead lift with my toe by way of reprimand, I'd made up my mind to put my love life in a "box" seal it and concentrate on my work. I gave myself a severe talking to.

As I got into the car park, there it was in all its glaring ugliness. The face of the car looked like the face of someone you'd never tire of kicking. It resembled a cross between a chrome-toothed guppy fish and a fridge freezer from the 1970s. Why anyone would buy one I have no idea. It was a top of the range LS600H, the H standing for "hybrid". I walked up to the car and it opened. It had a new-fangled keyless system that recognizes a driver as they approach it and unlocks the doors. Its ugly face lit up momentarily as the headlamps and indicators flashed. I opened the driver's door and got in.

This keyless entry thing was going to be a nightmare for an over anxious owner. After all, how could a driver be certain the car was locked? When you walk up to it, it opens, when you walk away, it locks. Knowing Lexus they probably have a department to deal with people traumatized because they can't check whether their Lexus is locked or not. Inside it was the usual Lexus fare:to me, leather that looks like plastic, plastic that looks like cardboard. I don't really know how they get leather to look so synthetic, but I was going to have to find something positive to write about. I decided to take it for a spin around the block, to get used to it.

Those nice people from Lexus had even included a button that said "start" so I gave it a go, nothing happened. I pressed it again, this time a little harder, something happened, but then it stopped. I was tempted to ring the grumpy guy and get him to take it back. Then I read the manual and started it. A little "Ready" light came up in green that meant that the car could be driven. Why not a big flashing sign saying "You can now move away". Being a hybrid vehicle, it was quiet. Spookily so. I selected "Drive" and accelerated out of the car park.

Once on the open road I began to warm to the car slightly. It had a decent sound system and Elton was soon booming out of its competent speakers. Elton chanting "Saturday, Saturday, Saturday night's all right for fighting," made me reflect further about who to invite to the Mercedes dinner. I had to get it sorted out. I decided to ring Martin. Lexus had patched in my mobile phone details and soon Elton had shut up and Martin was talking.

"Hello mate," he said, "what's up?" (This is Essex.)

Martin and I had worked together for many years before I became a writer. He was a safe pair of hands in financial services, a great storyteller, a loyal friend and I valued his judgment I ran through my dilemma of who to invite.

There was a brief pause and he said, "Invite them both."

"Martin, how on earth can I invite both of them to one 'do', I only have one companion ticket?"

"No you fool," he said, "invite them both and then decide which one you want to take. To my mind, neither of them sounds that promising. Or, why not just go on your own mate. There's bound to be some nice, single girls there and anyway, I thought it was a work thing?"

"Well it is," I said, "sort of." 'Hmmm,' I thought. "Okay Martin, thanks for your advice, I'm not sure I'm going to take it but I'll let you know what happens." Click – back to Elton who was now singing "Sorry seems to be the hardest word".

I was getting used to the controls on the Lexus and had decided that I did like something about it; the control panel was practically three-dimensional in quality and I was dwelling approvingly on the detail of the instruments when something caught my eye. It was the flashing orange of a Belisha beacon. Studying the dashboard instead of the road whilst driving is patently not to be recommended. There was someone on the crossing and they were directly before me. I stamped on the brake pedal. The Lexus, fitted with every anti-locking device known to man and no doubt satellite controlled by a technician in Tokyo, stopped instantly, inches away from the person on the crossing. To my great relief they remained upright.

'Oh my God!' I wanted to put my head in my hands. How idiotic of me to focus on the dash whilst driving in town. I flung open the car door, rushed round to the front.

"I'm terribly sorry, it's a new car, I'm really terribly sorry, are you okay?" A pair of huge oval shaped brown eyes glared at me. They belonged to Shilpa.

"You!" she exploded. "This is the second time in a day that you've practically sent me flying, this time with near fatal consequences. If you don't want to see me again Simon that's fine but you don't have to run me over."

People had started to stop and look. Some were leaning on their car horns and wondering who the useless driver was.

I quickly got back into my car as Shilpa had marched off. I was shaking. What a twit I felt. Back in the car the stupid Lexus had switched itself off so I had to re-start it. I wanted to follow Shilpa and see if I could give her a lift but it took a while to work out again how to start the car. She'd long gone. I hit the accelerator and got back to the flat as quickly as the speed limits, allowed.

As soon as I was inside I put my hands over my head, crouched down and jumped about the living room in Basil Fawlty mode. If I'd been wearing a jacket I would have pulled it over my head and frog-hopped insanely about the room as Basil did when things went wrong at Fawlty Towers.

"What a twit, what a twit, how stupid of me! Fancy nearly running someone over and that someone being Shilpa – Shilpa of all people! What an utter berk, she'll never want to see me again, she must think I'm the biggest tosser going and that fucking car, I hate it!" I wanted to send it back, to ring the grumpy guy, get him to come back and collect it. "I hate it! I don't know why I took the assignment, I hate my agents, and I hate everybody."

Then the phone rang.

"Hello," I said distractedly. There was no reply. "YES," I said crankily. Loudly. There seemed to be some sort of delay. I thought 'Please don't let it be one of those telephone calls about claiming compensation for personal injury and road traffic accidents.'

"Hello England," said a soft, Irish voice.

"Niamh?" I must have sounded puzzled.

"Hello, Simon." A pause.

"Niamh, err, um hello."

I forgot that I was *John Cleese*, slipped back into *Hugh Grant* and said

"Well, to what do I owe the pleasure?"

"Well, I just had a break between patients and, um, I thought I'd give you a ring."

We hadn't discussed her work much in Venice. She'd explained early on that she'd had some tiresome experiences socially and generally avoided telling people she was a dentist. She described how when she was introduced at parties to guests, some would open their mouths, start pointing at their teeth telling her they'd had work done, been unhappy with it and asking what she thought of the treatment!

I'd kept quiet about my own painful experience of root canal treatment when she'd said this. I also hadn't discussed her work with anybody else on the Venice trip in case they sought her advice.

She'd said "When I'm on holiday, I'm on holiday and I don't like to discuss my work. Most people hate dentists anyway and tell me their horror stories about being traumatized as a child, quite apart from showing me their teeth. So I don't mention it."

Niamh continued. "Yes, so I had a break and I thought I'd give you a ring and see what you're up to." There was a pause. "What are you up to?" said Niamh.

I was standing bolt upright and grinning not prepared to disclose that I had just nearly run Shilpa over. Shilpa who?

"Well I'm just writing or trying to write about a car, um, I'm test driving a car and I'm writing about it for this magazine."

"Oh really, what sort of car?"

"A Lexus," I said.

"Oh, I like them," she said. "My friend's got one."

"Really? Well, yes, it's quite impressive actually, solid braking system, fine sound system and attractive control panel, I was only just thinking how decent it was!" I made a sign of the cross. "Niamh it's so nice to hear from you."

Then on impulse I said, "I've got an invite to a car thing at a Mercedes Benz launch, gala dinner. I'm sure you're busy and it's a long way to come, but I'd actually love you to come over. Its black tie 'do' and you know, well, um, would you consider coming over? You would be welcome to stay with me. I have a spare room," I volunteered.

There wasn't much of a pause, Niamh said "Well, I'd be delighted to come, but I'm not sure if I can, when is it?"

I scurried round the flat frantically trying to find the invite. I'm pretty disorganised with paperwork but I eventually found it. "Well, it's um, 28th January, so that's in, well, um, what, just over three weeks?"

"Well, I'll see. I'd better go because I've a patient now, but perhaps we can have a chat at the weekend, I'm not doing much. Just popping over to see Mum and Dad in Dublin, but let's have a talk then. I'll let you get back to your Lexus."

I rang Rick.

"She won't come. She's just being polite Simon, you're going to have to start getting real," he said.

I told him about Shilpa and nearly running her over on the zebra crossing.

"You berk," he said. "Niamh won't come over from Ireland, of course she won't. But you're not going to be able to invite the Indian one either. Why don't you just go on your own? You could meet someone there." I was cross now

"She bloody well will come over from Ireland and she's reorganizing her diary and we're going to be discussing it at the weekend." I heard my voice rising in pitch. "She's already decided what she's going to wear; I'm going to pick her up from Heathrow and so, bollocks."

"You're lying again, aren't you Simon?"

"No, I'm not," I retorted unhappily in a shrill voice. I just couldn't control it.

"I don't know why I bothered to phone you, I'll see you for fish and chips.

"Don't be late, bring the Lexus and try not to prang it on the way or run into some other poor pedestrian."

I was tempted to tell him to "fuck off" but I didn't. I texted Shilpa straight away. "I am so sorry about this morning and the crossing, please forgive me, I'm very, very, sorry. Simon." To my surprise, I had a text immediately from her.

"That's okay, don't worry accidents happen. Shilpa x."

Well at least she sent a kiss so maybe all wasn't entirely lost. I'd decided that though I approved of the Lexus's braking system and dash and had enjoyed the sound system I couldn't think of anything else positive to say about it. It was big and marketed as a luxury model but its interior was disappointing, neither comfortable nor stylish. I hated the grille and it had several superfluous and irritating specs. For inspiration I went onto the internet. There must be someone who liked it.

I found that there's a Lexus "Owners Club" and their threaded messages suggested they were a jolly bunch. Perhaps I should entertain the notion that cars that do their jobs quietly (very quietly in this case) efficiently and reasonably economically are just as exciting to some drivers as great looking but temperamental Alfas.

Whilst doing research I had come across one interesting fact about the LS 600h. Apparently Paul McCartney's had one. That did it for me. I officially disliked it. As far as I'm concerned the Beatles are dying in the wrong order. We are left with Ringo and Paul. I'd have preferred it to be John and George. They were the real talent. Paul's taste in wives and cars seems questionable. At least Ringo had the sense to marry the lovely Bond girl, Barbara Bach.

I was going to struggle to cobble something together for the article and I wasn't going to compromise so as not to offend. I rang my agent and said, "Forget this, I can't do it. I can't do it without telling a load of porkies and I'm not doing that. It won't get past the PR people and I'm sending the car back."

He told me to think about it and give the car a few more days. I rang the grumpy guy and told him to come and get the car.

"Okay," he said. "Be there tomorrow afternoon."

The rest of the day I hunkered down on the mezzanine floor and worked through other assignments. I didn't want to go out, see anyone or think about anything, particularly the emptiness I felt. My love life was going nowhere and I felt depressed.

Later that night I was slumped on the sofa watching TV. There were more adverts than programmes worth watching. It occurred to me that television advertising for cars, fairly mundane now used to be fantastic. Remember the advert for the Saab car that turned into a jet fighter? And who can forget those adverts in the '80s with Paula Hamilton and the Volkswagen Golf, the one particularly where she ripped off her pearls and left her fur coat on the parking meter but kept her Volkswagen Golf? Brilliant. Reminiscing now about ads with girls rather than cars I thought of the Chanel advert with Nicole Kidman – "I'm a dancer," she purrs. That advert so appealed I Sky-plussed it. How tragic is that? As if on cue an advert for a new perfume by Kylie Minogue appeared on screen. A perfume that smells of Kylie Minogue! If Georgina Grey had a perfume, it would smell of strawberries.

Since dating and being in the market for buying perfume for girlfriends I've found that "celebrity perfumes" are whole-heartedly disliked by women. I'd imagined they would think "Well, they're a celebrity, they smell of this, I'd like to as well," but they don't, they think "My boyfriend wants me to *look like* the celebrity!" There's no point in buying celebrity perfume unless it's for a young or teenage daughter. Women seem to detest them.

Next was an advert for Aer Lingus. I wondered if Niamh would come over from Ireland and whether I should offer to pay for her fare and put her up at the hotel. And if she stayed with me, should I repeat the offer of the spare room? I concluded that I should really.

I ambled into the spare room which had the usual debris of spare rooms. There was a bed somewhere underneath boxes of God knows what that I'd meant to go through and sort out when I moved in. The "contents of the marital home" as it's called by solicitors. I'd kept everything, even my old school books. I still have my briefcase full of school books from the day I left school. As if I'm ever going to be asked to work out what the area of a triangle is, or what Pythagoras' theorem actually means.

If Niamh was coming over I couldn't offer her the spare room if it was impossible to sleep in. Perhaps I could find somewhere to store the debris at least for the duration of her visit? I started to organize the mess of boxes, LPs, spare bedding, pictures, and my RAF uniform. I'd always thought I might get a recall. There it was pristine, cleaned, hat, uniform, gloves, uniform shoes, along with motorcycle helmet and gloves, boots and boxes and boxes of photographs. I hadn't had a bike for a while, but always promised myself that someday I'd buy a replacement for my last wheels, my beloved Honda 550/4.

Of course, once I started looking at photographs the rest of the evening disappeared. I gazed at photographs of me as a baby; a young boy; my Mum and Dad; wedding photos, my early married life and oh, all those happy and heart wrenching ones of the children as babies, toddlers and on and on. Katherine had suggested that we divide them equally. She was very fair like that, along with everything else really. Gosh, the memories. I went to bed with a heavy heart and emotional, sad we hadn't been able to make the marriage work.

As I fell asleep I reminded myself that it was fish and chips tomorrow. Still at least they were going to pick that bloody Lexus up.

'Death trap' I thought. Lexus take note – this refers to the driver, not the car. In all fairness, the car had performed so well in crisis it had spared Shilpa.

Friday morning. I made it to the gym. 'God,' I thought, 'what am I going to tell Melanie? Shilpa's bound to have told her about the zebra crossing incident.' I was sure everyone in our small town had heard about it. I had been half expecting a Police Officer to knock on the door. It was probably on CCTV, on YouTube – "Killer Lexus Loony". On the way to the gym my mobile phone went off, it was Mr Grumpy from Lexus.

"Oh, yeah, Mr Taylor, yeah, we'll be round to pick your car up a bit later than we thought." A cocky voice, he might as well have been saying "you've really inconvenienced us". "Yeah, we'll be with you about 5 o'clock." He didn't even wait for me to speak and confirm but just hung up.

Fair enough. When I got to the gym I was scrupulously careful about negotiating the corridors but I didn't see Shilpa or meet anyone else en route to the main hall. Melanie strode directly over to me.

"What happened yesterday?" she asked.

"Oh no," I said. "I just feel so stupid, and Shilpa of all people." She was smiling.

"Well, she was okay this morning. You've just missed her. She was laughing about it. Are you going to ask her out again?"

"Well, I want to, I mean she's fantastic, but I just feel such a twit."

"Oh Simon, don't be ridiculous, nothing happened and you weren't half an inch away from her anyway, you weren't even on the zebra crossing. You just weren't looking where you were going, were you? There's no harm done, just get in touch with her and have a chat."

"Really," I said. "What, she really wants to see me again?"

"Yes, just ask her."

"Well, I've got this Mercedes Benz thing to go to and… " it all came gushing out.

"She'd love to go I'm sure. When is it? Just ask her," she said.

"I will, I will, I'll ask her. Oh thanks so much Melanie, I feel so much better."

"Right," she said. "Let's start getting some of that Christmas turkey off your belly."

'Charming,' I thought.

Interlude

That afternoon I had to go and see my solicitor James about the divorce. It's so miserably complicated, isn't it? Decree absolute, nisi, whatever. My solicitor's a great guy. I went to school with him and he's an old friend as well as my lawyer. He's always been straight-laced. I think he was born wearing a three-piece suit, shirt and tie. James is by nature cautious, quietly spoken and as for his choice of car? I think they actually designed Rover 75's for James. He's had at least three in a row. He probably kept Rover going till they went out of business. Rover 75's were James' top favourite car.

I decided to take the poxy Lexus with me and on the way there had to acknowledge that I was being too harsh about it; it was powerful and economical and I was learning to appreciate how quiet it was and how this allowed me to enjoy Elton at full blast. As I pulled into the firm's car park I noticed that James' familiar, elderly Rover 75 wasn't there. Parked in his usual space was a brand new Porsche 911. It was red and a convertible, beautiful. I went into reception and Monica, the receptionist who has been there forever welcomed me.

"Oh, hi Simon, James will be with you shortly, take a seat."

"Thanks very much," I said.

"Would you like a coffee?" she asked.

"Yes, please."

I picked up the nearest magazine – 'Horse and Hound' from about 1982, I'd read it before. It's not a sparkling read, things move rather slowly in James' practice, but that's what I suppose you want from a solicitor isn't it?" Solid traditional conservatism.

As Monica brought my coffee over, I asked nonchalantly, "So who owns the Porsche in the car park?"

"Oh that, you noticed?" she remarked.

"Yeah, could hardly not notice, gorgeous, whose is it?" I said flicking through the magazine and sipping my coffee.

"Oh, that's James's.

"What!" I retorted almost dropping my cup. The magazine fell from my hands. "James's? I mean, the Porsche, the red Porsche?"

"Yes, it's James's. He's had it a while and is really enjoying driving it. Great colour huh?"

"James has a Porsche?"

"Yes Simon, James has a Porsche."

"No!"

"Yes, he's very proud of it. We've all been out in it. Anyway, he's free now, so go in he'll tell you all about it I expect." She indicated in the direction of his office.

James was behind his desk as usual, but wasn't wearing a pin stripe suit; he was wearing a blazer and an open neck shirt, no tie! I'd never seen him without a tie; I'd never seen him without a suit, even at school! I think he wore his tie even during PE.

"James?" I said, uncertainly.

"Hi Simon," he said, bounding towards me.

He'd lost weight, a lot of weight, his hair was well cut. Styled! Was it darker? He had new glasses, the thick lensed tortoise shelled pair he'd always had, of a style dating back to our schooldays were gone to be replaced by stylish designer rimless spectacles, probably German.

"Thanks for coming. Good to see you," he said.

I was stunned. I didn't know what to say. I wanted to say, "Where's James?"

"Where's James?" I did in fact say. I don't think he heard however. He was in full flow.

"Just be a moment, to run through these," indicating a small pile of forms and ignoring my question. We did the run though, in double quick time. "Sign here, sign there."

"I'll get that off to the court," he said, "should hear in a little while."

"James," I said. "What's with the Porsche?"

"Oh, you saw it? Yeah, well, I thought I'd treat myself, you know."

"Really? What's brought this on?"

"Well, like you, I'm single now."

"What?" How could I have missed this? We hadn't been in touch or had a drink in some time. In fact, when I thought about it, it was probably an entire year since we'd socialized.

"Well," he took a breath. "I don't like to mention my private life during our appointments and we've not seen one another in a while have we? Laura and I had some really tough times and we finally separated a while ago. So, yeah, I'm single. Moved out, decided to ditch the old car. Got time for a spin in the Porsche?"

"Have I?" I said. "Definitely."

We headed out of the "staff only" rear exit from the office directly into the car park. James's Porsche was in front of us. "Jump in," he said. As he reversed out he exclaimed, "God, who's parked that Lexus? They're ugly aren't they?"

"Yeah, I know," I said. "Tell me about it."

As we went bombing along the lanes a short distance away from his offices, James told me that his own marriage, like mine had come to an end about three years before. He and Laura had limped along sharing a home but there was no life left in their relationship. They didn't have children and had reached a point where they realized that they were just going through the motions of being married. He'd moved out in September.

"What's going to happen?" I asked. "Is there anyone else?"

"Oh no," he said, "I've seen a couple of girls casually and had some fun but nothing serious, but I'm pretty busy so I've signed up with one of those agencies."

"What, an internet agency?"

I didn't think that James knew anything about the internet but how daft was that! He obviously did as he emailed me letters from Katherine's solicitor and his replies routinely. He was a professional so of course he would be familiar with IT. Why hadn't he mentioned this? Anyway, he'd signed up to an introductory service.

"Yeah, I've had a couple of dates already," he said. "You ought to give it a try, Simon I'll give you the number. It's a bit expensive though.

"Yeah?" I didn't like to ask, but I did anyway. "Really, when you say expensive James, what do you actually mean?"

"Well, I think I paid about six grand."

"Six grand?" I said. "Six thousand pounds!?!"

"Oh yeah, well they're all about that."

"Six thousand pounds! What do they do? Arrange introductions on board the QE2?"

Well they're going to find me someone. It's for professional people, bespoke and discreet. It's all very detailed. There's psychological profiling involved. It cuts out a lot of messing about and the six thousand pounds, well what price would you put on your future happiness, Simon?"

Now that was a phrase that James hadn't come up with himself. I was sure that it was one the Agency had used in their "discreet" advertising.

"Well, I know, it's a tough one to answer, but six grand, Jesus! Seriously, who are they going to introduce you to James – Miss World?"

The Porsche was lovely. I'm not a great fan of Porsches either, but it was fabulous, compared to the Lexus. Powerful obviously but also stylish, comfortable and well engineered. I said goodbye to James back at the car park and drove back to the flat. Time was cracking on and I'd had a text from Rick saying he was going to come over early because he wanted to have a look at the Lexus.

I drove sedately on the way back and cringed as I went past the zebra crossing where I'd nearly flattened Shilpa. When I got back to the flat, Rick was already in his car waiting. He'd pulled up moments before me and was talking on his phone. I sat in the Lexus until he finished his conversation and watched as he sauntered over appraising the car.

"They're ugly buggers these things, aren't they?"

'Does nobody like the way Lexus cars look?' I wondered. I'm sure they must do because they sell loads of them, it must just be me and my friends. "It's very clever though, Rick," I said, "It has a battery propelling the drive train."

"What like a milk float?"

"Well, yes, well no, not like a milk float, no, much more sophisticated and when the battery runs out the engine charges it up."

"Really?"

"Yeah, it's very clever."

"How loud's the stereo then?"

"Pretty loud." I gave him a blast of Elton, 'must remember to take the CD out,' I thought.

"How fast does it go?"

"Hmm, hops on a bit when it's cranked up."

I kicked the door shut and we went inside.

Really that's the sum total of what most guys want to know. How fast a car goes and how good the sound system is? Millions of words I've written about cars and it all comes down to that really. And of course the main thing is, is it sexy? Will I look good in it? Can I attract women? Pathetic? Women are draped over the bonnets of cars at motor shows and even in this politically correct age, the message is, "if you buy the car you can sleep with me". Women that read motor magazine articles in my experience want to know about reliability, economy and second hand values - I know Katherine did when we looked at buying our family cars and she reviewed write ups.

Now, I know I'm going to get letters, but that's the truth of it, isn't it? And I wonder why I don't get many more assignments from car magazines. I was amazed that Mercedes Benz had actually invited me to their event and that reminded me, I needed to call Shilpa and ask her. But should I ring or would it be better to text her? Should I e-mail her? Did I have her e-mail address? Yeah, I've got to do something, I decided, and I should do it soon. Once I get into the flat so that she has enough notice.

Barry had texted to say he was on his way as well, coming early to also have a look at the Lexus. I made some coffee and Rick and I were just sitting down at the kitchen table when the buzzer went in the flat. I glanced at the kitchen clock and it was coming up to 5 o'clock. 'Must be the grumpy guy from Lexus,' I thought. I was tempted to open the window of the flat and drop the keys down, on his head if I could aim straight. Then I remembered I needed to go down and get the Elton John CD and check I hadn't left anything else in it, like my wallet. I'm always doing that by the way as well. The voice at the end of the buzzer said.

"Hello Mr Taylor?" A refined female voice, definitely not' Grumpy'.

"Uh, yes," I said, thrown.

"Hello, I'm Sharon from Lexus."

"Err, Sharon?"

"Yes, I've come to pick up the LS600h you've been testing."

"Oh, yes, err, right, um well, would you like to come up?"

"Yes, of course."

I went back into the kitchen.

"There's a girl from Lexus, she's on her way up the stairs, and unless Barry gets here pronto he's going to be too late to see it."

"Up the stairs?"

"Well, in the lift if she's in luck. I know it was working for us, but it's so bloody useless, that's probably the last time today it will work. I don't care. She's on her way up. She sounds nice."

"Oh right," said Rick, then "You know you can't tell from people's voices what they look like Simon, particularly women? She's probably going to be awful."

"Why do you always say that Rick? She sounds very pleasant, refined in fact. She probably went to Roedean or somewhere like that."

"Roedean? What's Roedean?"

"Well, it's a school, isn't it? It's a girls' finishing school."

"Well, I don't know, I'm not really up on girls' schools."

"You know Roedean, they do that thing, they play that game, what's that game with a sort of big tennis racket and a ball?"

"Lacrosse?" he said.

"Yeah, that's it," I said, "Lacrosse."

I don't know why we were having this ridiculous conversation about over-sized tennis bats. I opened the door and there was Sharon from Lexus. She was of course gorgeous. A redhead. She smiled and introduced herself and explained that she'd come to pick up the car."

"Err, do come in, er, this is my friend, um, Rick. Well, when I say friend I mean friend I don't mean anything else by that he's just a friend and he's just popped in to see me!" She looked bewildered, not surprisingly.

"Um, yes, we are just friends having a cup of coffee and we were just, in fact, in fact... " desperately trying to gather my thoughts, "err, in fact I was just explaining to Rick, what a fantastic car the Lexus is."

Rick's eyes widened.

"Err, um, and in actual fact, Rick in fact, err, is, well, we were talking about him buying one, weren't we Rick?"

Rick took a while to reply. "Err, yes, well..."

"Oh, really," said Sharon enthusiastically. "Strange, because we got the impression back at the office that you weren't too happy with the car, um, is that the case?"

"No," I said, "no, I love it, I absolutely love it."

"Oh there must be some mistake, sorry, so you're enjoying it and have you written the article yet, can I read it?"

"Err, well, no," I said, "I haven't quite finished the article yet, but, um, I will be sending it in via my agent and if you'd like an advance copy I'd be happy to e-mail it to you."

"Oh yes, of course, I'll just jot my e-mail address down for you."

Gosh, this was going well. Whilst Sharon rooted round in her bag for a piece of paper and a pen, she gave me one of her cards, "Sharon Wade, Co-ordinator. Lexus, Public Relations Department." Clearly Grumpy wasn't from this department. Tall and with her red hair she looked like she should have been a member of a girl band. She had trousers on and a fleece, a black fleece with the Lexus logo on and a rather natty scarf tied round her neck, smelt lovely, looked lovely. Late 30's? I didn't know what to say.

Rick was staring at me. I wished he wouldn't. Not quite so obviously.

"Well, I'd love to read your article, Mr Taylor, and... perhaps if I could just have the keys for the car now?"

"Err, yes, yes, yes." I turned into Basil Fawlty. "Yes of course, of course." I grabbed the car keys. As she spun round to go out of the flat she noticed the invitation to the Mercedes Benz do.

"Oh," she said. "Are you going to that? I hope you don't mind me asking."

"Oh this," I said, "Oh this from Mercedes Benz, oh err, No, I'm so keen on Lexus that I'm not really bothered about going, I get invites all the time to these sort of events. Why do you ask?" I enquired.

"Well I am going," she replied.

"What, to a Mercedes Benz do?" I queried in a rising falsetto.

"Yes, I am freelance. My business card is one Lexus have printed for me but I am not an employee. The PR agency I work for gave me the invitation, we all get invited to one another's do's and yes, it's a shame I won't see you there then."

"Yes, um well, a real shame."

I forgot all about the CD of course, gave her the keys, and she was gone. I came back into the kitchen.

Rick had heard every word. He raised his eyebrows smirking. "You berk."

Barry arrived too late for a spin in the car. We headed off for our usual fish and chips, their usual interrogation of me and Agony Uncle wisdom on how I should keep busy, focus on work, not make more of an idiot of myself than I could possibly help etc. etc. Thank God for friends!

When I arrived back at the flat I got down to work. On the Lexus article.

An Unexpected Invitation

The phone rang. I was in the middle of writing and the landline was ringing. The ringtone in the flat's loud and shrill and startles me, especially at night or early in the morning. It was only 9pm though. Rick had called my mobile moments earlier moaning about Tottenham losing a game. I had just settled down again to work when I was interrupted once more.

"Hello, Simon," said a vaguely familiar female voice. I couldn't place who it belonged to. A neutral, educated voice, the type used to advertise watches or cars, like a broadcaster reading the news. Then I got it, it was Ingrid.

"Ingrid, goodness I haven't heard from you for a while." I hadn't.

Ingrid had worked some years earlier at James's firm as a legal executive. She handled commercial work in-house and had advised me on a couple of contracts a while ago. We'd got on well, met at a mutual friend's party and had a brief liaison. I'd lost touch with her after she left James' firm. Yes, our "fling" was whilst I was married. It was in the dying throes of it, the drifting no-man's land between the marriage fading, ending and my moving out. I know it doesn't make it any better.

Ingrid and I had remained friends. Our relationship had a brief "enjoy by" date. She was also then married, unhappily but had no plans to end it. She wanted some attention, sex and company. That was all. That was okay by me. In fact, we weren't suited for anything more. That was then, however.

Things had moved on for Ingrid and as she was now explaining, she was in the throes of getting divorced too, had bought her own flat, was leaving legal practice and had already started re-training to be a personal trainer. Part of her divorce settlement was going to be a holiday home in Barbados that she and her husband had bought with an eye to their eventual retirement. It needed a lot of work doing to it, but her whole life was going to change. She was planning to move into the holiday home, project manage the building works and work as a personal trainer for wealthy ex-pats.

"Well, I'm glad you've got life sorted out," I said, "I'm still muddling through with mine. Anyway, it's lovely to hear from you and thanks so much for keeping me updated."

She'd found my number from a friend of a friend and had been given my new phone number and email address. Rather tantalizingly, she said "I would like to talk to you about something, else Simon. It's a bit delicate."

I'd said, "Well, yes, of course, you can talk to me about anything."
We'd previously acknowledged that whilst we were fond of one another,
aside from her being married and seeking to remain so, we weren't
compatible. She wanted a different sort of life to me and at 38 years she
was quite a lot younger than me, didn't have children, whereas I did. Even
if she had wanted a long-term relationship, which she didn't, there were
just too many things that were never going to make it work. We were
better friends than we were lovers.

"Are you still a member of the RAF club in London?" she asked. "Yes,
of course," I said. "In fact I'm meeting my publisher there shortly, on
Tuesday."

"Well, I'm planning a trip to Town and I thought I'd do a bit of
shopping and it would suit me to come then, so maybe we can meet up
then and have a spot of lunch, a glass of wine, how does that sound?"

"Fabulous," I said.

We agreed to meet after I'd seen my agent and she rounded off the call
with a "Lovely, look forward to seeing you."

I was intrigued, but with everything else going on, especially this
Mercedes thing, I didn't think much more about it. I presumed she might
want some advice about marketing, perhaps some contacts. Maybe she
was thinking of setting up a company? Ingrid was now in the orbit of my
current network of friends and I consoled myself with the thought that
even if I couldn't help her out personally with her problem, I probably
knew someone who could.

She breezed into the foyer of the Royal Air Force Club in London, long
chestnut hair loose about her shoulders. She wore a vivid green blazer
with gold buttons, a short black skirt with black high heels and was
carrying a large black and gold bag shaped like an envelope. She smelt of
Yves Saint Laurent *Rives Gauche*. She caught the eye of some rather
crusty looking Air Marshalls waiting in the foyer at the time. She was
deeply tanned.

I started off as Hugh Grant again, "Gosh, Ingrid you look fabulous,
where on earth have you been?"

"Oh I've been out to Barbados quite a bit, checking on the house. I've
been going to the gym every single day doing this trainer course."

"Well, I hope you can have some lunch," I said. We went into the main
dining room and sat down. The RAF club, whilst being discreet, isn't
exactly a romantic location. We looked to all intents and purposes like a
business couple. Because of the formal dress code at the RAF club, I had

worn a suit and tie together with my RAF cufflinks. Ingrid's envelope-shaped handbag looked like a blingy briefcase. She got straight to the point.

"It's lovely to see you," she said brightly.

"And you. How can I help?" I replied enthusiastically.

"Well, as I said to you on the phone, it's a little delicate, but I'm sure you'll understand and before I go any further, if you don't want to do what I'm suggesting, it won't affect us at all, we'll still be friends, but I'm dying to… well let me explain."

She continued in breathless detail of how, since separating from her husband, some six months previously, she'd been "not exactly questioning" her sexuality, as she put it, but aware that some brief encounters with girls whilst she was at boarding school, were on her mind. She'd recently signed up for her intensive personal training course and met Katie. Katie was an airhostess and was openly bi-sexual, but she, that's Katie, wasn't sure whether she was truly bi-sexual or whether she was lesbian. I hope you're keeping up with this? The sober and formal surroundings of the RAF club seemed highly inappropriate for the conversation we were having. I was glad that the elderly Air Marshals sitting some distance away couldn't hear what was being discussed at our table.

"It's all very, well, interesting, Ingrid, but I'm not sure where I fit in," I said when she had finished. She raised her eyebrows.

"Well, quite simply Simon, we thought that we could all, well you know… " Ingrid now lowered her gaze and seemed strangely hesitant.

"You know what?" I said genuinely puzzled.

"Well… if we all got together Simon, to, um explore these issues, um… "

The penny suddenly dropped. "You mean the three of us?"

Ingrid nodded: for a long time, just nodded.

"So Ingrid, just so I'm absolutely clear on this, you want me to meet with Katie and you and give it a go?"

"Yes," she said bluntly.

I didn't know what to say. Now I know, you're probably thinking that I'm making it up. This is fiction right? I'm not. And I did hesitate, I wasn't sure. Friends had mentioned threesomes, as people often do in jest, but I'll be honest I'd never fantasized about being with two women. Now here I was, being invited to consider it as a serious option for myself. I was never sure what the other girl was supposed to do really. Aside from the crawling all over bodies part, perhaps make a cup of tea? Cheer from the side-lines after mutual congress or something? I realized what little imagination I had. Ingrid spoke.

"Simon, do you fancy coming shopping with me or what? Are you going to let me know? What shall I tell Katie?"

I'm not normally reticent, maybe it was the surroundings. "Well, yes," I said. "I can't come shopping, but um, I will let you know."

"Yeah, of course, well you let me know."

I paid the bill and as we headed to the door she said, "If you are interested, perhaps we can meet up soon. Maybe in the next couple of weeks? I'm heading back to the Caribbean at the end of the month. Oh and that's the other thing, where? Perhaps we could meet..."

"No." I stopped her, anticipating her suggestion. "We cannot meet here."

I expect people do have sex at the RAF Club but not experimental threesomes. Since Ingrid had mentioned that Katie was an airhostess and their course was over in West London we decided that if it was happening, a hotel near Heathrow would be a good idea. I still couldn't quite believe that: (a) I'd been asked and (b) we were now actually planning where to meet. (c) I had agreed having no idea what Katie was like. What if she didn't like me? What if I didn't like her? What were the arrangements going to be? I started to panic again.

Ingrid could tell I was thrown. She gave me a kiss on the cheek and said, "Look, don't worry Simon, I'll sort out all the arrangements, it will be great fun."

I managed to hail down a taxi for her just outside and having declined her offer of going shopping as I'd work urgently needing completing, realized how much I also needed the opportunity to walk to Green Park tube station to consider her invitation. My head was spinning. When I reached Liverpool Street there was a delay for the train home. I phoned Rick.

"What's up?" he answered cheerily.

"Well," I said rather breathlessly. "You remember Ingrid?"

"Err," he said, "Ingrid, what one was that?"

"You know Ingrid the legal executive, worked with Simon my solicitor?"

"Oh yeah, vaguely, why?"

"Well, I've just had lunch with her in London at the RAF club."

"Oh right, yes." Rick seemed uninterested. He was eating.

"And she's asked me, well, she's put it to me, well, she wants me to..."

Rick seemed irritated now. "What, what does she want you to do? Shag her?"

"Well, sort of… "

"What do you mean, sort of?"

"Well, she wants me to, yes, but with a friend… "

"With a friend? Can I come?"

"No, you twit. She wants to bring a friend… "

"What another bloke?!?"

"No." I was beginning to wish I hadn't phoned. My head was actually hurting now. "No, just listen. She's got this friend, she's doing this course and she's met this girl, an airhostess and..."

"Another girl? So, she wants you to join her and another girl in bed?"

"Well, yes, I was going to try and put it a bit more diplomatically, Rick, but yes, that's what she wants me to do."

There was a pause. "You lying sod," he said. "You're always like this when you go up to London and get pissed."

"No," I said. "I'm not making it up. Of course I'm not making it up, why would I make it up?"

"Well, because you're so crap at chatting up women, don't forget I was there when that very nice girl from Lexus turned up at your flat and you were useless. I find it very hard to believe that Ingrid, who is a legal executive and clearly smart, wants you to have sex with her and an airhostess. Look, Simon, if you're just trying to do this just to try and impress me, forget it."

"No, no," I said. "You've got it all wrong, I'm not doing that, I just don't know what to do."

"What do you mean, you don't know what to do?"

"Well, I don't know whether to say yes or not." Another pause.

"What do you mean you don't know whether to say yes? Bloody hell, if you don't want to go, I'll go!" he said.

"Apparently," I said. "It's a top male fantasy."

"Yes, it is."

"Well, is it yours?"

"Well, yes, I think so, providing they're twins."

There was no point in carrying on the conversation any further. "Look we'll talk about it on Friday okay?"

"Simon you're mad and must be pissed." Click.

On the way back on the train I couldn't stop thinking about it. Had I really heard what she'd said? Had I misconstrued it?

A text from Ingrid seemed to confirm that I hadn't. It read simply "Hi Simon, thanks so much for lunch. I've had a chat with Katie; she's dying to meet you. Are you free next Thursday at 3 o'clock? X"

Was I? I thought. Was I really going to go through with this? I checked my diary on my phone. Yes I was. Sod it, I thought. Let's give this top male fantasy a try. I just texted back, "Yes, let me know where you want me to be. PS. what's the dress code?" This wasn't a joke; it was what I was then genuinely worried about. First impressions and all that and an airhostess I'd never met but was expected to become intimate with!!

I still had about over a week to go before the planned liaison, 'if it happens' I thought. I forced myself to focus on who I was going to ask to come to the Mercedes-Benz dinner, now under a fortnight away. I had decided to adopt Martin's suggestion of inviting everyone after all. Niamh hadn't confirmed and was almost certain to say no. She seemed far too organized to make any last minute arrangements and had more or less said she couldn't get away.

Apart from the occasional text from Shilpa, I hadn't arranged another date with her. Melanie had said I should just ask her out and that she'd enjoy being taken to a Gala Dinner, but I'd done nothing about it. The woman from Lexus would be going, but she would be on another table and presumably there to generate work. She would be surprised to see me there now anyway. She was attractive though. I had her email address and wondered if I should email her the article on the Lexus, now finished and mention that there was a change of plan, I was now going to the event.

As I headed back to the flat, I decided to do some research about threesomes on the internet. Now if you are going to do this, be prepared. There is an awful lot on there and malware like porn sites. It's true that it is a very common male fantasy. I don't really know what mine is – something involving pink knickers definitely, for the avoidance of doubt, not *me* wearing them – there's lots of that on there as well. I'm not prudish but I just don't understand why some men, however interested in girls, their underwear and the feel of certain fabrics would want to wear women's clothing. The statistics are interesting and reveal that most men that do dress up are heterosexual. But as long as they're happy and not harming anyone, its fine.

I opened my emails whilst on the computer. I was still receiving messages about joining a dating club with personal introductions through arranged events. I must admit I was intrigued. Whilst I was contacting women I seemed pretty hopeless at getting anywhere with them. With hindsight, my friends were right, I was just panicking; it was middle age panic that I was going to be on my own, forever. That I wouldn't meet anyone and enjoy a functioning long-term relationship.

The site that kept emailing me was called *Across the Room* and its formula had proven to be "notably successful" at least according to their own blurb. There had recently been some television advertising of it. It's based in Essex and the Home Counties and the proposal made in the email involved clients meeting at a designated hotel or restaurant. The agency would invite an equal number of men and women guests who would circulate and socialize during dinner. It appeared well organized and designed to enable members to meet a variety of people without the stress, awkwardness or hassle of having to make initial choices about dining companions. To join the Club clients were required to provide a detailed profile and complete a questionnaire that contained an array of enquiries. The joining fee was reasonable though this was the Company's "Silver Service" option. There was another level of service – the "Bespoke Introduction Service" with the fee available upon personal request designed to appeal to higher net worth individuals.

The personal information sought by the company for club events was presumably obtained with a view to ensuring that a fair proportion of the guests would be chosen to complement the tastes and aspirations of one another. And the mechanics of the introductions? The detail of the plan for dining involved the men moving tables between courses. So they would eat their starter seated as allocated by the organizers, between ladies, move to a second allocated seat on another table for the main course, then again for dessert, coffee and liqueurs. The events included live music, a band or a disco with every guest having a dance card! – can you remember those? I do.

When I was a cadet in military college we had formal dances where we had the opportunity to dance with the girls from the military academy along the road. It was the only available female company we had access to during training. We each had a numbered dance card and the lads were expected to ask the girls to be put on their cards, noting the girl's names on their own card by the number of dance. When the number of the dance was announced the idea was that you found your partner and off you went. Rather clumsily in my case, as I remember. I did a lot of treading on feet and quickly learned that "I'm sorry my dance card's full" meant "piss off". Really!

Across the Room had a similar arrangement except that it was expected that each guest would start off with six people on their dance card. The men would have an entry for each of the ladies seated beside them for each course and after that could ask anyone they chose. The idea appealed and I thought, 'well why not?' It was madness really, with everything else going on. Barry would be bound to advise me to stop and think for a moment and say it was a daft idea because (a) when was I going to get the time? and (b) did I really want to spend my time with a lot of like-minded desperados, trying to put a brave face on being single?

I completed the on-line application form, inserted my credit card details and sent it off. I'd also got an e-mail from Niamh. "Hi, Simon," it said. "I thought you might like this photo." I clicked on the attachment. There was a picture of Niamh at work. I was immediately struck by how like the wonderful Mrs Pike she looked, in her long white lab coat. She had goggles on and gloves and one of those blue, bib-type things, that looked like she was just about to tie round her patient's neck. Underneath she'd written, "One of the girls in surgery had taken this during a training session, thought you might like it." She did look lovely. Then she put, "PS, when is the Mercedes do?"

I replied straight away, "Thanks so much, Niamh, you look wonderful." I decided to leave out the bit about her looking like Mrs Pike. "It's on the 28th; I'd love you to come. Can you?"

She e-mailed back straight away, "I'll see what I can do, at work, on the phone shortly."

Great. I wondered if she really would come. Should I not invite anyone else now as Martin had suggested? What if she doesn't phone? What if she doesn't come and I'm on my own? Should I ask Shilpa as I had been planning? Should I e-mail Sharon?

Fish and chips that Friday was dominated by the threesome issue. Rick was convinced that I was lying and Barry was concerned about the moral issues involved, not least those of sexually transmitted disease.

"Simon, why on earth do you want to do this? Why have you agreed to it?" he said I had to admit that I felt a bit sort of sluttish, really, and said, "Well, you know, thought it might be fun."

"And who is this girl that Ingrid knows?"

"Well, I don't really know really. I know she's called Katie and she's an airhostess."

"Is that all you know about her?" He persisted.

I studied my fish and chips closely. "Yes," I mumbled.

"And you've agreed to meet them and have sex with both of them?"

"Well, it's not quite like that," I said lamely.

"You said it was," retorted Rick instantly.

"Well, yes, well I don't really know. I've never done anything like this before."

Barry became stern. "Well, I'm pleased to hear that. You should have a really good think about this Simon. What if you get something? And for a Catholic, the non-wearing-condoms-as-it's-against-my-religion thing is a bit ridiculous, isn't it?"

"Well, in truth," I said. "I really don't think it's going to happen. I haven't heard from Ingrid, she spoke about meeting up next Thursday, but I'm not sure."

"There you are," said Rick. "I knew you were lying or making it up. I suppose you're going to try and say she cancelled it now or you just didn't hear from her."

I was beginning to get really fed up with them. "Yes, okay," I said. "I'll let you know."

"What about the Mercedes thing, who's coming?"

"Well, I've decided to invite them both."

"Both of them! What, the Indian bird and the Irish one?"

"Yes."

Barry was indignant. "Simon, what are you doing? Why are you inviting them both to one event? What if they both say yes? What are you going to do then?"

"Well they won't, will they? And I spoke to Martin and he said it was a good idea."

"So you thought you'd just do it?"

"Well, it's just the... well, I don't know. I've not really been in this position before."

Barry seemed genuinely upset and said, "Look Simon, you've invited people out before. You're going to this Dinner, whatever it is. It's clearly a formal posh 'do' and you need someone to go with you. But for God's sake, invite one person, if they say no, and then invite someone else. Don't just invite everybody. You're completely mad and far too desperate to meet someone."

I hadn't dared mention *Across the Room.* As I said before when you're single your private life isn't really your own. It's everybody else's. I rang Martin and told him about the threesome.

"You lucky sod," he said.

"Have you ever done it?" I said.

"No, I haven't. You're such a jammy git, Simon, I remember Ingrid. I met her once when she came to the office, do you remember?"

"Yeah, I do."

"Is she still nice?" he asked.

"She is," I said. I described her suntanned legs, crossing and uncrossing at the RAF club. "Well, let me know how you get on," he said.

"Vesuvius" as code for "get me out of this" had now been unanimously adopted with the boys and in the event of the meeting being a success, we'd agreed I'd simply text "Tsunami" It was Thursday and I was in the car heading to a hotel on the outskirts of Heathrow. Rick repeatedly reminded me about texting "Vesuvius" if I wanted to get out of it. He would then leap into telephone emergency "Mounting" Rescue!

As the signs for Heathrow appeared on the M4, I began to get really nervous.

I had worried endlessly about what to wear to the meeting with Ingrid and Katie. What do you wear to a threesome? Okay, what do you wear if you're a middle-aged naturally anxious sort of guy? I'd made the excuse that I may drop back and see my publisher at the RAF club so I wouldn't look ridiculous wearing a suit. I just felt more confident like this. I'd settled on the same grey Gucci single-breasted suit that I'd worn on my date with Stephanie. I doused myself in Issey Miyake *Sport.* It seemed appropriate.

Ingrid had confirmed that she was on her way and she was coming straight from her personal training class, so she would just be in a tracksuit. It had been a long while since I'd had sex with Ingrid and I didn't know whether that might happen if Katie didn't show up. It all seemed pretty mechanical. As I got closer to the hotel, the satellite navigation indicating I was just three miles away, I started to feel rather grubby and well, a bit ridiculous really. A mixture of anxiety, anticipation, lust and desperation. I pulled into the car park and decided to phone Rick.

He just said, "Don't tell me, you've called it off?"

"No," I said. "I'm in the car park."

"Oh, right."

I told him the name of the hotel. "Okay," he said, "I believe you, I believe you're there, but I'm sure it's not going to happen."

I said, "Well, Rick, I don't think it's going to happen either, mate, to be honest. It will be nice to see Ingrid again anyway. I'll have a drink with her and I may call back via the club. If you want to join me there, it'll be no problem. I'm sure it'll just be a quick drink with Ingrid so I'll give you a call when I'm finished."

"Okay, no problem," he said. "Be careful, if it does go ahead, enjoy."

As I came off the phone from Rick and whilst still sitting in the car, I got a voicemail message. I dialled the Vodafone voice messaging service and it was Martin.

"Simon, if it all goes ahead, you lucky bugger, get stuck in, ha, ha." And that was it.

I started to feel more cheerful now, less apprehensive, headed into the very large foyer and sat down, ordered a cup of coffee from the waitress service there and waited for Ingrid. I didn't have to wait long. She came at speed through the automatic doors. She looked lovely, if a bit sweaty. Her hair was scraped back into a ponytail and she was carrying a gym bag and mobile phone. She had on large pink trainers, which seemed slightly at odds with the rest of her look of just plain black jogging bottoms, black tee shirt and grey top. I gave her a kiss. "Well it's lovely to see you. Can't believe we're actually doing this. Are we going to do it?" Ingrid ordered tea.

"What do you mean are we going to do it?" she said in a very dignified voice. "Yes of course, we've been looking forward to it."

"And, um, Katie, she's on her way is she?"

"Well, strangely enough, I haven't heard from Katie, she sent me a text this morning saying see you at the hotel, but I've texted her couple of times and haven't heard back."

I was relieved, genuinely relieved.

"Oh, well," I said. "Not to worry, um, shall we, um..."

"Well, I haven't booked a room."

"You haven't booked a room?" I said.

"Well, no I hadn't heard from Katie and you know, to be honest Simon, I thought you were going to bottle out."

"Me bottle out?" I said indignantly. "Course not, I've been really up for this."

"Hmm," Ingrid seemed slightly unconvinced "I'll text her again." Ingrid zapped away on her mobile phone with amazing dexterity. "There you are, sent."

"Anyway," I said. "Tell me a bit about your plans and the house in Barbados."

"Oh, yes," she said. "Well, I should finish this course in a fortnight and then I intend packing the last of my things up, putting stuff into storage and heading out. You can come out and stay if you like. When I was out there last I took some photos. They're in my bag."

She placed some photos on the coffee table next to our drinks. The house looked delightful, colonial style with a veranda and set in a large garden. The pool was empty, apparently in need of relining and the grounds were to be landscaped whilst the house was to be rewired and decoration.

"I've decided to use one of the outhouses and turn it into a gym for my business," she explained.

"What about your love life Ingrid?" I asked.

"Oh that'll sort it out. I've had a few dates," she replied breezily.

"Have you been on any introduction agency websites?" I asked.

"What, dating websites?"

"Yes."

"No, they're just for saddoes aren't they? No, I'm not worried about meeting anyone, I've been too busy, and well, there's this thing with Katie."

"Tell me about the thing with Katie then, what's been happening?"

"Well, you know, I've felt attracted to several girls over the past few years. I find Katie very appealing and as I'm getting on, I thought I should decide whether I want to be with a girl, have a girl as a girlfriend."

"So, you and Katie are more than just friends?"

"Yes, I thought I'd explained that. But I'm not sure if either of us can be without a man in the end. As a sexual partner. That's partly why we thought we'd try this."

Human sexuality is complicated isn't it? So there I was about to be with two girls involved in a sexual relationship with one another but who now also wanted to have sex with me. Not individually, together at the same time. What was the sort of, well, etiquette? I mean, I'd never done anything like this before and I was still confused as to what, if anything, Katie was going to do, or what I'd be required to do to Katie if she ever turned up. I had a vague idea about going with the flow, no pun intended, but that was really about it.

Ingrid decided she needed the toilet and disappeared to find the Ladies, leaving her gym bag and photographs strewn across the coffee table. There were lots of people milling about in the foyer of the hotel and I wondered if any of them, or the reception staff more to the point would guess at what we were doing.

I was being paranoid. People are far too concerned with their own lives to be interested in what other people are doing. I told myself to relax. If Katie turned up, fine, and if she didn't, well, that would be fine too. Ingrid was soon back.

"Any news from her?" I asked. She delved into the pocket of her tracksuit top which she'd left over the back of her chair.

"I don't think so," she said. She picked up her mobile phone and as she glanced at it, looked towards the revolving door and said, "Ah, here she is."

I stood up immediately, a sort of a reflex action. Katie was petite. She had short brown hair and was wearing black trousers, a white shirt and a black cardigan, flattish black shoes. She was pulling a small suitcase, her flight-case presumably. She had a very pretty face and a slight but athletic physique. I could see why Ingrid was attracted to her.

Ingrid and Katie embraced, kissed one another and exchanged greetings. I just stood in my suit feeling uncomfortable. Ingrid then introduced us. "Katie, this is Simon I've told you so much about."

I shook Katie's hand and said, "Hello, I'm very pleased to meet you," in my best BBC voice.

"Would you like a drink? Tea or coffee?"

"Oh, yes please, coffee," said Katie.

She had an accent, but I couldn't quite place it. I later learnt that it was a Welsh accent though she hadn't lived in Wales for a long time. When the coffee arrived, she spoke about being an airhostess; why she was re-training to be a personal trainer also; that that was how she'd met Ingrid. My mobile phone was on vibrate and in my pocket and it had vibrated a couple of times. I guessed it was Rick trying to get hold of me. I ignored it.

Katie then glanced down at the photographs on the coffee table. "Oh, are these of your house in Barbados?" she said animatedly.

"Yes," said Ingrid. "I was just showing Simon before you arrived."

"Oh, it looks lovely."

"Yes," I said. "It does doesn't it, and apparently we're both invited."

"Oh yes, Ingrid had mentioned that," she said.

I'd not been to Barbados or any part of the Caribbean, but had always wanted to go.

Katie told me she'd been a couple of times and that long haul flights were popular with flight attendants and offered the best working conditions. Things were going well, the conversation was natural and flowed and I began to relax and enjoy myself. I couldn't seriously believe we were going to do anything apart from enjoy conversation over coffee and possibly a few drinks. I felt content simply being in the girls' company.

Then Ingrid spoke. "Right, so what are we going to do? Are we going to get a room or not?" She flashed a slightly nervous look across the table at me.

"Yes," I said. "Well, we're all here aren't we?"

Katie then seemed reticent. She bit her bottom lip and studied her shoes for a bit.

I decided to intervene and said, "Look, if you're not happy about doing any of this that's fine. Don't feel you've got to go ahead with anything for my benefit." I was going to say "my part" but stopped myself.

Ingrid spoke. "Look, let's just get a room and go and see what happens."

Katie then smiled and said, "Yes, that would be fine, but I don't think I can do anything without a drink, a proper one I mean." She giggled.

I stood up and said, "What would you like to drink?"

"Scotch," she said. "A large one."

"How do you take it?"

Katie glanced at me and said without hesitation, "Straight up!"

We laughed. I had a glass of wine, Ingrid, a gin and tonic and Katie, a Scotch on the rocks.

Ingrid took her drink and headed to reception to organize a room. She came back with a key. "All done," she said.

"What do we do? All go up together?" I said. "Won't that look as if we're advertising?"

"Simon, there's so many people about. No one's looking at you or us."

We piled in the lift together. The wine was starting to have some effect but not enough to prevent me feeling suddenly nauseous. What if I wasn't able to perform? I'm not comfortable at being seen naked, I feel self-conscious and fat, and I'd never done it with somebody actually watching me have sex. I mean what was going to happen? I felt awful. I later learned that Katie was just as nervous and was just about to say that she wasn't going to go ahead with it when we reached the room. It was a larger than normal double with a king-size bed, a seating area with a small low coffee table, a separate TV, fridge, standard sort of up market executive hotel arrangement.

The dynamics seemed to change once we were inside the room. Katie became more assertive. I slipped my suit jacket off and hung it up in the wardrobe, undid my tie. Ingrid came over to me and we started to kiss, Katie sat down in the chair opposite the bed. This was the bit I was really unsure of. How was it actually going to work?

Kissing Ingrid seemed to be enough of a distraction for me to try and forget that Katie was in the room and soon we were on the bed. Ingrid had taken off her tracksuit trousers and comically large pink trainers. She had knee high white socks on and white sports knickers. She pulled her chestnut hair free of the band keeping it in a ponytail and soon we were tumbling about on the bed. Katie was still seated on the chair opposite. I didn't know whether she was just going to watch or what really would happen next. It did seem to be a bit bizarre and I wasn't wholly comfortable. I decided to just concentrate on Ingrid as I pulled her towards me.

I could see Katie out of the corner of my eye and after a while I noticed that she'd undone her trousers and had her hand down the front of them. Presumably down the front of her knickers, although I couldn't see that.

A few more rolls round the bed and I caught sight of Katie again, this time she had her cardigan off and her white blouse was undone. She had her other hand in the top of her bra. Ingrid had now taken her top off. She was wearing a sports bra which looked look like a swimming costume at the back. Not sexy but sportily functional. But never mind, things were starting to hot up between us. I began to fondle Ingrid's breasts, although I was still fully clothed. Aware that Katie was watching us closely, my anxiety returned.

I decided to break off and go to the toilet. "Sorry about this," I said and dashed off.

In the bathroom I had a long look at myself in the mirror. "What on earth are you doing?" I asked myself. I was beginning to feel unsure again about the whole thing though it was good to be with Ingrid and Katie seemed content sitting in a chair playing with herself and knocking one out. Were they going to get it together? I'd discussed the idea of girls liking girls to my trainer, Melanie and she said it was quite obvious why lots of men find the thought of two girls arousing, that's because they fancy girls, fancy girls' bodies and expect other girls to fancy them as well. I'm not sure if that's true. Anyway, here I was in this unlikely situation. I came out of the toilet to be greeted to a sight I shall remember forever.

Katie and Ingrid were on the bed, they were completely naked, apart from Ingrid who still wore her knee high socks. Ingrid's all over suntan was in sharp contrast to Katie's white porcelain skin, as was Ingrid's long chestnut hair by comparison with Katie's short, cropped style. They were in the "69" position. It was an arresting sight, but left me with a dilemma, I didn't know what to do.

I didn't know whether it was my turn to sit in the chair, make a cup of tea, order some more drinks, or what to do? Though I'd only been in the bathroom briefly, they seemed to be in a pretty high state of arousal. Perhaps they just wanted to get it together with one another without me there.

With a long moan, Ingrid lifted her bottom and Katie moved from her side to between her legs. She knelt on all fours, so her small, perfectly shaped pale bottom was in the air. Ingrid looked at me and smiled at Katie's bottom. I knew what to do then threw off my clothes and leapt on the bed. The ice was well and truly broken. After a long session of both girls having each other and me having both girls in different positions, we were exhausted.

At one point we all lay on the bed on our backs in a row. I was tempted to order room service then remembered there was a mini bar. I felt quite self-conscious, went to the bathroom, and had a quick shower. I slipped my mobile phone into the bathroom and texted Rick, "Tsunami squared!"

A text came back immediately, "Liar!" on the screen.

I'd sort of half got dressed, shirt on, went back into the main room and offered the girls a drink. I like mini bars, there a vague sense of excitement when you open one to find what's in there. It's like looking into the future, isn't it? You can see what a can of coke is going to cost in thirty years' time from your local supermarket. There were three miniatures bottles of white wine, with just over a glass each. I poured a couple out and then Katie said, "Oh, no, nothing for me," glancing at her watch that she hadn't taken off during our shenanigans. "I'd better be going, I'm flying."

"Really?" I said.

"Yes, I'm off to New York. I'd better get ready."

She walked into the bathroom and took her suitcase with her. Ingrid and I sat on the bed, Ingrid started to get dressed as well, pulling her sports bra over her head and searching the bed for her knickers.

Then Katie came out of the bathroom and said, "It's ridiculous me getting dressed in there, you've just seen everything." We all laughed.

Whilst the threesome was enjoyable what happened next was for me equally as exciting.

Katie undid her suitcase and got out her hostess uniform. She hung up her jacket and skirt, got out a new blouse, quickly found the iron and ironing board, ironed the blouse and then started to get dressed. She had a selection of knickers in her travel bag and put them on the bed. I asked if I could choose a pair for her to wear.

Ingrid laughed, "Oh yes, I remember being with Simon, I always had to wear pink knickers.

"Well," Katie said. "Afraid you're out of luck, I don't think I've got any pink knickers with me but you can certainly choose."

I chose a ruffly pair of white knickers, but they were rejected on the basis that they would show under her tight skirt.

"How about these?" she said holding up a pair of cornflower blue briefs.

"Oh, they're nice," I said. "Yeah, put those on."

Having pulled those on she opened a new pack of hold up stockings. Unlike those Niamh had worn in Venice with lace decorative tops, these had plain elastication. She wore a white bra and dressed in the rest of her uniform she looked fabulous. She re-did her make-up; putting a lot on she looked vastly different. She styled her short hair round her ears, sprayed lots of perfume in front of her and stepped into the cloud of *Miss Dior*. Wow!

I was rampant. I don't know what came over me, "Katie," I said. "Before you go, do you think I could, um… ?"

"What?" she said.

"Well, do you think we could… ?" Ingrid was indignant.

"You aren't going to shag her again, are you? Oh, no, that's not part of the deal. It's the two of us together not individually."

"What?" I said. "Well, how does that work? I've… " Katie laughed.

"Well it's very flattering, and I'm glad you like my uniform so much, but one, I don't have time and two, I certainly don't have time to take this uniform to the dry cleaners and I haven't got a spare skirt with me."

In the foyer of the hotel I shook Katie's hand formally and said I'd been very pleased to meet her and hoped to see her again and that she had an enjoyable flight. She giggled. We both grinned at the comedy of the farewell.

Ingrid glanced at her watch, "Oh gosh, I've got to get back as well. Thanks Simon, great one." And was gone. Why do the women I know dash off so quickly after sex? As I got back into my car and drove back up the motorway I felt exhausted and pleased with myself in a dirty sort of way.

In between trying to sort my love life out, life was carrying on pretty much as usual. I was seeing the children, writing, eating fish and chips, going to the gym. I had realised something. Rick and Barry were right, I was desperate to meet somebody, but then apart from Sharon, the Lexus lady, I really didn't meet women in connection with my work. It was clear that unless I engaged actively in the dating scene I wasn't going to stand a chance of meeting someone.

I doubt if I'm going to get much sympathy from any male readers, having just described the three in a bed romp, but it was true: the reality was that unless I went on the internet, joined a dating agency or was involved with an organization like *Across the Room* how was I going to meet a woman who wasn't my dentist; personal trainer or a cashier at M&S?

I felt less guilty about the three in a bed thing having had a text from Ingrid saying, "What a laugh, and great fun. Lovely to see you. Katie is going to be in touch when she gets back from New York. Perhaps we could all go out for dinner? Xx."

'That would be a first,' I thought, 'two dates and one dinner.'

Speed Dating

I played back the messages on my landline. I hardly used the phone these days relying predominantly on my mobile. The messaging service's blue indicator was blinking on the cradle alerting me to a missed call. There was a message from Lexus. I held my breath. Hopefully the lovely Sharon. It wasn't from her but a call from Lexus's publicity department, asking when my article was going to be ready. My agent obviously hadn't passed the copy I'd managed to write onto them. I thought of Sharon. Should I email her?

Niamh had said she'd phone, but so far she hadn't. I decided to phone Shilpa. Speaking to Shilpa on the phone was difficult. I always got the impression she was doing something else, painting her nails, watching TV, reading a book? She appeared distant, yet when I was with her she was warm, friendly and focused on me. I mentioned the Mercedes dinner to her but she avoided committing herself, her reply a vaguely casual, "well, yes that would be nice."

I should be more forceful and say, "do you really want to go or don't you?"

We were interrupted by someone knocking on her door, or rather ringing the bell from her gate. She promised to call back, but she didn't.

In addition to the message from Lexus there was a message from *Across the Room*. "Eleanor" was calling to enquire whether I'd like to join them this Friday night at a local hotel for a speed dating event. I had expected an invitation to a formal dinner and didn't know for certain what speed dating was so I looked it up and discovered that it's an organised event and way of meeting lots of people quickly and deciding which, if any, were ones you'd like to meet again. The clue is in the title. It sounded fun so I rang back, spoke to Eleanor and said that I would be interested.

"Wonderful," she said. "It'll give us a chance to meet, have a chat with you and see if you'd be interested in our Bespoke Introduction Service. This was the expensive one, although hopefully not as expensive as my solicitor's.

"Is it dear?" I asked tentatively.

"Well, I'm sure you can afford it," she said cheekily. I wasn't sure I could but decided I would go along to the speed dating event. This was a big mistake. Since discussing my experience with others, I have yet to meet anyone who has had a positive experience at a speed dating event, let alone met someone worthwhile. In theory I can see it's a good idea, after all, it doesn't really matter how you meet somebody, or where you meet them, just that you meet, so the more people that you encounter, the better.

The evening was to take place at a hotel owned by the proprietor of my favourite restaurant, *The Riverside.* 'How bad could it be?' I thought. It's only just a few drinks, no meal or anything, just meeting and talking to people. How wrong could I be? I told the guys that I'd be dipping out on Friday as I'd be going to the speed dating event. Rick was clearly disappointed. He wanted to hear details of the three in a bed thing.

"Any photos?" he said. "Not of you obviously."

"No," I said, "we didn't do photos. It was much more civilized."

"Really?" he said. "I'm surprised. Oh, well, enjoy your speed dating, if you get fed up myself and Barry are going to go to the 'FishnChickn' anyway. You can join us there for coffee later if you want."

I had the usual dilemma about what to wear. What makes an instant impression? I decided against the clown suit and got out my trusty blazer. Should I wear a tie, should I not? I settled on a tie. I feel more confident dressing formally in new social situations, but as soon as I arrived, I realized I'd made a dress error. In fact I was grossly over-dressed, most of the other guys wearing tee shirts and jeans. I looked like a disapproving uncle.

Eleanor came bounding over to me. "Are you Simon?" she enquired.

"Yes, I am," I admitted.

"Oh you look very smart," she said. "I'm glad you've made the effort."

She looked at me, "So many men don't. Such a mistake!" I felt reassured by that till I realized she was probably just humouring me and being kind. "This is our first speed dating event," she said.

"Well, it's my first time as well," I replied, "so just let me know what you want me to do."

"Are you okay walking in on your own?" she asked in a low voice.

"Well, yes, I can walk," I said puzzled, "Why?"

"Well some people can be uncomfortable about walking into a room full of people on their own, I'm happy to accompany you," she explained.

"Well, no, that's very kind," I said, impressed with her discreet offer of support.

I wandered into the main dining room where the event was to be held. There were two groups, men and women. I wanted to go and join the women to be honest, I mean what was the point of going into a speed dating event and standing with the men? But I wasn't sure whether that was the protocol and I didn't feel I should break ranks. There were no other men talking to the women so I joined a group of men. I'm not very good at traditionally blokeish male conversation knowing nothing about football, not being fond of beer and uninterested in golf or cricket. Fortunately of course I like cars.

Inevitably I ended up talking to somebody at the bar. He was a chatty happy-go-lucky Cockney-type whose opening line to me was "Blimey, mate, you going to a wedding or something?" He was wearing jeans and an Arsenal football club shirt and sporting a muddy blue tattoo of a serpent on his right outer arm. I wish I could do that. I don't mean show off a tattoo or wear an Arsenal shirt, but be comfortable enough to wear anything. I made some lame excuse about just coming from the office.

"Oh, right," he said. "Well you don't need to worry, you don't need to dress up for these sort of occasions, it's only the do's that Eleanor insists you wear a shirt and tie."

"So have you been before?" I said.

"Oh, yes," he said. "Been to loads of do's. First time she's done speed dating, though, so I thought I'd give it a go."

"How long have you been coming to these things?"

"Ooh, about five years."

"Five years?" I said. "Have you never met anyone in five years?"

"Oh, yeah, I've met loads of birds."

"Anyone special?"

"Yeah, a few nice birds."

"Not settled down then?" I enquired, already knowing the answer.

"No, sod that for a game of soldiers. Tried it once, didn't like it. You?" he asked.

"Well, I'm separated, only recently actually, last few months so I'm here trying to meet someone."

"Sod that," he said. "Sow a few wild oats, mate." He nudged me in the ribs.

My eyes were drawn to a group of women who were standing some distance away from us. The girls had made more effort than the majority of the men seemed to have. There were quite a lot of legs on display and their side of the room was thick with perfume. More and more people were arriving and it was getting difficult to hear or make myself heard while conversing. To my intense relief, another couple of guys turned up wearing suits, or shirts and ties, so I didn't feel entirely alone, though the majority were in jeans or Chinos and tee shirts.

Eleanor gained everyone's attention by blowing a whistle loudly three times and the hubbub stopped. She introduced herself and then described what we were to do. On the tables in front of us there were place names for the men. The men were going to sit down and the women were to come along in an organised fashion and sit and chat with us for seven minutes. Then she would blow the whistle again and all the ladies would move along to the next seat. Everyone would get a chance to speak to everyone else for seven minutes. There would be a comfort break after 35 minutes.

Now, I'm no mathematician, but looking at the number of people in the room, I thought this was going to be a tall order. We were to start in 15 minutes to allow for the comfort break. The hubbub started again.

I decided to order a glass of wine and moved towards the group of men wearing suits rather than the other end of the bar, occupied by the jeans and tees. Not that I'd got anything against them. They were clearly having a good time, talking amongst themselves and seemed more relaxed already than the "suits". My Cockney friend was guffawing loudly.

'Why can't I be more like him?' I thought wistfully. I took a large gulp of my wine. Eleanor blew the whistle again.

She announced that there was going to be a further delay as it had started snowing and a number of clients had phoned to say that they were going to be late. To accommodate them, we were now to start at 8.30pm, fifteen minutes later than expected. The temperature that week had been descending daily. Since the poxy Lexus had gone back I was using my Alfa Romeo again and I had already switched on the heated seats a couple of times. I decided to use the extra time by chatting to one of the suits. There was a chap next to me at the bar, tall, about my age, wearing a suit and tie that looked like a new purchase from M&S, (I quite like their suits and ties and the tie resembled one I'd nearly bought on my recent shopping trip to Lakeside).

I am glad I hadn't purchased it now as that trip was the doomed "Jane" excursion. I would have always associated it after with that episode and it would probably have languished at the back of my wardrobe, as a permanent reminder of that fateful day.

"Hello," I ventured, to M&S man.

"Hiya," he replied.

"Is that your Alfa out the back?" he said.

"The grey one?" I ventured.

"Yes."

"They look smart," he said and I said that I was pleased with it. He took a gulp of what smelled like G&T from a tumbler, and then said "They're rubbish though aren't they? Attractive but unreliable... does yours break down often?"

My reply of "Well no, I've been very happy with mine actually," seemed to fall on deaf ears. I'm not sure he heard or was even interested in my reply.

"You can't beat the Japs for cars though can you?"

I decided that we probably didn't have that much in common. I smiled, half nodded and shook my head at the same time deciding to try and engage with another suit.

Before I could make my excuses though he said "It's like women, you know." He wasn't looking at me.

"Really?" I said.

Then he pointed to a lady standing across the room from us. "Take her for example."

I was startled; he seemed to be having a conversation with himself.

"Which one?" I asked.

"Floral dress, black handbag."

I looked in the direction of the ladies and thought I identified the lady in question.

"Her, she's attractive, her name's Mary," he said. "I've had a few dates with her."

"Good," I said looking around for someone to rescue me. He didn't acknowledge my reply.

"Yeah, had a few dates with her, expensive one's mind. I even serviced her car for nothing." He explained that he worked in a garage. "It was all going well, at least I thought so, and then she introduced me to her daughter."

"Oh," I said, "that's nice."

"It wasn't," he retorted instantly. "She was a right little bitch."

"Err, well, it was nice talking to you," I said, backing off slightly.

"My names Jim. I am going to go over and talk to her...tell her what a bitch her daughter is." It occurred to me Jim probably wasn't on his first G&T.

"Is that a good idea?" I said, but he had slammed his empty glass down on the counter and set off across the room towards Mary.

I spoke to the next closest suit. "Hello, I'm Simon," I said and offered a hand.

"Ed," came the reply along with a firm handshake.

"See you've just been talking to deadly Jim."

"Have I? At him, yes but I am not sure what it was all about."

"He is obsessed with the girl over there. Mary," he said nodding in the direction of the floral dressed lady.

I found myself repeating a phrase from Venice, adapted slightly. "So, what's his story?"

"It's quite simple really," said Ed. "He's nuts about her, she went on a first date with him, got pressurized into a second one. She doesn't like him, neither does her daughter but he just won't take 'no' for an answer." Whilst this mini soap opera was playing out the stragglers from the A12 arrived stamping snow from their shoes and in a few moments we were underway.

As directed by Eleanor I sat at one of a number of small bistro type tables. Each of us had a notepad, pen, piece of A4 folded card that I was to write my name on.

I thought it would be jolly to write something other than my name, so I wrote "Hello, I'm Simon." It wasn't. Everyone else just wrote their names.

Once all the men were seated, Eleanor instructed the women to choose their tables. She told us she would blow the whistle in 7 minutes and then the changeover should take place. She asked if everyone understood and there was a murmur of assent. She blew the whistle and then what I can only describe as an Olympic style sprint by some women to individual men began. I wasn't one of them. I noted with some dismay the jean wearing tee and football shirt fraternity seemed to be doing conspicuously better than the suits.

In the melee of people standing up, rushing about, moving chairs to greet women, I tried to look optimistic and to my relief I saw a lady standing beside me. I stood up immediately aware that I recognized the floral dress. It was Mary. The navy blue floral dress was identical to one my wife had owned. She had short dark hair, was of medium height and build, early 40s I guessed. She had dark eyes, and wore dark make up. She had a rather stern look. I began to move to reach for the chair behind so that I could guide it under her allowing her to sit down. However she grabbed the chair before I could reach it and sat immediately. Without any preamble or introduction she hissed.

"What did he say to you?"

"Who? I was trying to pretend I didn't know who she was talking about.

"Jim," she replied, "I saw him talking to you earlier."

It was pointless trying to pretend but I didn't want to get drawn into any unfolding mini drama, so I replied breezily, "Oh, him, we were just chatting about cars. I write a bit about cars and Jim told me he worked at a garage."

She seemed willing to accept this but told me that Jim knew nothing about cars and had completely "bollocksed up" her Mercedes. She seemed to relax then and warming to me, introduced herself. She apologized for being so abrupt and told me how cross she was about her dates with Jim and his refusal to leave her alone. She said that if he continued to cause scenes she would complain about it. I told her I thought she should do so. She then asked if he had said anything about her daughter. Before I said anything she told me that her daughter had rescued her from the second date.

"Plumbing emergency?" I proffered.

She smiled. "No, my daughter had locked herself out of the house... needed to come and get me. I had to leave." She smiled again. "The few minutes he spent with my daughter were awful. My daughter wasn't impressed as he spent some time peering down her blouse, and then told her that she had clearly got her figure from me." There was a loud blow on the whistle.

Mary stood up immediately. "Oh, I am sorry Simon," she said looking down at my card. "You seem very nice and all I have talked about is Jim... perhaps we could talk later."

"That would be lovely," I said and stood up as she left.

Before my bottom could touch the seat, another lady arrived. A striking redhead with fiery green eyes. Tall, wearing an *orange* dress. Red hair, orange dress, green eyes. The thought 'explosion in a paint factory' passed through my mind.

She seemed very confident. "I am Abigail," she boomed. She had a glass of red wine in her hand. This was deposited on the table with such force I was sure the stem would break. This was clearly a lady on a mission. Before I could even tell her my name she asked, "What do you do?"

I explained that I was Simon and a writer.

She made no comment. "I work in credit management control," was all she said.

'I bet you do,' I thought rather unkindly. It had crossed my mind that she probably didn't work in the fashion industry and could be colour blind.

There was no conversation from that point on, just an interrogation. "Do you have any children?" she quizzed.

"Yes," I said, "they are grown up now – I was a child bride." I quipped, hoping for a laugh. I was disappointed; she grabbed her glass of red wine and took a gulp. "Do you want any more?" she asked.

"Wine?" I asked, confused.

"No, I mean children."

I explained I didn't as I already had two and they were almost grown up.

"Surely you would want to have children with a new partner?" she retorted. I was beginning to feel as though I was in the dock. I decided to use my "Get out of Jail" card and explained that even if I did want more children, I'd had a vasectomy, so it wasn't an option. I was wrong.

"Well, you could always have it reversed."

I prayed for the whistle and it blew. She didn't even say goodbye, just marched off leaving me feeling mildly traumatised. I know there are many women in their late 30s and 40s desperate for a child or more children if they have one or two already. I wondered what Abigail's story was.

The next lady who presented at my table wasn't really my type but I was hoping I could relax and just have a nice chat. She didn't introduce herself but shook hands. "Oh, you have nice soft hands," she said, "Clearly you don't do any work."

I smiled. "Well I suppose I don't, I am a writer," I said.

"So are you no good at all at DIY?" she said. I was perplexed. Had I missed part of the conversation? There was a lot of background noise. "DIY," she said slowly, 'do it yourself', you know, home maintenance, repairs and that sort of thing. Are you any good at it?"

Family and friends reading this would have been hooting with laughter on hearing this enquiry. To say that I am hopeless at DIY is a grave understatement. My idea of hell would be to have to go to B&Q in a Lexus. Trawling round IKEA is torture.

I would be interested to know if anyone has managed to assemble a wardrobe or cabin bed (with concealed pull out mattress) first time, without help from a mate or without much profanity at least. I wonder how many incompletely assembled items of IKEA furniture there are in the UK. There should be a support group for users with a habit of being unable to assemble their furniture.

"No, I am no good at DIY," I said, sighing.

"I didn't think so," said my companion. "Not with hands like those."

I thought we might move onto another topic. Where we lived; what we did; what books/films we liked, just the normal stuff I had been expecting to discuss but "No-Name" lady was having none of it.

She explained how she had to live with a partly completed kitchen. A legacy of a friend's husband's efforts on her behalf, who had only half-built the kitchen, then rather inconveniently, suffered a stroke. I apologized for being unable to help her out. The whistle was blown again.

I thought about getting up and leaving. This was a disaster and I'd had enough. I had talked to three women; one who wanted to let off steam about a stalker; a second who wanted a sperm donor and a third clearly only interested in a kitchen fitter.

Eleanor was making another announcement. "I forgot to mention," she said, "but it's obvious, if you would like to speak to someone when we start the disco, jot their names down on the notepad; give it to me and I shall organise it." My notepad was blank. I doubted I had been included in Mary, Abigail's or No-Name's pads. I glanced outside. It was now snowing heavily. Should I use this as a reason to cut short the evening? I decided to stay a little longer. I was not expecting my next guest. It was Jim.

"What did she say about me?" he asked insistently.

Before I could reply, or head for the door, which I was seriously considering, Eleanor appeared. I can't remember what she said exactly, but the content couldn't have been clearer – Jim was ruining the evening for everybody, particularly Mary. He was being obnoxious, had had too much to drink, should leave and a cab was on its way. Eleanor spoke firmly.

Jim didn't put up a fight. A security man took him by the arm and escorted him from the table. Eleanor smiled at me, apologized for what had happened and said that I should continue to enjoy the evening.

She glanced down at my notepad. "Didn't you hear my announcement?" she queried. "You are supposed to jot down the names of the ladies you'd like to meet again."

"Oh, right," I said, "sorry, it's all new to me, this."

Eleanor didn't persist with her enquiries, but turned to blow the whistle again. The next 21 minutes went very quickly. I was adapting to the protocol of quick fire questioning and summarized responses. I was asked again if I had got/wanted more children, what sort of car I had (easy this), how much money I earned and had saved, whether I had a pension plan, how large my house was and in what post code area. In fairness there was the odd enquiry about me and my interests but overall it was a demoralizing experience. I declined to stay for the disco, made my excuses and left. It was a winter wonderland outside and I wished I had a coat with me as I de-iced the car. Soon, Elton and I were heading back to the flat. Elton was singing "I'm still standing".

Since writing this I have discovered that this episode was perhaps unusual. Contrary to my straw poll amongst friends, it appears that on a broader analysis plenty of people enjoy speed dating and aren't plagued by companions desperate for a baby, a builder, or couples playing out domestic squabbles in public.

Though I hadn't had the best experience, it had been a night out and it was obvious to me that Eleanor and *Across the Room* had plenty of fans. Eleanor was discreet, organised, calm and capable. More than a match for Jim. On my way out I had signed up to go to one of their formal dinner dances. More of that later.

The Posh Dinner

The next morning I woke to that muffled cotton-wool silence that indicates a heavy fall of snow. Pulling back the curtains I could see cars skidding along the main road; wellies and hats worn by locals out and about and kids pulling sledges. I knew instinctively the local Asda would probably have run out of milk and bread. What is it about snow in the UK? Do we need extra bread when it snows? Milk? Rather than go out and risk injury trying to find milk and bread I didn't really need, I decided to get on with some work. There is something comforting about being indoors in the warm when it's snowing outside. By early afternoon I had finished an article, emailed it, paid a few bills online, and caught up with the kids on Facebook their entries making me laugh. My son, Daniel, alerted to his ancient Dad's existence courtesy of a posting online arrived with a bright smile.

"Hi Dad," he said. "It was on the news to look in on the old people in the community so I thought I'd drop round."

"Thanks Dan that's very kind of you," I said. Victoria, my daughter also called in. I was pleased to learn all the family were fine.

Amongst my emails was one regarding the personal introduction service offered by *Across the Room*. There was also one from Niamh. A couple of others were from motoring hack mates enquiring if I was going to the Mercedes dinner this Saturday. I thought to myself that I had to get myself into gear and sort the dinner out. In her email Niamh hadn't mentioned the "do" so I assumed that she wasn't able to or didn't want to come.

This left Shilpa as the only possibility. I headed off to the gym.

As it was Saturday, Melanie was there and whilst I was trying to make a decent effort on the ski machine she enquired how I was doing. I gave her a very breathless account of the speed dating event the night before. She laughed, especially about the kitchen fitter. She found it particularly hilarious that anyone, even on a brief first acquaintance might mistake me for one.

Melanie wanted to know if I had spoken to Shilpa recently and I told her that I had had a half conversation with her about the imminent dinner but she hadn't said if she wanted to accompany me or not. Melanie's brows furrowed. "Well that's not what I understand at all," she said.

Paul Fox

"She's bought a new dress, is having her hair done and is definitely expecting to go with you."

After my session, in the bar downstairs, I texted Shilpa. I asked her how she was getting on with the cold weather as a preamble and then if she was free for a coffee/lunch/dinner. Unusually I had a text by return.

She said she was indoors with the fire on. "Busy all this week, what time are you picking me up on Saturday? x."

I was getting used to Shilpa's style of texting. Brief, to the point but not unfriendly. As I sipped my cappuccino I felt pleased that she was coming. She would look fabulous in an evening dress I was sure and I would be proud to be seen with her. I sent her a text explaining I was organizing a taxi, and said I would be at hers by 7pm. "It's black tie and I am very pleased that you are accompanying me and I am looking forward to seeing you on Saturday, x." It took me ages to compile the text. My aim had been to copy Shilpa's crisp, informative textalogue, but I failed woefully. I still sent it.

I rang my local taxi firm, booked a car and managed to speak to Jim who drove us to the gym on New Year's Eve.

"Hi Simon, so where you off to mate?" he asked.

I told him.

"Very nice. Are you going with that gorgeous Italian lady?"

I didn't correct him and explain Shilpa's origins. She had told me she was often taken to be European because she was quite light skinned.

Flushed with success, I wandered over to the cleaners to collect my dinner jacket. This is a favourite item in my wardrobe. It was from "William Hunt" of Savile Row. As far as I know it's the only link I have to Graham Norton as he has an exact same jacket that he's worn on his TV show. It's got a multi-coloured silk lining with blue piping ("ticking" I thinks it's called) around the sleeve and lapels. Apparently this gives the jacket more definition when in the glare of media lighting and it's a common trick used by celebrity tailors. I think I read this in *GQ magazine* and whilst I am not a celebrity, don't have to hide from paparazzi and I don't even have nosy neighbours I can show it off to, it's still my favourite dinner jacket.

My trainers were sodden with snow and I was beginning to slide around as I headed back to the flat. It had started to snow again. Indoors and on autopilot I switched on my flat-mate TV, jogged up to the mezzanine floor and switched on the computer. Joanna Lumley contributed to the noise filled flat, "You have email," she purred.

It was Rick, writing "Hi Simon, proper brass monkey weather here, what's it like where you are?"

Before I could reply, the phone rang. It was Rick. "Did you get my email?" He asked.

"Yes, I was just about to reply, I've just got in from the gym."

"What do you want to go to the gym for, in the fucking snow?" he said bolshily.

"Well… I like the gym and it's not snowing inside the gym."

Rick came back with "Did you see the Indian bird?"

"I take it you mean Shilpa, and no, but I am on Saturday because she is coming with me to the Mercedes do."

There was a pause. I anticipated some smart reply, or any reply, but from the noises on the line I could tell he was eating his lunch. "Spud u Like not coming then?" he eventually volunteered.

"I presume you mean Niamh. No she's not." Another pause. Was he still feeding?

"I said she wouldn't come, didn't I?" he said triumphantly.

I spoke testily, "Yes that's right." I wanted to add "Yes, yes you were right all along and I was wrong and no she's not coming so happy now?" but I managed to restrain myself.

"So what excuse did she come up with?" he said.

"Why so curious?"

"Well I'm just taking an interest in your life, anyway what's the matter with you – not on your period are you?"

I had to make something up, because Niamh hadn't exactly given me any excuse. The issue of her coming had just been left hanging in the air. I tried to explain to Rick that she was a busy dental professional and I wasn't privy to her diary, her family commitments, social engagements or the weather in Ireland, and that in any event I was going with Shilpa.

Rick seemed to have run out of insults. He said he'd see me on Friday anyhow subject to the weather.

"I'm not getting Beryl out if it's bad – the salt plays havoc with her bodywork."

"Beryl" isn't Rick's girlfriend – well not a conventional one anyhow. She's his beloved car – a Ford, quite a decent Mondeo, but not in the first flush of youth – lovingly looked after by Rick. She had been his constant companion for more than ten years.

"I bet your Alfa's disintegrated in this snow," he quipped, as he ended the call with, "Bye, old boy."

By mid-week it was still freezing and more snow was predicted for the weekend. I decided to risk the roads and drive to Lakeside to buy a gift for Shilpa when I met her. She'd gone to the expense of buying a new dress and I was getting fed up with the inside of the flat. I thought she might appreciate a present.

On arriving at Lakeside it struck me that I am not that good at buying women presents. What can you buy them? There are only four things I have ever bought the women in my life, flowers, perfume, chocolates and underwear.

I could get some flowers on Saturday morning and that was still an option. Perfume is tricky because (a) the celebrity ones just aren't appreciated and (b) fragrance is such a personal item to buy for someone unless you know what they like. I thought Shilpa would be displeased if I got her "wrong" with perfume and I was equally certain she wouldn't hesitate to tell me! Underwear was out as it was only a second date and it's such an intimate purchase. I might, given that the relationship was thus far platonic, get a slap across the face. Not a great way to start an evening.

Buying women's underwear can be a minefield for men. In my experience what we like, they often don't. Girlfriends might wear stockings and suspenders or fancy hold up stockings, the ones with frills or lace at the top to please us, rather than from choice or for their own comfort or convenience. Lots of fancy underwear shows through clothing, especially evening dresses and most women hate this. Underwear was definitely out.

So that left chocolates.

I headed for *Hotel Chocolat*, the shop that has about as much to do with confectionery as luxury watches do with telling the time or supercars have with transport. Don't get me wrong, the chocolate is good quality, the stores are coolly stylish, the staff are informed and friendly and the carrier bags scream "luxury purchase!" That's the point of course. You get to buy a fantasy lifestyle item. I settled on a heart shaped box of Champagne truffles, opting for gift-wrapping, a luxury bespoke bag and handed over my American Express credit card. Hopefully I could move onto more personal gifts once I got to know her better.

It's a shame about celebrity perfumes. I liked the idea of buying *Nicole Kidman* if there was one and if Shilpa truly didn't like it, I could always spray it round the flat as air freshener I bought a couple of things in M&S noting with approval that they still had milk and bread despite the fact that it had been snowing heavily.

In spite of the weather Rick ventured out in Beryl and our first fish and chip evening in a fortnight was underway. Our usual smiling waitress arrived at our table in an almost empty restaurant. She mentioned she had missed us the week before and asked us what we wanted to order. It was a pure formality as each week we ordered exactly the same meals: I always had the regular fish and chips, Rick the large cod and large chips, a pickled onion, mushy peas and bread and butter and Barry ordered his usual meat and potato pie and chips. On occasions Rick would order a pie or roast chicken to take away as well and he'd eat this at home cold.

Talk turned to an account of the speed dating and an update of the Mercedes plans. Barry, a builder, was quick to appreciate my issue with "No-Name" and her kitchen dilemma.

"Why would she want to go to a speed dating event to find a kitchen fitter? I would have gone and done it for her. You should have given her my number, I specialize in half-completed jobs."

"So does Simon," Rick quipped.

"What does that mean?"

"Well how daft is this? You're going to all the expense of taking the Indian bird to a dinner tomorrow when you could easily have met the Lexus lady there at no expense at all. How half-baked is that?"

Barry turned to Rick.

"You're not very romantic are you, Rick?"

Rick thought for a second "No, probably not," he conceded.

Barry came to the rescue again telling me how Shilpa sounded fantastic and he was sure we'd have a great time.

"Any news from the Irish bird?" said Rick.

It was strange but I hadn't thought of Niamh. I hadn't heard from her all week nor received an email during that time. As I said goodbye to the guys in the car park I thought I should send her a text. "Hi Niamh. London calling. What's the weather like over there?"

I was pleased to get a reply promptly. "At Mum and Dad's. Speak later x."

I told myself I wouldn't hold my breath.

On Saturday morning it was still bitterly cold. The newspapers and TV stations were describing the coldest snap in years and predicting snow imminently. As I walked back from the gym mid-morning I noticed that even the weak winter sun had made no difference to the carapace of ice on my car. Niamh hadn't called or texted last night. I decided not to ring her. I had mixed feelings – guilt about going with Shilpa but slightly resentful that Niamh wasn't even prepared to call or text as promised.

As I was going to be eating a four-course dinner that evening I decided to make myself a light lunch.

Fish fingers with grilled cheese on top. I can highly recommend it. It's my signature dish and I didn't want to use up one of my M&S dinners for one in case I needed them because of bad weather and being holed up in the flat. I was halfway through it when the landline rang. I picked up the static wall mounted handset from the kitchen console. It was now 12.15pm.

For some reason I was expecting it to be Rick, but it wasn't, it was Niamh. She was on her mobile and there was lots of background noise. Her lovely, soft Irish tones worked their magic and filled my head.

"Oh hi Niamh, are you still at your parents?"

She laughed, high-pitched, higher than normal-pitched laughter.

"No I'm not – I'm on the shuttle bus."

'What?' I thought. 'What's an Irish shuttle bus? I thought she had a Toyota…'

"Yes, I'm on the shuttle bus. I thought I'd surprise you completely, but have decided to call so you can pick me up from London City Airport. That's not too far from you is it?"

I froze, my fish finger falling from the end of my plate lay marooned in a pool of melted cheese. I suddenly had no appetite and pushed the plate away distractedly.

A scene from Tom & Jerry came to mind – the cartoon bit where Tom gets hit with an iron by Jerry, and slowly cracks appear then his body falls apart into a heap on the floor. I felt like Tom.

I didn't know what to say, but needn't have worried. Niamh was in full flow explaining that she had been due to see her parents in Dublin today, but they had asked her to change the arrangement as they had old friends visiting, so she had found a flight from Cork to London City Airport and was on her way!!

"I've packed my white and gold evening dress, you remember, the one you liked so much on Boxing Day and I've even packed my nightie. I'll give you the flight number so you can collect me… Simon… Simon… " Niamh was still excitedly giving me details. "Just coming into the terminal buildings; I will text you the flight details in a moment; are you sure you are okay to pick me up or shall I get a taxi?"

I sat in a daze, staring at the wall. My heart was racing, my mind had stalled. I wrapped my arms round my head; crouched down; and bunny hopped around the living room.

"Oh no... Oh no… Oh Nooooooooo!" – Basil Fawlty again. Why was I such a total twit? Why hadn't I kept more in touch with Niamh and found out for certain if she was coming or not?

It was now 12.40. Whilst I was in meltdown, Niamh had texted her details: "Aer Lingus AL276 arriving City Airport 14.40. Just got hand luggage, so meet you 3pm. Confirm collecting me please xx." I was trying not to panic but I couldn't help it. I rang Rick without thinking. I had to talk to someone.

"Hello old boy," he said. "You getting ready then? You've only got seven hours to iron your shirt and slap on moisturizer..."

"Shut up," I snapped, "I've got a problem!"

"What's that then, apart from the obvious one, like being you?"

I gabbled that Niamh was on her way, I was taking Shilpa to the dinner and that Niamh was expecting me to pick her up from London City Airport in a couple of hours.

"So what's the problem?"

"Shilpa's got a dress and is expecting me at 7pm to take her to the dinner and Niamh is arriving at 3pm with her dress and expecting me to take her to the dinner and neither one knows about the other..."

"Well," said Rick, sounding calm and reassured.

"Ring Shilpa and say you are not well." "Right,"

I said.

"Will she buy that?" I asked

"I don't know – I don't know her. When did you last see her?"

"The other day in the gym..."

"Well ring her and tell her you've broken your leg."

"I don't think that's going to work."

"Well ring Niamh and tell her you've broken your leg."

"She's about to get on the bloody plane," I exploded.

"Well don't get cross with me, I thought you said she wasn't coming. Well tell Shilpa Niamh's your sister from Ireland."

"What, am I supposed to take both of them? I won't be able to keep them apart and that is a useless idea. You're not being any help at all are you? What about if you come over here Rick? I can say you are some long lost relative with an interest in cars and you can come to the dinner too, so there'll be the four of us."

To say Rick wasn't keen is another understatement. "I'm not fucking doing that!" he said.

"Why not?" I screamed.

"Well one, I don't want to go out, two, I don't possess a monkey suit, three I am not taking Beryl out and four... I just don't want to go."

"Well you owe me Rick," I said. "You could just be a long lost retarded mute if you don't want to talk to them, just a relative who is a bit odd staying with me."

"Look Simon," he said, "I know you're in a fix, why not ring Martin, he'll go and he lives closer to you."

"I can't do that, Martin's married and you're not," I hissed, resisting the temptation to say "not surprisingly." I decided to be forceful. "Look Rick, just get over here as fast as you can. I've got a spare DJ you can wear and we can think of something."

"So you're going to be with the Indian one are you which means, I'll be stuck with the Irish bird. I know nothing about Ireland. What am I going to say?"

"You're mute remember? Just get Beryl out and come over now."

"Are you really going to make me do this?" he said.

"Yes, now!"

"Okay. Leave me a key."

I headed down to the car and put the demister on full blast. I had about 45 minutes before I had to leave. Leaving the engine on and the car warming I returned to the flat and did a frenzied domestic workout, flinging clothes into cupboards and the washing machine, filling the dishwasher and doing a very basic hoover of the flat. I had a crashing headache, both temples pulsing with pain as I tried to work out what on earth we were going to do.

It wasn't going to work, Shilpa was expecting to go with me and so was Niamh. I was going to have a panic attack. What about the sleeping arrangements? Shilpa lived just along the road and had given me no indication she was preparing to stay the night with me.

If I was going to get away with the charade, Niamh was going to have to be in on some of it. Could I get away with saying I was distantly related to Shilpa, possibly my granddad had befriended one of her relatives during World War II; then there were the chocolates, the pre-booked taxi. Could I say I had invited her because I was feeling low at being let down by Niamh and Shilpa was prepared to accompany me as a family friend aware of my disappointment? It was going to be a nightmare.

The mobile rang. It was Niamh. "Hello, hello. Simon?"

"Hi Niamh." Click. The call ended. I tried to call her back. Nothing. Then again. Nothing. I was on speed dial trying to retrieve her. I had to leave. Driving gingerly on the slippery iced side and local roads I made it onto the A13 eventually. The windscreen wipers and my head were pounding away in unison. It was –2 degrees and snow was falling. My mobile phone rang. Frantically, I pressed "accept" on the steering wheel. "Niamh," I yelled. There was a pause.

"Hello, is that Mr Taylor...?" The phone became silent. The weather was affecting the signal. It was probably just an annoying sales call anyway. I was driving tensely along the A13 as fast as I dared – only about 40 mph though.

As the City Airport sign appeared on the motorway there were hazard warning lights on stationary cars and several people pushing a couple of vehicles to the hard shoulder. An accident. Blue flashing lights of a traffic officer Land Rover appeared in my rear view mirror. The airport was still miles away. The phone rang again, a male voice, as before

"Mr Simon Taylor… is this Mr Simon Taylor."

"Yes, yes, yes," I said, "it is… " The line died again. This was so frustrating. I was stationary in the car and checked my phone. The screen said, "number withheld" so I was probably right in the first place. It was from someone selling something or perhaps news from Nigeria that a distant relative living there had bequeathed me money in their will and if I would only send £980 as fees for the district probate attorney the substantial bequest would be in my account within days!! A scam in common currency. I tried to ring Niamh over and over again. No connection. She would still be in the air.

In my panic I hadn't switched on the radio or CD – my default setting on getting into the car. I was approaching the slip road to the City Airport when it occurred to me to switch on the radio. I heard the tail end of the weather and roads report. The Dartford Crossing over the Thames was shut and there were reports of innumerable accidents, road closures, delays. I realised that the window of opportunity was closing. As soon as Niamh was in the car it would be too late to speak to Shilpa or Rick.

I had flown from City Airport a number of times. It's my local UK airport and a favourite so I knew where to go to park. It was very quiet. Just a few cars dotted along the usually busy dual lane car parking area.

With the engine still running I put my head in my hands. What a mess. I had cocked it up so badly.

'There is a lesson to be learned here,' I thought miserably. The phone rang again.

"Is that Mr Simon Taylor?"

Oh God, not again. "Yes, this is Mr Simon Taylor. What do you want? No I don't want to buy a time share, I am perfectly happy with my energy supplier and I support the Red Cross with donations."

The chap at the end of the phone was silent. Then he said "I am sorry but I think you may be mistaking me for someone else Mr Taylor. My name is Alan Cook ('Who?') and I am phoning on behalf of Mercedes-Benz Public relations department. ('What?')

"Yes?" I said.

"It's about tonight's Gala Dinner. I have some bad news I am afraid. As a result of the extreme weather many guests have been forced to cancel and since a number of airports have closed we can't fly our special guests over from Germany. I am afraid that this evening's special event is cancelled. I have been trying to call you for a while now and am sorry.

"What!?" I spluttered.

He was fulsomely apologetic, clearly under the impression I was distressed at his news. He explained that the dinner would be rearranged, probably during the summer and promised to email me an invitation. He said they would send over a new shape S Class Mercedes and the PR Agency wanted me to provide a review. He was going to be in touch with my agent. Was I interested?

All I could think was 'Thank God.' I rang Shilpa immediately and gave her the news.

She was unsurprised and said that she knew that the A12 was blocked in a number of places. She said that as she had a new dress, she hoped I would take her out somewhere to wear it soon. I said that I would be delighted to do that and that I would call her later when I had thought of somewhere to go. I said I would see her at the gym. She was perfectly fine about it all.

'Bingo!' I thought. I would now be able to enjoy the lovely Niamh all to myself in the flat, or possibly, we could go up to the RAF club, roads allowing, for a special treat. I left the car to walk to the terminal building to wait for Niamh to arrive. A normally aware person would have been quickly realized several things. That there were very few cars in the car park, most of those being liveried taxis. The runway, close to the road and car park had no planes taking off or landing. The terminal building had a number of travellers but the usual clamour of the airport was absent. A member of staff told me that the airport was shut due to ice on the runway. No planes were landing or taking off.

Stansted was also shut leaving Gatwick and Heathrow alone serviceable and open. I wondered if Niamh's flight would have been diverted to either of these. The information desk staff conferred when I asked but said that this was highly unlikely. Cork airport had been closed for about 2 hours. Her flight number was not showing as cancelled or at all on the monitor. I didn't know what to do.

I didn't know how I felt. Relieved, disappointed, stupid, confused and cold were all options. I hunched over and headed back to the car. I tried phoning Niamh again. It wasn't long before I had an answer though. In the car I had tuned into LBC London News, a talking station I usually avoid. A breathless, excitable commentator confirmed all London airports including Heathrow and Gatwick were closed.

I kept trying Niamh. Nothing. I decided to head back up the A13 whilst I still could, snow now falling thickly. I was almost back at the flat when she rang. "Simon, Simon I'm so sorry, my flight's been cancelled due to the bad weather. I've been trying to call but there's been no signal and I am back home now. Just me and the cat. We'll have to make it another time."

"We will," I said fervently. "It was lovely of you to think of surprising me," I fibbed. As I arrived back at the flat I saw Beryl in my car space. Rick! In all the "excitement" of the drive to the airport I'd forgotten to phone Rick and update him. I opened the front door and there he was, not in my dinner jacket but in something he'd owned since 1979. Wide lapels, flared trousers, frilly shirt, velvet bow tie – a vintage classic. He looked like John Travolta's fatter older brother from "Saturday Night Fever."

"Well, where is she?" he said, checking behind me. "Still down in the car park unloading her backpack?"

I explained calmly what had happened and acknowledged that I probably should have phoned him to say he didn't need to bother coming over, or disinterring the cobwebbed trunk in the attic with his mothballed suit in. I thought he was going to punch me, and I couldn't have blamed him. But, he didn't. He took off his velvet bow tie and jacket and said simply, "You berk."

No Sex Please

The bad weather hung around for a good few weeks. I had the heating on fully in the flat and was getting used to de-icing the car each morning and the daily dash across to the gym, dodging filthy puddles of water and lumps of ice. Fish and chips had been on hold because of the bad weather and a bout of flu suffered by Barry. Time pretty much stood still.

I had had a couple of phone calls from Niamh, the odd snatched conversation with Shilpa at the gym when we spoke in vague terms about going out for dinner when the weather cleared up, I was relieved to see the guys the following week for only the second fish and chip meal of the year. As I had little to report on the dating front, the conversation turned to hobbies.

Now I don't know why but hobbies are now considered to be a little "nerdy" and on the dating sites now, no one talks about hobbies, but "interests" and how you spend your leisure time. "Hobbies" are rather old fashioned concepts bringing to mind enthusiasts modelling galleon ships out of balsa wood using matchboxes and collecting stamps.. But I was beginning to worry that when asked about my interests I could only truthfully respond, or rather not, with "cars, girls and fat-fighting" at the gym. I needed something more substantial.

I decided to enlist Rick and Barry's help. I announced rather grandly and to pretty much anyone in earshot at our table: "I've decided I need a hobby."

"I thought you already had one?" said Rick.

Barry looked startled.

"No I haven't!" I protested.

"Yes you have," said Rick, "being a berk." He was referring to the monkey suit debacle from which I guessed he was still smarting. I ignored him.

I explained that I felt I needed a proper hobby, one I could do reasonably competently, be proud of, describe to girlfriends and maybe even involve them in.

"So you basically want a hobby in your endeavour at getting girls to take their knickers down?" said Rick.

"Well, no," I said.

"Well, yes," said Rick and Barry practically in unison.

Undeterred I grabbed a napkin and a pen from my jacket pocket and began to make a list of potential hobbies. With the guys help I created a short list. First on it was football. Rick's idea. After all it's what most guys are interested in, in fact it seems to me to be what most of the country is interested in. That was easily dismissed. It wasn't a serious option as I genuinely dislike football. I've tried but I just can't get excited about it. If England are playing in an International game I want them to win, in fact I expect them to win. Rick and Barry are keen fans and I often have to endure long sometimes heated conversations about the blessed game. Rick supported Tottenham Hotspur – also called "Spurs" for some strange reason and Barry, well he is a Chelsea fan and was always going on about going to Stamford Bridge. This is even more confusing because Chelsea is in London and Stamford Bridge in North Yorkshire. I crossed out "football".

Barry had suggested I could do "football lite" and join the "prawn sandwich" brigade, those "fans" who don't actually have any interest in the beautiful game but go for the corporate hospitality. In the end we all agreed that this was pointless, elaborate and expensive and that football as a contrived interest was a non-starter. Talking of starters and indeed prawns, I'd just finished mine – a proper prawn cocktail, made in a wine glass, with seafood sauce and lots of unnecessary lettuce. I am not keen on green foods.

Next on the list was golf – a game, hobby or pastime? This is enjoyed by millions of men and women all over the world. With its own social and dress code and formal etiquette this was surely worth a try?

"I can see you suiting golf," said Rick. "It's an opportunity to wear funny clothes in public."

"You are on dodgy ground there," I said "Remember, I've seen you in your monkey suit."

"Guys, guys, don't start on that please," Barry said, explaining patiently that golf is a great game because its handicap system allows all abilities of player to enjoy it and compete. He added that as so many women play it could be a good way of meeting someone.

"You mean totty," Rick interjected.

A perfect pursuit – clothes, codes of practice, women. There's a problem though: I think it's arguably the most tedious game ever devised. Granted I'm not sure what you're supposed to do, apart from getting a ball and hitting it into a hole with a stick. The idea is to do this for up to three hours or more whilst walking over courses that extend for miles.

Now the walking and environments appeal, but every golf club I've ever been to I've found that firstly, it's rarely possible to park closer than half a mile from the clubhouse as all of the parking bays have signs like "Captain/Vice Captain/Previous Captain/Captain's wife/Previous Vice Captains wife/Previous Captain's wife's friends" etc.

Secondly, once you eventually make it inside the "Clubhouse" there are more signs – and I am not trying to be rude about any particular Club here, they're everywhere – with prescriptive messages such as:

"Will members please move away from the bar when they have ordered drinks."

"No golf attire in this area."

"Captain's permission required to play during freezing weather."

This is in the club itself. I was in mid flow about the signage when Barry interrupted me.

"Look Simon, you have to be sensible. If you actually play you might be pleasantly surprised and there is the social side too."

Our main courses had arrived and having crossed out "golf" I had an inspiration. I had thought of something I genuinely fancied having a go at. I told the boys I had had a brilliant idea.

"Amaze us," said Rick dourly.

"This is it, something that's not nerdy, lots of people do it – what about fishing!"

"Fucking fishing," said Rick. "You mean sitting on a riverbank for hours on end freezing your bollocks off!"

"It's not really you is it, and it's a bit out-doorsy?" offered Barry.

"No, no," I said, "not that sort of fishing – the sort that James Bond does in *Live and Let Die*.

"Well I know you fancy yourself as James Bond," said Rick.

"Not even as James Bond," said Barry.

"Did he ever go fishing?" said Rick

"Yes, yes," I said, "in the film he goes fishing with Dr Quinn, he straps himself into a seat and they speed along chucking food into the water to attract the fish."

"Dr Quinn," said Rick waving his fork – a large white clot of cod on the end of it.

"When was Dr Quinn ever in James Bond?"

"No, she wasn't Dr Quinn then," I said, "I couldn't remember her name, she was Solitaire in the film... anyway that looks brilliant. I fancy having a go at that definitely. Where do you think they do it?"

"Jane Seymour," said Barry thoughtfully.

"Big game fishing, that's called."

"Great," I said, "Do you think I could do it in a local reservoir?"

The guys went on to explain, unnecessarily sarcastically I felt, that "big game fishing" got its name from the fact that you were hunting "big" fish – shark, swordfish, sailfish, tuna etc. none of which would be found in the tropical waters off the Essex coastline. I'd have to travel a lot further than that to indulge this hare-brained fantasy. I conceded the point.

Over dessert we rummaged around for others. Bowling – not old enough/don't like the outfits. Cricket – defeated by the scoring/hated it at school. Darts – dangerous/don't like lager. Rugby – terrified me at school. I shudder at recalling that the only thing I really learned was never to get the ball, and as for all in the bath afterwards, no thank you. I love it when England win but participation was not for me. Trainspotting – liked the film but don't possess an anorak.

As I trudged back to the flat in the snow I started to review my options again. There had to be something else. Try as I might I just couldn't think of a non-nerdy pastime or hobby I was interested in. Apart from tennis.

I was so bad at rugby, football and cricket at school, that one farsighted (or frustrated) and progressive PE teacher decided that the more "sensitive" boys amongst us could play tennis. When I say "boys" I mean me and Eric. Just the two of us. Eric had asthma and loathed all sports with a passion. I had no excuse apart from being constitutionally uncoordinated, with an odd pair of legs and systematically useless.

Playing school sports made me utterly miserable. But playing tennis was different. This was the first PE I had ever felt excited rather than actually anxious about participating in. Tennis saved me and it got even better when the school decided that since there were just two of us playing the game, it would be ideal if we could play with others, at (you won't believe this but it's true,) the local Catholic Ursuline Convent School for Girls, St. Joseph's.

The noble idea was that we would progress at tennis as a result of the abilities of the girls and we could become more competent and competitive. I spent a long time watching the girls hemlines rise to reveal their knickers. I was expecting to see Chris Evert style frillies but the girls wore uniform bottle green or brown serge big knickers – but hell – they were knickers.

The initiative didn't last long, probably due to complaints from the girls' school. Too soon wheezy Eric and I were back grappling with odd shaped balls and silly "mid-offs". But Eric had the last laugh. He now owns an airline in the Caribbean. Truly.

I made a mental note to self 'join tennis club'. Friends who are members have since told me that most tennis clubs are a hotbed of extra marital shagging. They should be listed as one of the warning signs of a wife's impending affair. The others of course being:

1. Losing weight.
2. A sudden interest in waxing legs, pits and intimate parts.
3. New underwear purchases.
4. Dropping someone's name into conversation randomly
5. Acquiring new friends that you don' know.
6. Showering after a night out you're not invited to.
7. Buying a new mobile phone whilst keeping an old one.
8. Joining the tennis club.

The Mercedes function hadn't been rearranged but the Company had been in touch to arrange delivery of their new shape S class saloon (Sedan) for me to evaluate and the weather had started to brighten up. I was enjoying daily workouts at the gym and had arranged a date with Shilpa for the coming Friday and had had a few emails from Niamh.

The Mercedes handover was efficient. The car was delivered together with a DVD for me to watch about its functions. Unlike Lexus I do quite like Mercedes and the new Mercedes S class occupying my visitor's car parking space dwarfed my beloved Alfa. It was a bit "shouty" in a "look at me" way that modern Mercedes are. The DVD revealed that you can personalise the new car by choosing details such as the time you would like the interior light to stay on when parked; how long the headlights should stay on whilst you walked to your front door; whether you wanted the registration plate light to remain on during the above and if the answer was yes, for how long? Commendable but I suspected designed by someone with few friends, who'd never had a girlfriend who just might be well advised to take up a hobby.

I booked an Italian restaurant in nearby Great Baddow for Friday and decided to use the Mercedes to take Shilpa there. She had sent me some encouraging texts – phrases like "looking forward to seeing you" and "lovely to hear from you" and even to my great delight, "can't wait for Friday." These were definitely less bland than those I was used to getting.

My son came to see the car and being a teenager instantly showed me additional functions from the on-board computer menu including the heated, ventilated and massaging front seat options. I took him for a drive in the car and we headed off to Lakeside.

The big car needed fuel and I made certain Daniel identified the diesel pump as it would be just like me to fill it up with unleaded. I wanted to see how the car performed on the mix of twisty "A" roads and the M25. I was hoping the M25 would not be like a car park. It wasn't and after taking it along the stretch of motorway at legal and admittedly 100 mph, I realised that it was here that the car really scored. It was quiet, meatily powerful and even at 100mph there was plenty of acceleration left. If looking for a car to cross Europe quickly in, this was it. The star at the end of the long bonnet is a permanent reminder that life isn't treating you too badly.

At this stage I was wondering how much I should tell my 17 year old son about my dating. It's difficult to know when to introduce the subject of going on dates, meeting someone other than your child's mother. I would expect him to tell his mother. I should perhaps tell her myself out of courtesy that I was dating.

What's the etiquette? I decided to mention that I was seeing a lady from the gym for the second time that Friday. He seemed unperturbed, said, "Okay dad, that's cool, have a good time," and that was it! He wasn't obviously embarrassed or uncomfortable and I was impressed at his mature response.

On the way back to the flat Dan showed me how to use the in-dash six CD changer audio system. Baffling for anyone over the age of 25 to work out perhaps but a piece of cake to a 17 year old. There had been a sale at HMV at Lakeside and I had treated myself to a couple of CD's, one was a compilation of Adam Faith songs and soon Adam was belting out "What do you want if you don't want money?" jarringly at odds with the car's luxurious interior.

I'd been lucky enough to meet Adam Faith before his premature death. He was an immensely entertaining and friendly guy. We were both interviewed on one occasion by the BBC and I met him in the green room, where the aim is of course to relax you before a broadcast. I remembered him from "Budgie" the TV series in the 70s and my Mum playing his records during the 60s when I was growing up. This was the first of several meetings.

On this particular occasion an incident occurred involving a female broadcaster. I won't mention her by name. She was walking around the green room introducing herself to the guests including myself and Adam. We're not used to seeing our newsreaders' legs, and my goodness, did this woman have legs! She wore a very short skirt, was perfectly made up and attractive and Adam, being Adam, was quick to elbow me and say "Cor, look at the legs on that. Wouldn't mind those wrapped round my neck!"

I spluttered and nearly spat out my coffee. But there was worse to come.

If you've not been interviewed on TV you may be surprised at the technical paraphernalia involved. Though the hardware is much more discreet today, broadcasters and interviewees have to wear a microphone.

Adam and I were both wearing suits and ties. We were soon asked to be "miked up". A small microphone, like an oversized tie clip was placed on my tie, the lead was taped to the back of the tie and pulled around the back of my jacket and a plug attachment was left dangling to be inserted into a small plug on the interviewing sofa later.

We were then free to return to the green room with the mikes in place with the wires hanging down the back of our jackets. Soon after our newsreader/presenter herself returned from being miked up. The technical staff had placed her microphone high up on her jacket lapel and the wire or mike-pack was trailing down the back of her shapely legs.

I am told that what happened next was 'pure Adam' who was known for being "mischievious"!

There were two sofas in the centre of the room with a coffee table between them. Adam sat on one and I sat opposite him. They were fairly wide apart and we were having an on/off conversation whilst scanning our notes. I was asking him about the series he had been in and telling him about my Mum's love of his songs.

He had also managed 1970s pop star Leo Sayer. Remember him appearing as a clown on *Top of the Pops*? In mid-sentence our newsreader walked between us. As she passed, Adam, quick as a flash grabbed hold of the mike pack and raised the wire quickly aloft, revealing tiny white knickers. She wheeled round, grabbing at her skirt.

Adam dropped the wire quickly. He glared at me and said, "Simon, what did you do that for?"

I was speechless, I didn't know what to say. The presenter said nothing but gave me a withering look. To this day, when I see her on TV I remember Adam. One day hopefully I will get to tell her that it wasn't me. It really wasn't.

The phone ringing was a signal to return to the present. It was Rick.

"So you're going out with the Indian bird then… where are you taking her?"

I had decided to give Rick as little information as possible as it would no doubt come back to haunt me. I explained that we were just going out for a quiet meal at the Italian.

"Not an Indian then?" he said.

I tried not to laugh.

"You are not taking your Indian then for an Indian?"

"No, I am taking her for an Italian," I said patiently.

We both laughed. He wished me a good time and then asked after Niamh and whether I had heard from her. I told him we'd been emailing and he made a few more crass remarks about potatoes and Guinness, then signed off in his usual chummy way. "Okay old boy. Have a good one."

The next day, pulling up at Shilpa's home I was full of anticipation about the coming night and what it would bring. I hit the buzzer. Shilpa answered immediately.

"Hi Simon, I'll be out in five."

I waited by the car for her to appear. She didn't keep me waiting long and I wasn't disappointed. I handed over the Champagne Truffles. "I thought you might like these," I said.

"Oh Simon, that's lovely," and she grabbed me and gave me a kiss. She looked stunning.

She had on a wine coloured skirt, tapered at the knee into which she had tucked a floral blouse in vibrant shades and black cropped jacket, buttoned up against the cold of the January evening. Against her dark skin the outfit looked amazing. She had high heels on and the instep of her black shoes was burgundy to match her skirt. Her make-up was expertly applied in the Asian tradition of "pooling" her eyeliner in the inner corner of her eye and leaving a tail of liner on the outer corner of her eyes, elongating the natural almond shape.

"New car?" she asked.

"No, no just one on test that I'm writing about."

"Hmm, very posh," she said.

I leant over and switched on the massage seat for her.

"Oooh... oooh," she exclaimed. "I definitely want one of these."

The Italian *Il Lupo* in Great Baddow had a small car park and it was a squeeze guiding the Mercedes into it without the parking sensors screaming – overly sensitive and designed for the American market and wide streets. The sensors were going off continuously as I manoeuvred it into position in a space just adequate to accommodate it. Being a bloke that hadn't read the instruction manual or paid sufficient attention to the

DVD, I felt sure that they could have been adjusted for Essex sized car parking spaces, but these functions and adjustment of the sensors had eluded me thus far.

I am, as you know, fond of Italian restaurants. The menus are easy to understand, none of that "jus" drizzling, no grilled tripe with trios of odd vinegars. My favourite dishes are the hearty peasant ones – pizza, pasta and of course, spinach cannelloni. The desserts are to my liking too – my favourites, tiramisu and Italian ice cream.

Shilpa was fabulous company. The dining room was lit by candles and flames danced around her beautiful oval shaped eyes and light was reflected in the silver of her jewellery. Shilpa had a way of moving her head from side to side slightly as she listened to me talking. It was reminiscent of an Indian dance routine, though obviously far less exaggerated in style. It fascinated me.

As I was driving I had decided to have just a splash of white wine with my meal and after a small glass was drinking San Pelligrino. The white wine we ordered was in an ice bucket beside our table and once I had drunk my allocation, the waiter filled and refilled Shilpa's glass. Soon the bottle was gone. As we were ordering our desserts the waiter came over to remove the empty bottle. He enquired if we would like another.

"I wouldn't have thought so," I started to say. But before I could finish Shilpa asked if she could have a glass of Champagne with her dessert. She had ordered panna cotta with raspberries. A glass was ordered.

The conversation was fluid and effortless. She spoke of her family, her marriage, being divorced and she seemed interested in me. I was aware that something else was happening. We were beginning to flirt with one another.

At one point Shilpa reached over the table and held my hand. She excused herself from the table after dessert and was gone for ages. I replayed some of the conversation. She had said that this was a weekend when her daughters were with her husband, so she was alone. She said she didn't enjoy being in the house on her own.

I wondered if these were signals that I might be invited in for coffee. But I knew she didn't drink coffee. Green tea? Should I invite her back to mine or was that too forward an invitation Was I misreading what I thought could be cues?

When she returned to the table she looked even more amazing. She had reapplied her lipstick and there was a bloom to her.

"I was beginning to wonder where you'd got to," I said.

"Oh don't worry about that," she said airily. "I always take ages in the loo. I have that fear of walking into a public place with my skirt tucked in my knickers, not that I have to worry about that tonight."

My eyes widened.

"I'm not wearing any!" she added coquettishly.

Before I could speak, though I didn't really know what I was going to say anyway, our waiter reappeared. He enquired whether we would like any coffees or liqueurs.

"I'm not sure," I said, turning to Shilpa "Would we like any liqueurs or coffee?"

"Yes please," said Shilpa. "I'll have a glass of port."

"I'd better have a coffee," I said to the waiter.

"We have a choice of port," the waiter addressed Shilpa, "which would you like?"

Without hesitation, blinking or casting an eye at the proffered menu, Shilpa replied, "The most expensive one."

The waiter glanced at me for confirmation. I assented with a nod. I decided to push my luck. "Do you often go out without your knickers on Shilpa?" I asked, intending to give the impression of authoritative schoolmaster, mockingly disapproving. I suspect I sounded more like a limp John Alderton.

She took a large sip of Port and gazed at me with her huge brown eyes. "Well to answer your question truthfully: I don't often go out without my knickers on, but, yes, I do sometimes go out without my knickers on. So, my question to you Simon is, do you think I am telling the truth or not?" She was playing with me now.

As usual, I didn't know what to say. I knew it was going well, very well. She was sexy, smart, single and flirting with me.

"Shall we go?" I asked.

I paid the bill. It was considerably more than I was expecting. I'm not mean and rarely even check restaurant bills if I'm honest, but this was well into three figures for just the two of us. The Italian was an up-market bistro but Shilpa's single glass of port had cost over £14.00! "Does this include service?" I had asked. It didn't.

Arriving back at Shilpa's I was full of anticipation. That's an understatement of course! I was brimming with it. Conversation had continued on the drive home. At one point Shilpa leant over and kissed me. Was I going to be invited in for "coffee"? There's always that moment when you think that something might happen, it's on your mind, your response is planned but you have to wait to hear the words. The wrought iron gates protecting Shilpa's house were open. As I pulled onto the drive next to her gleaming 4x4, I didn't have to wait long before she spoke.

"Simon, I've had a wonderful evening, thank you so much."

I slipped back into Hugh Grant mode and said, cheesily, "Well it's been my pleasure... " Here it comes...

"Would you like to come in for coffee?" she said. Well, that's what I wanted her to say, but what she actually said was, "Well goodnight Simon, have a safe drive home."

I was stunned and didn't know what to say. "Err..."

As Shilpa reached for the door handle I leapt out of the car and in the nanosecond it took to reach her side I was scrabbling for something to say. I was so disappointed, had expected to be invited in, but I knew I couldn't appear rude or pushy. Arriving at the passenger door I was too late, Shilpa was already on her feet. All I could say was, "Err thank you, it's been great. I'll text you."

It had indeed been great up until then. As Shilpa reached her front door I jumped back in the car, slammed it into reverse and was just about to launch out of her driveway when she waved. That wave people do when they want you to put your window down. I was tempted to drive off. I could feel a huff coming on. I didn't of course.

Instead I lowered the window and Shilpa came over to the car. "Oh, did you want to come in?" she said.

She was like a cat playing with a bit of fluff... I was the fluff. I was relieved though. Little did I know that this was a carefully orchestrated game. She was testing my reactions, teasing. It was later of course that I realised this.

"I'd love to," I beamed.

I threw the gear leaver back into drive, parked and literally ran into Shilpa's house. The interior was light, cool, Scandinavian in style. Very expensive solid wood, no veneers. I followed Shilpa into her kitchen. Solid wooden floor, sunken mood lights, marble, hand-made kitchen. She had one of those cookers that look like the grille of an expensive German car. Left alone I'd probably starve before working out how to use the thing.

"What can I offer you," Shilpa asked, beaming. "Coffee, or something stronger?"

I began to feel nervous, for no real reason particularly, but nervousness stalks me and in that second, it overwhelmed me.

Shilpa took the initiative. "How about a glass of Champagne? There's some in the fridge. Open it and pour a couple of glasses out, I'm just going to the loo."

As she walked past me, she kissed me on the cheek. My confidence was restored. I didn't turn into Hugh Grant, John Cleese or Sid James. Reaching into the fridge I pulled out one of three bottles of Champagne there – Veuve Cliquot. I wasn't Simon any more I was Bond... James Bond. I even straightened my tie, popped the cork and poured two generous glasses of champagne. When Shilpa returned I turned into Roger Moore, raised an eyebrow and handing her a glass I said, "To us, Moneypenny – or rather – Shilpa!"

There was a highly charged sexual atmosphere. Our eyes did meet and I gazed at her. She was so attractive. Her lips were glossily red with what I presumed was more re-applied lipstick.

"Shall we go into the lounge, it's this way," she indicated, with a glorious movement of her head. I followed her through a doorway without a door and down a short flight of steps.

'Odd,' I thought, 'who has a downstairs?'

Then I realised that the house was built on the side of a hill and the back of it was completely open to what would have been extensive views.

The lounge was vast. I counted at least five large white leather sofas and to one side what looked like an electronic fireplace. Shilpa pressed a button on a remote control unit and flames appeared in the fireplace along with soft coloured lights. It was impressive. It occurred to me that Shilpa was going to have a problem coping with my flat with its dodgy lift and bizarre interior.

"Well, it's some place you have here," I said casually, trying to hang onto Roger Moore. Shilpa didn't reply but waved her hand in front of a sound system on the wall. A smoked glass door moved noiselessly aside.

A few more clicks on the remote control in her hand and the room was filled with music. Diana Ross, singing "Today I saw somebody who looked just like you."

Shilpa pressed yet another button on the remote and the curtains began to close, silently, smoothly, gliding towards one another. I felt as if I could be in a Bond movie. I had gulped most of my Champagne. Shilpa had drained her glass and poured herself a second and had finished that too. I didn't know whether to help myself to a second glass. Was I driving, or perhaps staying?

As I reached for the bottle, having decided on a splash of a second glass she said, "I hope you're going to behave yourself Simon. I mean, just because you're here doesn't mean that anything's going to happen."

I didn't say anything. She leant towards me though and gave me a kiss, a proper kiss, a long proper kiss and then she pulled me backwards towards a white sofa before pulling off my jacket, I wrenched off my tie. She threw her black jacket off as we kissed then urgently pulled her floral blouse out of her skirt. Her shoes had gone flying in the first tumble. Then, there was a pause and we both seemed to come up for air.

"Well Simon," Shilpa said. "I think we'd better both calm down. Let's have another drink."

She grabbed at the bottle and spilt some of its contents on the carpet. The housewife in me wanted to wipe it up but it didn't seem appropriate, James Bond wouldn't have done it. I refrained from mentioning it and neither did she

Soon we'd returned to our fumblings which were becoming more intimate. Diana Ross was in full flight now and Shilpa was lying on one of the white sofas, her legs raised, ankles crossed and her heels resting on the back. Her skirt had ridden up to her waist. She was wearing stockings fastened with a white suspender belt and despite our conversation in the restaurant she was in fact wearing underwear. I had assumed she wasn't wearing any hosiery, but to my delight she was. Fine denier stockings with a white suspender belt and she was wearing knickers, white with lace. 'Expensive,' I thought.

"So you are wearing knickers?" I said, trying to summon up John Alderton.

"Of course I am. What sort of respectable Indian girl goes out without them?" I decided to push my luck a bit further. "Well would you like to keep them on, or would you perhaps be more comfortable without them?" I smiled, not expecting a reply. I didn't get one. Shilpa took a long gulp of Champagne, devouring completely another glass. She raised herself up slightly and slid into the corner of the sofa, lifted her legs straight up again and then put her thumbs in each side of the waistband of her knickers. She started to push them down her legs towards her upturned feet. I couldn't believe my luck. I stood up quickly unbuttoning my shirt and the waistband of my trousers, which had become rather tight.

'The boys in the fish and chip shop won't believe this!' I thought.

But what happened next took me completely by surprise. The waistband of Shilpa's knickers had just cleared the cheeks of her bottom. She then stood up quickly, pulled her knickers back into place, started to stuff her blouse back into her skirt. I was confused. I thought perhaps we were heading to the bedroom. But Shilpa's expression had changed.

"I am sorry Simon," she said, "I just can't do this. It's too soon and I just can't do it."

"What?" I said. Then I checked myself, it was the wrong response. I quickly fixed the waistband of my trousers and tucked my shirt in hastily. I looked for the shoes I had kicked off. Although she hadn't said so, I felt she wanted me to leave, and soon. We walked to the front door in silence. My head was spinning. Not just from the Champagne. I wanted to ask what I had done wrong, so I did, on our way through the kitchen. I did. "Shilpa, what have I done wrong?"

She simply repeated the words she had astonished me with in the lounge. I don't even recall saying goodbye or making any reference to calling or seeing her again.

In what seemed like an instant I was back in the car on the driveway. I was despondent, confused, frustrated. What had gone wrong? Had I assumed too much, been too pushy? She had made the first, second and third move. It was Shilpa who had removed her clothing and some of mine.

'I'm just rubbish at this stuff,' I thought as I drove off.

Fish and chips that week was a sombre affair. I had enjoyed my dinner with Shilpa and I had wanted us to have sex, but obviously the time had to be right, and for her, it was not. But I felt as though I had messed up and was at fault. I just couldn't shake off the belief that it was my fault.

Rick, typically, summed up the situation in one unflattering comment. "Prick teaser!" he said vehemently.

"Isn't that rather harsh?" said Barry.

But Rick was unrepentant. "You are joking. He's brought her an expensive meal, she's invited him in, and he's got his meat and two veg out."

"Who ordered the pie?" interjected our waitress looking startled.

"She's taken her knickers down... " Our poor waitress looked shocked and moved away quickly from the table. "Then she's come over all Mary Whitehouse and thrown him out," he finished. "Paying for a meal, expensive or not, doesn't mean she has to have sex," said Barry quietly.

"Well," I protested, "she didn't exactly throw me out."

The atmosphere was charged, as Rick settled in for the kill. "She's bang out of order," he said emphatically glaring generally in my direction.

"But it's not quite as simple as that is it?" said Barry. "She had the right to decide if she wanted to have sex and she decided she didn't actually. Where's the harm in that?"

"Well why didn't she fucking well decide that on the driveway and not in the lounge with her knickers half way down?" said Rick.

It was a fair point I thought. "Maybe she decided that she didn't want sex, but she did want some affection and physical contact with Simon," responded Barry, the Voice of Reason.

"So, she can decide at any stage whether she wants sex – even if it's at an advanced stage of an encounter?" said Rick, refusing to give up and I so wished that he would just shut up.

"And what about him?" he added. Rick pointed another piece of cod in my direction. "He doesn't have any say in this? Did you want sex?" said Rick, quite loudly.

The poor waitress, on the horizon retreated back into the kitchen. I wondered if she was going to tell her manager and get us thrown out or perhaps call the Police. We needed to apologise.

"Well, yes of course I did," I said.

"That's the problem," said Rick. "She can decide whether she wants to end the evening with sex or not, but what about him?" It felt alien for Rick to be on my side. "He's also paid for dinner."

"Yes, but he's not paid for sex," said Barry.

This was obviously right but Rick insisted that I had been invited in, Shilpa had played with my affections "And," he added, "your todger, then sent you packing!"

The conversation rambled on, several staff looking on with interest or possibly alarm. After we had eaten and apologised to our waitress, I trudged back to the flat. I hadn't heard from Shilpa so I decided to check my emails. I was pleased to see one from Niamh asking me for an update generally on things but specifically what I was doing on the forthcoming May Bank Holiday.

Bank holidays are feasts when you have a full time job – like a free gift. When you are self-employed it's different. They're just another day, only with congested roads, filled car parks, the gym either eerily empty or chaotic with casual visitors and an array of relatives of members, often youngsters.

I wasn't sure if Ireland had the same Bank Holiday dates as the rest of the UK so emailed Niamh to find out. She replied immediately.

"Ireland isn't in the UK Simon. We are a separate country and have been for some time!"

'A bit facetious,' I thought, though I hoped it was meant to be a joke.

"Were you a total failure in geography at school?"

"Well I was, but only because I could never find the classroom," I quipped back.

Niamh responded with an offer. She invited me to visit if I wasn't doing anything. The UK bank holiday date applied to her invitation. She would take holiday leave as well to make it a longer break. Her missive ended by wishing me "Goodnight xxx."

Ireland

Standing on Rick's drive was a black Range Rover Vogue Autobiography. I had just stepped out of it. The latest test drive for a write up. My suitcase was packed and somewhere in the cavernous boot and I was running through the controls with Rick.

"It's all fairly standard," I said, "You can't move the gear lever unless your foot's on the brake, lamps here, indicator there."

"What's that? Rick interrupted me. Pointing to a large black box between the front seats.

"A fridge," I said

"A what?"

"A fridge," I repeated

"You are joking aren't you? Why do you need a fridge in a car?" he said. I ignored him.

"You are going to be alright driving this?" I asked him, getting cross. I had accepted Niamh's invitation, booked a flight from Luton to Waterford and was on my way via Rick's. He was to drive me to the airport and keep the car for a long weekend as my designated mid-life "consumer" for research purposes and insured accordingly. That was the idea anyway. I was beginning to regret the arrangement involving Rick and the car.

"Why's it got a fridge?" Rick repeated annoyingly.

"I don't know, I suppose it's for wine, or water, or bars of chocolate or for your sandwiches. Can we get going please?" I said "It's probably easier if I drive."

Rick obligingly sat in the passenger seat and we headed onto the M25 towards the airport. He had missed a couple of fish and chip dinners and was keen to catch up with things.

"So, you're off to see the Irish bird and you've given the Indian bird the Spanish archer?" (Essex for "ElBow").

I was now very irritated. It wasn't his entire fault. I was already feeling sensitive about the airport experience.

I took a deep breath and said "It's nothing like as simple as that. I've seen Shilpa at the gym a couple of times and we've had coffee. It's all fine. I'm seeing Niamh in Ireland for the Bank Holiday, as I've told you. We're going to dinner tomorrow night and she's going to show me around. That's all."

"So you're not going to shag her then?" Rick said.

"No Rick, I am not as you so charmingly put it, going to 'shag' her. I am spending a weekend in Ireland with a friend and that's it." I'd had enough of Rick's prurient insistence about the intimate details of my love life and now also had a tension headache.

"Has this thing got any music then?" Rick asked almost certainly sensing my annoyance.

"Yes, AM/FM radio, six stack CD, USB connector for your iPod and twelve speakers," I said.

"All a bit wasted on Elton then," he replied.

"Oh fuck off!" I said, as we pulled into the airport terminal. I quickly disembarked, fished about in the boot for my case, gave Rick a few last minute instructions about the car and wishing him a happy driving experience, headed off into "Departures". I gave Rick a backward wave before disappearing from sight. Rick had assured me he knew how to drive the car.

His parting remark as I left him was "Just one thing Simon, why is there a fridge in this motor? Go! And don't overdose on potatoes and Guinness!"

The tedium and anxiety of checking in, security and passport control over, I headed into the light, airy departure lounge at Terminal 1. I made straight for the bookshop.

I always do this; another default setting I have, probably a hangover from travelling to the States frequently during my early working life. Although the flight from Luton to Waterford was only a little over an hour, I still wanted to buy a book.

Rick's daft clichés about potatoes and Guinness had made me think. I knew nothing of the potato famine, but I am interested in history and I wanted to find a book about the country I was about to visit. If possible, something with a historical focus.

Seated on the plane, I began to read. I had found a book that was about Irish history which had a chapter on the famine. I read that the horror of the disaster was on a scale I hadn't imagined. Two thirds of the population either died of starvation, illness, or were forced to leave Ireland to try to avoid privation and death.

The cause of the famine was a disease, potato blight, which rotted crops in the field before they could be harvested. I couldn't stop turning the pages. The famine occurred at a time when the English were still shipping food out of Ireland to feed the British Army in India. As the pilot announced that we were about to land and issued a welcome, I felt a pang of guilt about being English.

As I prepared to disembark, my thoughts turned to the coming weekend. For all my bravado about this being a matey cultural weekend with a few of her friends thrown in for entertainment, I was of course hoping that I might sleep with her, the memory of her pink knickers in Venice still fresh in my mind.

The formalities at Waterford Airport are scant and friendly. There's no carousel for luggage and cases are piled high with a guy helping to distribute them.

The same guy, or so it appeared, was also Passport Control and Customs. It seemed to set the tone of Ireland and as I came through the arrivals door to meet a smiling Niamh, I knew that I was going to have a great time.

She was smartly dressed, wearing a cream coloured light raincoat over a close-fitting polo neck jumper with a denim button-through skirt. She had tall black boots on, her blonde hair loose. There wasn't a hint of awkwardness. She rushed toward me, planted a kiss on my cheek and greeted me. I showed her the book I had read on the plane.

"Hmm, perhaps not your finest hour. But come on now, let's get you some lunch," she said.

We drove into Waterford in Niamh's Toyota Celica and I was soon captivated by Ireland. It was as I had imagined it. In the rural areas it's wholesomely green, calm, rolling gently into a vista of hump-backed hills and watered valleys. No wonder it's called the Emerald Isle.

Niamh's accent seemed even more Irish than I had recalled it being in Venice. She was explaining that she had booked us into a local restaurant that evening. Her home was a three-storey townhouse on the outskirts of the town decorated in warm colours.

Standing in her hallway with my suitcase, my nerves returned. I don't know why – I was comfortable and Niamh was charming and relaxed.

"Put your suitcase upstairs, Simon and I'll make you a cup of tea. I know how keen you English are on your tea," she laughed.

Now to a normal person the direction to "put your case upstairs" would have probably led to a reply such as "Where to?" or "Can you show me?" or "If it's okay, I'll just leave it here." I am sure Niamh was about to show me where to put the case, but the phone rang. Again, a normal person would have waited for her to finish her call before asking about where to go.

I didn't. I left her to take the call and headed upstairs. On the landing there were four doors, three closed and one open. I later found that one closed door led to a bathroom, the two others to bedrooms and the one open door was to Niamh's bedroom.

I could hear Niamh on the phone describing to the caller that yes, she had collected me from the airport and yes, we were going out to dinner to a restaurant called *The Castle* I wasn't sure what to do. Should I leave the case on the landing and return downstairs? Indecisive to the end, I stood on the landing holding my case, uncertain about what to do next. Niamh appeared at the top of the stairs. In her soft southern Irish drawl she said, "So you've not chosen a bedroom yet then, Simon?"

Basil Fawlty replied.

"Well no er, I just wondered, err, no well hmmm..."

Niamh laughed.

"Well just come and get your tea."

She showed me around. It was a lovely home.

"I don't know how you like your tea," Niamh said, as we sat down to drink.

"Well actually, I like tea but I prefer coffee."

"Well Simon, that's your problem," said Niamh, "You're more American than English."

"Really!" I protested.

"Yes, you're like the one out of Frasier – Niall. He's always tense and fretting about something – too much caffeine in his system."

"Well how do you know about Frasier?" I said.

Niamh, realising where I was going with this, said "Well Simon, we have television in Ireland... " slowly and deliberately. "The old country's come on leaps and bounds since we sorted the potatoes out." We both laughed.

She took a sip of her tea, then asked me what I'd like to do now I was in Ireland.

"I'm here for the views, the cultural experience and I don't mind, I am happy to be guided by you."

"Really?" said Niamh, "The cultural experience," she intoned. She seemed amused and unconvinced. I suggested that perhaps we could do some sightseeing, go to church on Sunday if she felt she'd like to. She said that would be fine and that there was a church – St Francis – in Waterford where we could attend Mass if I liked.

"Is that St Francis of Assisi?" I enquired.

Niamh took a sip of tea. "I believe it is," she said simply.

The atmosphere was crackling with humour, and something else. It felt charged. Electricity? Niamh had removed her raincoat and she shook her hair. Her button-through skirt seemed to have more buttons undone than I remembered from the airport. Her legs were bare but she still wore her long boots. A few minutes ticked by without either of us speaking. We just looked at each other, slightly shyly on my part. I wanted to say something, but I didn't.

After a long pause, Niamh said, "So you're here for the culture then Simon?"

"Yes!" I said, in a strange, high, stringy voice… Robin Gibb of the Bee Gees?

Taking another sip of tea, Niamh replied, "That's grand, but I thought you were here for the… shagging."

I didn't need to say anything in reply. I launched myself from the chair onto the sofa where she was sitting. Hands everywhere, kissing her neck, the buttons of her skirt seemed to flip off and the skirt opened up fully, but the waist button was stubbornly in place. Niamh pulled her polo neck over her head revealing a red lacy bra, her button-through skirt now undone to the waist, showing lacy, red knickers: a matching set. Hoping that this wasn't going to be another Shilpa experience, I lifted Niamh's bottom and pulled her red knickers to her knees. I needed some confirmation to continue and I soon got it.

"You're a horny bastard aren't you Simon?" she said. After kissing her breasts and caressing her smooth honey-coloured thighs, I fondled and stroked her. She pulled me towards her and I entered her to the hilt. It felt fantastic to be inside her. As I came I felt the tiniest pang of guilt at pretending to Rick that I only had friendship and culture in mind in visiting Ireland.

Niamh disappeared to the bathroom. Returning, she said with a smile "Well at least that's sorted out where you're going to sleep." We both laughed.

To my eternal shame I texted Rick. It was a short text: "Vesuvius!"

He texted back immediately: "Cultural tour. By my reckoning you've been in Ireland just over an hour and you've already shagged her!"

I replied "Not my fault. Just off to get some Guinness. See you at Luton on Monday. How's the fridge?"

He texted back: "Ha, great car, a guzzler of petrol though. See you Monday."

Now I could properly relax.

The Castle restaurant was in the middle of the medieval centre of Waterford, Niamh explained. It was only 2.30pm so she suggested going for a walk around the town. There was the usual array of pubs and coffee shops. We went into one of the pubs so that I could have a Guinness. Though it was still only afternoon someone was playing the violin, or "fiddle" and there were people dancing. A few more glasses of "liffey water" later we were walking back to Niamh's home when an older lady who had passed us, stopped and scurried back to stand in front of us.

"Is that yourself Niamh?" she enquired of my companion.

"Ah, hello Mrs Bailey," said Niamh "how are you?" She was apparently unfazed by the astonishing enquiry.

I am sure that you are thinking that no Irish person has ever said, "Is that yourself?" like no Welsh person has ever said, "Whose boots are these shoes?" etc. But Mrs Bailey did. I was completely charmed.

Niamh introduced me as her friend, Simon, from England. Without a further word Mrs Bailey took hold of my arm and insisted that I should meet her family. She pointed to a nearby café then addressed a smartly dressed young couple amongst the seated group. "Anthony, its Niamh and this is her friend, Simon, from England. You know Niamh, my dentist?"

Anthony greeted me and introduced his wife. The elegant young lady beside him tilted her head towards me.

"Can I introduce my wife?" he said. "Her Serene Highness Princess Theresa of Austria."

I took the words in: "Her Serene Highness… " And something about them led me to believe that this was the truth and not some scene from a pantomime scene. Instead of saying something crass as I had been instantly inclined to do, I took her hand, nodded my head and said respectfully, "Your Serene Highness."

This surreal moment was interrupted by this lovely young woman. She said that she was delighted to meet me and asked how I knew Niamh.

Before I could reply, Niamh said, "We are casual acquaintances, your Highness, we met on holiday. Simon is here researching a book."

"Ah, a writer," the Princess said, "how interesting."

"Not really," I said. I had the impression that Niamh was keen to end the conversation and move on.

"Enjoy your day," she said to the couple, "and goodbye Mrs Bailey."

We wandered back to Niamh's house. I expressed my surprise at the meeting and was keen to know more. Niamh explained that Anthony, a commoner who had once worked in a pizza parlour before making his fortune and becoming a millionaire had married Theresa – Princess Theresa of Austria about a year before. She was the great granddaughter of Archduke Franz Ferdinand. The wedding held in Salzburg was celebrated as a national event and the country had virtually come to a standstill as it engaged in celebrations.

We dawdled along the route to Niamh's, talking and laughing. I felt completely relaxed now. As we stumbled through her front door we were soon in each other's arms.

"I don't think we've got time for this Simon," she said, "the taxi will be here in twenty minutes."

"Oh I am sure we do," I said. "I can fit into the smallest of time frames." I pulled down her scarlet knickers and bent her over the dining room table.

"My Mother warned me about men like you," she said.

A quick shower and shave later, I began to dress in my suit when some headlights flashed in the driveway outside.

Niamh was in the shower and she shouted to me to tell the taxi driver to wait for a few minutes. I opened the front door, walked the short distance down the drive and approached a large, ruddy-faced man seated in a taxi.

He wound down the window down but before I could speak he said "Now, you're not the dentist arrgh ya?" I had to concede this.

"No," I said, "the dentist is just getting ready, would you be kind enough to wait a few minutes?"

"Sure I can," he said, "There's no rush on this earth. Where are you from then?"

"I am from England."

"Well you hid that well, I'd never have guessed," he said drolly.

"So you and the good dentist are off to *The Castle*?" he went on.

"Yes we are, what's it like?" I asked. "Is it good?"

"Well it's not for the likes of meself, but I am sure you and the good dentist will enjoy it."

I excused myself and returned to the house. Niamh was just coming down the stairs. She looked fabulous in a pale cream dress topped with a black woollen cape, black stockings and very high-heeled black patent shoes. She carried a black patent clutch bag and smelt delicious. She told me it was *Chanel No.19*. I told her she looked ravishing and that the taxi was waiting.

I opened the back door of the taxi for her.

"Hello Sean," said Niamh. The two were clearly acquainted.

"So you're off to *The Castle* with your friend from England then?" asked Sean. "Well I must say you're looking grand."

Niamh thanked him graciously. She did indeed look grand. As we approached the medieval castle in the old town in Waterford, I gazed openly at Niamh and thought how lucky I was to be spending time with her. Her hair was held in a ponytail and there were frilly wisps falling over her ears. She seemed to shine.

Sean pulled up outside *The Castle*. Looking in the mirror and switching on the internal light he indicated the fare was ten Euros. I reached inside my wallet and gave him a ten euro note and then a five euro note indicating he should make it twelve. He thanked me and I made my way to the nearside of the car to let Niamh out.

As Sean passed her the change her dress rode up to reveal lacy topped stockings. I felt sure Sean had seen. He looked at me, then back at Niamh and said, "You know, I think I am seeing things I probably shouldn't." We all laughed.

The restaurant specialized in seafood: langoustine, Dublin bay prawns, salmon – all gloriously fresh. It was ideal for me. Not too heavy, light and cooked without excessive cream or heavy buttery sauces, which I don't enjoy. Between courses when Niamh excused herself to go to the bathroom, I glanced at my mobile phone. I'd forgotten to let the children know about my arrival in Ireland and felt guilty, so I sent them a quick text. There was a text from Rick, saying, inevitably.

"Any more eruptions?"

"Just one," I texted back.

"You're just showing off now," he retorted.

When Niamh returned to the table the conversation took on a more serious note. She spoke about how much she loved her work, but that she often felt isolated, even lonely. She wasn't in touch that much with her family and there were long nights and many evenings on her own. She had tried joining clubs, done some dancing, dabbled at golf but she still felt pretty much on her own.

I spoke about my marriage, my children, and she was very sympathetic and listened intently when I discussed my divorce and how I missed them. After dinner we walked into Waterford, a popular venue for stag and hen nights.

We managed to find a traditional Irish pub again with more fiddlers and more dancing. A great atmosphere. It was by now well after Midnight and after the excesses of the day; travelling, drinking, shagging, I was beginning to droop. Niamh confessed to being tired too, so we agreed to go home and arm in arm made our way to a nearby taxi rank.

Sean was at the head of a line of taxis. He enquired about our evening and we said it was "grand" – we'd enjoyed ourselves. Soon we were falling into Niamh's cast iron bed with its eiderdown cover. Although I wanted to wear pyjamas as I'm shy about my body and being naked makes me feel exposed, which of course I am. Grossly exposed. I settled for just a pair of boxers. Niamh showered and in the half-light of the bedroom slipped in beside me. She had on a camisole and French knickers. I was extremely tired and though it felt fabulous to actually be in bed with Niamh, the conversation became oddly formal again as she turned to me and said.

"Well goodnight Simon. I hope you're enjoying Ireland?"

"I am," I assured her. "Thank you for the invite. It's a wonderful place and you are beautiful."

I hoped I hadn't snored. The next morning, I felt mildly jet lagged, even though the flight was only an hour. I guessed it was dehydration. Niamh was up before me and I could hear the sound of the radio on in the kitchen, doors opening and shutting, and a soft constant "phing" sound which I took to be the refrigerator. I took my dressing gown out of my case and headed downstairs.

"Morning sleepyhead," said Niamh. She was wearing a satin dressing down, royal blue in colour with a deep cream/beige border and a wide cream belt. She still had bed hair and a pair of satin slippers on. Without any make-up, she was just lovely. "Would you like coffee, Mr Taylor and how would you be taking it?" Niamh poured out a large mug of coffee and we sat at a small bistro table outside the kitchen on a small patio area. It was cool but not uncomfortable. "Do you want to go to Mass?" asked Niamh. "Because if so, there is a lovely church in the centre of town and we have plenty of time to wander around and have coffee. Mass isn't till 11am." I thought this was a good idea.

"And what about something to eat? Will you be having the full Irish?" Not being a great breakfaster – a cup of coffee and a bowl of "wheetie bangs" – the generic term used in the Air Force for any breakfast cereal – is usually enough for me. The full Irish I learned includes white pudding, as opposed to our black pudding. I can't say for sure since both sound pretty revolting and I have never eaten either but apparently, I am told they are both delicious if you like offal. I believe the black version contains pig's blood. The white? I don't want to know. Niamh produced a basket of croissants, warmed gently, just as I like them. I smiled to myself as she seated herself opposite me.

"Well," she said, tilting her head to one side jauntily. "If we are going to Mass at 11am we'll have to leave at half ten. It's now a quarter to ten so we'll have to get a shift on. You've time to read the paper – *The Irish Times* – which I have delivered whilst I get dressed."

"Any other options?" I asked hopefully. Niamh caught my drift immediately.

"You know Simon, you're a horny bastard!"

I tried to look shocked, mockingly offended but couldn't manage it. "I'm not sure about that," I said. "Just a healthy appetite."

"A healthy appetite – that's what you're calling it are you?" she said, smiling. "Simon you've not been here 24 hours yet and you've had me five times already."

I wasn't sure if this was a mild complaint – and I hadn't been counting. Was it five? "Get inside, I'm not giving the neighbours a free show," she said.

We stumbled into the dining room and she said, "You know I don't know that we should be doing this before Mass."

"Ah well," I said, slipping off my dressing gown, "I think the old Catholic rules dictated that we shouldn't even eat before going to Mass, hence the tradition of early Mass." Before the conversation could develop, Niamh slipped down my boxers and took my cock in her mouth.

'What a fantastic negotiator,' I thought.

As I stiffened inside her, I couldn't help thinking, what an amazing time I was having and what a lucky sod I was. 'Have to ease up a bit though,' I thought to myself. I was getting slightly sore and my hips were beginning to ache.

As Niamh came up for air, I fell onto a dining room chair behind me. Her dressing gown was open I and could see that Niamh still had on her camisole and French knickers from the night before. She slipped her legs over mine and sitting on my lap, facing me, I slipped aside the crotch of her knickers and began to pleasure her. She moaned, moved my hand aside then shifted her hips so that I entered her.

'Handy things, French knickers,' I thought. 'No need to take them down… perhaps that's what they were designed for.'

Niamh moved up and down against my thighs, put her hands around the back of my head and looking into my eyes and whilst concentrating hard, smiled and said again, "You're a horny bastard, aren't you?"

Showering, shaving and dressing quickly, I joined Niamh, now dressed, to head off to Mass. Now, if you're Catholic and haven't been to Mass in Ireland you are in for a treat. If your experience is like mine, it'll be a hoot. Niamh and I sat about mid-way down the aisle of St. Bernard's in Waterford. This being her local church, Niamh nodded to a few people but didn't introduce me. I wondered if Her Serene Highness, Princess of Austria might be in attendance, but didn't see her.

At 11am precisely, the parish Priest (Father Pat – who else?) walked up the aisle. "Walking" isn't quite accurate – he was striding briskly up the centre aisle. As he sped along, he opened a hymn book and bellowed without any preamble, "Hymn 179."

There was an orchestrated scramble for hymn books. I dropped mine – clumsy – and had to start again, riffling through the pages. I can't remember the title of the hymn, it was one I had never sung before and didn't know. It was rather dirge-like. I don't think anyone else knew it either judging by the hesitancy and lack of communal timing.

Niamh glanced at me quizzically as if to say she didn't know it either. To my amazement, the Priest waved a hand aloft, made a cutting gesture with both hands and said crossly, "Ah forget it!"

No one seemed remotely fazed by this. Then he announced "I have no servers, no organist and no Communion assistant, so you'll all just have to bear with me."

The service proceeded at a cracking pace – standing up, kneeling down, standing up again, making the sign of the cross – his homily or sermon lasted about 3 and a half minutes and consisted of him telling as many jokes as he could around a vague theme of Masses of Intentions (i.e. the practice of paying a contribution to the priest's income by dedicating a Mass for a departed loved one).

He described how a widow had come to see him and asked for a Mass to be said for her recently deceased husband.

Now, as the Priest put it, "he (the dead husband) was not the best of fellas, overly keen on the Liffey Water, with a roving eye and a fondness for the ladies (Niamh looked sideways at me at this juncture) and not a lot else to commend him."

"Father," she had said, "I would like you to dedicate a Mass for my husband." holding out a ten euro note. "I took the note and thanked her," said the Priest.

"You may have to wait a while for the Mass, Bridie," I told her. "It will be at least six months before I can say it." She snatched the ten euro note back, stuffed it in her purse. "Ah don't worry Father, for sure he'll be burned to a crisp by then."

The congregation roared with appreciative laughter. This was new to me. I'd never heard such a response in church before. And that was it really – quick, funny, bread, wine and absolution in under 25 minutes.

After Mass we went to see the "Dunbrody." This is a replica of one of the many ships that a vast number of Irish residents left the country on during the potato famine in the 1840s – known as the "famine ships". I had wanted to know more about the famine, hence the purchase at the airport and Niamh without knowing this had arranged this trip before I had arrived. We joined a small queue and boarded the ship via a narrow gangplank. The first thing that struck me was the small proportions of the ship.

On board were a company of actors dressed in period costumes. Some were in rags, others dressed relatively finely. There were children as well. The acting was superb. Visitors were encouraged to ask questions and the actors remained resolutely in character throughout. One woman, wearing a rough shawl around her head and holding onto two tiny, immaculately behaved – too quiet – children, narrated a story about being evicted from a smallholding when her husband had died, by an absentee English landlord. She told how a cousin who had settled in New England had sent her the fare to leave Ireland. They were travelling third class and were sharing a single bed in a cabin with ten others in it. They all had to come up on deck to get fresh air and went to the toilet over the side of the boat. She was worried about her children's health and was frightened about the journey ahead, which she knew to be arduous.

After the short show was over, Niamh and I moved down to the lower decks. Here, a middle class lady in an embroidered black gown and coat was holding court. She was telling how her husband, their four children and herself had had enough of Ireland and were leaving for Boston. They had decided to sell their grocery shop as "No one had any money to spend in it," but they had managed to sell it for a good price to an Englishman. She was saying that Ireland was finished and their future lay on the other side of the Atlantic in the New World. She seemed less representative of the emigrants that I had read about but nevertheless it was a moving and powerful tribute to so many Irish who had been forced to leave Ireland. This lady's cabin bore all the comforts of home, a comfortable bed, sofa and a "comfort wardrobe" as she put it. One of the third class passengers was acting as a maid. By comparison, the cabins that the third class passengers shared were little more than a double size wardrobe – enough to accommodate two triple height bunks but nothing more. No "comfort wardrobe" for them. The experience was professionally managed and compelling. I again felt guilt at being English. I wondered how much children back home knew of this chapter of history and the role their ancestors played in it.

Soon, we were on our way back to Niamh's house. We'd decided against going out and Niamh said that she would cook. I quickly texted Rick. "Having a great time, staying in with Niamh tonight." A text was instantly returned and predictably "Potatoes?"

I was tempted to send one back saying "Don't even joke about it!" I just replied, "Coq au Vin."

Another instant reply: "I knew there'd be coq in it. Not sick of it yet then?"

Fortunately for me, Niamh wasn't sick of it; in fact, to the point where, during one particularly vigorous session her bed collapsed. We didn't suffer any injury, just looked at one another and laughed...

And then my trip to Ireland was over and Niamh was driving me back to the airport. As it had been in Venice, it was difficult to leave her and we didn't say much as we drove the short distance to Waterford Airport.

"Shall I say goodbye here in the car," she said, "or come into the airport?"

"I would like you to come in, we could have a drink before I go," I replied.

So we sat in the small upstairs bar at Waterford Airport. We raised a toast and said, "God bless Ireland." In an instant I reflected on the wonderful time I had spent with Niamh. It had been for me a perfect weekend. Fabulous company, good food, and lots of lovely sex – what more did I want? Of course, me being me, I did want more, here was someone I felt very warmly attracted and now close to, but I couldn't gauge how she felt. Was there going to be anything more? As my flight was called we stood up and headed to passport control, such as it is at Waterford Airport – the same chap checking me in, being passport control and the baggage handler – a true multi-tasker.

I wanted some confirmation about the future, a future? Looking back it was foolish. It had been wonderful and I should just have accepted it as that. But no, I had to ask.

"Are we starting something?" I asked, holding Niamh around the waist.

She threw her head back, roared with laughter and said, "I think you've started something, I'm going to have to get a new bed for a start." She had skilfully avoided answering the question. She just kissed me and said, "Have a great flight; I'll be seeing you Simon."

As I came through arrivals, Rick was there waiting for me. I had managed to cheer up on the plane and bounded over to Rick, who was half way through a Mars bar. He just looked up casually and said "Hiya, had a good time? Oh, good... " He seemed mildly uninterested. "The car's this way."

As we drove back along the M25 I filled Rick in about how wonderful Ireland was, how wonderful she was: "I'm definitely going to see her again. I could move to Ireland and write from there." After all with the internet and return flights at only £49, it would be easy.

None of this seemed to impress Rick very much and he simply looked at me sideways and said "So what is she doing now? She's gone to bed with an ice pack down her knickers, has she?"

I didn't answer that but said, "Well I'm definitely going to see her again, she's fantastic."

"I can't wait to meet her," he said unconvincingly.

Well He Would, Wouldn't He?

I'd had a couple of emails from Niamh, low key, friendly. Was it my imagination or was she being rather restrained? I felt sure that I was going to see her again and that we'd embark on a proper relationship. However things rarely go to plan, especially for me. I had pretty much forgotten about Shilpa until I met her at the gym.

As I came round the infamous hairpin bend in the corridor she was coming the other way. I pressed myself against the wall exaggeratedly and grinned sheepishly. She grabbed my arm and said, "Simon, I've got to see you." I was slightly taken aback, but agreed. After I'd finished my workout, I showered and headed downstairs to the café where Shilpa was waiting. She was direct. "Look, I feel really bad about what happened when we last met. It was too soon. I shouldn't have invited you in and I would like to see you again."

"Well, I'd like to see you again," I said wanting to be kind and thinking of Niamh. "We should just go out for dinner sometime and forget it ever happened. There's no reason why we can't be friends," I said.

"I think we could do better than that, Simon, why don't we go away for the weekend?" she said.

I have to admit I didn't know what to say, I mean was I in a relationship with Niamh, so should I say no? I quickly assessed the situation and thought, 'Well, Shilpa's obviously trying to make amends for the other evening, not that she had to and well, it's unlikely anything would happen.' Of course a cautious man would undoubtedly have asked questions and considered the suggestion with care. I just agreed to go away with her for the weekend. We didn't discuss when, where we might go, for how long or what the sleeping arrangements would be.

Shilpa just got up said "Okay, I'll be in touch," gave me a quick kiss and was gone. Why is it that all the women I know dash off quickly?

Rick and Barry were seriously unimpressed. Fish and chips that week led to a tirade of jokes about Ireland.

Barry asking lots of sensible questions like "Who is she, did you find out more about her, has she got any family, will she be coming over from Ireland, when will we meet her?" The sort of questions that a sensible, right thinking, middle-aged man would ask.

Rick simply joked inanely about potatoes, Guinness and shagging.

I thought I'd better mention the Shilpa thing because if I didn't, it would be a source of further aggravation later. It was better to get it over with.

Fortunately, Barry helped me out. "Did you see anything of the Indian lady?" he said, almost on cue. "Ah," I said. "Well, yes, I, well…" I tried to find the right words and immediately Rick caught my eye and said, "Well what, don't tell me you're not shagging her as well now?"

Barry Gibb replied, "No, I am not, I'm just..."

"I'm just what?" demanded Rick.

"Well, I thought I might dash away for a weekend with her."

"What?" he said, "I thought you were supposed to be all loved up with Niamh?"

"Well," I said, trying to explain. "Shilpa feels bad about the other week."

"What? When she blew you out, or rather didn't?" Rick said.

I ignored him. "And we just thought we'd dash away somewhere."

My story was so feeble I decided to concentrate on my cod and chips and let Rick and Barry make of it what they wanted. Of course they were right.

There was no way I should have agreed to go away with Shilpa but I had and having agreed to it, I really didn't think anything would happen between us. Shilpa had sent me a few texts and an email saying that we could either go away the coming weekend or we'd have to wait a little while.

Why is everything so complicated? I thought if I agreed to go quickly, then when she changed her mind (as I believed she might) I could concentrate on Niamh who'd let me know that she wouldn't be free for a few weeks. She hoped after that she could come over. There, that makes sense doesn't it?

But, Shilpa had organized the weekend. She had called the following Monday to say that if I could book somewhere I could pick her up next Friday morning and that she'd be mine until Sunday evening! It sounded quite promising. But she wouldn't go through with it, would she? I booked a decent hotel on the internet in East Grinstead. I specifically asked about their cancellation policy and really couldn't get that excited. I really didn't think we would be going and I felt guilty about Niamh. And there was another reason why I didn't feel we'd be going. I was feeling unwell.

By Wednesday I was dosing myself up with Lemsip, ibuprofen, echinacea, vitamin C – in fact anything I could get my hands on. I don't suffer from colds, I only ever get flu and my remedy is:

a) Tell everyone I know about it in some detail.
b) Complain about it to family members repeatedly as they are more forbearing than anyone else.
c) Take every cough, cold and flu remedy as often as I can manage (don't try this at home) and drink as much fresh orange juice as I can hold.

I'd even missed going to the gym. By Thursday I was beginning to panic. I was supposed to pick Shilpa up at her house the next morning and whilst I wasn't coughing and spluttering, I was aching a lot. I should have spoken to Shilpa, explained the situation and been relieved of the stress and guilt. But no. I didn't feel I could so at 11.30am the next morning I was outside the electric gates of her home. Rick and Barry had been disgusted that I was going away with her and now I was feeling pretty uncomfortable with the idea, but determined we had to go. I thought I couldn't let her down. I had listlessly packed a dinner jacket and a few clothes. If I go away by car for a weekend I usually fill it with most of my wardrobe, giving myself plenty of options for changes of clothing. But not on this occasion. I just couldn't be bothered.

Shilpa met me on the driveway.

I was so tempted to say, "Look I don't feel well, this probably isn't a good idea," but I didn't. I hadn't got a car to write about so I was using my Alfa.

"Will there be a hanger to hang my dress up in the back?" asked Shilpa.

"Yes," I said and fiddled about with a fabulous cream, beaded evening gown that I knew would look good next to her dark skin. Stuck in the car for just over an hour I didn't learn a great deal more about my passenger really. The "other night" wasn't mentioned, she spoke some more about growing up in England and her memories of India and how much she was sure I would like Bollywood films.

The hotel we were staying at was a Country House hotel, quite luxurious and we were soon checking into our room. It was a small suite and had a very large bed, two small sofas, an enormous television on the wall and a bathroom that was as big as the bedroom. It had a walk in shower and a deep roll top bath in the centre of the room. It was like the Flake advert bath. I was still feeling unwell but trying to shrug it off and not really succeeding. It was only about lunchtime. Shilpa put her arms around me and kissed me. I was feeling nervous and wondered whether this was a good idea at all, and if so what was going to happen. When I responded she broke away and said, "Goodness I'm hungry. Shall we go down to lunch?"

There was a roaring fire in the comfortable lounge/bar and we had a light meal, Shilpa drank a couple of glasses of wine and then we headed out for a walk around the grounds. The hotel had provided Wellington boots and Barbour jackets, which we needed.

I was starting to feel a little better and Shilpa put her arm through mine and her head on my shoulder as we walked. The gardens were extensive and the crisp air had a beneficial effect. As my head began to clear my thoughts turned to what might happen when we returned to our room.

Shilpa was looking at her watch and suggesting that we go back there to get ready for dinner. It was about 4.00pm and we had booked a table for dinner in the hotel for 7.30pm.

Now, if you are a girl reading this, 4pm to 7.30pm is quite a while to get ready for dinner. Or is it? Katherine my-ex was a pretty fast mover at preparing for an evening out. She could be ready to leave home within about half an hour of heading into the bathroom. Niamh, albeit on a slender acquaintance seemed able to shower and get ready to go out in a similar time frame. My nearly adult daughter on the other hand could take two to three hours to get ready to go out. Then the penny dropped. Shilpa wanted to go back to our room so we could get things out of the way.

Once inside the room, Shilpa clearly decided that this was it. Off came her jeans, I was slightly disappointed to note that she wore plain, white cotton knickers. I started to undress as well. Taking the initiative she led me over to the sofa and sat down. Her head was level with my waist and I thought 'Ah, this is good.' I bent over and kissed the nape of her neck and started to unbutton my trousers.

Shilpa looked up at me with her big, brown oval eyes and asked "What are you doing Simon?" I froze, quickly buttoning my trousers up again.

"Um, I thought..."

"Yes, I know what you thought," she said. "Look Simon, I want to make something perfectly clear, we are here for two nights and we've got plenty of time for that, I just want to get ready."

I felt as if I had been slapped. My head began to throb instantly. Shilpa strode off to the bathroom and I sat down heavily on the bed.

I wanted to go home. How had I got it so wrong? She had agreed to spend two nights in a hotel with me, had been happy for me to choose the Hotel. And one room (I had checked this with her). We could have had two rooms. Was she agreeing to sex? Was I rushing her? I was tempted to text Rick, but decided against it. And anyway, I couldn't just go. I couldn't sulk and leave her in a hotel. I moved to the sofa, flicked on the television and tried to bury myself in Sky News. I sat there for a good 20 minutes. Shilpa was still in the bathroom.

I was beginning to calm down when she emerged. I ignored her. She pottered about, wearing a white fluffy robe, and she had her clothes and underwear in her hand. She put them down on the bed and then found some jewellery. I didn't say a word. Just stared straight ahead and pretended I was listening to what Kay Burley was saying on Sky News. I'm good at sulking and I was having a mega sulk.

Shilpa looked at me and smiled, when she smiled she looked fantastic. Her soft mouth opened to reveal those gleaming white teeth, her wide oval eyes gazed at me intently. "I'm just going to have a bath," she said seductively. I glanced at her and then back at the TV.

"Ah-ha," I was tempted to add "Enjoy" but didn't. Shilpa stood there for a second and then headed for the bathroom. At the door she turned and said, "I thought you might like to join me?"

'Great!' I thought. I leapt up from the sofa, moved towards the bathroom, throwing my clothes off as I went. I eventually caught up with Shilpa as she was standing alongside the enormous bath. The bath was nearly full with exotically fragrant bubbles popping on white foam surf as more water poured into it. She turned to face me and without a word undid her robe and let it fall to the floor. She was now naked. She had a fantastic body. Slim but curvy and with perfect small breasts, she was completely shaved everywhere and gave me a look as if to say "What do you think?"

I was too busy taking my clothes off to say anything. I was a lot more nervous about showing my body than she had been and let's face it, middle aged men's bodies often aren't all that great to start with, especially mine.

Shilpa didn't say anything but stepped delicately into the bath and sat down. I eventually managed to take my trousers and underpants off all in one go, with them mixed up together, wondering whether I should separate my pants and my jeans? I picked them up, started to unravel them, dropped them and then climbed inelegantly into the tub. I had wondered what Shilpa had been doing in the bathroom for 20 minutes before she had issued her invitation, then I realised she had taken a full sized bottle of Champagne from the mini bar, drunk over half of it and poured out the remainder into two glasses. She had orchestrated this seduction. I'd gone from seeing nothing of Shilpa to seeing everything in an instant. I started to feel anxious. The bath water was uncomfortably hot. My head was throbbing.

"Cheers," said Shilpa, leaning over, clinking her glass to mine.

"Cheers," I said. I put my glass down and floated over to her, started to kiss her, took one of her brown nipples in my mouth and very gently slipped a finger inside her, expecting a favourable response and feeling myself harden.

Shilpa spoke. "I'm not having sex in the bath, Simon."

I started to feel dizzy, partly because of the alcohol, partly because of the water and partly because I didn't know what to do any more. If she didn't want to have sex, what did she want to do? Had I offended her by touching her too intimately, too quickly?

I didn't say anything, I should have, but I didn't. I climbed out of the bath, pulled on a fluffy robe and headed back into the bedroom. Kay Burley was still talking. I lay on the bed and wondered what I should do. Was it my fault? Was I doing something wrong? Why had I agreed to go? About ten minutes later Shilpa reappeared. She had washed her hair and now had a robe and a turban as a towel around her head.

"I just didn't want to have sex in the bath, Simon."

"No okay," I said, "that's fine," rather crisply.

To my surprise, although nothing now could really surprise me, Shilpa climbed onto the bed next to me. I was feeling very confused. I didn't say anything, she just lay next to me on the bed watching Sky News.

After what seemed like ages, she leaned into me and kissed me hard on the mouth. Do I respond, what should I do? Shilpa then flung open her dressing gown and started to play with herself, finger darting in and out. She started to rub her own breasts, at this stage I thought I should probably join in but I was hesitant. What was the right thing to do? We seemed to be going from nothing to everything and then back again. I started to kiss her on the mouth, began to relax slightly, felt myself get very hard and then moved on top of her.

"No," she said, "not like this." So I gathered her legs up and rolled her on to her tummy.

"No, I don't mean that," she said and rolled back again onto her back. "I need you down here."

She pushed my head down to her pussy and I started to lick away. Soon Shilpa was moaning quite loudly and I began to think everything was going to be okay. I just carried on. She didn't seem the type to fake it but she seemed to be approaching orgasm very quickly, which pleased me. Then she stopped. I moved up level with her again, I just wanted to please her, to know what she wanted, to have her and I also really wanted this to be over. It might sound fantastic, but it wasn't. And for the first time ever, I began to worry about what I was doing. Shilpa was now lying on the bed, completely naked, her legs wide apart, clearly indicating that she wanted me to enter her. And I couldn't. At the point Shilpa had finally wanted me to have sex with her, my confused body refused to co-operate. It had never happened before, truly, it had NEVER happened before. I didn't know what to do or say. I wanted to cry.

Realising, Shilpa got up from the bed, went back into the bathroom and I heard her mutter, "I knew it was too soon." I felt terrible. I wanted to die. If I could have run out of the hotel room, I would have done. How I managed to get through dinner I don't know.

Shilpa looked lovely, her cream dress beautiful against her brown skin. She had completed the outfit with cream coloured stockings and suspenders and a tiny cream G-string. But I wasn't interested in eating and our conversation was formal. I felt tense and miserable.

By the time we got back to the bedroom I said, "Look I'm not feeling very well," and tried to sleep on the edge of the bed. It was in sharp contrast to my experience of being with Niamh. It was my own fault. If I wanted a relationship with Niamh I shouldn't have been in bed with Shilpa. Perhaps this was my God's way of teaching me a lesson.

The next day I felt terrible, through lack of sleep, anxiety and the remains of a cold. It was the worst weekend I'd ever spent with a girlfriend. Was it her fault, was it my fault, were we just sexually incompatible?

Driving back in the car Shilpa had an opportunity to ridicule me about the events of the weekend, but didn't. Looking back I realise that she wasn't ready, didn't want a relationship and we should have called it a day there and then. She was without doubt staggeringly attractive, but we were completely ill matched. It happens and I should have accepted it.

The drive back seemed terribly long. As I reached the flat after dropping Shilpa at hers I phoned Rick and told him what had happened. He came round immediately. I went through every detail with him.

Predictably he said "She's just a bitch, forget her. You've still got the Irish bird after all."

The Worst Date Ever!

And did I learn my lesson? Did I recognize after the worst weekend I had ever spent with a girlfriend that I should avoid Shilpa and make what I could of my relationship with Niamh? No, I didn't. And why? Because I was weak and stupid and enlightenment came later. A couple of weeks after our dreadful weekend I found myself, once again on my way to Shilpa's to pick her up!

Martin had phoned and asked whether I fancied going to a "do" at his golf club. It was a social evening with a band, buffet meal and drinks. I was welcome to bring a friend. I hadn't seen Martin for a while so accepting his invitation would give us an opportunity to catch up.

I hadn't heard much from Niamh at this point and was feeling low. Her texts and emails had petered out. She hadn't returned phone calls I'd made and we had no plans to meet up in the foreseeable future.

I reasoned that whilst sex with Shilpa was pretty rubbish, she might make an agreeable companion at the Club social event, assuming she wanted to see me again. The memory of the weekend had dimmed and it had seemed like a good idea to at least enquire if Shilpa wanted to join me. It wasn't a good idea. I was at mid-point on a learning curve and there was more horror in store.

Shilpa had appeared pleased to be asked. When I arrived at her place and pressed the intercom at the shuttered gates, she didn't answer. I pressed again, this time for slightly longer.

Eventually a rather startled sounding Shilpa answered and said that I should come in.

I parked on the driveway and walked to the front door where normally she would be waiting. She wasn't. The door was slightly ajar. I went into the lobby, and the kitchen, she wasn't there either. What should I do? Go downstairs to the lounge? I decided to wait. And I waited and waited. I knew she must be in somewhere in the house of course because she had let me in.

Eventually she appeared. She looked distracted, slightly vacant. Something was wrong, or was it just me? She seemed marginally less groomed than usual; her sleek dark hair slightly awry, perhaps in need of a wash? I could tell that she had just sprayed herself with perfume, overdone it possibly? She didn't say much as we headed off to the golf club and I was relieved to see Martin in the doorway of the clubhouse.

Paul Fox

Martin, as always in good spirits, expansive and friendly. "Hi guys," he said. "Hello gorgeous," he enthused as he grasped Shilpa and enveloped her in a bear hug.

The club lounge was busy. A few members and guests were formally dressed but the majority wore smart casual gear. There was a four-man band, a lead singer, a couple of guitarists and a keyboard player. They were reasonable, playing a selection of middle of the road standards and "elevator" type stuff. I felt relaxed and was chatting away with a small group of old friends who had gathered round our table.

I hadn't noticed Shilpa filling her glass and refilling it. Repeatedly. As we were seated with plates from the buffet I realized that she had drunk an entire bottle of wine and was pouring a large glass from a second. We were only just eating our starters. She hadn't spoken much either. I had asked several times if she was all right and introduced her to several of my friends. She had said she was fine, listened to conversation without contributing much and seemed subdued. Or was she bored?

What happened next was wholly unexpected. It ranks to date as without doubt the most embarrassing experience of my life. Even the memory of it whilst writing this makes me wince. In this conservative venue and at this rather intimate gathering, Shilpa announced that she wanted to dance. There wasn't a cleared space that amounted to a dance floor and it wasn't that sort of evening. No one else was dancing. The band were having a break whilst food was served

I was eating and really didn't want to dance. Shilpa was having none of it. She dragged me to my feet and stood where everyone could see her, ankles and knees together doing a sort of sixties type dance, arms waving in front of her, head bobbing from side to side. I shuffled next to her, moving my feet and looking at the floor acutely uncomfortable. Then, without warning Shilpa leapt cat-like towards me, put her arms round my shoulders, lifted both legs in the air and wrapped them around my waist. Her stocking tops and knickers were on clear display to everybody, she then jiggled up and down. I held her tightly and realised from the gasps around me that this impromptu display wasn't appreciated.

I tried smiling, I registered Martin looking on astonished but it wasn't over yet, oh, no! I told Shilpa I thought we should sit down. I was pretty assertive.

She replied loudly and very emphatically "No fucking way!" Then she jumped down from me, squatted down so her head was level with my waist and moved her face and chin into my crotch and then up towards my

190

chest. People started to get up and leave. I was rooted to the spot, aghast. She started to simulate oral sex on me at which point I grasped her, lifted her up and attempted to sit her down in her chair. She resisted, swayed, regained her balance, swore at me and slapped me full on the face. I wanted to die. Again!

Two stewards came running over. "You need to take this outside, now!" they said. I grabbed Shilpa's arm, "No fucking way!" she shouted again, very loudly.

Martin came to my aid. "I think you need some fresh air," he said calmly, amazingly calmly considering the circumstances. I was so grateful to him.

As we manhandled her into the foyer Shilpa let loose with the foulest language I'd ever heard. She was like a thing possessed. She refused to get in the car with me, drunkenly called a taxi, stormed off, fell over twice and was violently sick. I eventually managed to get her in the car. Her clothing was in disarray; her stockings ripped to pieces, hair strewn across her face.

Driving back to her place it all made horrible sense. Whenever we'd gone out she had had a lot to drink. On the ill-fated hotel trip, there was a large amount of alcohol consumed, including eventually that weekend the entire contents of the mini bar. Apart from a sip of Champagne I hadn't drunk at all. Tonight she'd obviously she had a lot to drink at home before she'd even got in the car. What on earth was I going to tell the guys at fish and chips? Would they already know. Were we on YouTube?

Rick stared at me in disbelief when I described the sorry tale of what had happened at the golf club. He wasn't often lost for words.

I did add that the next day Shilpa had been full of apologies. My mobile phone filled up with texts from her, saying how terribly sorry she was and she knew that there was no chance of us having a relationship now. She even sent me flowers and chocolates!

"So she should be," said Rick who seemed genuinely concerned and upset for me. It had been a dreadful experience. "What did Martin say?" he asked.

Martin had been a true gentleman. He rang me the next day and tried to make light of it. "Don't worry, Simon," he said, "it was the best laugh we had in ages. I'm going to put the CCTV tape on YouTube. We'll make a fortune!"

Rick returned to his cod. Barry wasn't with us that night as he'd gone to a family party and as Rick demolished his large cod, large chips, mushy peas and bread and butter, his concern degenerated into customary ridicule. "So, Simon,' he said, ruefully, "Let's have an audit of where you are then with all this dating. So far you've spent a small fortune going to Venice and meeting the Irish bird, encountered a bunch of saddoes including someone looking for a kitchen fitter at speed dating, been duped by a married bird on a dating site and my particular favourite – met a mad, frigid piss-head on a blind date."

I tried to argue, unsuccessfully, but Rick was right. That was the sum total of where I was. Whether having a serious relationship with Niamh was on the cards or not, I didn't know. I was very attracted to her but wasn't at all sure that she wanted a long-term relationship with me. Looking back the easiest thing to have done would have been to have asked her, but being me that was far too difficult.

Our usual long-suffering waitress came over and smiled. "Was that alright for you two?"

"Yes, thanks," we spoke in unison. As I said goodbye to Rick in the car park, I decided I had to do something positive and sort myself out a proper girlfriend. I fired up the computer. If you sign up for a dating agency on line, you tend to get invitations from associated sites. And since I had actually been to an *Across the Room* event, apart from the speed dating evening, I was still receiving regular emails from them, inviting me now to one of their formal dinners or to join their bespoke introduction service. I had registered for further information about the dinners. What I received looked interesting. There were a series of attractive local venues with forthcoming organized events. I found my credit card and paid to go to their next dinner dance. It was at a hotel on the Essex/Hertfordshire border – the next day! I'd already paid the annual fee for the Club so the cost was for the dinner booking. I still wasn't ready yet for further details of the bespoke introduction service. An e-mail came back immediately confirming my place.

I went to bed that night wondering if I might finally meet someone. That would shut Rick up!

I thought of Niamh, as I often did at bedtime. Would I see her again? I missed having contact with her but I felt optimistic about the forthcoming dinner. Could this be where I met my someone special? Where she might find me?

Across The Room

Dressing for this one was easy, I got out my 'Graham Norton.' The only other decision was whether to wear a wing collar or a normal collared evening shirt. I settled on the latter, a satin bow tie and got out my best Kurt Geiger evening shoes. Freshly showered, shaved and doused in after shave I headed off towards Stansted airport and the *Down Hall Hotel*. I'd been there once before for a conference and although it's only probably about ten miles from Stansted airport, as the crow flies, it's tricky to find and the satnav was struggling. Elton was constantly being interrupted by commands. "At the next roundabout, go straight on and take first exit" and "In a hundred yards, go straight". What on earth does that mean, how can you go straight on and take first exit?

Of course I do know why most sat navs are confusing. It's because they are engineered by Americans, a race who have never seen a roundabout and for whom every road is straight. How they hit the moon with their satellite systems I'll never know, but to my relief, the imposing pillars of the entrance gates were soon in my headlamps.

I struggled to park as there were a lot of guests. As usual, I was early. The dinner was 7.30pm for 8pm and it was 7.20. I had time to sit in my car and take in the view. I was slightly wary about going in early and bumping into another Jim and what about Mary? Had she managed to escape from Jim's clutches?

I was too anxious to sit outside for long and made my way into the hotel's entrance hall. After registering with Eleanor I was handed a glass of champagne. Everyone was dressed up. There were so many fabulous dresses! I had to have a good chance of cracking it this time I thought, there was bound to be somebody here I'd get on with.

Over the rim of my Champagne glass I scanned the room. As I was standing with the other "suits" or rather "penguins" as we were all dressed formally in evening wear, it became apparent that several of us were looking at one particular lady.

She had long, dark brown hair, which reached almost to her waist, a black evening dress which was a fishtail type design, halter neck with a deep V at the back, edged with what looked like diamonds. She had on a fantastic pair of Christian Louboutin high-heeled evening shoes. I love those shoes, the ones with the red soles, a bit overdone now but very sexy.

The Christian Lacroix shoes with the pink soles are more exclusive now apparently. 'How well would they go with pink knickers?' I thought.

The chap next to me had noticed me looking, "She's not bad, is she?" he commented.

I turned to one side and smiled, "No, not at all." This guy was older than me, maybe in his sixties, distinguished looking, a full head of white hair, expensively dressed. I'd already clocked the gold Rolex and Jaguar key ring. "Yes she is, rather," I said. "I'm Simon," I said, offering a hand.

"Bill," he said, tucking his Jaguar key ring into the pocket of his dinner jacket. "You won't get anywhere with her," he said, "She doesn't even dance with people. She'll probably go after the meal."

Bill, I learned, was a regular attendee at the dinners and he filled me in on what to expect of the night to come. I knew this from the website information write up but I let him tell me anyway. "You see what happens, Simon, is that we guys move round the tables, so everyone's got a place to sit. After the first course you'll move to another table for your main and another for your dessert. Everyone has a dance card and you ask the women on the left of you and the right of you on each table for a dance so when the music starts you'll have six partners to dance with. After that it's a free for all."

"Oh right," I said. "Dance card." remembering those military college dances of the early 1970s. I decided to pump Bill for information about the lady in the Christian Louboutin shoes. "Do you know her?" I asked.

"Well I've sat next to her a few times he said. "Louise," he said, "gives very little away conversation wise."

"She's very attractive," I said. Louise now was standing with her back to me, she had a lovely figure, very curvaceous and she looked slightly tanned as if she'd just come back from holiday.

I decided against a second glass of Champagne as I was driving and stuck to orange juice. I was relieved not to bump into Jim and mildly disappointed to see that Mary wasn't in attendance. I was feeling relaxed and confident as the gong sounded and we were ushered into the main dining room, lavishly decorated with warm toned furnishings, fresh flowers and chandeliers dimmed to cast a flatteringly soft glow. The effect was enhanced by candlelit tables. It was impressive. There was a table plan as we went in and I quickly found my name.

"Where are you then, Simon?" Bill said to me.

"Um, table 5, I said."

"Oh," he said, "you're honoured."

"Why's that?" I said.

"A single digit table number means you are most favoured. You never know, you might be sat next to the lovely Louise."

I tried to find her name on the list but was manoeuvred out of the way by other guests thronging into the hall trying to locate their seats. There were at least thirty tables and it took me a little while to locate table 5. I found my place, having glanced at the names next to me. I wasn't sitting next to Louise but perhaps she'd be sitting elsewhere at the table. I checked myself, I was here to have a good time not just settle on meeting one lady I'd happened to notice. If what Bill said was true, I didn't stand a chance with her anyway.

The lady to my right arrived; she was a "jolly hockey sticks" type, probably a few dress sizes up from Louise, with very short, almost cropped, grey hair. She introduced herself, sat down and then ignored me for the rest of the evening. I don't even remember her name. Obviously something in my "Hello, I'm Simon" must have offended her as she just sat hunched up with the guy next to her.

Fortunately the lady on my left was sociable and friendly. Caroline was a GP. She was charming and had a sweet heart shaped face, lovely blue eyes. She wore an elaborate evening dress which I guessed was probably quite expensive but apologised for her appearance explaining that she'd come straight from her surgery, changed in a room at the hotel in haste and apart from a dab of lipstick hadn't had time to put any make up on. She kept running her fingers through her hair, saying, "I didn't have time to do anything, I must look a right state!"

She didn't and I told her so. I explained I was new to the dinner scene but believed that it was etiquette that I should ask her to dance and place her name on my dance card. I said I hoped this was okay but explained that it was only fair to warn her that I was an inept dancer and there was a reasonable prospect that she'd require medical attention from being trod on or worse, knocked over.

"That's alright Simon," she said, "I appreciate the risk assessment but I'll be pleased to dance with you. After all, I have ready access to bandages and splints if necessary!" As the lady to my right had spent the whole time with her back to me I decided that I wouldn't even enquire whether she wanted to dance. The first course – smoked salmon – was over and the seasoned operatives on the table were now glancing at the next table they wanted to sit at.

You see, that's the trick: although at the "starter" table everyone has a designated place, at the second and third tables, the men fit in where there is a space between ladies. Being a newcomer to the dinners and dim, this was lost on me. I spent so long saying goodbye to Caroline that there was only one space at the next table between two women who knew one another. In fact they knew each other so well they carried on their conversation across me throughout the entirety of the first course – Chicken Kiev. I am not a fan of this dish. Quite what the appeal of a chicken breast stuffed with molten garlic sauce, the temperature of lava is I don't know? Whilst it was demoralizing to find myself between women who barely spoke to me, it gave me an opportunity to observe those dining at surrounding tables. To my delight I noticed that the lovely Louise was seated at the table I was destined to move to for dessert.

My aim was to finish the main course and sprint over to bag a seat next to Louise. Unusually, it was an oblong table and Louise was sitting on the end. Another lady was seated opposite her, so there was effectively only one seat next to Louise. That was the seat on which I had set my sights. As Eleanor was getting to her feet to announce the change, I was up and running but as in most things I am a mere amateur and far too polite. Somewhere in the maze of tables and chairs, I lost my advantage and ended up sitting about as far away from Louise as was possible.

A lady opposite who looked pretty fed up, told me a litany of her troubles (work/relationship/children problems) I nodded feigning interest whilst stabbing irritably at my Pavlova, when she finished her tale of woes she simply disappeared. There wasn't anyone to my right and the lady on my left was another "back turner", so out of a possible six dances I only had one name. What on earth would Rick say?

Was it was my imagination however or was I being idiotically optimistic? I thought I'd noticed Louise glance in my direction a couple of times and smile. Or was she squinting?

Coffee was served and dispensed with and the music started. Eleanor was on her feet again explaining that the men should now be heading back to the first person on their dance card. In my case the only person on my dance card. Caroline. She was waiting at table 5 for me and we took to the dance floor.

"I've never danced with a GP before," I said. She was an excellent dancer, took decisive steps which I found easy to follow and we managed a couple of uneventful laps to "Shall We Dance?" then headed for the bar. To my surprise Caroline ordered a Scotch and when I asked how she took it, she said, "Straight up." I smiled remembering how Katie drank hers. I had an orange juice. Caroline observed, "So you're not drinking, then?"

"No," I said, "I rarely touch the stuff."

She smiled. "Liar."

"No," I said, "I'm really not tonight. I'm driving. You?"

"No, I'm staying."

"Oh I didn't think that was an option."

"Yes," she said, "when you book, you can book accommodation and *Across the Room* do it all for you."

We weren't supposed to be seated in the bar at this point, but I was relieved to notice that Caroline hadn't made it onto anyone else's dance card either and spending time chatting to her restored my faith in the evening. She was good company. But a part of me (and you can guess which part) was keen to make Louise's acquaintance. Caroline became engaged in conversation with a chap that she knew who'd joined us at the bar and I excused myself and went back into the main dining room where the dancing was in progress.

The lovely Louise was heading off the dance floor and in the direction of the bar, within a couple of seconds she would be in front of me. I quickly tried to gather myself and find James Bond or Hugh Grant. I had to say something, but what? She was now only a few steps away. She looked fantastic. She had a deliberate walk, confident, head held high, chest out and I decided to go for it.

"Err, hello," I said, grinning. It wasn't James Bond or Hugh Grant, but a slightly distracted Basil Fawlty. Fortunately it didn't put her off replying.

"Hello," she said, "are you new?"

"No, I'm Simon," I said rather stupidly.

"I'm Louise," she said.

I very nearly blurted out, "Yes, I know!" but fortunately didn't. "Are you heading to the bar?" I enquired "If so, I'd be happy to come with you and buy you a drink."

"Well," said Louise, "that's very kind of you, but I am actually going to the Ladies and you definitely can't come in there with me. I've still got a couple of dances left but maybe you could buy me that drink later. That would be very nice of you," and she smiled. Without waiting for a reply, she strode off to the cloakroom.

I wanted to shout out "Jurassic Park!" (Like Alan Partridge!) Not only had I spoken to Louise, I was going to have a drink with her. All I had to do now was while away a few numbers before what's known as the "free dancing" starts. I was beginning to enjoy myself and so it seemed was everyone else. Many of those at the dinner dance were staying overnight at the hotel and enjoying the opportunity to drink and relax. It was also apparent that lots of the guests knew one another – a singles event for singles but also couples and groups of friends. I later learned some people continued to attend events organized by *Across the Room* even though they were in relationships with partners they had met through being registered.

Eleanor came up to me and asked how I was getting on.

"Great," I said.

"You didn't dance much, Simon."

I decided not to enlighten her about my dinner companions, but I said that I was looking forward to dancing with Louise later.

She looked slightly quizzical. "You've met Louise, then?"

"Well, briefly," I said, "I wasn't sitting next to her during the meal, but I'm hoping to have a drink and a dance with her later."

Eleanor hesitated. I sensed she wanted to say something. I looked at her directly and wondered if I should ask her if there was something I should know.

Caroline then joined us and the moment was lost. "I saw you two dancing earlier," said Eleanor. The sub-text seemed to be "Are you going to hit it off? Do I need to go and buy a hat?" Caroline and I laughed, but I only had eyes for Louise, who had returned from the ladies. She brushed past me like a perfumed goddess, touched my arm and said, "As soon as I finish these dances, we can have that drink."

'Cosmic,' I thought, 'lovely jubbly. I'm getting good at this,' I congratulated myself. 'I'm very lucky, she is so lovely.'

It wasn't long before Louise walked into the bar, it could have been a scene from a film and if this were one it would be the simplest scene to shoot. I'm sitting on a bar stool and Louise comes into the bar looking for me. As our eyes meet she walks over and takes the seat next to me. She gives me a look as if to say "Well, what happens now?" She was there beside me now.

On cue, my nerves returned. "Err, what would you like a drink?" I mumbled.

"Well, I'll have a glass of Champagne if you're asking," she said.

I know I shouldn't have done so but I ordered two glasses. We clinked glasses and she spoke, "Well, nice to meet you Simon, I take it this is your first do?"

I did my usual gushing: "Yesthisisthefirstdoivebeentoandireallythink it'swonderfulyoulookeeversolovelyandiloveyourdress."

Louise was taken aback, unsurprisingly, but just said, "Thanks, I wasn't sure about the dress, it's a bit tricky to sit down in."

"Why's that?" I said.

She gave me a slightly cross look and said "Well, it's got a split right up the front, in case you hadn't noticed."

Oh, I'd noticed alright.

"And I'm worried my boobs are going to fall out of the side." She was remarkably candid and I relaxed. We started to talk. About family, jobs, music. She worked as a PA to a Managing Director of a large department store. She'd two children, similar ages to mine, and although she didn't look it, she was well into her forties.

I completely lost track of the time. I was captivated by her. I could see behind her in the bar several guys who seemed to be trying to attract her attention. Two actually approached her and asked if she would like to dance, completely ignoring me.

'How rude!' I thought. I mean, I do understand it is a singles event, but I was clearly engaged in a conversation with her. Was I perhaps being unfair by monopolizing her? Then I shook myself. "Faint heart" and all that.

I could hear the DJ playing slow songs next door and I leapt at my chance to hold Louise in my arms. "Would you like to dance?" I asked.

"Love to," she replied and soon we were slowly rocking gently together to the sound of "I Only Have Eyes for You", the Art Garfunkel number. I was thrilled, intoxicated by her. She leaned in pressing against me. I was worried that I was starting to get an erection. I was. I moved away from her, but Louise held me close, looked into my eyes and said "You're pleased to see me then?"

It was half past one in the morning. Most guests had left or were seated on the outer fringes of the room or at the bar. We stayed on the dance floor. All slow dances now. I'd told Louise I needed the practice and she had laughed. The hotel staff eventually began putting chairs on tables signalling comprehensively that the night, so far as they were concerned, was truly over. Bill had left earlier, pulling on his coat he gave me thumbs up as he left and headed towards his Jaguar.

Eleanor interrupted us: "We're off now, you two seem to be enjoying yourselves," she said. It was time to go. I didn't ask about seeing her again, I just jotted down my mobile phone number on a piece of paper. Louise did the same thing, we'd already established that we wanted to see each other again. She lived in Billericay in Essex which wasn't too far from me, it was a "no brainer".

We even sorted out where and when we'd meet during the week and as I got to her car with her she kissed me full on the lips and said "Can't wait to see you again Simon."

I flew home. My Alfa had wings. I couldn't sleep, I couldn't eat the next morning. I must have texted her fifty or sixty times by the time our Wednesday dinner date arrived. Rick had been less than enthusiastic as I gushed about Louise on the phone to him.

"So what's this one called then?" he said indistinctly as usual eating something as he took the call.

'Why does he do that? I must ask him,' I thought. "Louise," I said.

"Oh right, what does she do?" he said casually.

"She's a PA," I replied. I was tempted to say ,"Try picking holes in that!"

"Another Piss Artist, well you don't want one of those again; I'd have thought you'd had enough of that with the mad Indian one."

"No," I said getting irritated. "She's a Personal Assistant."

"Who does she personally assist?" Rick said.

"I don't know why we're doing this," I said. "You're not interested are you?"

"Yeah, yeah I am," he said. "Who does she look like?" said Rick, feigning interest.

"Well, I'm glad you asked that," I said, "I think she looks a bit like Kelly Brook."

"Oh I like her," said Rick, suddenly sounding more interested, "she's got enormous tits!"

"Well I'm having dinner with her tomorrow night," I said, "and I can't wait. And before you ask, there's no need for you to sit by your phone. I won't be having a plumbing emergency, but I will text you if it all goes well."

"Alright old boy I'll look forward to the code word. Tsunami."

The next evening I was sitting in a lay by in Billericay. Quite why I was in a lay by and not pulling up outside Louise's house, I didn't know. Maybe it was me being too forward again, she clearly didn't want me to know where she lived. She'd made a rather lame excuse about her daughter being at home. I fully acknowledge that involving teenage children can prove tricky in the early exploratory days of dating but there was something about this arrangement that seemed a bit odd and looking back it was a sign that perhaps Louise wasn't quite what she seemed.

We headed off to a small French restaurant after Louise sauntered up to the passenger door of my car, leaving her own in the layby. It must have looked strange to passers-by. But the meeting and meal were a success. We got on really well, had plenty in common and similar likes/dislikes.

She enjoyed reading and we discovered we shared a favourite author, F Scott Fitzgerald of *Great Gatsby* fame. Elton was amongst her favourite singer/songwriters. She enjoyed watching old films; travelling; walking; eating fish and chips. She laughed, I laughed and soon it was chucking out time.

Back in the lay by I leant over for a kiss, she pecked me on the cheek, grabbed the door handle, said, "Bye Simon," and disappeared into the night.

I felt a bit cheated, but shouldn't have done, after all this was only the second time I'd seen her. She was lovely. The next six weeks were full of dates with Louise. I forgot about work. I'd see her at lunchtimes, after work, we'd go to the cinema and one Sunday we went for a picnic at a local beauty spot, the reservoir at Hanningfield.

Going for a picnic can of course be romantic. When Louise suggested it I foolishly offered to do the food.

This was a problem when the time came to organize it as I didn't think that fish finger sandwiches would travel too well. I looked around the kitchen. An audit of the fridge revealed a Kitkat, a bottle of Champagne and a half empty tube of "squirty" cheese (with prawns). I had half a loaf of aged bread and some crackers too. The Champagne and Kit-Kat might come in handy but I had reservations about the cheese in a tube.

I was trying to finish an overdue assignment and I hadn't time to shop and organize a hamper of food. I rang the gym. I have to acknowledge that to most people phoning a gym for food wouldn't make much sense, but the staff at the restaurant there regarded me as "family" and I was sure they'd help out if they possibly could.

When I explained my dilemma and that I needed a few sandwiches, Rob, one of the chefs offered to assist. "Don't worry Simon we'll organize the picnic for you. Be ready in an hour."

The picnic provided a picture-perfect scene. The nice people from Mercedes had leant me a new SL sports car to write about, though I don't know why as I was two assignments behind already. Louise looked fantastic in a white cheesecloth dress, cork soled high-heeled sandals, and her long brown hair tied in a ponytail. She smelt gorgeous.

As she sat on the tartan rug overlooking the water at Hanningfield I wanted to sing. The gym had done a great job and not only provided a feast but everything we could possibly want for a refined upmarket picnic.

Proper wicker basket, china plates, linen serviettes, silverware. And the food – cucumber sandwiches, Spanish omelette, chicken satay, pork pies, homemade cake. They'd thoughtfully supplied a rug and even a couple of cushions from the restaurant for us to sit on. Louise's legs were bare. I'd learnt over the weeks that she used an expensive fake tan. It gave her a natural looking warm glow rather than an orange tint like David Dickinson or an Oompa Loompa.

As she sipped her Champagne and crossed her legs, I got a flash of her white thong. She always wore thongs. We talked and laughed. We never ran out of things to talk about and whilst this was delightful there was a problem developing. The only reason I knew anything about Louise's underwear was because of what she told me she wore and the occasional flash of it as she got out of the car. Louise's underwear was off limits.

In fact, apart from the odd peck on the cheek, there had been nothing more intimate between us. I had held her close several times and tried to caress her, but she had moved away before anything more could develop and did not encourage further contact. After a couple of weeks and a couple of dates I hinted at how much I would like to make love to her and her reply was, "Oh we've got plenty of time for that." After another couple of weeks went by I mentioned it again.

"I just take a little time to warm up."

The lack of Code "Tsunami" had of course alerted Rick and Barry to the situation.

Barry was pleased that I wasn't leaping into bed with Louise and that we were taking time to get to know one another. He didn't realize that it wasn't me taking my time, it was Louise. Over the last fish and chip supper Rick had remarked "Not got her knickers off then?"

I bristled and replied, tersely, "There's plenty of time for that Rick, she's explained to me that she just takes a while to warm up."

"Hmm," said Rick, taking aim at his cod, "you could say that, or you could say there's something wrong." And just as he speared himself onto a piece of cod, he said, "She's not a bloke is she?"

"Don't be ridiculous!" I said.

And whilst gazing at Louise sprawled out on the tartan rug it was blatantly apparent that she wasn't a bloke, I was getting very twitchy. I wanted her, I wanted her so much, I was beginning to feel slightly obsessed about this. I took every opportunity to be close to her. Though we didn't talk about sex, bizarrely we did discuss where we'd like to live, and looking back I recall going to look at a house with her.

I decided to broach the subject again. "We are getting on so well, Louise and I think the world of you."

Louise immediately held up her hand, "I know where this is going," she said, rather crossly. "This is about sex isn't it?"

"Well Louise, I would like to, wouldn't you?"

"You've made that quite clear and well, yes I would, but as I've explained, I just take a while to warm up," she replied. Sensing that I was getting annoyed and not wishing to ruin the day, she leaned close to me and said, "Soon, Simon."

"When?" I said.

Her answer surprised me. "Now!"

"Now?" I said. "What, on the rug?"

"No," she said, "We can go back to yours can't we?"

"Come on then," I said, scooping up the remains of the picnic, throwing the tartan rug in the boot of the Mercedes and pulling away before Louise was fully belted into the front passenger seat. "Steady on!" she exclaimed. "We want to get there in one piece."

I screeched to a halt outside the flat. Normally, I would have made sure that the roof was back in place on the Mercedes, but the 20 seconds it took to fold back into place seemed 20 seconds too long so I left it, bundled Louise into the lift (Yes! It was working) and less than 20 minutes from when Louise had said, "Go" we were in the bedroom back at the flat. We rolled around the bed kissing each other. As I dived for the buttons of her dress, Louise pushed my hands away, stood up from the bed and slowly and rather gracelessly undid her dress and let it fall to the floor. Underneath she had on a plain white bra and thong. She had a gorgeous body. Then something unusual happened. Instead of starting where we left off, Louise just lay face down on the bed next to me; I was distracted of course by her shapely bare bottom.

I started to caress the back of her neck and run my fingers down the back of her spine. I was so hard I was beginning to feel dizzy. Louise didn't move, didn't respond, what should I do? Should I carry on? So I did. I started to undo the strap of her bra and she moved away, then I moved my hand down to the back of her G-string and started to pull it down and that was it, something snapped! It wasn't her G-string. Louise leapt from the bed, "I'm sorry Simon I just can't do this."

Oh God not another Shilpa!

She threw on her dress, found her bag and left. I scrambled on clothes, followed and met her in the car park. She repeated herself over and again and seemed genuinely distressed.

"I'm sorry I just can't do this."

I said, "Don't worry; I'll drive you home," I was mentally retracing our encounter to see what I'd done wrong.

"No, no," she said. "I've a friend who lives nearby, Angela, I'll go and see her."

I thought this was odd. She'd never mentioned a friend living near mine before, but she had mentioned an "Angela". Stuff like "Angela and I went shopping" and "Angela makes lovely home-made ice cream". I'd assumed she was a work colleague.

"Are you sure?" I said, feeling bad. "What if she's not in? I'd be happy to run you home."

"No, no," she replied, and she marched off in the direction of the station.

Back in the flat I didn't know what to do. I felt awful. Tense, distracted and upset. Louise was perfect in so many ways but something wasn't right.. I couldn't work out what had gone wrong; I'd waited, been patient and it was her timetable in the end – she was the one who'd said "now" not me. I texted her, "Are you okay?"

After about an hour I got a reply. "Yes, I'm fine, I am sorry Simon and I will give you a ring tonight."

It was Sunday so I decided to head off to Mass. I needed to get out of the flat and wanted the comfort of going to church. There was another attraction. I'd been standing next to a lovely lady called Judy for several weeks. I'd also seen her in the gym and having coffee with friends in the restaurant. We hadn't really said anything to each other, just nodded and smiled in passing and on meeting at church. I think Judy assumed I was in a relationship with Shilpa because often when I was in the gym I talked to or went to the restaurant with her. But even Judy's charms couldn't cheer me up this Sunday evening. At half past eight Louise phoned. I gushed, "I'm so sorry, I'm so sorry."

Louise immediately silenced me and said, "No, I'm the one who's sorry and I'm the one who owes you an apology."

"I'm sure that's not the case," I said. "Why don't I come over and get you and we can talk about it?"

"No, Simon I just want you to listen."

Louise went on to explain in detail that since her early teens she'd had thoughts about sleeping with other women, which she suppressed. She'd married and had her two children. There had always been problems with sex with her husband and since they parted she'd had boyfriends. She'd also had girlfriends and of late I'd been the only boyfriend for a while. She'd also been "dating" as she put it, Angela and it seemed – to add insult to injury – she'd been having sex with her. Louise explained that she was confused; she still liked male company, she thought I was charming and wonderful, and "a lovely man". I was the first man she felt she might be able to contemplate a serious relationship with but she hadn't been sure. Sparing me nothing, she then went on to explain that actually being on the bed with me, she'd realised that she wanted Angela. She didn't want to have sex with me.

What could I say? I told her I was sorry and that I appreciated her explaining to me what the situation was and I wished her well. There was little else to say. I fell into bed exhausted and surprisingly slept rather well. I knew I was going to have to come clean with the guys, but put it off until the following Friday.

Rick's reaction was predictable: "Fucking bitch," he said. "What a fucking bitch!"

"It's not like that, Rick," I said.

"How is it not like that, Simon?" said Rick. "So she's a dyke, she knows she's a dyke and yet she's leading you on, couldn't she have told you beforehand and what about this introduction agency, I bet they knew!"

Remembering Eleanor's reaction on learning that I had become friends with Louse, it occurred to me that perhaps she knew something.

If she suspected Louise was bi-sexual or gay she would have been unable to tell me. She would have been bound to respect her privacy. And how would she know unless Louise had told her?

Louise had told me that she'd kept her relationships with women and Angela confidential. She hadn't been on any lesbian or bi-sexual dating sites. I wondered if there was a *Gay and Lesbian Across the Room* and if so whether in fact Louise was a registered member of both.

I tried to be annoyed, but I just couldn't. Louise and I are still friends and I have since accompanied her to her works Christmas "do". She hadn't felt that she wanted to introduce her girlfriend to colleagues. So I gained a friend, but was still on the quest for a girlfriend.

The Naming of Parts

For the next few weeks I felt pretty fed up. I'd had a few emails and texts from Niamh, mentioning vaguely that we should get together again, I couldn't even summon up much enthusiasm for her really. I'd made it up with Shilpa and we'd had the occasional coffee together, but romantically I'd lost interest in the dating websites. What to do?

The answer seemed to present itself when I received a letter from *Across the Room* inviting me to join their Introduction Agency. Though I had had reservations about the agency, I'd become reconciled to the obvious difficulty Eleanor would have had in disclosing personal information or concerns she might have had about Louise and I had no actual knowledge that she knew of Louise's bi-sexuality and lesbian leanings or relationship.

I filled the forms in, found a recent photo and posted it that afternoon. As an existing client I qualified for an introductory discount. It was quite a lot of money, but I'd come to the conclusion that I needed dedicated professional help in identifying a prospective partner My researches suggested that an agency that sought to match clients using comprehensive data made sense.

James had been in touch since my visit to his office and had met a lady he'd been seeing for nearly four months. He was clearly delighted with her and happily making plans for a long haul holiday a deux. He said that I should try an introduction agency even if this meant paying a sizeable fee.

Eleanor would personally select clients she thought would be suitable for me from the extensive database of clients that the company held. She would then forward comprehensive details and photographs so I could decide whether to make contact or seek alternative opportunities. This would continue until I met someone and we both wished to pursue a serious relationship. She would need to have more information from me and I needed to complete a series of profile questionnaires. I could dip in and out of the programme over a 36-month period. It seemed to be a no-lose situation.

'I could do with one of those,' I thought.

Once I had completed the profile information all I had to do was sit back and wait for the details to drop through my letterbox. I couldn't wait. I spent two hours completing a detailed profile, scanned four recent photographs and emailed the lot to Eleanor.

The next morning I found I had a letter from Ireland. It was from Niamh who explained that she had tried to call on a couple of occasions but hadn't got through, that her computer was being repaired, that she'd been unusually busy at the surgery and had decided to drop me a line. It was several months since my wonderful trip to see her in Ireland. She wrote that she was going to her parents in Dublin this weekend and would phone me on Sunday for a chat.

'Great!' I thought, maybe things with Niamh could work out after all. I phoned Rick.

"So the Irish bird's back on, is she?"

"Well I do like her," I said, "and I did have a wonderful time when I went to see her, so why not?"

Niamh explained when she called that Sunday that she had some holiday time owing and had a locum organised for a fortnight at the end of the month. If I had nothing else planned I was welcome to visit her in Ireland again or she could come over and see me. What did I want to do if anything?

Well, what *did* I want to do?

I thought of inviting her to stay with me but felt squeamish and inadequate about such an arrangement. After all I'd gone to see Niamh in a beautiful medieval city in Ireland and spent time in her lovely three-storey town house. She'd be coming to a modern new town in Essex to stay in a rather bizarre and oddly furnished flat. Then I had a brainwave. "Why don't we just dash off on holiday, I could do with a bit of sun." We had two weeks to organise it.

"That'd be great," said Niamh. "Seeing as my computer is broken, you organise it."

We quickly worked out the dates. I went online and two weeks later I found myself inside terminal 3 at Gatwick, waiting for Niamh to arrive from Dublin. I'd managed to find a weeklong holiday in Corfu and had booked it. In a series of planning phone calls, Niamh had explained that she'd been working twelve-hour days at the surgery and could really do with a holiday.

Rick had driven me to the airport, "What you going to fucking Corfu for?" he'd asked.

"Well it's quite simple Rick, Niamh has been working really hard..."

"Unlike you," he interjected.

"She's having some new equipment fitted at the surgery and she's got a week where she's got a locum in, so it makes sense to dash off on holiday."

"So it's all back on?" asked Rick.

"What do you mean?"

"The Irish bird is all back on." I knew what was coming. "You've finished with the mad Indian bird? Louise has decided to stick with her girlfriend, or should I say *lick* with her girlfriend?" Before I could answer Rick launched into one of his awful jokes.

"Oh, on that note, what do you call a lesbian dinosaur?"

"I don't know," I said, dreading what was coming.

"A Lickalotapus," he said. Then he leant over and nudged me with his elbow, the car swerving slightly on the M25. "Send that to Louise, I bet she knows."

"I don't know why we have to have these conversations," I said.

Rick wouldn't be deterred. "I do think it's quite funny though because you've actually confirmed that she really prefers girls."

"How do you work that out?" I said.

"Well, she's dating you and a girl and she's decided that the girl's better." Of course he was right.

"Anyway," I said, "that's all in the past now."

Rick said, "You've always really liked this Irish girl." And as we pulled up at Gatwick, he helped me with my bags and said, "Have a great time, I'll look after your car for you."

And here I was, Gatwick North Terminal and waiting for Niamh's plane to arrive. I didn't have to wait long. She looked different. Her hair was shorter: it was tucked behind one ear. She looked tired. Still lovely. She wore white linen trousers, flat, white and gold sandals and a navy, cotton jacket and white tee shirt, in holiday mode.

There wasn't long to go before we were checking in for our Corfu flight. I'd never been there though I had travelled to mainland Greece years before with Katherine, I doubted that Corfu was going to be very different.

Niamh had been before with a girlfriend, the phrase "with a girlfriend" gave me slight pause for thought but I decided not to be paranoid and definitely not to tell Rick.

The flight to Corfu took just over three hours and as we settled into our seats, I realised that the seating arrangement was slightly unusual. I was seated next to the window, Niamh next to me and there was a third, as yet unoccupied seat. But in front of me the row of seats was offset so I could easily get out of my seat and walk past it with the fuselage on the left and get past Niamh. Shortly before the plane took off, an elderly gentleman occupied the third seat, he was smartly dressed and immediately started chatting to Niamh, ignoring me.

"And what part of the Emerald Isle are you from?" he asked.

Niamh explained that she was from Waterford; somewhere he knew, and they chatted for a while. He didn't introduce himself to me, speak to me or even look at me.

'How rude,' I thought. And Niamh was making no attempt to introduce me either.

Feeling slightly irritated, I decided to start my book. I'd bought the new James Bond continuation novel *Devil May Care*, by Sebastian Faulks at the airport. It was engrossing and the flight passed quickly.

As we were disembarking from the aircraft Niamh explained to me that the elderly gentleman was on a regimental reunion and that he knew Ireland and she'd reminded him of his daughter.

'How lovely,' I thought. Obviously I didn't remind him of anybody.

Corfu, if you haven't been, is lovely. The landscape is a combination of lush green and scorched barren brown. It was very hot. The hotel was oddly built, effectively in two parts, the beach side where we checked in and a larger, more modern part, which was to my disappointment on the other side of a main road.

It was even worse than that: it was a main road disappearing around a bend. We had to take our life in our hands to get to our room, which was comfortable and reasonably furnished, but accessed via a lift and then a landing. The prospect of dicing with death every morning to get to the beach or the dining room didn't appeal. I decided to see if we could move rooms.

The receptionist was unsympathetic. "Well, this is the room you booked," she declared.

"Yes, I know," I said, "but I didn't realize it was going to be the other side of the road."

"It's stated clearly in the e-mail and in our terms and conditions." In fairness it was, but obviously I hadn't read them.

Fortunately Niamh intervened, performed a charm offensive on the receptionist who agreed we could move for a small additional fee to a bungalow on the beach. We had a look and it was ideal. It was effectively a detached room, with a large bed, a small veranda outside and a bathroom and it was on the edge of the beach.

The hotel arranged for our bags to be moved across and as it was late afternoon Niamh and I decided to take a walk into town. I can't remember what it was called, but it was about fifteen minutes along a busy road.

There don't seem to be any traffic laws in Corfu. Cars, trucks and sometimes coaches would be weaving in and out of pedestrians, motor cyclists, tourists on scooters, but it seemed to work and at least whilst we were there, we didn't witness any dreadful accidents. Finding a bar, which wasn't too difficult, I decided to try the local wine, Niamh did indicate that I would regret it, but nonetheless I went ahead.

"Cheers," I said to Niamh, "happy holidays! You do realize, holidays are what we seem to do? After all, we met in Venice and here we are in Corfu."

"Yes," said Niamh, taking a gulp, "here's to a wonderful holiday, Simon." Then surprisingly she took on a sterner look and said, "Now Simon, I think we need a few rules."

'This will be fun,' I thought. I hadn't seen Niamh in a schoolmistress type of way.

"I don't get much holiday and I'm unlikely to go on holiday for the rest of the year, so I do just want to rest."

"Fine with me," I said, "and I've brought a few books and my laptop and I will need to do some work."

It wasn't going quite as well as I thought, but no matter.

"We're all inclusive aren't we?" said Niamh.

"Yes," I said, "we are."

"Well why don't we try and eat out every other night to see a bit of Corfu?"

"All fine so far," I said.

It was going to be fantastic. Why had I been so impatient? I should have realized that Niamh was so busy and had little time or energy after work to call. She was not as keen on e-mailing and texting as I was. Why hadn't I just waited for her? Been more relaxed? She was clearly the one. I didn't want to tell her but I'd already been checking out house prices in Ireland, I couldn't believe how expensive they were!

As we wandered back to the hotel, we had a look at a small gift shop and Niamh purchased two or three post cards. I'm rubbish at writing postcards. I buy them but never write them.

"Who are they for?" I asked as we wandered along the busy road, dodging buses and cars.

"Mum and Dad," she said, "my sister and a girlfriend."

I flinched again. I decided to change the subject.

"Ah," I said, trying to be serious and probably sounding again like John Alderton. "Do you think I should have a contact number for your Mum and Dad or your Sister? Maybe you should have the number of my children or Rick."

"Why?" said Niamh, suddenly a little frosty.

"Well, in case there's an accident or something or you were unwell. Wouldn't it be sensible for me to have a contact number?"

"I'll be fine," said Niamh.

I thought I was just being sensible. The prospect of an imminent collision with one of the cars hurtling towards us seemed to focus my mind on accidents.

Dinner that night was a buffet arrangement in the hotel: Greek meats, lots of salads, yogurts and local resinated wine. After a few glasses I started to get used to it though I wasn't sure if I would grow to actually like it. We walked back along the beach to our bungalow arm in arm and Niamh showered; she liked to shower.

As it was so warm she simply wore a pair of what I call "bed knickers" and a sleeveless cotton top. I didn't quite realise how tired I was and Niamh had said the same thing, so we did have sex, not as enthusiastically as we had before but still lovely. I was so pleased to be with her. I noticed that she had a particular smell, it was a pleasant smell. It wasn't strawberries like Georgina Grey from school, Niamh always smelt so fresh.

One advantage of our Corfu location was that there was little street lighting, I could see the stars clearly through the patio doors of the bungalow as I listened to the waves gently crashing on the beach. This was going to be great holiday, I thought. The boys at the fish and chip shop would be so jealous. I fell soundly asleep. The next morning I woke early, Niamh was still asleep and I decided not to disturb her. I grabbed some shorts and a tee shirt and headed out onto the beach.

To the right of the bungalow, towards the main part of the hotel, I could see the hotel staff preparing for breakfast. You could either eat inside the hotel or on one of the small tables set out on the beach itself.

I ran into the sea and had a swim. The water was completely transparent, the sand was golden almost white and looking back at Corfu from the sea, it was much greener than I had realised on the drive through from the airport.

Looking out to sea, we were very close to some mountainous land, I tried to work out what it was, mainland Greece? It turned out to be Albania and later a waiter explained that during the communist occupation of Albania lots of people tried to swim the short distance across, but it's not as easy as it looked. Very strong currents and very deep water meant that many were not seen again. But the ones that did make it quickly found work, shelter and a new life in Corfu.

By the time I had got back to the bungalow Niamh was in the shower. She came out of the bathroom with a towel wrapped round her and a turban around her head. Why do women do that, is it something they teach you at school? I've never known any man able to do it. "Morning," she said, bright and breezy in a very Irish way.

"Morning Niamh, I've just been for a swim. The guy was telling me it's Albania over there."

"Really?" said Niamh. She pulled on a bikini and fastened a sarong around her waist, grabbed her hat and we were soon arm in arm walking along the beach to breakfast. We opted for one of the tables on the beach. It was delightful but you had to help yourself to fruit juice and coffee which I found rather annoying since there were a lot of waiters about. Niamh confirmed that she wanted fruit juice and coffee so I headed off into the main part of the hotel.

There was a small queue at the juice machine and as I struck up a half conversation with a German guest. I looked back at Niamh and waved. She waved back. There was something in her hand: it was a pen. Then she looked down and started to write. She's writing her post cards, I thought.

When I returned to the table, complete with a couple of glasses of juice and some coffees on a small tray, Niamh seemed slightly distracted and as though she wanted to say something. Oh boy, did she want to say something.

Almost on cue, Niamh straightened in her seat, looked straight at me and said "There's something I want to talk to you about, Simon."

'Oh God,' I thought. 'I can't be in trouble already surely? We've only just got here!'

"Something wrong?" I asked.

"Uh, no," said Niamh. "But I think we should be honest with one another and I wanted to talk to you about last night."

Last night, last night, I was scrabbling in my brain, what had happened last night? We'd had dinner and we'd had sex. Instead of keeping my mouth shut like a normal person, I opened it and said, "Well, all fine with me!" and gave her a thumbs up, rather stupidly.

"Yes, said Niamh, "that's what I wanted to talk to you about."

I couldn't believe what I heard next. Niamh went on to explain that we'd had lots of sex when I saw her in Ireland but she'd wanted to say something then and as we were going to be spending a full week together, she felt that she should explain what she wanted.

It was a very direct conversation, although not really a conversation as I wasn't really saying anything. Niamh was explaining that she was enjoying sex with me, she had no difficulty in reaching orgasm, I nodded politely at this stage, but she felt that well, it's difficult to put into words really, I'm still not entirely sure what she meant, but she seemed to be criticizing me for thrusting too hard once inside her. I mean, I'm no expert, but thrusting is all part of sex surely? But if that's what she wanted, or didn't want, then I'd be happy to go along with it.

Just when I thought this embarrassing conversation was drawing to a close, Niamh turned over a piece of paper in front of her, it turned out to be a paper serviette.

'That would explain the pen,' I thought.

Niamh wasn't writing post cards to her friends or parents, she was drawing a detailed sketch of her vagina. I stared at it: I couldn't believe she'd actually drawn it in some detail and even arrows with a narrative naming of parts. Niamh's lips were moving, the ones on her face that is, I wasn't taking in what she was saying, it was all to do with more pressure here, less pressure there.

I just wanted the conversation to end and I just finished it with, "Well, whatever you want me to do or don't want me to do just let me know." I felt like adding, "At the appropriate time, not at breakfast with a diagram."

Quickly Niamh turned from gynaecologist back to Niamh again. "Now what shall we do today?" she said.

I was still stunned. I was going to say "Well, how about sun, sea and sex?" but I didn't. "Just relax," I said.

"Great idea," she said, "I'll make a start on my book."

I've told this story to pretty much anyone who will listen and the women I've related it to fall into two camps. One camp's view is "Good on her, she's telling you exactly what she wants and ramming it home with a diagram" (excuse the pun). The other groups' opinion? "Well, yes she was right to say what she wanted, but it was not the right time or place and a diagram, well it's just not necessary." Of course I told Rick on my return. I expected unalloyed scorn or perhaps rage. Rarely does he double up with laughter, but he did on this occasion. When he had regained his composure he said, "What, you're that bad at it she had to draw you a fucking diagram, literally?"

Back on Corfu, the rest of the day passed without incident and nothing was mentioned about the diagram. We spent the day by the bungalow stretched out, reading, drinking, sunbathing.

I went for an occasional dip in the sea. I'd look up from the sea just to see Niamh reading her book, waving occasionally. She'd brought a few dental manuals with her and made it quite clear she didn't want to have any conversation whilst she was reading these as they were continuing professional development texts, which was fine.

That evening we decided to go into the local town again for dinner. Niamh had put on a bright blue sundress, with a halter neck, she had already begun to catch the sun and looked wonderful, her slightly freckly complexion aglow as she sat down opposite me in the restaurant.

We'd had sex just before we came out to dinner, I'd taken Niamh from behind as she knelt on the bed. I had felt inhibited and didn't quite know what to do. Whether to carry on; whether she'd tell me if I was doing something wrong or not. I tried to recall her diagram and directions. Once I'd entered Niamh I decided to let her have control and without saying anything she took the initiative and pushed her body back against me. At least this was out of the way.

I was tempted to ask for the diagram for my own continuing professional development and then I realised that the serviette must have gone back into the kitchen by mistake. I wondered if they'd seen it and thought it was some sort of comment on their food; perhaps we'd better avoid the dining room from now on!

The following few days were similar in pattern; we'd get up; go to breakfast; return to the bungalow; read, swim and sunbathe all day until it was time to get ready for dinner. Sex was lovely and I forgot my inhibitions and the diagram. I felt I was beginning to get to know Niamh slowly though I still felt she was being reserved. Sharing a small space like a hotel room for a week served to highlight the fact that we didn't know each other that well.

The mobile phone signal in Corfu was intermittent, but I still managed to send texts to the children, the guys from the fish and chip shop, my two uncles and Martin.

Niamh didn't touch her phone at all, it remained inside the safe in the room. She certainly wasn't keen to keep in touch with anyone from the old country. What happened next took me by surprise. Behind the bungalows, towards the road, there was a small pool, so if guests didn't fancy going in the sea they could have a dip in the pool. Being more fidgety and sociable than Niamh I wandered back and forth from the pool, to the sea, to the bungalow several times. I'd achieved nodding acquaintance with several of the guests, including a friendly German from breakfast the first day.

One day on a trip to the pool I noticed a guy just sitting on the side, sunbathing. As I walked past I looked at him and smiled.

"Hello there," he said in a broad Irish accent.

"Hello," I said, "you're Irish." Stating the obvious.

"Yes I am," he said.

I offered my hand "Hello, I'm Simon."

"I'm Pat," he said.

"Oh my girlfriend is Irish," I said. I didn't know whether to call Niamh my girlfriend or not, but what else could I say?

"Oh really," he said. "Where's she from?"

"Waterford," I replied.

"I'm from Dublin."

"Oh, her parents are from Dublin I said. Come and say hello."

Now perhaps I should have stopped and thought. Here was a complete stranger and I was taking him to introduce him to Niamh, who had already told me she wants to read her book and not be disturbed on holiday.

On turning the corner Niamh looked up from her book. "Niamh, I want you to meet someone," I said.

Niamh tipped her sunglasses on top of her head but said nothing.

"This is, err, Pat."

Niamh took a long while to answer. "Hello Pat," she said rather coolly eventually.

Pat offered a hand, but Niamh didn't take it.

"I'm from Dublin," he said.

"Really?" said Niamh.

"I understand you're from Waterford?"

"I am," said Niamh, decidedly frostily.

I realised I'd made a mistake.

We both just stood there. Niamh remained lying on the sun lounger. Without saying a word she tipped her glasses back into place and started to read again. I didn't know what to do.

None of this seemed to bother Pat though I felt very awkward, he simply said, "Well, nice meeting you, see you for a drink sometime."

As he wandered off Niamh said nothing, just carried on reading. Sensing another diagram coming on I decided to head for a swim.

"I'm just off for a swim," I said, "Perhaps you'd like a drink when I get back?"

"Ah ha," said Niamh, not glancing back. When I got back from my swim I started to dry myself off and changed into some shorts.

"Shall I go and get us a drink?" I said to Niamh, expecting her to give her usual reply of "Yes please, I'll have a Diet Coke."

But on this occasion she slammed her book shut, disappeared into the bathroom, came out wearing a cream see through sun dress over her bikini, picked up her bag, grabbed my arm and we walked into the hotel. Shunning the outside bar and heading for the corners of what can only be described as a snug, Niamh seemed to soften and taking a gulp of sparkling wine, she said, "I'm sorry about that Simon, I'm very wary of lone Irishmen."

Niamh went on to explain that her family had been involved in an incident in Northern Ireland. That's all she would tell me apart from the fact that although nothing had happened to them, as a young teenager at the time, she had been acutely aware that Ireland was a divided country and people were dying for being on the wrong side. She wouldn't elaborate. She also said, "That guy knew I was Irish as well, because he was behind me in the gift shop the other day. Why didn't he introduce himself then?"

I nodded and apologized, I had no idea that she had all these worries and wondered whether the troubles are still an issue for many?

Niamh seemed remote and she seemed to be drifting to that unhappy place – the memory of the "incident". Then, collecting herself, she drained her glass, plonked it noisily on the table and said, "Right, let's get ready for dinner, where are we off to?"

We didn't really have much of a plan. Instead of turning right out of the bungalow and walking along the beach to the main part of the hotel, this evening we turned left and just walked hand in hand. Niamh wore a gorgeous salmon-coloured sundress and had tied her hair back with a pink hair scrunchy. She carried her shoes. I too was barefoot carrying my sandals. We came across a small restaurant, family run and beachside on a wooden terrace with white table cloths and the usual jugs of wine replacing wine bottles.

As we ate the tensions of the day lifted.

"So, barring lone Irishmen, are you having a good time?"

Niamh smiled and said, "Yes of course, I am, I'm having a wonderful time."

"Well, it will be hard to say goodbye at Gatwick," I said."

"Yes, it will, said Niamh, "but we've both got work to do and we'll have to return to our normal lives, so let's just enjoy it while we can."

My anxiety returned. It was Thursday evening and we were leaving on Saturday. While I'd grown closer to Niamh, the 'L' word hadn't been mentioned. Of course it had been mentioned in intimate moments in as much as "I love that" and "you are lovely", but the "I love you" phrase remained unsaid.

Was I in love with Niamh? Looking at her across the table it would be difficult to imagine that any man couldn't be. I was trying to force the issue and looking back I realized this and that I should have relaxed and allowed things to develop between us – or not? I'd seen Niamh in several situations. Seeing her tense and anxious about the lone Irishman today and angry with me, I thought that this could be Niamh as cross as she would probably be likely to become. But oh boy, was I wrong! Tomorrow was another day entirely.

It started without issue. I'd received a few texts including one from Shilpa that arrived at a fairly inappropriate moment. It was only a friendly enquiry asking how I was and when would I be back and had I forgiven her for the golf club incident. I didn't tell Niamh the text was from Shilpa so she may have thought it was from a girlfriend as I'd normally announce who texts were from, the children, Rick or Barry. This time I didn't.

I sent a text message to her, saying, "Yes, forgiven, back Saturday."

Shilpa replied immediately saying, "Great, perhaps we can have a coffee together?"

I should have left it there of course, but I replied "Looking forward to it."

Why was I doing this? Here I am contemplating being in love with Niamh then agreeing to have coffee with Shilpa. It occurred to me that Shilpa had made the transition from girlfriend to friend and I reasoned that I couldn't see anything wrong with it. I still didn't discuss the texts or Shilpa with Niamh however. After breakfast Niamh slipped into her white bikini. Her skin was tanned and shone as she applied oil and stretched out languorously on a sun lounger on our decking.

It was an exceptionally hot day. I pottered about the beach and the pool and dipped in and out of my book. Niamh remained on the lounger toasting under the hot sun and reading. We had a couple of drinks, a light lunch, served at the bungalow on its veranda. At about three o'clock, I had a long swim and dried in the sunshine in moments. When I returned to the veranda Niamh was lying on her tummy, feet dangling over the edge of her sunbed with her head in a book. Her bottom was beautifully shapely. I had a rush of desire. I really wanted her. Sensing my presence, Niamh turned her head, looked over the top of her glasses and said, "What are you thinking?"

"Err, nothing," I said. "Just wondered if you wanted a drink or anything."

"What time is it?" enquired Niamh.

"Err, it's about 4 o'clock," I said.

Niamh slipped off her glasses, folded her book up and said, "I think I'll have a lie down." Then she stood up and stretched, smiled at me.

"Oh, err, well I think I'll come with you," I said.

As soon as we got inside the chalet, we reached for one another and tumbled onto the bed. Niamh pushed me onto my back, straddled me with her back to my head, bent and took me in her mouth. I was treated to the most fantastic view. Her bottom, perfect skin, dimpled, cream in contrast to her brown thighs – what a lucky boy I was!

Niamh then slipped off her bikini bottoms. I was rampant. She was rubbing herself and pressing her hips into my thighs. I pressed her bottom hard towards me and rocked her body whilst I pulled her hand away and applied pressure to her clitoris. She responded enthusiastically and came quickly. I turned her around and entered her from behind. She was very wet. I came almost instantly.

Afterwards I fell asleep. I must have been very soundly asleep. I woke with a start, the room was in darkness, Niamh wasn't in the bed with me and some lights were coming on outside.

I quickly pulled my shorts back on, opened the sliding door to the veranda and there was Niamh, now with a sarong over her white bikini. In fact, over only the top half of her bikini; the bottoms were still on the bed. I quickly looked at my watch and ran my fingers through my hair and said, "Gosh, I must still be jet-lagged, what time is it, I'd better get dressed for dinner, where shall we go?"

Niamh didn't reply, just carried on reading her book.

I thought she hadn't heard me and continued. "Well it must be the wine or the sun, I don't normally fall asleep like that, I don't know what came over me." Niamh still didn't reply.

Sensing a mood, I announced, "Well I'll dash in the shower and have a quick shave, back in a minute." I was soon back standing on the veranda, wearing my favourite white holiday jeans and a blue Chambray striped shirt. I too had caught the sun and my skin felt warm and as if the nerve endings were on the outside of my body. I'd quickly splashed on a bit of Chanel aftershave.

"So, where shall we go for dinner, stay in the hotel or do you fancy a wander?"

Alarmingly, I became aware of a low rumbling sound. Niamh stood up, it seemed as if a tremor was coursing through her body starting at her feet. When it reached her mouth, it opened wide and she bellowed "So, you want to go to dinner now, do you? Before I had any chance of replying she continued with a stream of abuse. I couldn't understand what I'd done wrong, I know I'd fallen asleep, but I was on holiday and she could have woken me up.

I started to apologise, "I'm so sorry about falling asleep," I said.

"It's not that I'm cross about, Simon," Niamh yelled, "but when I say I'm going for a sleep that isn't a cue for you to shag my arse off."

"What? I said shocked.

My mind rewound the scene. It was Niamh who had made the first move, she'd performed oral sex on me, she was the one who had taken her bikini bottoms off. If she'd said, "I'm not in the mood, I just want to sleep," I'd have let her of course. And the sex had been careful, considered. I wasn't drunk. I had had no doubt she was happy to participate in what was happening, although it was true that we hadn't had a conversation about having sex I had no idea that she was doing anything except taking a full and active part in normal everyday sex, conscious of what was happening and engaging fully in this. It was obviously a misunderstanding.

I felt very upset. I couldn't reconcile what had happened with her totemic reaction.

I didn't want to argue, especially on our last night. I apologized profusely and then finished up with, "Look, it's our last night, we don't normally argue, I'm very sorry about what happened and can we put it behind us?"

Fortunately Niamh calmed down, relaxed, eventually smiled, headed back into the bungalow and got ready for dinner. If this was a film I would now be looking into the camera, holding my palms up and saying "Women!" I tried to be cross with her, but I just couldn't really. I did remain upset at the notion that I had somehow taken advantage of her though.

We decided to stay in the hotel for our last evening. There was a band in the dining room and we had a fabulous time dancing to sounds of the 80s. Niamh had saved the best dress till last, a close fitting white knee length dress with a fitted tight bodice. It showed off her tan fabulously. As we walked along the beach our quarrel seemed to have been forgotten and I complimented her on how lovely she looked.

"Thanks Simon," she said. I thought she was going to apologise about the incident earlier, but she didn't. Instead she said, "You'll like these as well." Looking around quickly to see if someone was looking and with one yank she pulled her skirt up above her waist. She had on a tiny pair of pink knickers. A peace offering?

"Fabulous," I said.

Too soon the holiday was at an end. Rick was waiting for me at Gatwick. Niamh had managed to organise a flight back to Dublin leaving only 25 minutes after our arrival. Normally of course, I would expect Rick to be late and I wanted to leave my final goodbyes until absolutely the last minute.

As Niamh and I stood at the entrance to International Departures, and the crossroads with the short term car park, she said before I did, "Well, I guess this is goodbye Simon, I've had a wonderful time, you've been great company and I got all my work done."

I wanted to say – and I had rehearsed it. "I think you're wonderful Niamh and you are everything I want. Let's just give it a go, I love you." As I was about to open my mouth, I heard a familiar voice.

"Hello old boy," said Rick, who'd parked the car and was walking into Arrivals.

I wanted to scream at him, "Go away, get back in the car!" but of course, I couldn't. "Err, hello Rick" I said "err, um can I introduce my friend Niamh?"

"Hello dere!" said Rick in a terrible Irish accent, Niamh didn't reply just raised an eyebrow and offered a hand.

Rick wouldn't be put off. "Did you find any potatoes and Guinness," he said, "in Corfu?" Fortunately Niamh saw the funny side. "We've had a great time, Simon's told me all about you," she said.

"Really?" said Rick, looking slightly hunted.

Niamh looked at her watch. "I must dash," she said.

Rick interjected "Back to the old country."

And in a flurry of passports, tickets, suitcases leaving a trace of Chanel perfume she was gone.

I turned to Rick. "You berk!" I said.

Introduction Agency

Driving home from the airport, Rick brought me up to date on what was happening. Whilst Niamh and I had been bopping to the sounds of the 80s in Corfu, he and Barry had been tucking into fish and chips.

"You must have had a good time, because I didn't get many texts from you." He said. Before I could reply he said, "She's cracking looking, that Irish bird, isn't she?"

"Yeah she is, isn't she?" I said.

"Yes, you're a lucky chap there Simon. So when are you seeing her again?"

I wanted to say "Well, if you hadn't barged in just at the moment I was going to tell her I loved her and then I'd know."

So I did what I always did in those circumstances, I lied. "Yeah, I'm going to go out and see her in a couple of weeks, maybe spend a week with her."

"Oh right," said Rick, "what, are you going to help out at the surgery are you?"

"She's fantastic," I said.

Without listening to what I was saying Rick said "You know who she looks like? Jerry Hall."

I said, "No, Geri Halliwell." Which she now did somewhat with her hair shorter

Back at the flat there was pile of post. Rick declined the offer of coffee and left after a chat about the car. Before I open my post after a holiday I put it in bundles, brown envelopes are obviously bills, white A4 envelopes are normally from my agent. These were in the heap lying on the kitchen worktop beached amongst a litter of glossy flyers and the usual unsolicited crap that bulks out the post these days. There were also four A5 envelopes, heavy gauge posh cream coloured envelopes. Not realizing their significance I left them till last. I thought they were probably invitations to pre-launch receptions for cars. After phoning my children and Katherine, who I still check in with after holidays, I settled down and opened these envelopes.

Inside each was a personal introduction, to a female client of *Across The Room* whom Eleanor had evaluated I might find attractive and possibly a compatible companion. Three were quickly dismissed. You just know whether you find someone attractive or not don't you? One looked a distinct possibility. I had received a brochure with a profile and a set of what looked like professional photographs of a lady in a green evening dress with long, wavy blond hair. She had large blue eyes and looked very attractive.

But why was I even looking at this? After all hadn't I decided that Niamh was "The One"? We were suited in lots of ways. She was smart with a great sense of humour, when she wasn't angry with me. We shared similar interests and I was confident she enjoyed my company. I thought we'd be building on this and whilst it was still early days I could see that it could work out long term. I did find her occasionally unpredictable but I'd struggle to find anyone better and apart from one kick off over inappropriately timed sex and the dodgy introduction to the lone Irishman, I felt the holiday had gone well and we'd become close. I was sure we'd see one another again soon and that there would be many more holidays.

Despite this I read on. The brochure was introducing "Rebecca" from King's Lynn, Norfolk. She was a school teacher in her early 40s, had one child, was divorced, enjoyed the "finer things in life" defined in her profile as going to the theatre, dining out, travelling, reading and playing tennis. She was looking to meet a gentleman with a view to a long-term relationship, possibly marriage.

'Hmm,' I thought, the others I binned, but I left Rebecca's brochure on my desk. I reasoned that I could have been interested if I hadn't already decided to marry Niamh.

Fish and chips that week went well. I showed the guys my photographs of Niamh on the beach and a video of us dancing to sounds of the 80s. At least, Niamh dancing as I strutted enthusiastically with my thumbs in the air. I hadn't realized till I viewed the footage that our movements weren't vaguely coordinated.

Barry tolerantly offered a polite commentary, the sort friends often make when holiday snaps are inflicted on them; "Ooh that's nice, good shot and that's scenic." And of the video "Christ Simon, I'd delete that. Even I'm embarrassed by that."

Rick asked inevitably "Got any photos of her with her tits out?"

I didn't, but I had taken one photo of Niamh (with her consent) as she was getting ready to go out one evening. She had her back to me and was brushing her hair. She wore a pair of lacy black knickers and as I took the photograph she glanced over her shoulder at me and gave a cheeky smile. It was a great photo and I'm sure she wouldn't have minded the boys seeing it. I then spoke about how things were going, maintaining the pretence of going over to Ireland to see her, meeting her parents, getting married perhaps? etc., etc. was conscious that I was digging myself into a deep hole, but I reasoned that it didn't really matter because all of this would happen.

Barry saw through the fantasy immediately. "So before you went, when you were seeing the mad Indian bird, you were complaining Niamh didn't keep in touch much. Have you sorted that out?" he asked.

"Definitely," I said "100% better, we jabber away all the time on the phone." In reality I'd spoken to Niamh a couple of times and she'd been charming, saying how much again she'd enjoyed the holiday. She didn't discuss where a next holiday might be. I'd also had a few texts from her, not many but a few and although in these we'd written about me going over to see her again, we hadn't got as far as putting a date in the diary.

As the weeks passed, I threw myself back into work. I saw Shilpa at the gym and we had coffee together. She had said (again) how dreadfully sorry she was about the Golf Club incident; explained that she hadn't been feeling well and had taken cold remedies without realizing how these might interact with alcohol. She mentioned having a "few glasses of wine". I wasn't convinced she had much insight into her capacity to drink, but had to acknowledge she seemed genuinely remorseful and she looked wonderful.

Now I could say here that Niamh and I had settled into a routine of phoning each other regularly, exchanging long, loving emails and cards in the post, but that would be a lie. My contact with Niamh was becoming more infrequent and whilst I was test-driving a fabulous Jaguar XF, I realised that I hadn't heard from her for nearly a week.

I went through the usual – maybe she was ill, maybe she was busy – I sent her a few texts, didn't get a reply. The following day I sent an e-mail and then another, still no reply. I decided to send her a card, I'd got some small notelets from my last visit to the Royal Air Force Club and jotted her a note in my best handwriting (in truth my best handwriting is still very bad), just saying I hadn't heard from her and I was worried and I hoped I hadn't offended her and could she please get in touch. I even checked out flights to Dublin and to Waterford and wondered whether I should just get on a plane. After all, she was happily going to surprise me. I still heard nothing. It was now nearly ten days since I'd heard anything at all and I reflected on how little I knew about her. I didn't know her parents' names, where they lived, her sister was called Jane or Janet I think and she lived somewhere near Dublin.

Paul Fox

'That narrows it down a bit,' I thought, 'can't be that many Janet or Janes living somewhere near Dublin'. And what could I say if I phoned up – "Hello, I've been shagging your sister and she hasn't contacted me?"

I was beginning to feel a bit desperate. Then I remembered that Niamh had sent me some photographs of her surgery and a link to her website. I quickly trawled through some old emails, I congratulated myself on remembering and soon I was dialling the number. Niamh didn't answer the phone. A female voice answered giving the surgery name.

"Hello," I said "can I speak to Niamh?"

"Dry Riordan is with patients at the moment, can I help you?" said the Irish receptionist.

I realised I was going to have to identify myself so I just said, "I would like to speak to her; it's Simon, can I leave a number?"

There was a long pause and then an even longer one, I thought about hanging up.

"Oh," said the receptionist, "she's just become free, hold on, I'll put you through."

There was a double click on the line.

"Hello," said Niamh, "Simon?"

"Hi Niamh," I said "I'm sorry to bother you at work, I hadn't heard from you and I just wanted to check you were Okay."

"I'm fine, said Niamh, "it's me who owes you an apology. Look Simon this isn't the time or the place, but I just can't do this. I have your lovely card and your emails and your texts, but I just feel that we are looking for different things. I do think you're wonderful Simon, but you're looking for a wife and as I said to you in Venice, I don't really do that sort of thing. I'd love to see you again but it's got to be on the clear understanding that we're not going to have a long-term relationship."

I didn't know what to say. Being honest I had suspected before she said it that this might be the case. I had hoped I was wrong and that the absence of contact was explicable. But deep down I had felt she might feel differently about a commitment.

All I could manage to say was how very disappointed I felt. Niamh went on to say that I wasn't being realistic, we lived in separate countries. She didn't plan on regularly spending time away from her practice and home. I started to splutter about how I could consider a move to Ireland and then she added.

"You've children. I know they're growing up but you need to be with them. It would never work Simon."

I had to accept that no, it probably wouldn't. It should do and I'd love it to, but it probably wouldn't and the conversation ended with us agreeing to remain friends. I'm pleased to report that we are. I hear from Niamh every so often. She's a wonderful person; a great ambassador for her country and I'm so pleased that I met her. We were in truth looking for different things.

Fish and chips that week was a gloomy affair as I recounted my tale of woe to the guys, even Rick seemed genuinely upset. It didn't put him off his large cod, large chips and mushy peas for long though, and by way of consolation, Rick-style, he punched me hard on the arm announcing "Well, I'm sure you'd have got fed up with all that Guinness after a while."

Barry said sensibly. "Just look at it this way Simon, you met a lovely lady, you've had some great times with her and you've remained friends, you can't really ask for much more."

And of course, he was right.

I went into a bit of a decline after that though, started missing out visits to the gym, bought and drank more wine than usual and played lots of sad Elton John songs. Everyone has a break up song haven't they? Mine? "Don't let the sun go down on me"!

After a couple of weeks or so of feeling pathetically miserable I was beginning to bore myself. I made up my mind to get on with some work. Being clumsy I managed to start the computer, then knock the keyboard on the floor along with most of the paperwork on the desk.

Swearing, I bent to pick the dropped papers up and saw Rebecca's face and blue eyes staring at me from a photograph I'd placed on a pile of post a fortnight before. I re-read her details and one phrase struck, "long-term relationship or marriage".

It was staring me in the face, literally. Here was someone declaring openly that they wanted a long-term relationship and would consider getting married. I read the part of the brochure that I hadn't read before, it explained how I could get in touch with Rebecca. "If you'd like to talk to me please text me first. There was her mobile number.

As it had been more than two weeks since I'd received Rebecca's details through the post I felt certain that lovely Rebecca from Norfolk would be fighting off people to have a long-term relationship with. Still I decided to send her a quick text. As usual it was something cheesy, "Hi Rebecca I got your details from *Across the Room*, you seem very nice. Simon." I had an immediate reply.

"Hello Simon, its Rebecca here, thanks for your text. Yes, I got your details as well and wondered when you'd be in touch."

'Bloody hell,' I thought, and fired off a few more texts. I knew King's Lynn well. My parents had retired there and I've still family, an Uncle, living there. I'd opened a bottle of wine and then decided to send her a cheeky text. "We're getting on so well," I said "do you fancy talking on the phone?"

"Of course," she said, "phone me in half an hour on my landline," and gave me the number.

I couldn't wait for the thirty minutes to be up and I carefully dialled her number. There were only two rings and then a soft, "Hello?"

"Hello Rebecca," I said, "it's Simon," a slight tremor in my voice.

"Well it's nice of you to call me," said Rebecca. "What's taken you so long?"

"Well, yes I am sorry," I said, "I didn't realise there was a time limit."

"Didn't you read the instruction pack from Eleanor?" she said.

"Err…" I was contemplating lying, but had to admit I hadn't read this, in fact I hadn't even opened it. Rebecca came to my rescue and said "But no matter, it's nice of you to call tonight. I was just in the bath when I got your text."

I decided not to comment on that. The conversation went well and we spoke for a good half an hour. In fact it went so well that I suggested meeting up. There was a pause and I thought I'd pushed my luck too far.

Rebecca said "Well, I'm going on holiday the week after next and I've got a lot of marking to do from school."

I said, "Don't worry if you're busy."

She said, "Well, we could meet up Sunday."

"Sunday?" I said, "Why don't we meet for lunch?"

"Well, that would be great."

I couldn't believe my luck. "You're in King's Lynn," I said, "so shall I come to King's Lynn?" I knew the journey so well.

"No it's not fair if you do all the driving," said Rebecca. "Why don't we meet half way?" In the confusion I couldn't think where to meet. Then suddenly Rebecca said, "How about Saffron Walden?"

"Fine with me," I said. "Are you sure that's not too far for you to drive?"

"No not at all," said Rebecca. "I get fed up being stuck here all week, see you at *The George* at 12 o'clock on Sunday."

"Fabulous," I said. "That'll be great," I gushed, "I can't wait."

Rebecca laughed, "See you then, Simon, I'm off to bed now."

"Wow, wow, wow." I jumped round the mezzanine floor. "She sounded fantastic, she looks fantastic, she wants a long term relationship and she lives in fantastic King's Lynn!"

My parents had moved there 25 years ago and while the kids were growing up, it was a great place for weekend visits, especially since it provided us with in-house babysitters and an opportunity for a rare night out. It has a wealth of good restaurants. We loved exploring the Tuesday market place, the small villages outside of King's Lynn on the coast. Cromer and Hunstanton particularly. Happy memories.

Getting to sleep that night was difficult. There was something about Rebecca, our conversation and her response that gave me confidence about this relationship. I knew I was vulnerable after Niamh's rejection and realized it could be a rebound reaction. I needed to slow it down. I tried not to panic about what to wear as it was only Friday night.

Sunday morning arrived soon enough and I'd had a few texts from Rebecca. I was having an ongoing anxious debate with myself about what to wear and this time what car to take, as apart from my own Alfa I was now test driving a BMW 6 series convertible.

It was black with a black hood and very light cream leather upholstery. What car would be better for a first date? Some people don't like BMW drivers, what if Rebecca was one of them? She'd definitely see the car as we were meeting in the car park, but then it would be a lovely drive with the top down and would make an impression, not that the Alfa wouldn't, but they are very much an acquired taste. I settled on the BMW.

I couldn't decide what to wear, my usual anxious dilemma. It was warm. I tend to have a default setting of blazer, jeans and shirt for Sunday lunch out but felt I should dress up. At the back of my wardrobe I found a summer suit, sand coloured and linen. I teamed it with a white shirt and a Dunhill pale blue and sand tie. I put on a pair of suede loafers.

With the top down, my sunglasses in place and Elton on the CD auto-changer singing "Come down in time", I was heading for Saffron Walden. I sent Rebecca a quick text, "Just leaving, see you there." She sent one by return "See you at 12, I'll be driving a black Mercedes."

I found the pub easily and waited in its spacious car park for Rebecca to arrive. I decided to leave the roof of the car in position. Why was I feeling so tense and anxious?

Then, there she was, a black Mercedes pulled into the car park. A door opened, I stood up and got out of the car and started to approach her, then

I realised it was a bloke on his own not Rebecca, at least I hoped not. I smiled awkwardly at the bearded chap and swiftly got back into my car.

Twenty agonizing minutes went past. I kept looking at my watch and then my phone. Maybe she'd decided not to come and I'd be eating humble pie instead of fish and chips this Friday. Then, a second black Mercedes, a sports car pulled into the car park.

I recognized the blond curly hair from the photographs. Rebecca found a place to park, opened the door and I approached her. She wore a black dress with a cream silk blazer, high-heeled black shoes, perfect make up and a shy smile. Those lovely blue eyes were even lovelier than her photograph suggested. I just didn't know what to say, she was attractive, elegant and graceful. Every small move she made seemed to be carefully considered. I was pleased that I had put on a suit and tie. We both extended our hands at the same time.

"I'm Rebecca..."

"I'm Simon... " Rebecca seemed nervous. too "Well, I found it okay," I said. "I haven't been here for ages."

"I was late leaving," said Rebecca speaking at the same time as I did. She smiled then. "I'm sorry but glad you're still here."

We engaged in small talk as we made our way into the pub. As we walked into the dining room there was a staffed podium for checking into the restaurant. Rebecca was quiet, but that was fine.

"Hello," said the receptionist, bright and breezily.

"Hello," I said, "I've got a reservation for lunch, Mr Taylor."

"Would you like to go to your table now or have a drink at the bar?" she asked.

I turned to Rebecca, she'd pulled her hair into a pony tail and it lay over her left shoulder and as she looked at me I almost gaped on realizing how very good looking she was.

"Err, would you like a drink or shall we go straight to the table?"

Rebecca seemed to hesitate for a moment. "Well, shall we go straight to the table?" she said.

It was a large dining room and we sat in an alcove which afforded us some privacy. There's always an awkward moment when you're on a first date; after having spoken on the phone, there's the anxiety of first meeting and then the slightly awkward initial formality of being alone as a couple. A voice inside me was saying 'Don't mess this one up, Simon.'

As if on cue Rebecca reached down into her handbag and pulled out a brochure. It was the brochure about me from *Across the Room*. I hadn't thought to take mine – I mean did we need it? Rebecca seemed to be interviewing me, checking the details of my brochure, how many children I had, what I did for a living. After this initial discussion was over, a waitress arrived at our table and said we could help ourselves from the carvery.

"Carvery?" I said.

I loathe carveries; if I'd known the restaurant only offered a Sunday carvery I wouldn't have booked it. I tried to cajole the waitress into queuing up and getting our meals for us, but to no avail.

"Sorry Rebecca," I explained, "if I'd realized it was a carvery we wouldn't have come here."

"Oh, that's okay," she said sweetly. Soon we were queuing up with the other diners. I don't know why I have such a dislike of carveries; if you're going out to dinner why would you want to queue for food. It reminds me of waiting in line for school dinners? If I'm going to a restaurant I want someone to bring my meal to me, not trek off to collect it myself.

All this fortunately seemed lost on Rebecca. Whilst in the queue we didn't speak. She faintly smiled a couple of times, but that was all. Of course, on cue my nerves returned and looking at the food, bulky slices of a massive turkey, joints of chicken, a bloodied beef joint, I suddenly didn't want anything to eat at all.

The chef turned to me. "What can I get you sir?"

I turned to Rebecca. "After you," I said.

"No, no after you," she said.

I started to feel dizzy; I really dislike witnessing other people's food piled up on plates. Regretting booking this dreadful place, I finally settled on some grilled salmon, a Yorkshire pudding, gravy and a portion of mixed vegetables. Rebecca looked slightly askance at my choice of food, but didn't say anything. She ordered roast beef and two veg.

When we returned to our table Rebecca's questions continued. I didn't object as I felt she was probably talking as a means of relaxing and as a preliminary to conversation. She had now moved onto financial issues. She announced that she owned her home, a house, and she didn't have a mortgage and her car was paid for.

It wasn't very relaxing for me but I supposed this was how it should perhaps be. If you're contemplating embarking on a potentially steady relationship then serious questions do need to be asked; whether this was the right time I didn't know. I sort of mumbled through my financial questionnaire. I told her about my rented flat and that I was expecting to receive some capital from the marital home once it was sold. I had to explain that the BMW was on test, I had my own Alfa Romeo that was paid for. "How much do you think that's worth?" Rebecca chipped in.

She reached into her bag again, I thought she was going to get a pen out and make notes or mark my answers.

'It's not going well,' I thought.

Fortunately it wasn't a pen but a set of photographs in clear plastic wallets. Rebecca appeared to soften and relax; she smiled. "I thought you might like to see some photographs of me and my family," she said. There were photos of her daughter, her Mum and Dad, a few of her on holiday, in her garden and then some fabulous ones of her; modelling type photos, in various evening dresses.

I adopted Barry's comments: "Ooh this is nice, that's good one, nice scenery", etc. When I got to the formal photos I couldn't help saying "These are fabulous photos."

"Yes," said Rebecca, "I had them done professionally. When I joined the agency I thought I'd better have some done."

'Gosh,' I thought, 'this woman is on a serious mission.'

I'd managed to push my salmon round my plate, had a few mouthfuls of soggy Yorkshire pudding. I hadn't touched the vegetables.

"Not very nice?" enquired Rebecca.

"I'm just not that hungry," I said. And that was true.

"Shall we skip dessert and just go for a walk?" she asked.

"Oh that would be lovely," I said gratefully.

I quickly paid the bill and we went for a walk round Saffron Walden. When people are dismissive or rude about Essex, Basildon and the "Sugar Hut" they forget that the county has some very attractive villages and this was one of them. The sun had come out and being outdoors seemed to signal a fresh start, a better one to the date. I felt more relaxed and in control of the situation and was thrilled when Rebecca linked her arm with mine as we walked along. We looked into a few antique shops then found another pub, sat down outside and ordered a glass of wine each. It was then that Rebecca began to talk and open up.

Smoothing her blond hair and flicking it to one side again she enquired "You think I'm being too cautious don't you?"

"No, not at all," I lied.

"I've just had my fingers burnt that's all. But you seem genuine enough," she offered.

I wanted to know more about Rebecca; not just whether she had a mortgage or not. She went on to explain why she was single. She'd been married for nearly twenty years, her husband was very successful, and a Director of a large family owned agricultural business. About five years earlier she had discovered that he was having an affair. That's why she was divorced.

"Just like that?" I said.

"Well I couldn't live with someone who'd had an affair could I?"

"No, of course not," I said squirming.

She went on to describe how she'd found out; how her husband had inadvertently dropped his mobile phone in his car whilst he was a passenger in a car driven by his 'other woman.' Rebecca was the last person he'd called on the mobile and his call to her hadn't disconnected. As a result she could hear him talking with his girlfriend about amongst other things, their illicit sex that afternoon and their plans to meet next.

I could imagine Rebecca listening to the call, frozen to the spot, her blue eyes widening. When he got home he tried to keep up the pretence claiming that he'd been with a client for lunch. They had had a blazing row and he had left.

She said that being on the wrong side of a wealthy businessman wasn't easy and for reasons that she didn't go into she explained that she spent some time after this living with her parents. They owned a farm just outside King's Lynn and that was where Rebecca and her sister had been brought up. That was the first time she mentioned that she had a sister.

"A sister?" I said.

"Yes, she lives in London, I don't see her much."

We decided to continue with a walk. It was approaching 5 o'clock. I didn't want to leave her.

Unlike Louise, Rebecca was warming up, she had linked her arm with mine as we walked and patted me on the knee jokingly a couple of time. She was far more friendly, relaxed and talkative as noon became late afternoon, though my impression was that she was a little serious perhaps. I was tempted to ask "Shall we go on to dinner?" but as we rounded the bend to the car park, Rebecca said.

"I'm going to dinner at my parents," she said, "otherwise I would have liked to stay longer."

"Oh that's fine," I said, "I do understand, I've had a wonderful day."

And I had.

Rebecca kissed me briefly and said, "I'm going away for a week on holiday with my daughter next Saturday, but I may be free during the week if you'd like to meet up?"

"Definitely," I said, "how about Wednesday?"

"Love to," she said and she got in her car, put the window down and said "I've had a wonderful day, Simon, see you on Wednesday. If I get back at a reasonable hour, I'll give you a call."

I climbed into the BMW, reached for the sound system. Elton boomed out "Country Comfort".

I was ecstatic: here was somebody who was not only attractive, but serious about having a long term relationship.

I was tempted to phone Eleanor; I had her mobile number, but thought it would be unfair to intrude on a Sunday. I rang Rick from the car phone.

I didn't even bother saying "Hi", I just went straight into "She's fantastic!"

"What one's this?" he said.

"You know, the one from the dating agency, Rebecca."

"Oh right," said Rick, "so you're no doubt in love with this one. What's her name?"

"Rebecca," I said.

"Wasn't that a book?" Rick said.

"Yes I do believe it was a book, I'm surprised you know that. It was a book by Daphne du Maurier and was also a film."

"Doesn't she go mad?" said Rick.

"Who?" I said.

"Rebecca."

"What, Daphne du Maurier's Rebecca?"

"Yes, she does; in the book and in the film. So she's alright then, is she?" said Rick, trying to feign interest and failing. He was definitely eating now.

"She's really lovely, she's better than alright and she's really keen on me AND we're meeting up again on Wednesday."

"Where does she live?" said Rick.

" King's Lynn," I said. Her parents have a farm in the country.

"Oh well, it's not as far as Ireland is it, or Calcutta?"

I ignored that. "I'm going to see her on Wednesday, then she's off on holiday on Saturday with her daughter."

I filled him in on some of the details. I knew what was coming. "Has she got big tits?" said Rick.

Now I'm not really into breasts at all, being far more interested in legs and bottoms, but I had noticed that Rebecca was very well endowed. I later found out that she wore a size 30FF bra, which as my ex-wife said is some going and yes, they were real. I confirmed to Rick that yes, she did have big tits and even I had noticed them.

"Christ!" he said, "They must have been huge for you to notice them. Well, they'll be wasted on you," he said.

"Look Rick," I said, "I didn't ring you up just to talk about her tits!"

"Okay," said Rick, "I'm trying to be enthusiastic, but every time you get really excited about someone they turn out to be mad, why is this one going to be any different?"

I tried to defend my position but didn't succeed very well, finishing off with "Well, you'll see, she is absolutely lovely."

"Okay Simon," Rick said. "See you for fish and chips on Friday. You'll have no doubt seen the lovely what's-her-name again!"

That evening the landline rang in the flat and it was indeed the lovely Rebecca. She thanked me again for a wonderful day. We had a laugh about my odd choice of meal and she explained that her parents had been very curious about me, what I was like. She said that she had told them that I was charming and that we were going to meet up again on Wednesday.

I was enormously relieved. Here at last was a "normal" person with parents and a sister. A girl who liked me, who was looking forward to seeing me.

I'm not saying that other women I'd met hadn't liked me but with Rebecca there seemed a purpose. She wanted me to get to know her and her family. We both hated being on our own, a fact we'd established within minutes of meeting. We appeared to enjoy similar lifestyles; had discussed interests in common. We were equally keen at this point to know more about one another.

Where should we meet on Wednesday? Rebecca had already thought about it. The school she taught at had organized a teacher training day in Cambridge on Wednesday; she'd be finished at about 4 o'clock and we could meet up after that at the hotel where the conference was being held – the *Royal Garden Hotel.*

"That would be wonderful," I said.

After we agreed that, Rebecca yawned expansively.

"I'm so tired," she said, "and I've had such a wonderful day. I've had a bath and I'm looking forward to going to bed."

The word bed seemed to hang in the air a bit.

"Have you got your pyjamas on?" I said.

"I don't wear pyjamas," said Rebecca, "in fact I don't wear anything in bed."

"Really?" I said. "That's interesting; doesn't it get rather cold in King's Lynn?"

That was as far as the flirting went and after saying goodnight I had a real job getting to sleep thinking about Rebecca's blond curly hair spilling out on the pillows of her bed, on her own.

It had been such a serious meeting I hadn't really thought about knickers, but I was hoping she had some pink ones. Then I checked myself – she was a school teacher in a rural town, her Mum and Dad owned a farm, she'd been badly hurt and so I was prepared for her to be a little cool on the sex side and that was fine. I made a mental note not to flirt with her too much on Wednesday. I really didn't want to mess things up.

Monday morning came and I decided to get my outstanding assignments out of the way; get to grips with work so that I could concentrate on seeing Rebecca on Wednesday. I'd already made a reservation for dinner at the *Royal Garden Hotel*.

I thought I'd better start writing about the BMW. It was going back on Thursday morning and staring at a blank page, it was difficult to know what to say. It was powerful, comfortable, boring, diesel, I couldn't imagine who would want to buy one, at £65,000, but there must be a good market for them in America. As I sat at the computer on the mezzanine floor, the phone rang again.

'Rebecca?' I thought.

It was my Uncle Colin. He greeted me with his usual, "Hello, daft nephew." He was my favourite Uncle, the one who lived in King's Lynn. How strange that he should phone. "Are you still alive?" he said.

"Ah, yes, sorry Uncle Colin, been meaning to phone. I phoned a couple of times and you were out."

He asked whether I'd been to Ireland again. I brought him up to speed with Corfu and Niamh's decision that it wasn't going anywhere, but I'd met the lovely Rebecca and she lived in King's Lynn.

"Whereabouts?" he said.

"I'm not too sure, I haven't got her address, but I'm seeing her again on Wednesday."

"Ah, that sounds good," he said. "Well keep me posted and don't leave it so long next time."

We are really quite close and I felt guilty when I thought about how much energy and time I'd devoted to my love life this past year. I hadn't been keeping in touch with my few family members nearly as often as they deserved. Even the children had had little attention lately.

"Shame about the Irish bird," he said. "Anyway, see you Simon."

I managed to rattle off a few paragraphs about the BMW and emailed them to my agent. I kept the criticism to a minimum and concentrated on the car's good points. I did criticize it for being ugly and I'm pleased to say the latest version is a lot prettier, maybe they took my criticism to heart.

That evening I determined to make contact with the family so I called Katherine and the children and chatted about what I was doing and asked for their news.

I told them about Rebecca. My ex-wife commented that a lady from King's Lynn would be ideal as I knew the area so well. Katherine was discreet and, perhaps unusually for an "ex", supportive of my attempts to find a suitable partner.

I've led a charmed life.

The next morning I got up early and went to the gym in my continuing bid to whittle down my waistline. In fact I arrived so early they hadn't even opened up. After a few minutes standing about in the cold, the doors were unlocked and I made my way to the changing room. I was quickly joined by one of the regulars – Steve.

Steve's one of those regulars who more or less lives in the gym. He is a huge guy; Massive arms and legs. I always feel like a ten stone weakling when I stand next to him (even though I weigh a lot more than that.) He's normally cheerful, but this morning was different. Instead of asking how I was and talking about cars, he just kept his head down.

"Hi Steve," I said, to which I didn't get a reply. He just put his kit bag in a locker and went into the gym. I joined him a few paces behind. I felt as though I should say something. He got on the rower and I got on the ski machine, and apart from the TV blaring out Sky news, there was silence. It was most odd. Maybe I'd upset him, but that wouldn't be the case, surely, maybe he's read some of my reviews, maybe he's got a Lexus. I decided to go ahead and investigate.

Steve didn't look up as I approached. "Steve, are you okay?" I said gently.

This giant of a man stopped rowing, spun round on the seat of the rower, put his head in his hands and said, "No Simon, I'm really not okay."

'Dear God,' I thought. "Steve," I said, grabbing one of his huge shoulders, "what on earth has happened?" As he looked up at me I could see he had tears in his eyes. I squatted down beside him, what could it be? "Are you unwell?" I said. "Has there been an accident?"

He shook his head slowly from side to side. It was a long while before he spoke and we were alone in the gym before he finally blurted out "It's Chelsea!"

"Chelsea?" I said, wondering if it might be his daughter or his wife. And then I looked at one of his tattoos. The largest. "Chelsea FC" was emblazoned down one of his arms.

"Chelsea?" I said, "The football club?"

He just nodded. Holding back the tears, Steve explained that they'd been knocked out of the European Cup or some other such tournament.

I didn't know how to feel; pleased that a person named Chelsea wasn't ill or had some dreadful accident or annoyed that Steve had evoked such concern in me over a football team. Maybe you're reading this and you're thinking, "Well, he had every right to be upset; he's a long term supporter of Chelsea and he's upset. I can understand that."

Well, I can understand disappointment but wholehearted misery and grief! Maybe I'm just different from most other men.

After making sure Steve was okay and well enough to continue, I returned to the ski machine. I noticed there was someone else in the gym now; using the bench press with some degree of enthusiasm. Shilpa. I decided to give up the ski machine and walked across the floor to talk to her.

"Hi, Shilpa," I said.

"Hi," the eyes flashed back.

We had a breathless conversation about nothing in particular. I didn't mention Niamh or Rebecca and as we walked back together into the main area of the gym to use separate pieces of equipment, Shilpa said something rather surprising. "I know it's a few months ago now Simon, but I really can't forgive myself about the golf club, I want to make it up to you," she said.

"Don't," I said, "don't worry, it's all in the past; all forgotten." I didn't want anything to get in the way of spending time with Rebecca.

Before I could say any more she said, "Let me know when you're free and I'll make you dinner."

"Really?" I said.

"Yes," she said, "come round and I'll make you dinner."

'How lovely,' I thought, she had crossed over from being a potential girlfriend to being a friend, what's wrong with two friends having dinner together? I went back to the ski machine and started again.

As Tuesday passed, I'd had a lot of phone calls and texts from Rebecca. I explained to her that I'd booked dinner at the hotel and I would be happy to meet her whatever time she liked.

"Well, why don't you aim to be here at say, 4.30pm? Dinner's not till 7.30pm – I'm sure we can think of something to do."

I decided not to make any comment being on my best behaviour. There had been a few comments like that: not wearing anything to bed; Rebecca referred to her large bosom occasionally; having trouble keeping them in; finding underwear to fit her. I didn't make any comment at all, or indulge in any sexual innuendo, just played it straight bat.

On Wednesday I started getting ready about lunchtime. Barry had phoned for an update, which was unusual. I explained to him in sober and reserved terms how lovely and suitable Rebecca was and how we were meeting up in Cambridge shortly. I told him I'd update him on Friday at fish and chips.

Then Barry gave me some really good advice, which of course I ignored, "Just take it easy, Simon. Find out about her, don't rush in."

Hmmm, we'll soon see where that got me.

Bearing in mind that this was an afternoon in mid-summer, in England, for some reason I decided to wear another suit: my grey Gucci suit, a white shirt with French cuffs that had cost a fortune and my favourite blue tie. There was no need for me to wear a suit, but I just felt that I wanted to. Cambridge is only about an hour from where I live, so of course I was early.

As I pulled into the car park of the *Royal Garden Hotel*, I remembered I'd been there before. It's a favourite conference venue and Martin and I had been there years before, attending a course on Professional Development for financial advisers.

Martin, of golf club fame, and I had decided to travel together that morning and I remember driving round the car park trying to find a space. It must have been a good ten or fifteen years previously that we were there but I recalled it clearly. I remember Martin rattling on about golf as I found a space and parked.

As we were both leaving the car, collecting our briefcases and putting suit jackets on, I became aware of an older, middle-aged man approaching my car with some dispatch. He looked angry, came directly up to me, banged his big fist on the side of my car and shouted, "What the hell do you think you're doing?" Before I could reply he said "I've been waiting ten minutes for this space!"

I hadn't noticed his Volvo, he'd made no attempt to pull into the space, and his behaviour seemed totally out of order.

Martin took command of the situation but instead of explaining anything or seeking to justify my actions, he simply walked round to the man and said, "Look mate, have a day off, just get lost."

To my surprise, he did and just walked off in a huff.

If you're reading this book, I'm sorry I just didn't notice you there. It felt bizarre pulling into the car park all these years later; I am still wary about middle aged men drivers in car parks, even though I am one now.

It was just after 3.30pm and fortunately this time I found a car parking space that wasn't in a war zone and eased the BMW into it. As I unclipped my seatbelt I was aware of someone tapping on the window.

'Oh God,' I thought, 'Not the same bloke, he's not been waiting here for 15 years to get his revenge!'

It was Rebecca.

I leapt out of the car, I wanted to be reserved but just couldn't. I grabbed hold of her and kissed her, fortunately she responded.

"It's lovely to see you Simon, I've been thinking about you all day. We finished early."

She looked stunning, she had on a close-fitting floral summer dress, which came to about mid-thigh, and it was mostly blue with white flowers on. Her shoulders were completely bare but on her finger dangled a short red jacket. She had red shoes and bare legs.

Rebecca's ample bosom seemed to be bursting out of the top of her dress. She shrugged on her jacket and then gathered all of her long hair from inside the jacket and threw it once again over one shoulder. "It's so lovely you're early," she said, "the conference finished a while ago and I just happened to notice the car."

"Wow," I said grinning broadly "school teachers have changed since I was at school!"

"Oh I haven't had these on all day," she said, "don't be silly. I've just changed in my car." My eyes widened.

"Yes, it was a bit of a struggle," she said "especially with these," Rebecca cupped her bosoms in her hands. "There's almost not enough room for them."

I decided to remain tight-lipped and make no comment at all. "Be cool," was my motto.

I swallowed hard and simply said, "Its ages since I've been to Cambridge."

Rebecca gave me a look as if to say, "I thought we were talking about my bosoms," then said, "Well, we've got loads of time before dinner, what would you like to do?"

Looking at Rebecca's fantastic figure, long hair and tanned legs, I knew exactly what I wanted to do, but in keeping with my discreet approach I didn't mention it. "Shall we have a look around Cambridge?" I said, "And you can show me the sights?"

"Love to," said Rebecca, grabbing my arm again. She clearly knew the city well and we walked along by the river, stopped for a while by a metal map of the city, in itself is a small sculpture.

There are some great shops in Cambridge. Beautiful clothes shops, independent bookshops; bespoke shoe shops; lovely cafes. Then there's the River Cam. A popular excursion in Cambridge involves hiring a flat-bottomed boat, a punt, which is propelled along with a long pole; it's a fabulously romantic thing to do and I was tempted to suggest we hired one. For about ten seconds. Knowing how clumsy I can be I was sure we'd probably end up in the river with the punt on top of us. We had a glass of wine in a pub overlooking the stone bridge in the centre of the city. I couldn't take my eyes off Rebecca.

"I need to do some shopping while I'm here," she said. I remembered with some disappointment that she was going on holiday on Saturday.

"Great, I said, "I love shopping."

"Well, I need to look at a few outfits and I need to get a bikini, so shall we do that?"

We headed off into the centre of the City, went into several shops and Rebecca tried on a few outfits, sundresses, a couple of evening dresses. Then we went into Karen Millen and something amazing happened. I picked up a few dresses and Rebecca complimented me on my taste and then said, "I think I'll try this one on." It was black and gold dress with a couple of sewn-in petticoats underneath a full skirt. There were shoes and a bag to match. There were two changing rooms opposite one another, and an assistant waiting at the entrance.

"I'd like to try this on," said Rebecca.

"Yes of course Madam," said the efficient assistant.

Rebecca went into the first changing room and didn't pull the curtain fully across. She wasn't standing in front of the opening, but there was a full length mirror in which, from where I was seated, I could clearly see her.

'My God,' my heart started to thump, 'should I move?' Yes, I should that would be the gentlemanly thing to do. Should I draw attention to the fact that she hadn't pulled the curtain fully across? Well, yes I could do that, but I didn't want to cause a fuss. In the changing cubicle Rebecca slipped off the red jacket, and then undid the floral dress by way of a zip along the side, pulled it down and off. What a sight, I nearly passed out. Underneath she had a small white G-string and a very large lacy white bra. She stepped into the Karen Millen dress, turned round and zipped it up, moved the curtain back and stepped out.

"What do you think?" she said.

I couldn't speak, I just couldn't get the image of her amazing body out of my mind. She had everything, she was small but had long legs, big boobs and a shapely bottom.

"Fantastic!" I finally spluttered.

"I like it as well," she said. She returned to the changing room and this time pulled the curtain completely across. When she came out fully dressed, we headed for the checkout.

"I'll get it for you," I said.

"Oh no Simon, you can't. I can't allow you to do that."

"I'd love to," I said. So she let me without any further protests. It cost an eye watering £275.00. But she was worth it.

Next she wanted to buy a bikini. According to Rebecca, it's more difficult buying swimwear than dresses. Most shops only sell bikinis in dress sizes.

"What's the problem there?" I said.

"Well Simon," said Rebecca, moving into school mistress mode, "in a dress I'm normally a size 8, but because I've got such big boobs, in a bikini I need a size 16 in the top and for the bottom I need a size 8, so sometimes I have to buy two bikinis. Apart from certain specialist shops," she grinned, "that cater for big girls brought up on farms. It's all the fresh air."

I was tempted to ask whether her boobs were real or not, but before I could reply and seeming to be able to read my mind, which was a worry, "They're real," she said.

"Are they?" I said. "I'll take your word for it."

"Well, you don't have to Simon," she said, "you can have a feel."

I couldn't believe it; we'd only had one glass of wine. In the middle of the street, Rebecca held her jacket open and said, "Go on."

I thought Rick wouldn't have hesitated like I did. "Which one?" I said.

"Either one," she said.

I gently and briefly gave her right boob a squeeze. I'm no expert but it didn't feel like silicon, but I may have just been feeling her bra. We found a lovely boutique-type lingerie shop that Rebecca knew well. She found a maroon bikini and asked to try it on. I didn't think they'd let you try on swimwear but the assistant didn't seem to be fazed at all and said, "Yes of course, just keep your knickers on."

What a fantastic shopping trip this was turning out to be. Unfortunately I didn't get an impromptu show of Rebecca trying on the bikini as the changing room was upstairs and, by the look on the assistant's face, I was to remain where I was.

After paying for the bikini, it was time to head back to the *Royal Garden* for dinner. It was a lovely occasion. Rebecca abandoned her formal interviewing style and we enjoyed the meal and one another's company. She was forthcoming and told me more of her former husband and their marriage. I told her everything; including how my marriage had ended. How we were the classic couple drifting apart; we'd married young, had children young and then seemed to have nowhere to go. Our table was narrow and in a quiet corner of the restaurant. Our heads were nearly touching as we conversed.

Rebecca seemed astonished that I was on such good terms with my ex-wife; she said she rarely spoke to her ex-husband. She explained in more detail about the acrimonious terms of the divorce; how she had to fight tooth and nail for a settlement that was probably a lot less than she should have received. She was going on holiday with her daughter to Egypt on Saturday and we wouldn't see each other for a week and a half. She hadn't mentioned anything about me to her daughter and said that at this stage, texting and phoning might be difficult. There was going to be a pause in our burgeoning relationship.

With hindsight it was no bad thing. The distance and the fact that Rebecca wasn't just round the corner and was going on holiday with her daughter meant that we had time to pause, reflect on what had been said and how we felt about one another. I knew how I felt, I was totally bonkers about her. She seemed to be equally enamoured.

It was now past 11 o'clock. Rebecca had to go to work next day and it was over an hour's drive to her house. We headed back out into the car park and after paying the exorbitant parking fee, headed to our cars. Mine was parked near to Rebecca's. I blipped the key fob, so my lights flashed and the interior light came on.

"Have a wonderful holiday," I said, holding her in my arms.

"Thanks, Simon," and we started to kiss passionately. Rebecca spoke "Perhaps we should say goodbye inside the car."

She got into the passenger side and I dived into the driver's side. Soon we were kissing again, hands all over. I ran my hand up Rebecca's long legs and her white G-string became clearly visible as her dress rode up.

"Should I go any further?" I thought. "Probably best not to."

After lots of intimate kissing and fondling, Rebecca regained her composure.

Driving home from this wonderful day in Cambridge I felt as though I'd met "the one".

I know what you're thinking, how many times have we been here before? Could Rebecca be that different? Well she was and it seemed to me that perhaps the biggest difference was that she was seriously looking for a steady relationship and in the end, perhaps marriage. She'd hinted at that at our first meeting and said again over dinner today, "I'd love to be married again."

"So would I!" I'd wanted to shout.

As the M11 flashed by, and the large BMW 6 series that was going back tomorrow seemed to stretch its legs, I thought to myself that I needed a plan this time. I needed to organize my life properly not stumble from one disaster to another.

If I wanted a chance to marry Rebecca, if she turned out to really be "the one" I had to get my act together. Being single might sound great to lots of hitched and bored husbands but it wasn't in my experience.

Tomorrow I had the meeting with BMW to hand the car back, a date at the gym with my trainer Melanie, some writing to do and my son was coming round. Friday gym in the morning and fish and chips in the evening. Rebecca was off for a week from Saturday. I had a whole week to sort my life out, tie up loose ends.

That was my plan. I was focused on making it a reality. It was going to be easy, wasn't it?

Decluttering – Part One

The buzzer in the flat assaulted my senses at 8 o'clock the following morning. I had finally switched off my phone in the early hours. I'd had some amazing texts from Rebecca and once again had found it hard to sleep. I dragged myself out of bed, pulled on jogging bottoms and a T shirt and answered the intercom.

"Hello, is that Mr Taylor?"

"Yes," I said, "is that BMW? Yes, come on up," and gave the door release a punch. I opened the door of the flat and was surprised to see not one but two men. Both smartly dressed in dark suits.

One of them spoke. "Good morning Sir, we're here to collect the 6 Series."

"Oh yes. Come on in and I'll get the keys."

'Strange there were two of them,' I thought.

"What do you think of the car?" enquired one the men.

"Yeah it's okay," I lied, "and I'll be sending off my article to your press department."

The other suit offered me a clip board "If you could just sign here, please Mr Taylor," "What's this for?" I said.

"It's for the 7 Series."

"The 7 series?" I said

"Yeah, we've got instructions to pick up the 6 Series, and drop off a 7 Series."

My head was spinning. "Um, okay," I said, "um yeah right, um..."

I realised then how far behind I was with my work and what little attention I was giving it. So I've now got a 7 Series to play with and as the suits refused coffee and returned to their base I headed for the gym.

The changing room was relatively busy. Steve had got over his acute disappointment at Chelsea being knocked out of whatever competition it was and was his usual smiling self. "Hello Simon," he said cheerily.

"Oh hi Steve," I said, "you okay now?"

"Yeah fine, you got a new motor then?" he said.

I explained that unexpectedly I'd received the new 7 Series to write about.

"What a job!" he said.

I headed for the rowing machine and tried to settle down and establish a working rhythm. My thoughts were all over the place. It had occurred to me that my plan to "organize" myself meant explaining to the guys that our next supper was going to be my last fish and chip Friday. I couldn't maintain the Friday routine with the boys when this would be the first opportunity each week to get together with Rebecca.

Yes, sacrificing 'FishnChickn' Fridays was the right thing to do. I'd still see plenty of them and keep in touch by phone and when Rebecca and I were settled we could have a dinner party for Barry and Alison, his wife and Rick and well, Rick and… well I'm sure there would be someone he could bring. There'd always be Beryl.

I was going to ring my Uncle Colin as well and explain to him I would be spending much more time in King's Lynn. King's Lynn.

I'd moved onto the running machine now and was remembering my Mum's telephone call to me. It had to be in 1987.

"I've got something to tell you," she had said importantly.

"You're pregnant?"

"Don't be daft Simon – no. Your Dad and I are moving."

"Moving! Where to?" Mum and Dad had always lived in Grays, they were in their late 50s. Mum had talked about moving for years but nothing had happened. She always seemed to want to move from somewhere to somewhere else, but it was all just talk.

I recall I gave a sarcastic reply "Oh really, where to this time?"

" King's Lynn," my Mum replied.

" King's Lynn," I said, "what do you want to move there for?"

"Well, we've always wanted to live there, we've always wanted to live in Norfolk."

"Really?" I said. "This comes as news to me."

But sure enough they did move to King's Lynn and to everyone's astonishment settled easily, made new friends and were contented. And as visiting family, as I've described, we enjoyed spending time there. It's been the location for several feature films. *Revolution*, starring Al Pacino, *Atonement*, with James McAvoy; *The Fourth Protocol*, with Michael Caine and Piers Brosnan and *The Duchess*, with Kiera Knightley and amazingly parts of *Out of Africa*, with Meryl Streep to name but a few.

Sandringham and its estate are just along the road and there's the whole of the Norfolk coast to explore. The only drawback is that there are no motorways in Norfolk so whether 1 drove like a bat out of hell or Captain Slow from *Top Gear* I couldn't really make any serious dent in the journey time of two and a half hours each way from where we lived in Essex. Nevertheless I have happy memories of many weekends spent in King's Lynn.

Rebecca had described where she lived in King's Lynn and I knew it well. It was a suburb called North Wooton. I could just imagine what her house looked like. She'd given me the address and I'd looked it up on Google Earth. It was a large detached house with a double driveway and double garage. The satellite image even showed Rebecca's Mercedes outside. Though I'd not been there, I knew exactly where it was.

"Simon, Simon… " Someone was talking to me. I looked up and it was Shilpa.

Reminiscing about Norfolk I hadn't noticed her coming into the gym. I got up from the rowing machine. As always Shilpa was to the point.

"What you doing on Saturday?" she said.

"Um, well, err, yes, um, well nothing," I spluttered.

"Good," she said. "Pack a bag, dinner jacket and pick me up at say 3 o'clock."

"What?" I said.

"I want to put the golf club behind us, make it up to you, so I've booked a night away."

'What about Rebecca?' I thought. 'I can't do that!'

Shilpa seemed to read my mind. "It's just a thank you, it's a hotel I've been to before that I know you'll like. I've booked a twin bedded room so you don't have to sleep with me. But it's a fabulous place and I'd love you to come." She touched my arm and said, "I'd feel better."

I didn't really say yes or no but we know don't we, that I was going to go? As I got on the bench press I thought to myself, 'Well, I'm not in a fully-fledged relationship yet with Rebecca and it is the week to sort loose ends out and Shilpa is a loose end.'

Yes that makes perfect sense and I'm sure as you're reading this you're thinking the same. What's wrong with two friends having dinner and putting things to bed. I mean sorting things out and I'll be straight with Shilpa and Rebecca, actually maybe I wouldn't mention it to Rebecca. I mean, I could hardly say no could I?

Showering off after my gym session and coming through the main part of the gym I saw Melanie. "Hi Simon, you okay for a session tomorrow?"

"Yes," I said. And in a gossipy aside, "Got loads of news."

"So I understand," said Melanie, tapping the side of her nose with her finger. "Shilpa's told me all about her plans for you."

"Ah, yes, well I'm not really sure if I'm going."

"What do you mean?"

"Well I've met someone else, Rebecca and I'm not sure I should go or not."

"Oh God, Simon," she said, "she's been talking about this for ages, it's all booked, she'll be ever so upset."

"Okay," I said, "look I'll see you tomorrow, I'll explain everything."

Walking back to the flat I decided to look at the 7 Series BMW that had been dropped off.

Why was I getting these great big barges to write about? Perhaps I should read some of the emails from my agent. Like the Mercedes S class, it seemed to dwarf my Alfa. It's got a Massive grille at the front of it that looks like it's eaten a Range Rover. I'd brought the key with me, so hopped inside to try and familiarise myself with the controls, still shuddering about nearly running Shilpa over in that dreadful Lexus, plugged in my mobile phone to the Bluetooth and as I pulled out of the flat car park, I rang Rick.

"Hello old boy," he said. "No Tsunami message last night? So it didn't go that well with Miss Big Tits from Norfolk then?"

"Morning Rick," I said, "how charming of you to refer to Rebecca as 'Miss Big Tits from Norfolk'."

"Well I'm only stating the obvious aren't I? She has got big tits and she does come from Norfolk doesn't she?"

I explained my dilemma about Shilpa's invitation, not so much an invitation, as a command, forgetting momentarily that Rick had a pathological dislike of Shilpa since the escapade at the golf club. There was a silence, then Rick erupted.

"What are you doing even speaking to the fucking mad Indian bird, let alone agreeing to spend a night with her in a hotel?!"

"Well," I said, playing for time.

"What's she got planned in the hotel? Is she going to get pissed and stab you?"

I tried to explain but I knew it sounded really lame. "She just wants to apologise and set the record straight and I thought..."

Before I could finish Rick said "That's the problem Simon, it all goes wrong when you think. She's completely mad, just say no and keep your cock in your trousers until Rebecca gets back, it's only a week. Surely you can manage without sex for a week?"

"It's not about that at all and anyway, I didn't think you'd understand."

"You're right there. And you're mad," said Rick. Click went the phone.

'Oh dear, who else can I phone?' I thought. Martin. Dear old Martin – he's always on my side.

I reached for the controls of the telephone with BMW's famous i-drive. This is BMW's system that enables a driver to easily access the car's functions, including telephone, audio and Sat. Nav. It's like a metal mouse emerging from the central reservation and whilst it's great if you're left handed, I'm not and even a quick glance at the controls reveals that it's geared for the steering wheel to be on the left side. So here's a £75,000 car that you have to take your eye off the road to look down at the i-drive, which is a bit nuts.

Without managing to run anyone over this time, I managed to dial Martin's phone number.

"Lord Taylor," said Martin. Before I could speak, he said, "And before you ask, Simon there are no functions on at the golf club this weekend."

I laughed, a hollow laugh. Then I quickly explained my dilemma to Martin. He had a characteristically incisive way of putting things.

"Go," he said. "You don't know what's going to happen when Rebecca gets back, she may not even be going on holiday with her daughter for all you know. She might be trying to patch things up with her old man. And okay, Shilpa did make a bit of a scene at the golf club, but there have been worse and I think she's genuinely sorry. You know your trouble, Simon," he said, "you think too much."

Well that was settled then. I decided to phone Shilpa and get a bit more information about where we were going. If I had been in any doubt I had now made up my mind to go.

"Well, it's going to be a surprise," said Shilpa rather breathlessly. She had just come out of the gym.

I didn't want to mention that I'd been on the receiving end of one of her surprises before and I'd rather know a bit more about it. I pressed her for more information discreetly.

"Okay then," said Shilpa, "I'll tell you, we're going to Cliveden and that's all I'm going to say about it. See you Saturday," she said, "bring your dinner jacket and swimming trunks."

'Cliveden,' I thought, 'I know why it rings a bell – the *Profumo affair*.'

In 1961 the Conservative Minister for War, John Profumo, a talented and ambitious politician, married to the actress Valerie Hobson, had been to a house party at Cliveden hosted for an exclusive group of guests by the then Lord Astor. It was a privately owned stately home when Profumo met two girls, Christine Keeler and Mandy Rice-Davies. Keeler, just 19 years of age, was rumoured to be the mistress of a suspected Russian Spy.

Whether they were prostitutes or not I don't know, but there was a whole lot of stuff that went on around the swimming pool. Profumo had an affair with Christine Keeler. Having extra marital affairs isn't a crime of course, but from my history lessons and vaguely remembered newsreels, John Profumo's "crime" was to lie about this to Parliament. He declared that no impropriety had taken place. The scandal cost him his place in the Cabinet and he stepped down as an MP.

I recall he managed to hold onto his marriage and devoted himself to charitable works for the rest of his life. I only know this because I used to have a client who lived in a house that John Profumo had owned. He'd met him a few times and was greatly impressed by this gentle, thoughtful man, wondering how he'd managed to become involved in this extraordinary scenario, later the subject of the film *Scandal*.

So that's where I was off to with Shilpa? Well if she did get drunk and show us up again it wouldn't be the greatest scandal that Cliveden had seen. I was just getting used to the 7 Series and now going on a much longer trip than I'd planned, I didn't know exactly where to but had in mind that I'd probably end up at Lakeside Shopping Centre.

As I was deciding which exit to take off the roundabout ahead my phone rang. I searched for the button on the steering wheel, trying not to take my eyes off the road to answer the phone call.

"Hello," I said.

"Simon it's Barry, Rick's been on the phone, what's this about you going away with Shilpa?"

"Well yes," I said, "its' only one night and we're going to Cliveden."

Barry listened patiently as always before making any comment. "Well I don't want to interfere," he finally said, "but do you really think it's wise? I'm concerned about your safety Simon. Hopefully the golf course incident was a one-off for Shilpa. We all do stupid things occasionally, but if you're determined to go – and I'm sure you are – just be careful and make sure she doesn't have too much to drink. Are we still on for fish and chips tomorrow?"

"Yes," I said. It was too soon for a last supper! I would deal with the issue of future Friday meetings later.

"Okay, lecture over, Simon, see you there."

I was just pulling into a space in the Lakeside car park. Should I buy Shilpa a gift? When she said she was organizing it did that mean she was going to pay? I didn't know what the tariff was at Cliveden, but I could imagine it would be expensive. Maybe it would be an excuse to buy her some knickers. After all, the sex had not been great but at least in a non-biblical sense I knew her well. I was in *Ann Summers* when my mobile rang. I'd just bought two pairs of frilly knickers for Shilpa, one plain white frills and the other was blue with layers of white frills all the way around like tennis knickers. I did my usual joke at the checkout, "They're not for me, ha ha." And then my phone rang, there was a familiar deep female voice.

"Hello Simon." It was Ingrid. "Can you talk right now?" she said.

"Err yes," I said, dropping my knickers, or rather Shilpa's.

I scurried out of the shop, "Oh, hi," I said, "I haven't heard from you for ages. How's um, err… " I was trying to think of the airhostess's name, "…Katie?"

She said, "Oh fine, I haven't seen her for a while. I was just phoning to see if you could do me a favour."

"Well, yes of course," I said.

"I wonder if you could put me up for the night."

"Well, um, err..."

"Are you with anyone yet? Have you got a girlfriend yet?"

I decided not to explain my complicated love life. "Well, no, not really," I mumbled, "not a live-in one anyway."

"Well if it's okay with you, I've got to go to a works "do" near you in Chelmsford, don't particularly fancy staying in a hotel and I thought if it was okay, I could stay with you and we could catch up. You've got a spare room haven't you?"

"Err, yes," I said, "I've got a spare room."

"Well I've got a boyfriend now, Hamish."

"Scottish?" I enquired unnecessarily. "So you've gone for a man in a skirt?" I said. We both laughed. "Won't he mind you staying with me?"

"I'm not going to tell him," she said. "I'll be at yours on Sunday night if that's okay? I know it's a bit of an odd time but I'll explain when I see you. It'll be late, about 10 o'clock. Is that okay, are you sure?"

"Yes of course," I said, "I'll get the spare room ready."

'Well what's wrong with that?' I thought, 'putting up an old friend, nothing at all, just doing her a favour and it would be nice to see her again. I wonder what did happen to Katie.'

As I was walking back to the 7 Series, which was growing on me, I decided to stop for a coffee. I was in the queue waiting to order my "tall skinny decaf mocha with hazelnut syrup" – yes, yes I know it sounds metrosexual but give it a try (you'll like it if you have a sweet tooth) – someone tapped me on the shoulder. It was Judy, the lady from church.

"Hello Simon," she said breezily. Church had been on the back burner for a few weeks and I hadn't seen Judy at the gym lately. She glanced at my bag "What have you been buying?"

I looked down at the tell-tale *Ann Summers* carrier bag, they must have spent ages designing a carrier bag without the words "Ann Summers" on it, thinking it looks discreet, and it doesn't. It screams "I've bought something really sexy from Ann Summers!" Everyone knows that the pink and black carrier bags are from Ann Summers. We both looked down at the carrier bag and I decided to change the subject.

"How's Father?" I asked. I ordered my exotic mocha and asked Judy if she'd like to join me, she appeared to be on her own and indeed she was. Judy asked for a straightforward large cappuccino. I saw her raise one eyebrow when I ordered mine.

"Sounds exotic," she said. She smiled warmly. I thought how very pleasant she was. As we sat down together Judy answered my question. "Well, Father's okay, but he's a bit stressed, I'm glad I've seen you because you may be able to help. The church is having some work done on it as you know." I didn't, but just nodded. "And there's a Parish Council meeting due to take place there this Wednesday. His house is far too small."

"Is it?" I said.

"And we were just looking for somewhere else to go. Do you think the gym would accommodate us?"

"I should think so," I said, "they're very helpful in there. You could probably use one of the function rooms."

"I thought so too," she said, following this with, "Simon, you seem to know the management well, could you possibly ask about our Council's use of a room for me?" Judy was Head of the Parish Council. We chatted a while over our coffees. I didn't know much about her though she was friendly. We would chat after services and shared a pew, normally as I've explained standing together, but that was about the extent of our friendship. She asked me directly if I was seeing Shilpa. I decided not to fill her in on the detail but nodded and said I was still seeing her, "as a friend of course."

She seemed interested in me and asked about my work; the flat and how I was coping alone. I answered but before I could ask any questions of her she bent down, picked up her handbag and said that she had to dash. She hurriedly wrote down a list of optional times that the Parish Council would be able to meet at the gym along with her mobile number, saying, "Give me a ring if that's okay, otherwise we'll have to come up with some other ideas." She gathered up her several shopping bags. I offered a hand, she took it and gave me a kiss on the cheek: "See you Simon, bless you." and waved.

'She was actually really rather nice,' I thought, and it would be no trouble to do something to help out Father and the church.

I hurried around Marks and Spencer's. If Ingrid was going to stay on Sunday night it would be a good idea to get some food and wine in and if I was going away I needed some new pants and socks. Women's underwear is so much more interesting than men's? With women's underwear you get at least two pieces, three if you include a suspender belt and then there's the fabulous corsets, in silk, satin and lace. Men have pants, y-fronts, briefs or boxers. And vests! Novelty underwear is about as exciting as men's underwear gets and unless you're aged thirteen, it's awful. I've only ever worn white briefs, I suppose it goes back to my days at military college. I'm not very evolved.

Heading back to the flat in the 7 Series, it occurred to me that my usual uneventful life was cranking up and things were becoming busy. Fish and chips tomorrow with the guys, then Cliveden with Shilpa on Saturday. Ingrid was arriving for the night on Sunday and now I had to organise something for the church at the gym for Judy on Wednesday.

At this rate I was going to have to employ a PA. Was my dinner jacket clean for Cliveden? Had I taken "Graham Norton" into the cleaners? I'd have to check when I got back. Then I'd have to get a suitcase ready, check what I was going to travel in, have breakfast in.

Should I take pyjamas, as I wouldn't be sleeping with Shilpa? I needed to ensure there were clean towels for Ingrid, change the sheets in the spare room, have a dash round with J Edgar (Hoover) and I'd probably have to go shopping again to stock up on fruit juice, milk, etc. etc.

'Get a grip, Simon,' I told myself, 'you're just going away for one night, having an old friend to stay and asking the gym about a Parish Council meeting, most people have far more to worry about and deal with than this.'

I decided to call back in at the gym immediately and ask about the Parish Council meeting. That would sort out one agenda item.

"Sorry Simon," said Ian "but all the meeting rooms are booked. The local hotel has had a burst pipe on its lower ground floor and they've lots of people staying over who need meeting rooms. We just can't do it I'm afraid. I'm happy for them to sit in the restaurant, how many of them are there? Can't they just go to the priest's house?"

I decided to ring Judy.

"Hello," she said.

"Hi Judy, I'm at the gym, looks like they're already committed. How many of you are there and why can't they go to the priest's house again?"

"Well there's only going to be six or eight of us at the most. Don't worry Simon, I'll sort it out. Thanks anyway."

"Don't worry, Ian, I think we're all sorted. Thanks anyway," I told him.

"Oh," Ian said. Then, "Simon whilst I've got you, did you want to pay for your next six sessions of personal training? You're seeing Melanie tomorrow and for the next six weeks?"

"Yes, that'd be fine," I said, "great."

"That'll bring us into the dark nights," said Ian.

'Crumbs, it will,' I thought. It would be all that "spring forward and fall back" nonsense shortly.

"It'll be downhill all the way to Christmas then," said Ian.

'Christmas,' I thought, 'Christmas. I wonder where I'll be this Christmas, hopefully with the lovely Rebecca in King's Lynn. Perhaps my Uncle Colin could come round and join us as well.'

"Oh," said Ian, "someone was asking about you."

"Really?" I said. "Not a debt collector was it?" I laughed in case he didn't!

"No she's not a member here, I think she's read some of your stuff. Wanted your phone number. I said obviously I couldn't give her your phone number but you were a regular."

"Oh, right," I said, "what was she like?"

Ian smiled "Attractive in a sort of business-type way."

"It was probably someone wanting to have a go at me about something I'd written."

I didn't think any more of this conversation and headed back to the flat to start preparing. The first thing I had to do to tie up the loose ends of my life so I could embark on a long-term relationship bliss with Rebecca, was to finish the assignments I had on my desktop. I made myself a pot of coffee and headed up to the mezzanine floor to begin work. I'd pinned Rebecca's details to the back of my workstation and there she was, smiling at me from her photo. I decided to get my head down and just work. I finished the article on the 6 Series BMW and made notes on its successor.

Later that evening the phone rang, it was Uncle Colin. "Hello idiot nephew," he said, "what's happened with this bird from King's Lynn?"

I brought Uncle Colin up to date and explained that Rebecca was going on holiday, that she was lovely and that I thought we might end up spending Christmas together!

Then Rick rang. "You're not still going, are you?" he said.

"Well I am, look it's just two friends making up and having dinner together in a posh hotel. I don't know why you've got a problem with it."

"Because she's mad!" bellowed Rick. "Oh well, see you tomorrow," he said. "You are mad but I know you're going to go."

Then Rebecca phoned, she even sounded lovely on the phone. "I've got my Mum and Dad coming round later, Simon," she said, "so I thought I'd give you a ring now. I'm just packing, it's an early start Saturday. Thanks again for the lovely bikini, it fits perfectly. I'm wearing it now and thought of you."

"Got it on?" I said swallowing hard.

"Hmm, I thought I'd just try it on. The bottoms fit much better now I haven't got my knickers on."

I resisted the temptation to say something suggestive. "Oh good, that's nice." Useless berk! How inane. I decided to push my luck a bit. "So you finish school on Friday and then you're off on Saturday?"

"Yes that's right. Dad's taking us to the airport."

"So will you be doing any work on holiday?" I said, thinking of Niamh and her dentistry books in Corfu. "Well, I've got some marking to do," she said, "but I won't be taking it. We get back the following Saturday so I've Sunday to do it, it'll probably mean staying up late into the night, but I have to get it done."

"What happens if you don't do it?" I said. Without any hesitation at all Rebecca laughed and said, "I get my bottom spanked."

The blood rushed to my head, I think as I thought about Rebecca's lovely bottom.

"Well, I must dash, Simon," she said. I'll give you a ring tomorrow night."

"Well, I'm going out with the guys for fish and chips."

"What guys?" said Rebecca.

"You know, I told you I always go out on Friday night with my friends Rick and Barry."

"Oh yes," she said, "have a nice time and give me a ring when you get in."

I started the assignment on the 7 Series and sent an e-mail to my agent asking why I was test driving big "bargey" executive tanks, not lovely sports cars; quickly rang my ex and the children to check everything was okay with them.

It was nearly midnight when I headed to bed. I tried to sleep. I generally take a long while to get to sleep but Rebecca's comment about her bottom being spanked was occupying my thoughts. .

It had prompted an early memory. From the late1960s when I was about nine or ten.

I was a pretty annoying child, full of questions, irritatingly inquisitive and a bit of a handful for my Mum and Dad. My Mum always said that I was older than my years and by about nine years of age I was beginning to tire of playing out in the street with friends.

In those days we lived in a quiet street in a suburb of Grays. We were an ordinary family. I went to the local Catholic primary school where corporal punishment was administered routinely. I remember being caned by a nun on both hands when I was five for genuflecting on the wrong knee at Mass. It is true.

Nowadays the nun would be prosecuted for assault and rightly so. I didn't tell my parents but I still genuflect on the correct knee at Mass. Corporal punishment was in fairly common currency in many schools in the 60s though more threatened than actually administered thankfully. It wasn't used by my parents.

I woke up late and was in a panic that Friday morning. I'd yet to pack. I needed to do some ironing, a shirt for travelling in, a dinner shirt, another shirt for breakfast – or maybe I'd put on a rugby shirt. There was a pool of course: the very famous pool.

Would I get a chance to have a swim in it? Would it be closed – maybe now a shrine to the Profumo affair – and then there was Ingrid coming to stay on Sunday. I headed into the spare room, my son stayed there sometimes. I quickly gathered up the duvet and pillowcases and shoved them in the washing machine, dusted and hoovered, put fresh towels out, toiletries I'd bought in Marks and Spencer's into the downstairs bathroom and sat down to check my emails.

Over the last few months I'd had a couple of messages from Niamh and I was pleased to see her name in my inbox again. We'd settled into a comfortable friendship and perhaps that's really what we should have just aimed for in the first place, but I wasn't regretting my time with her.

The next e-mail was from someone I didn't know, just, "Hello Simon, I got your email address from a friend and I'm writing a book, I know you go to the gym and I wondered if we could meet up?" It was signed "Kirsty".

'How interesting,' I thought.

So I replied immediately, "Hello Kirsty, thanks for your email, yes I'd be happy to meet up and in fact I'm just off to the gym now." I'd delayed my early morning session with Melanie, in order to get some things done in the flat.

An email came straight back from Kirsty just as I was putting my trainers on. "I'll be near the gym, any chance of seeing you today?" 'How about coffee? Can do 12.30pm' I typed back.

'Great. See you in the coffee bar then?'

I was intrigued, I wondered what Kirsty would be like, she did indeed seem business-like and as the meeting was about a book I wondered if my coffee would be tax deductible.

Melanie was waiting for me in the gym. "You are going," she said, without any preamble at all.

"I assume you mean Shilpa's invitation. I am."

"Thank God for that," she said. "She's fretting that you're not going to go."

"Shilpa fretting?" I said. I couldn't imagine Shilpa fretting about anything.

"Do you know where you're off to?" she said.

"I do, Cliveden."

"She really wants to get back with you," said Melanie, as I stepped onto the ski machine.

"She wants to get back with me? We were never on," I said. "It wasn't a proper relationship."

"Well Simon, not that long ago you were besotted with her. I think you still are and if it hadn't been for the unfortunate incident at the golf club, I think you'd still be together. She's really sorry Simon, she wants to put it all behind her and start again, and that's why she's organised this night at Cliveden."

I explained to Melanie that I'd met the lovely Rebecca and how suitable she was and how she was looking for a long-term relationship. I told her about her bra size. I have no idea why I did this though unless it was meant to give Melanie pause for thought. Then again, perhaps it was simply because it impressed so many of my friends, male and female.

"Lucky cow," she said. "Well Simon," said Melanie, "it's very early days with Rebecca, just see how it goes with Shilpa, I'm sure you'll have a lovely evening."

The day passed quickly in a dizzying sequence of tidying, cleaning and packing. There was no sensible order to these chores though and I must have easily chalked up 10,000 steps in the hours before it was time to meet the guys at the fish and chip shop.

The whole thing, my love life was rolled out again for conference debate. Shilpa, Niamh, Rebecca, the golf club incident, Rebecca's tits, why I was mad, etc. etc.

I agreed a new call sign with the guys in case Shilpa kicked off again. "Broad Sword calling Danny Boy" would mean "She's off her face and I need help!" Though quite what was going to happen then, I don't know.

I phoned Rebecca when I got back to the flat, I felt slightly guilty. "Have a great time," I said.

"And you," said Rebecca. "What plans have you got?"

'Oh my God,' I thought, 'don't ask!' "Oh I've um, got to organise something for the church," I said. I felt pretty guilty then and just looked at my shoes.

I'd had a couple of texts from Judy, explaining that for all sorts of reasons the church hall and the priest's house were off limits and they needed somewhere to meet up. I'd already offered the mezzanine floor in the flat, but I couldn't see it really happening.

Rebecca signed off with, "I so wish you were coming with me on holiday Simon, I won't be able to phone while I'm there but I'll send you a postcard and I'll call the minute I get back. Oh and did you get my package?"

'Package?' I thought. "Err, no," I said.

"Oh not to worry," she said. "I'm sure it'll arrive tomorrow."

Sure enough I went to the post box and there was a red post office card telling me that the postman had tried unsuccessfully to deliver a package. I was able to collect it the next day at the post office. I was trying not to mess the flat up as I knew Ingrid would be arriving. I wasn't sure what time Shilpa and I would return on the Sunday morning.

I went to bed early and my thoughts again returned to the late 1960s, Rebecca and spanking. It had occurred to me that there was another connection between Rebecca, corrective treatment and the very young Simon.

As a 9 year old I had been friendly with Lesley, an older girl who lived up the road. Lesley went to the local convent school and she would have been about 16 years old when I was approaching my tenth birthday. I was fascinated with her.

We both went to the local church with our families and afterwards, if I was good (which I always was) I was allowed to go to Lesley's house and she would play records with me. The Beatles, the Who, Rolling Stones, Jimmy Hendrix. Elton hadn't yet made an appearance in the charts and was still playing keyboard/piano with Long John Baldry.

I'd been impressed with girls from an early age and as Lesley's bus got in later than mine from school I'd often wait for her to arrive and carry her books or satchel. She wasn't really a woman though she wasn't a girl either, unlike Georgina Grey whom I sat next to at school who was a kid like me.

Although looking back it must have been irritating for Lesley, having a snotty nine year old hanging about, she was never cross with me; and when I asked, "Can I carry your books for you?" she'd always say sweetly, "Yes of course Simon" and I'd walk along beside her, telling her what I'd done at school that day.

Her Mum and mine were friends, her dad was a bit, well standoffish and he also worked in a school. Then over a period of several days Lesley was late from the bus and I missed meeting her.

Because I hadn't seen her for a short while and I missed her, I mentioned it to my Mum.

"Don't go bothering Lesley," she said, "she's coming up to exams at school so she'll be really busy and won't want you hanging about." Of course I took no notice when an hour or so later I noticed Lesley walk past our house.

Now in those days the houses on our street had small back gardens. Running along the rear of these was an alleyway that could be reached by gates in the perimeter fences of our own and the neighbour's back gardens.

It had become a habit of mine to run along the alley and into Lesley's garden and knock on the back door. Her Mum always invited me in and Lesley would be eager to play me her latest Rolling Stones record or show me some of her "Stop the Bombing in Vietnam" stickers that I didn't really understand.

"Can I go and knock for Lesley?" I said to my Mum.

"No you can't," she said sounding exasperated. "I've told you she's studying for her exams and she'll have lots of homework to do so just leave Lesley alone."

Paul Fox

"Okay Mum," I said, "can I go and knock for my friend Sean instead?" Sean's house was only slightly further up from Lesley's. I had no intention of going to Sean's.

My mum said that would be okay as long as I was back for tea in an hour and no later. I tore out the back door and up the alley before she could change her mind. Within a moment I was walking up the back garden path of Lesley's house.

Approaching the back door I was aware of raised voices, I always knocked on the back door first, but as I got closer the voices grew louder.

I recognised her dad's voice. I couldn't quite make out what he was saying but he was shouting, something about boys and smoking and homework. I had my fist raised in mid-air poised to knock but there was something about the unfolding scene that made me pause. I sensed that I shouldn't knock on the door. Of course I didn't have enough sense to turn around and walk away.

The voices were coming from a room downstairs, the dining room I now know. This large room had French doors and though I realized I should leave before anyone saw me, I was curious and moved to one side of the opening to look into the dining room. Keeping my body out of sight and peeking in at the frame, I saw Lesley standing in front of her father. She was wearing her school uniform as Sixth formers did in the 1970s. White shirt, cardigan, and pleated skirt and knee high white socks. She was wearing quite adult shoes thought. Patent with heels. Her father was ranting at her and Lesley had her head down and kept trying to interject. I was fascinated, I knew I should move away but I just couldn't.

Lesley erupted and began shouting back at her father. "Well if I want a boyfriend it's my business not yours and yes, I've had the odd cigarette, but you smoke and so does Mum!" she yelled. Her father was incandescent. What happened next astonished me. Her dad strode across the room and stood in front of Lesley.

"I've had enough of this, young lady!" he said. He grasped and held Lesley's wrist and in one move hauled her across his lap. All I could see now was Lesley's bottom facing me, her legs kicking. He was going to smack her bottom!

"You're not speaking to me like that, young lady," he said, "no matter how old you are."

As it was the 1970s, Lesley's skirt was quite short and her white knickers were clearly visible. I don't remember her dad lifting her skirt up or whether it just fell over her back, but her dad was smacking her bottom very hard and soon Lesley was screaming for him to stop and saying that she was sorry. My eyes widened and then I ran. I ran down the garden, out the gate and back to my house. I couldn't believe what I'd seen. I'd heard about people getting smacked on the bottom, but it had never happened to me, nor did I want it to. I'd never seen Lesley's knickers before and maybe it was this encounter rather than Mrs Pike's pink knickers only a few years later that sparked my interest in bottoms, underwear and their mysteries.

I recall that Mum quizzed me as soon as I got home. "Where have you been?" she asked.

"Sean wasn't in," I said.

"You've not been to Lesley's have you?"

"Err no," I squeaked. I never did tell my Mum or anyone else what I'd seen. Rebecca's reference to her bottom being smacked had reminded me of the childhood Lesley episode.

Saturday morning I was awoken by chirping from my mobile. There was a text from Rebecca. It was only 7am so she had obviously had a very early start from King's Lynn.

Her text read "Hi Simon at the gate now, so will be switching my phone off, look forward to seeing you in about a week's time. Love Rebecca. xx."

I can't remember what I texted back but I think it was something cheesy like "Counting the hours until you return xxx," or something similar. Rebecca didn't reply.

I wandered downstairs and made myself a cup of coffee. I gave myself a stern talking to. "Right, this is it Simon, the clock's ticking, from now and until she returns you've got to get everything sorted and out of the way."

I was due to meet Shilpa up at half past eleven, collecting her to drive to Buckinghamshire and Cliveden. I no longer felt guilty about going, after all Shilpa was an old friend and there was nothing wrong with two friends having dinner together in a historic hotel, even sharing a bedroom? We had twin beds after all. I know it's hard to believe now, but I had genuinely convinced myself that we weren't going to have sex – I was saving myself for Rebecca.

I couldn't reconcile Melanie's comment about Shilpa wanting to retrieve a relationship with what I knew of Shilpa. I had been serious when I'd explained to Melanie that we hadn't actually had a "thing" or a relationship. I'd packed pyjamas.

And as for the prospect that she might want to have sex? 'Well' I told myself, 'I'm not an animal, I'm perfectly capable of controlling my desires.' Sex had been embarrassing and problematic in the past. I still felt squeamish at the memory of our last encounter. And so, no, we weren't spending time at Cliveden for dinner, bed and sex. We were going because Shilpa wanted to make amends for her behaviour at the Golf Club, for companionship and to say goodbye.

Do you believe any of this? I can't say I'm surprised. Did I – genuinely?

I decided to take the 7 Series BMW. It would give me an opportunity to take the car on a decent journey and variety of roads including a series of twisty country lanes. Once back I could finish the partly completed article. I had such a casual approach to the weekend that unusually I wasn't at all anxious about what to wear. I packed the Graham Norton jacket; a dinner shirt, bow tie and settled on dressing in chinos, a stripy shirt and a blazer.

The electric gates at Shilpa's were open and as I pulled in and parked beside her four wheel drive she appeared.

"Hi Simon, I packed this small bag but I thought we could hang my evening dresses in the back of the car."

"Sure," I said.

Then as an afterthought and several seconds later she made her way around to my side of the car, said, "Hello Simon," formally, giggled and kissed me on the cheek.

Shilpa had hung up two or three dresses; we were only staying one night! I thought she was perhaps as indecisive as I normally was about packing. She had a small suitcase on wheels and a larger bucket-shaped tote bag which I later found out contained her cosmetics and what she called her "girly" pieces.

We left to join the M25.

Shilpa was very chatty. 'Shall I tell her about Rebecca?' I wondered. After all we were just friends weren't we? I was tempted to but telling her in the car didn't seem to be the best time really. We chatted about the gym, she didn't mention the golf club, only asked if I'd seen Martin at all. I brushed it aside and said yes, Martin was fine. We never discussed it again.

"Have you got another new car again Simon?" she said looking around.

"No this one's on test. Do you like it?"

"Has it got those massage seats?"

"No," I said.

Shilpa found the controls for the electronically powered passenger seat and was soon fully reclined next to me, twirling strands of her long dark hair between her slim fingers. She wore skinny jeans, tucked into suede ankle boots, a tee shirt and a cashmere cardigan. She didn't have much make up on but she looked fantastic. "Well, Simon," she said, "are you looking forward to your treat?"

While she said that she was running a forefinger down the length of her body and over the zip of her jeans. I tried not to look at her and kept my eyes on the road.

"Yes," I said, "I've read up a bit on the history of Cliveden, I'm looking forward to seeing if the swimming pool where Profumo met Christine Keeler and Mandy Rice-Davies is still there."

"I don't know anything about that," she said, so I filled her in on the story and what had happened there. "Hmm," she said, "interesting."

Arriving at Cliveden is an event in itself. The house is located inside a huge estate. The first section of parkland is open to the public. Further entry into the grounds of the house itself is restricted for "Hotel Guests only". The driveway extends along a lengthy tree-lined avenue to a Massive fountain. Cliveden House is a country house hotel leased from the National Trust, overlooking the Thames with a series of gardens, formal, woodland and a riverside walk. Talk about having "wow" factor!

As I eased the 7 Series along the private road to the hotel I noticed someone waving. It was a liveried footman, beckoning us towards him. As I pulled up, he approached the car, opened Shilpa's side and said, "Welcome to Cliveden, ma'am."

I got out the driver's side.

"Welcome to Cliveden sir," he said.

"Thank you."

"Leave the keys in the car, sir and I'll arrange for your luggage to be taken to your room. Just remember to take any mobile phones and personal items with you."

"Gosh," I said, "thanks ever so much," diving into the back pocket of my chinos and hoping there was some money there. I found money for a tip and handed it to him.

Cliveden is probably the most impressive hotel I've ever stayed in. Uniformed flunkies everywhere, it oozes style and character. What it must have been like to have owned such a place when it was a private house I found hard to imagine. After signing in at reception we were shown to our room.

"You're not in the main house itself," said a slightly officious bellboy of about 50 years, "you're in the annex."

I glanced at Shilpa. After all, she'd made the reservation. Sounded okay to me, but I thought immediately of the hotel in Corfu and wondered if we'd be changing rooms on seeing where we'd been allocated. I knew Shilpa would be very direct if she wasn't happy with the booking.

We left the main house, turned a corner and saw a sign saying "Private Chapel" then passed under an archway and into a cool, stone built house.

Our names were on the door. "Simon and Shilpa".

'Bit odd,' I thought. 'What if we didn't want anyone to know we were here?'

The room, a suite was beautiful. Decorated in cool cream and gold furnishings with comfortable deep sofas, it had a raised lounge area and a large bathroom. And a vast double bed! Our bags and clothes were already in the room. I got out a fiver and gave it to the porter who had arrived to deliver my car key.

"Thank you sir," he said.

Shilpa addressed him, "Weren't you going to open the French doors for us?"

"Oh yes ma'am," he said, crossing over the expanse of deep gold carpet to the double doors. Opening them with a flourish, "Voila!"

There it was – the swimming pool – the same famous swimming pool that had been at the centre of the Profumo affair.

I turned to Shilpa, "You knew all along, didn't you?"

"Yes," she said and laughing, ran into my arms. "I knew you were a history buff," she said, "and you'd be fascinated about the pool."

"Can we swim in it?" I asked the porter.

"Of course sir, you're our guests, it's yours to enjoy."

When he'd left us I asked Shilpa about the bed. She said that she'd made a mistake and only noticed this when she'd picked up the booking details and read them a couple of days before. She'd rung to see if the reservation could be altered and it would have been possible to book a twin bedded room in the House but we wouldn't have been able to have the suite by the pool.

I didn't make a fuss! I told her that I thought the room magnificent and I was thrilled at the access it gave us to the pool. It was late September but it was a sunny day and relatively warm.

We decided to have a dip in the pool straight away. I should have realized what Shilpa had in mind because there had been a clue – the only things she'd told me to bring were my dinner jacket and swimming trunks.

"Quick," Shilpa said, "let's get in the pool, last one in pays for dinner."

I threw off my jacket, pulled my shirt over my head, ripped my trousers socks and pants off in one go and yanked on my trunks. Shilpa had only managed to take off her jeans and boots at this point and I was momentarily distracted by her white knickers.

Doing up the drawstring of my shorts, I ran out to the pool and jumped in. I regretted this instantly. It was freezing, positively glacial. I flapped about a bit, swam a brisk couple of lengths then climbed from the pool. In my haste I'd not bothered to take a towel with me. I was half way back to the room and shivering when Shilpa appeared in her white bikini.

"Is it cold?" she enquired.

"Bloody freezing!" I said.

"Simon you're such a sissy."

She strolled languidly to the edge of the pool, stretched her arms above her head, executed a perfect dive and swam ten lengths without a break then came to the side of the pool and put her elbows on the side. I was now wearing a luxurious deep pile robe from the room and I'd brought a couple of towels and her robe as well.

"Well, it is a little cold" she conceded graciously, "but you soon warm up. Are you warming up Simon?"

I leant down and kissed her wet forehead, "This is a fabulous hotel, thank you so much."

"Pleasure," she said. I took her hand, helped her out of the pool and wrapped her in a robe.

We sat down on loungers next to the pool and a waiter appeared from nowhere. "Would you like any refreshments at all, Sir, Madam?"

It was only about half past two in the afternoon but we hadn't eaten any lunch so we ordered sandwiches and as Shilpa said she wanted to celebrate with Champagne I ordered us a glass each. I resisted the temptation to order a bottle.

As we ate our late lunch Shilpa asked, "What shall we do now then? I've booked a table for half past seven so we'll need to start getting ready about five."

I had a suggestion. "Why don't we get dressed and have a wander round, I'd love to see the rest of the house," I said.

We gathered up our things, drained our glasses and headed into the room to get dressed. As soon as we were inside the door and whilst the French doors were still open, Shilpa stepped out of her bikini bottoms, untied the strings of her bikini top and rubbed her lovely, athletic, slim, toned body with a fluffy white towel.

Paul Fox

She sat on the bed, plugged in a hairdryer and started to dry her hair. The whites of her eyes flashed at me occasionally as if to say "Do you like what you see?"

I went into the bathroom, had a quick shower, dried myself off, came back and started to get dressed. Shilpa was still naked. The French doors still open. She wasn't in any hurry to get her clothes on. She made a half-hearted attempt at putting on some make up, the tension in the room was too much to bear. I knew that I probably shouldn't have done it and I hadn't any clear idea about what would occur but I took hold of Shilpa and pulled her to her feet and kissed her full on the mouth.

Shilpa immediately said, "Ah, I thought we were going for a walk?"

"Are there any other options available?" I asked.

Shilpa took me by the hand and pushed me down onto the bed, she knelt over me and we made love noisily and enthusiastically. It just happened. Well, it didn't of course, it was actively stage-managed by Shilpa who deserved an Oscar for her choreography skills. I was her supporting actor. I didn't deserve any award – a kick in the crown jewels from Rebecca arguably.

As she headed for the bathroom Shilpa turned her head and smiled cheekily. "I'm glad I didn't bother with twin beds," she said.

We wandered round the hotel for ages, it's classically British. I could imagine Kings and Prime Ministers, U.S. Presidents at every turn staying there. I know Churchill did. The House has been rebuilt at least twice and has witnessed some of the most historic events in this Island's history. It was once the home of Nancy Astor, Lady Astor, the first female Member of Parliament. There's a memorial commemorating a duel there in the 1600s.

We found the library and being a history enthusiast I was in heaven in the midst of its collection. Shilpa seemed happy enough looking at titles and I was soon engrossed. We ordered tea in the library. I was really enjoying myself but as the afternoon shadows started to appear I wasn't thinking about my striking athletic companion but about Rebecca.

I wondered if she'd text me when she landed. I glanced at the phone in my pocket. It showed I had one new message. 'Rebecca?' I thought, discreetly opening it. "Be at yours tomorrow about half 9. Will try and bug out of the party early. Bringing food n wine!"

I quickly texted back "Okay" and a kiss, hoping Shilpa hadn't noticed. It was nearly five thirty.

"I'm going to go and start getting ready," said Shilpa. "If you're happy here, there's no need to come with me, I'm going to have a bath and stuff."

"Okay," I said. I watched Shilpa's denim clad bottom wiggle as she left the room and smiled to myself. I carried on reading. About an hour later I headed up to the room, Shilpa was still in the bathroom. "It's me," I said. "Are you still in the bath?"

"Yes, come on in."

This would be an easy shot for a film, Shilpa in the bath, covered with bubbles, her hair in a turban. "You look comfortable," I said.

"Hmm, unlike most hotels," she said, "they've got a fabulous range of bubble bath and shower gel."

"Would you like a cup of tea?" I said, remembering that Shilpa didn't drink coffee.

"Yes please," she replied.

I looked round the suite for kettle, mini pots of milk, instant coffee and tea bags then realised that this wasn't the sort of hotel that encouraged guests to do anything for themselves. I rang reception. "Could we have tea for two?" I enquired, in my best BBC voice.

"Of course Mr Taylor, will that be Earl Grey tea?"

I covered the receiver with one hand and shouted to Shilpa, "Earl Grey?"

"Who's he?" she said with a laugh. "Yes please."

I lounged on the bed, flicked on the large flat screen TV and found Sky News. I could hear Shilpa getting out of the bath, then there was a knock on the door. I opened it and another uniformed flunkey sailed in bearing an outsized silver tray, complete with silver teapot, two cups, silver jug of milk and a silver contraption for squeezing half a lemon.

"Where would you like this sir?" he said.

"Err, just by the TV," I said. I rummaged in my pocket for another five pounds. He set the tray down and started to rearrange the cups and saucers. Suddenly Shilpa appeared in the bedroom, turban in place, but instead of a towel wrapped round her she held a towel just in front of her at her neck. The long towel covered her completely at the front. "Oh goody," she said, "tea, thank you."

The waiter seemed flustered and quickly made a hasty retreat. At the door he turned round and I gave him his five pounds. "Thank you sir," he said, looking down, then looking up again I could see his eyes widen. Quickly he turned and was gone.

When I turned round I realised what he'd seen. Shilpa was standing just slightly further into the bedroom with the towel still in place, but she was now standing in front of a full-length mirror, so looking at her you could see her bare bottom reflected in the mirror behind her. He certainly got more than his five pounds worth that day. I decided not to mention it. On reflection I'm sure she did it on purpose.

Watching Shilpa get dressed for dinner and sipping tea was a delicious experience. She pulled on a pair of silky French knickers, similar to Niamh's, but more close fitting and sat doing her make up for ages. I sat on the bed pretending to watch Sky News, but in reality I was watching her. I love watching girls get dressed. Eventually I made a half-hearted attempt at getting dressed, decided to shave again, went into the bathroom and ran some hot water. When I came back into the room, Shilpa had changed her knickers and was now sporting a lacy black pair and was pulling on a black suspender belt.

'Fantastic,' I thought.

She'd got on a black matching bra and began to gently long leg fine black stockings along the length of each long leg. I was fascinated. The stockings had a seam up the back and Shilpa carefully manoeuvred the seams into position. The contrast of the black underwear and Shilpa's brown skin and the dim lights of the hotel bedroom was a sight to behold (gosh, I hope they make this into a film).

I pulled on my evening shirt, slapped on some aftershave, *Aramis* this time; vintage, reminiscent of the '70s, still a favourite. I found my shoes and "Graham Norton".

Shilpa was stepping into one of her evening dresses having chosen a black satin floor length gown with a full skirt – lots of frothy black netting beneath this. She had black and silver shoes with a silver instep.

She rubbed something into her hands and ran it through her hair, I later found out that it was Moroccan Argan oil and it gave her hair a lustrous shine.

As we walked arm in arm down to dinner, heads turned and I knew they weren't looking at me. Shilpa had tied a small black silk scarf around her neck, which gave the impression of her wearing a choker. It was a perfect accessory to her outfit.

Little did I know that the coming months would lead me to feel very differently about items tied round women's necks. Tonight, innocent of such matters Shilpa looked truly stunning.

She had booked us into a new-style restaurant inside the main house. It was dramatically decorated in a minimalist style with bright red furnishings and décor. Unbeknown to her however this wasn't the main restaurant. There was one other couple in this dining room, but that was all.

In contrast there seemed to be plenty of guests heading into the far larger and more traditionally, soberly decorated main dining room. We were seated at our table and given huge menus, measuring at least four times the size of a magazine. Shilpa and I disappeared behind them. I couldn't make much sense of it. I later realised it was a tasting menu which involved ordering up to twelve courses.

Some of the options on the menu weren't recognizable: wild fowl, partridge, goose, chicken were fortunately amongst those that were. It was a fusion menu and included highly unusual combinations as well as choices that were in pots of ice.

I am a peasant really when it comes to food and what was on offer was going to be completely wasted on me. Peering round the enormous menu I could see that Shilpa appeared puzzled too. I waited for her to speak.

"This is a bit odd isn't it?" she said.

"Hmmm not really what I had in mind," I replied.

Now I would have stuck it out, I'd have ordered something after asking for some advice, politely sat there, paid the enormous bill, left and complained about it forever. When the waiter came over to take our order, Shilpa however slammed the menu down on the table with such force that a puff of air erupted from it and Shilpa's long hair wafted about momentarily.

"Can I take your order madam?" said the waiter, very politely.

"No you can't," said Shilpa, "this is not what we want at all; we want some proper food."

Sensing a problem, the Manager materialised. "Is there some problem?" he enquired, again very politely.

I didn't quite know where to look, I was still holding my menu half open, and there wasn't room for it on the table. I did think about putting it to one side down by my chair. Shilpa explained that the menu wasn't what we were expecting and we were unlikely to enjoy the meal

"That's no problem at all," said the manager, ignoring me completely on realising that Shilpa was in charge. "Would you like me to transfer your reservation to the main dining room?"

Without referring to me, Shilpa just said, "Yes please." The manager turned on his heels announcing he would return shortly, if we'd like to wait.

I finally managed to put my menu down and grinned at Shilpa wishing I'd had the nerve to take control of the situation as directly as she had.

The manager returned and spoke. "Your table will be ready in 20 minutes ma'am," he said finally glancing at me. "Perhaps you would like to have a drink in the lounge whilst waiting."

Paul Fox

Shilpa said, "Thank you."

I helped her stand up, she grabbed her bag and we walked back towards the main dining room and lounge. I wondered which of my friends would have the menu we had abandoned and realized that it would have appealed to Martin. He's a real foodie. I decided not to mention Martin to Shilpa as it might remind her of the golf club fiasco.

As we reached the lounge I wondered how much Shilpa was going to drink before dinner. "Do you actually want a drink?" I asked neutrally as possible as a waiter approached.

Shilpa looked at me, glanced at the waiter and said, "No, we'll come back in 20 minutes."

I wondered what she intended to do. As we turned and headed for our room, Shilpa just looked at me and said, "Hungry?"

"Getting that way," I said.

As I fumbled for the key to our room Shilpa spoke "I thought you might like a starter," she said.

As soon as we were inside the room she put her hands on Graham Norton's lapels and drew me towards her.

I instinctively started to kiss her and before we could fall back onto the bed, Shilpa reached under her dress, pulled her knickers down and then off with a flourish. Lying back on the bed she hoisted her skirt up and said "your starter".

I knelt down on the bed and inserted my tongue into Shilpa's waxed pussy. She didn't need to draw me a diagram of what to do; after a while she started to moan, a low contented moan. I kept up the momentum and pressure and soon she was thrusting her hips towards me as she approached orgasm; she grasped my hair and began to shudder throwing her head about before coming.

It was my turn. I unzipped myself and motioned towards Shilpa to take me in her mouth.

She lifted her hand up, waved and said, "Not that, I'll have to do my make up again, we haven't got enough time," then she just moved her knees up to her shoulder and said, "Fuck me." I obliged.

Looking at her watch, Shilpa sped into the bathroom and was out again within about 45 seconds. It wasn't until we were half way back to the dining room that she exclaimed "I forgot to put my knickers back on!" We presented ourselves back at the main dining room and the Maitre D exactly 20 minutes after we'd left.

"Ah yes," he said, "sir, madam would you like to come this way."

Shilpa and I exchanged a smile and I knew exactly what she was thinking – that we liked to come this way and that way!

We sat and ordered a glass of Champagne each. Shilpa's hair was pretty ruffled and I'd managed to not quite tuck my shirt into my trousers, so I expect the restaurant staff were under no illusions as to what we'd done with our 20 minutes. The menus arrived on one A4 size printed card. I was relieved. The meal was a success. I ate chicken with cepes mushrooms and finished with a delicious light Catalan cream. Shilpa had grilled sole and a frosted lemon dessert.

'What a lucky sod I am,' I thought. 'A night in a wonderful hotel with a beautiful woman.'

As the evening wore on we sat in the bar and chatted. We didn't get drunk and Shilpa didn't embarrass herself, though she did have some fun with me. We were sitting on a low couch by the door, her black stockinged legs were evidently a source of some admiration from several male diners.

As I went to the bar on one occasion Shilpa called out loudly "Simon," and as I turned round, she crossed her legs very quickly – like Kenny Everett used to do – giving me, hopefully just me, a flash of everything. When we returned to our room it was after one o'clock, Shilpa changed into an ivory coloured nightie and just as I thought we were going to maybe have sex again or fall asleep in the large double bed, she leant over and said, "Do you fancy a swim?"

"What," I said, "a swim? It'll be freezing! You are joking aren't you?"

"I never joke," she said. "I'm really hot and a swim would cool me down."

I immediately became anxious; although we weren't drunk we had had a few glasses of wine and Champagne each, the water would be extremely cold.

"Well, if you're scared," said Shilpa, "looks as though I'll have to go on my own."

I turned into John Alderton: "Now look here Shilpa do you really think this is wise?" I said.

But there was no dissuading her, she threw open the French doors and, still with just her nightie on, stepped into the cool September evening.

Looking back I don't know whether she was trying to prove anything or she just liked taking risks. I should have stopped her. At the edge of the pool, which fortunately was lit from underneath, Shilpa took hold of the hem of her nightie, pulled it over her head in one deft movement and dived in. There was a plop of water; the cold night air and this sudden element of danger had sobered me up. I held my breath until she surfaced, she swam to the end of the pool and back again and this time not allowing me to help her out, headed for the steps. Halfway up the steps she looked over one shoulder at me, panting. She was completely naked; the moonlight illuminated her body and her wet hair hung down her back like a dagger. The whites of her eyes and her teeth shone at me. I was more relieved that she was okay and I ran to her with her towel.

"You're such a scaredy cat," she said, "I feel much better now."

Maybe it's something about the pool, after all it had worked its magic on John Profumo all those years ago and it was doing the same now. Shilpa really was someone special.

Breakfast the next morning was a very grand affair and served at the back of the house overlooking the rolling grounds and manicured lawns, the river a blue ribbon border. We'd dressed sensibly in jeans noting that the dress code for the hotel sanctioned this but not "worn jeans" I was keen to look around the grounds. Many of the guests were more formally clothed. I felt slightly self-conscious in my rugby top, though it was a Ralph Lauren one.

Shilpa soon put me at my ease. "They don't care what you wear," she said soothingly, "as long as you pay the bill."

The service was as faultless as the food; breakfast was a relaxed affair and the view from our table was spectacular. After a handsome breakfast we walked hand in hand from the terrace onto lawns close to the House and towards one of the formal gardens.

It took two hours to stroll around the grounds and even then we hadn't seen all there was to see. I had been keen to see a Canadian Air Force memorial to their national airmen killed during the Second World War. There is a natural dell forming a theatre; formal and informal gardens, wooded areas; water features including a famous "Love Fountain" a parterre. At several points on our tour of the estate it seemed that we were in the middle of nowhere, yet we could hear the faint rumble of traffic on the M4, the occasional jet flying into Heathrow and from some positions see the River Thames and boats navigating its course. I could imagine passengers on board the passing aircraft looking down and saying 'That looks interesting, I wonder who owns that?'

Halfway round the grounds Shilpa decided that we should have sex out in the open, I thought she was joking at first, then realised she wasn't. I think she had been inspired by the "Love Fountain". I was quite nervous –

make that very nervous – and being in such a state is not ideal in these circumstances. We found a small relatively sheltered patch of lawn with shrubbery around three sides and a tree in front and I started to kiss Shilpa. "We haven't got time for all that," she said, "just get on with it!"

'So romantic!' I thought.

Shilpa quickly undid her jeans, pulled them down slightly. I undid my jeans and she took me in her mouth, suddenly I was aware of sounds all around me, I could hear people talking so they had to be close. I decided it wasn't a good idea. "Shilpa we just can't do this," I hissed, while her head was bobbing up and down.

"Come on," she said, "quick!" She lay on her back and lifted her legs up, still in her jeans, into the air. This wasn't funny. It felt like deliberate exhibitionism and I wasn't comfortable. I knelt down and tried to enter her but I just couldn't do it, "We're on show," I said.

Shilpa quickly stood up, pulled her knickers and jeans into place and said "You're such a coward, come over here."

In the deep undergrowth she led me to we were indeed more secluded and Shilpa pulled down her jeans and knickers again and simply bent over.

I took her from behind and although it was fun, it was also an anxious experience – what would happen if we were caught? They would throw us out, we'd be charged with indecent exposure, or I would. I mentioned this to Shilpa as she complained she was being stung by some stinging nettles.

"Don't worry about them throwing us out," she said, "we're leaving shortly anyway." Shilpa's risk taking was entertaining but alarming.

By one o'clock we were back in our room. To my astonishment, our clothing had been packed by the staff. Had they seen us in the undergrowth and were throwing us out?

Shilpa reassured me that it was simply a service provided by the hotel. Then I started to feel uncomfortable about the bill. Shilpa had insisted this was her treat, but God knows how much it was going to cost. I looked at the room tariff. I thought I was looking at the date but I wasn't. It was eye-wateringly expensive.

"I'm just going to get this," said Shilpa, "you stay here."

I started to protest. "Look Shilpa, it's really expensive, can't I pay or at least go halves?"

"No, no," she said, "it's my treat." When she came back from paying the bill she just said, "You can pay next time."

'Next time,' I thought. Ah, that's what we were here to sort out, or at least I had thought we were. There wasn't going to be a next time. I was going to marry Rebecca and I felt a twinge of guilt again. Why hadn't I stuck to my promise to myself, not to sleep with Shilpa?

The efficient staff had brought the 7 Series round to the front of the hotel, loaded our luggage into its boot and, with a handshake and a "Please come and see us again", waved us off. I drove out of the estate and headed for the motorway.

Shilpa seemed relaxed and happy. But as the motorway miles sped past I was feeling increasingly anxious. I owed Shilpa an explanation, what if she was seriously expecting a next time? It was a cowardly decision I know but I decided to wait for her to mention meeting up again. And she didn't.

We spoke again about the gym and friends we had in common there, about our children and work. What was I going to say to her when we pulled up at her home? The on-board car display linked to my phone told me that I had four new messages. I daren't click on them in case Shilpa saw them on the display in front of her. Then I remembered, Ingrid was arriving earlier than we'd originally planned. I accelerated. I needed to get back to Shilpa's as soon as possible, say our goodbyes and get to the flat.

When we arrived at Shilpa's she dived in her handbag, pulled out a large key fob and pressed it. The iron gates started to grind into motion and slid back.

She got out of the car. I went round to the boot and started to get her luggage out. Her mood had altered. She was quiet. Then to my enormous relief she said, "I'm sorry Simon, I would invite you in but I've got my girls here."

"ThatsperfectlyokaythankyouforawonderfulnightatClivedenandtheswimmingpoolandeverything!" I gushed. I wanted to avoid her saying anything about a "next," time for as long as possible.

And then, before I could say anything else, she spoke "I'm going to be busy over the next few weeks, so I'll perhaps see you in the gym Simon."

With that, she kissed me on the cheek, turned on her heels and disappeared into her house. I felt as though I'd been slapped. I realized instantly that she didn't want anything more from me. I had been dismissed! She patently had no real interest in any greater commitment than occasional meetings; probably at the gym, possibly the odd bout of sex and a casual friendship with perhaps occasional dinners in expensive restaurants; a companion for a party or black-tie event!!

I drove back to the flat at speed. On the way, I flicked on my messages; there were three from Ingrid. There was obviously some sort of dilemma.

She'd never fully explained why she was coming to stay with me, just that she was going to some do in Chelmsford. The messages were asking, "Is it still okay to stay with you?" and "What time will you be around?"

As I pulled up outside the flat, I quickly replied. There was a message from Judy as well, the lady from church. It read "Can you ring me please, regarding Parish Council meeting – Judy" and a kiss. I quickly replied to that, "Yes, just a bit busy at the moment, I'll give you a ring later, Simon x." Worrying about the Parish Council meeting was the last thing I needed.

Inside the flat, I unpacked my suitcase, hung up my jacket, double-checked that the spare room was okay, switched on the computer and made myself a cup of coffee. I checked the answer phone for any messages. There was one from my Uncle Colin saying, "Hello idiot nephew, you're obviously out, I'll try later." And one from Rick, just saying, "No messages, have you survived an evening with the mad Indian woman?"

I rang Rick.

"Hello old boy," he said, recognizing my number as he answered the phone.

"Hello old boy," I said.

"Did you have a good time?"

"Fantastic," I said. "Wonderful place, probably the best hotel I've ever stayed in."

"Did you shag her?" he said.

I mumbled a reply. "Um, well, well sort of."

"Sort of," he said, "shall we make that 'yes'?"

"Well, yes, I did actually," I said.

"What about Daphne from Norfolk?"

"You mean Rebecca," I said. "Daphne wrote the book."

"What book?" he said.

"Rebecca."

"Does she have big tits in the book?" said Rick.

I realised this was going nowhere. "Look," I said, "enough of all that, I've got Ingrid coming round."

"Ingrid," he said, "she's coming round? When?"

"Tonight," I said.

"Is Ingrid the one you had the threesome with?" he said.

"Yes," I said.

"Isn't she the dyke?"

"No, that was Louise, who is living with Angela."

"Ingrid is bisexual."

There was a long pause.

"It's bloody confusing," he said with a deep sigh.

I then went on to explain, as far as I could, that Ingrid was at some event in Chelmsford and was staying the night, in the spare room, I added pointedly.

"Well, I'm glad you're okay, are you going to be with us for fish and chips on Friday?"

I was sure I would I said. I had a loose end to tie up there.

"Do me a favour," he said, "text Barry and let him know you're alright, he was worried as well."

"There was no need to be worried," I said, "I'm perfectly okay. I just had a night away with a friend."

"Shagging!" said Rick, as he put the phone down.

I then turned my attention to Ingrid, why was she going to a "do" in Chelmsford on a Sunday night? I decided to re-read her texts again.

It seems that things with her and Hamish weren't going all that well and she was using the opportunity of working on a film, for a gym and personal training it offered, to spend the night away and meet up with a guy that she'd met on a training course. But she didn't want to stay at his and she just wanted to meet up with him and have a chat and whilst she was in the area, she thought she'd come and see me as well. It was all very complicated and odd but I decided to just go along with it.

It was mid-afternoon and I decided to watch some TV and relax, after all everything was ready. I might even have time to pop to Mass and see Judy about the Parish Council meeting.

As I channel surfed through the TV listings I wondered what story Ingrid was going to tell when she arrived. I thought of loose ends Shilpa was definitely a loose end resolved. I felt easier now that the issues between us had become clear. It was a relief she had taken the initiative I was avoiding.

Just as I was congratulating myself on having sorted this out the phone rang. It was Judy. She explained rather breathlessly that the Parish Council meeting venue had been sorted out and it was now taking place in the church hall.

"Oh good," I said, "so no worries then?"

"Well, there was something else I wanted to talk to you about, Simon." She talked at some length about me joining the Parish Council. I was flattered, but I just couldn't imagine when I would find the time; I'm not even sure what they do. I tried to be diplomatic.

"Well, it's very kind of you Judy," I said, stalling for time. "Let me think about it and perhaps we can have a chat about it at Mass?"

"No, Simon," Judy persisted, "I need to know. Look I'm at the gym, I'll pop round if you like. Is now a good time?"

There were still a few hours before I had to go and get Ingrid. "Okay," I said, "I'll put some coffee on."

"See you in about half an hour," said Judy, "I'm just changing."

There was no need for me to panic about tidying up as the flat was abnormally tidy thanks to Ingrid's visit. The computer was buzzing away on the mezzanine floor and while the kettle was boiling, Joanna Lumley piped up, "You have e-mail."

It was from an e-mail address I didn't recognise, it said something like "Front of House, Royal Egyptian Hotel". I thought it might be a spam message, but AOL hadn't thrown it out so I clicked on it. It was from Rebecca!

"Hi, Simon, I managed to find free internet access at the hotel, hope you get this. We are having a lovely time, hope you are." A pang of guilt. "Don't reply to this e-mail, I'll send you another one soon and phone when I can. Looking forward to seeing you again. Love Rebecca."

'Wow! She really does like me,' I thought. Would she if she knew about the lovely time I'd been having?

I was so pleased that I'd arrived at a rational conclusion about my relationship with Shilpa.

She was simply a friend. That was all she wanted from me and I hadn't been forced to hurt any feelings she may have had if she had wanted a relationship. The way things had been left suited us both. I could cherish the memory of the past 24 hours at Cliveden; Shilpa pulling on her black stockings; skinny dipping naked in the pool; romping in the bushes; dressed in her evening gown... imagine these scenes as if they were appearing on a screen.

Cliveden with Shilpa was a farewell to being a bachelor. As soon as Rebecca set foot on British soil it would be behind me. A lovely interlude. But one that was laid to rest, buried and in my past.

My mobile phone went off simultaneously with the landline ringing. I grabbed the mobile and picked up the landline. There was a text message from Ingrid and Uncle Colin was on the phone. He greeted me with his usual, "Hello idiot nephew."

"Hi Unc," I said, in my usual fashion.

"Are you okay, are you still seeing the bird from King's Lynn, when are you coming up?" he said all in one breath.

I decided not to fill him in on the events of the last 24 hours and the fact that Ingrid was coming round. I remembered he liked Ingrid as she gave him some free legal advice. He used to chat to her on the phone quite a bit.

I explained that Rebecca was back on Saturday and I was hoping to dash up and see her very soon and I'd call in and see him as well.

I had just put the phone down when the intercom buzzed for the front door. I answered it and Judy said, "Hi Simon it's me."

"Come on up," I said and gave the unit a long push. As I heard the lift whirring I did think that I could do without her visit really. I mean talking about church, what on earth could she want?

I opened the front door of the flat and as the lift doors opened, there was Judy smiling. It was just a business meeting after all, about the church. She wouldn't stay long.

Judy was certainly attractive though. She was always smart and expensively dressed when I saw her on Sundays. Now, whether as a result of her exertions at the gym or clever make up I didn't know, she looked positively radiant.

As she walked towards me, her short dark hair didn't seem as short as it once did. It was in nape length loose curls. She was wearing what looked like a Burberry raincoat in a stone colour, black opaque hosiery, black court shoes and as the mac was open, beneath I could see a red dress with a black belt. She was carrying a black bag and some gloves. She wore a scarf, a look I quite liked, reminding me of Katherine who often wore them.

Judy's scarf was tied in several knots high up round her neck. I know I keep teasing you reader, but this was a time when "tied round the neck" was quite innocent.

"Hello Simon," she said extending her hand.

"Come on in," I said.

"Oh this is unusual," she exclaimed surveying the vaulted ceiling and mezzanine floor. "What's that?" She indicated to the gallery area.

"That's my office. It hangs in mid-air, it gives me inspiration when I'm writing," I laughed. I made some coffee. "Go on into the lounge, how do you take your coffee?" I said, as she slipped off her coat. "Oh, just black please."

Sitting on the leather sofa opposite me, Judy pulled out a small file and notepad from her bag and started to explain why it would be a good idea for me to join the Parish Council.

I'd already decided that I wasn't going to join, I'm not a very good Catholic and I'm not accomplished at bureaucracy, but before you write in, I know Parish Councils do immensely good work.

Judy quickly drank her coffee. Like Shilpa, she had a way of tilting her head when she asked a question; her loose curls dancing as she did so.

"Would you like another coffee?" I said, thinking I could gain some time and formulate how I was going to body swerve her request without letting her down too harshly.

"Um, yes please, or have you got anything else?" said Judy, "I am a bit thirsty."

"Oh yes," I said, "I'd forgotten you'd just been to the gym."

"Well, yes I have been to the gym," As I wandered out to the kitchen again I heard myself say, "Fruit juice, glass of water, glass of wine?"

"Oh, glass of wine sounds nice," said Judy.

"White?" I said.

"Yes please."

I poured myself half a glass as well.

It's amazing the effect alcohol has on people.

After taking a few sips of wine, Judy seemed to forget all about the Parish Council meeting. She leant back in the sofa and started to talk. "You know Simon," she said, "I was thinking, how has someone like you ended up divorced?"

"Someone like me?" I said. "What do you mean someone like me?"

"Well," she said, "you're attractive, well read and articulate. I know you still get on with your ex, so couldn't you sort things out?"

I explained that it was my fault that we were divorced. We'd gone to counselling sessions several times and after my mother died I had decided that I didn't want to be in the marriage any more.

I looked at Judy directly and realised I didn't know anything about her at all other than that she went to my Church. I didn't know if she was married, had children, where she lived. I'm not one of those men that can tell from looking at girls hands what their marital status is.

"What about you, then," I said, "are you married?"

Judy scoffed, holding up her finger. "Yes," she said, "look, I'm married."

"Any children?" I said.

Judy took a large gulp of wine, when she had swallowed it she said, "No."

I decided to press that. "Why not?"

Judy cut me off immediately and said "No, no children," without expanding, so I didn't press her. She relaxed back into the sofa and crossed her legs.

The opaque tights weren't tights – they were over the knee socks, I got a flash of bronzed thigh.

She went on to explain that her husband worked in Saudi Arabia on a large engineering project as a partner for an International conglomerate. He earned good money, but his work commitments meant she rarely saw him. "How does that work?" I said.

Taking another large gulp of wine Judy said, "Well, it doesn't really."

"So, do you work?" I asked.

"Yes, of course. Well I don't really have to, but I'm a governor of a local school, do this Parish Council thing and I'm also a magistrate. Sort of keeps me occupied."

"And where do you live?" I said. "Are you local?"

"Sellyborne Road."

I knew the road, it was a prestigious development of individually designed detached homes. Houses on the development there sold for sizeable sums.

"So are you happily married, then?" I asked genuinely curious now.

"Well, I suppose so," said Judy. "I didn't realise when we got married that I'd see so little of my husband, but I suppose over the last ten years we've come to occupy different worlds literally and emotionally. I have friends and a life that he just isn't part of."

"Well, it must be very difficult," I said, "and do your voluntary jobs occupy your time fully?"

"Well, one thing I do," said Judy, "is I try to persuade people, who are blatantly not interested, to join the Parish Council." She smiled at me, waving her now empty wine glass. I'd been rumbled.

"Well, I wouldn't say I'm not interested Judy…"

"Well Simon, what would you say, just going through the motions? Don't worry," she said, "I'm at fault, I do get very lonely. My family live in Cornwall and even though I've lived here for ten years, I don't seem to have made many friends. So in truth I'm at fault, I'm sure that you have far better things to do than join the Parish Council."

I mumbled an apology.

"Well I suppose I must be going," said Judy looking round for her coat.

"Er, no," I said, "don't go yet, um stay."

"Are you sure?" she said. "I'm not holding you up at all?"

"No," I lied, looking at my watch.

I'd left my mobile phone in the kitchen; I'd heard it go off a couple of times whilst Judy was talking and as I wandered in to grab the wine bottle from the fridge, I hurriedly checked my messages. There was one from Ingrid saying, "See you about half nine-ish." Looking at my watch it was only half past four, so at least I could have another glass or two of wine in peace. I took the bottle back into the lounge, and Judy seemed to be at home, she'd kicked off her shoes and tucked her legs underneath her on the sofa.

"Have you ever been out to Saudi Arabia?" I said.

"Yes, I go all the time, the shopping's really good. Well, when I say I go all the time, I used to go all the time, now it's probably just twice a year."

"And how often does he come home?" I asked.

"Twice a year," she said.

"So you only see each other four times a year? How long for?"

"Two or three weeks at a time."

'It seems an odd way to conduct a marriage but they must both like it,' I thought. "You must miss him," I said.

"Well, I used to miss him," said Judy, moving one of her legs in the over knee socks down to the floor, "for all sorts of things, but now I've got a rabbit it's not as hard as it once was."

I couldn't believe what I was hearing, Judy who appeared so refined, so elegant, was now telling me about taking her frustrations out on a sex toy. She gave me a long stare, moved the other leg down to the floor, I got an even longer flash of thigh this time. Judy was flirting with me!

The internet dates had prepared me for knowing when someone was flirting and when they were not and she definitely was. I didn't quite know what to say so I didn't say anything.

Judy spoke. "I've some photos of Saudi Arabia, if you'd like to see them," she said, delving into her bag.

"I'd love to," I said. I sat next to her on the sofa, looking at the photos. I adopted Barry's way of looking at holiday photos. "Um," I said, "nice scenery, ooh that's nice." Now I'm sure you're reading this, thinking, "I know what's going to happen next, they're going to start kissing, have sex on the sofa," but no. What happened next took me completely and utterly by surprise.

Whilst I was looking at the photos of Saudi Arabia and trying not to be distracted by Judy, she suddenly grabbed hold of my chin, pulled it towards her so I was looking at her and said, "Shall we go to bed?"

I didn't think I'd heard her right. "Pardon?" I said.

"Well it's a straight forward question Simon, do you want me or don't you?"

"Well, I've actually got a girlfriend, Judy."

"Really?" said Judy "The Indian lady from the gym?"

"Err, no," I said "I haven't seen her for a while," I lied. "No, she lives in Norfolk and um, well, I, well she's not really my girlfriend, but she will be my girlfriend," I explained that I'd had a couple of dates with Rebecca.

Judy just smiled. "Well, I won't tell if you don't," she said.

Now, of course, any normal man would have politely declined Judy's direct offer, but being weak it won't surprise you to learn that we made our way upstairs to the bedroom. Judy hadn't put her shoes on but carried them upstairs. We didn't say anything, she reached round, undid the zip of her dress and let it fall to the floor.

Underneath she wore satin and close fitting waist high knickers. They were cornflower blue and matched her bra. She had a full and curvaceous figure.

I couldn't honestly believe what was happening. We started kissing and under the covers of the bed, I went to pull her knickers down but they didn't move. I gave them a harder tug, still they didn't move.

"You have to unbutton them," she explained.

I reached round the front of her knickers and couldn't find any.

"No, Simon, they're along the side."

I looked closely. At the waistband was a white pearl button and a bit like a kind of trouser fly of several smaller buttons underneath in a concealed fly, I'd never seen knickers like them, before or since. In frustration I quickly pulled them down Judy's legs and threw them out of the bed. They landed on a small side table. I launched myself into Judy.

"Well I didn't think I'd be doing this," I said to her.

Judy didn't say anything. She wanted me to have her in different positions, from behind, on top, laying on her side, it was very physical and completely unexpected. I was exhausted, when we eventually moved apart. After my recent encounter with Shilpa and the action packed workout with Judy my hips were beginning to ache!

Afterwards, I went downstairs and got us a drink. We sat in bed with glasses of water and a second bottle of wine drinking and talking.

"How are we going to square this with our Catholic consciences?" I thought. It was dreadful really, here she was a married woman, a magistrate, Chairman of the Governors, Head of the parish council and I'd been shagging the living daylights out of her for the past couple of hours.

"Well," said Judy, very seriously, "we'll both have to go to confession. My husband's coming back in a fortnight's time. I'll tell him that we need to organise an annulment and I think you and I should go and see the priest to discuss what we do next. Maybe announce our engagement in the New Year." She spoke without hesitation and appeared serious. Was she?

I gaped at her literally open mouthed.

She moved her head to one side again, "Well, you didn't think you were going to have sex with me and that would be it, Simon?" she said.

"Oh, well, I... " Hugh Grant was now spluttering for words. "Well, I..."

Judy moved her head to the other side then burst out laughing. "Sorry," she said, "I couldn't keep that up for long."

I laughed with relief. Then thought that in fairness, from what little I knew of her, being married to Judy wouldn't have been that bad.

It was now five to seven.

She seemed in no hurry to go. I just started to feel slightly edgy about the time but then why should I? Ingrid was only a mate coming to stay and it didn't matter to her if I had a girlfriend or not, but I felt Judy wouldn't have been keen to bump into anyone else, after I'd been bumping into her all afternoon!

"I don't do this sort of thing very often Simon," she said.

"Well, I'm pleased to hear it," I said in my John Alderton schoolmaster's voice.

"I'm sure I can rely on you being discreet?"

"Well yes, of course," I said.

Whilst we were laughing and chatting I glanced at the pillows of the bed. They were covered in mascara and make up, lipstick, semen. In fact the entire bed looked like it had been the setting for a porn movie. There were clothes strewn across the bedroom floor and Judy's odd but no doubt expensive knickers were crumpled on the bedside table accompanied by her bra, which had an odd way of fastening. Instead of doing up at the back, a wide lace ribbon bow between the cups at the front formed the fastening and the bra undid at the front. Bras that do up at the front should really be the norm shouldn't they?

She looked at her watch, it was now approaching quarter to eight. "I really must go Simon," she said.

Paul Fox

I went to the bathroom and when I came back Judy was doing up the buttons of her knickers. She fastened her bra expertly tying the ribbon at the front into a bow then dressed speedily.

I felt I should offer her the bathroom. "Do you want to shower before you go?" I asked.

"No, don't worry Simon, I'll have a shower when I get home."

As we said goodbye at the door I didn't know what to say to her really. It had been a real surprise ending up in bed with Judy.

What should I say? What can you say? "Thank you, that was awfully decent of you", "Tremendous sucking power Judy, thank you ever so much".

Judy just kissed me on the cheek, gave me a hug and said, "See you again Simon, have fun with Rebecca. She's a lucky girl," which I thought was very kind. She blew a kiss as the lift door closed.

I shut the front door of the flat, closed my eyes and let out a long sigh. Shall I tell the boys? 'Not yet,' I thought.

I was wearing my dressing gown still; it was now twenty past eight.

I had a quick shower and began to tidy up the bedroom.

Judy's clothes might have gone, but the bed told its own story, let alone the lipstick-stained wine glass and two empty bottles. But why was I bothered, Ingrid was just coming to borrow the spare room? I pulled on fresh clothes and decided I wouldn't change the bed. I straightened the covers slightly and pulled the door shut, put the wine glasses and coffee cups in the dishwasher.

I decided to text Rick – "Tsunami," – I know, not very gallant. He didn't reply.

I checked to see if I'd had another e-mail from Rebecca.

Every time I thought of Rebecca I felt a sharp tug on my heart and I felt genuinely guilty now. This was my week to tie up loose ends and Judy in my bed had been a wholly unexpected diversion. I'm sure that even to the most disapproving reader, this makes sense on some level, doesn't it?

I mean I had no intention of sleeping with Judy. No honestly.

The intercom buzzed. It was Ingrid, her deep voice saying "Hi Simon, are you in there? Let me in."

'God she's early!' I thought. I opened the front door and waited for the lift to decant Ingrid onto the landing. This was getting to be like a Brian Rix farce, or *Groundhog Day*!

Ingrid ran into my arms, carrying an overnight bag, jangling her car keys. "Are you okay?" she said. "You look a bit tired."

284

'I'm not surprised,' I thought, "I can barely walk," and there was a part of me apart from my hips that was just a little bit sore. "Coffee?" I enquired.

"Sod that, I'll have a glass of wine, I need one!" I poured out wine.

Ingrid left her overnight bag in the hall; she had one of those really expensive weekend cases, a Mulberry. I hadn't really had a chance to speak to her after the threesome with Katie several months before.

Swigging her glass of wine, Ingrid didn't sit. "Flat looks much better now you've got some furniture in it Simon," she said on a short walking tour.

She embarked on a monologue about Chelmsford and her plans. She was resuming her career as a legal executive but wanted to work freelance and part time so that she could also be a personal trainer. Being a trainer was a lot of work for not very much money but she enjoyed it immensely.

Whilst training she had met a guy who was opening a lot of gyms around the country. One of them happened to be in Chelmsford. She went on to explain that the guy was very keen on her; she wasn't that keen on him, but she was anxious to get a contract to work in the Chelmsford gym.

She didn't want, in her words, to have to "drop her knickers" That's why she wanted to stay with me. She'd told him she had plans to stay with an old friend.

The plans for turning the house in Barbados into a private gym as well as a home had foundered when she'd tried to apply for a full visa to start a business as a resident. There were endless bureaucratic issues to overcome. She had been put off the idea. She was just going to live in the house and enjoy it as a home.

Eventually, she settled down on the sofa, where only a little while before Judy had sat. I was conscious that I could still smell her perfume on me even after my shower.

"So Simon," said Ingrid, unzipping her boots, and lying on the sofa, "tell me what you've been up to."

"Um, not much," I said, "just quiet really."

"Really? Have you got a girlfriend then? It'd be unlike you not to."

I explained at some length about the lovely Rebecca, that she was on holiday and when she came back we were going to get married.

"Married?" said Ingrid.

"Yeah," I said.

"Bit quick isn't it, you've only seen her twice." She was right, of course. And yet marriage was where I believed my fledgling relationship with Rebecca was heading. Maybe an extreme position but that was how I'd built things up in my mind.

"Well, she's a lucky girl, you never asked me to marry you."

I don't know whether it was the bottle and a half of wine I'd by now consumed, the exercise, or the loss of bodily fluids, but I was beginning to feel light headed. "It wasn't really like that with us was it?" I said.

"Well not really I suppose," Ingrid admitted, "we're just friends that shag one another."

I tried to change the subject. "How's Katie?" I enquired. "Is she still um..."

"Bi-sexual?" said Ingrid.

"No, an airhostess," I said.

"Oh she's fine," she said, "we chat all the time. She's on the New York run so we've seen each other a couple of times, but not much."

"Have you slept with her again?" I asked conversationally. I knew Ingrid wouldn't find this intrusive or be remotely fazed by such a direction enquiry. "Yeah, I'm still not so sure I'm into girls really. As you know, I need a lot of pressure and thrusting to come. Katie had got one of those double-ended rabbits and we gave that a try, but I just couldn't stop laughing. It was so unsexy. Anyway, I had a text from New York and she said to say 'hi'." Her candour took me aback though I had asked the question.

Ingrid was in the "boxed off" ring fenced zone with Shilpa now. She was a "friend" – okay a friend I'd had sex with – but that was in the past. They were the sort of friends that I'd like to invite to an eventual wedding assuming that Rebecca wouldn't mind. I mean I get on well with women. Probably better than with men generally speaking, so it wouldn't be unreasonable to have my female friends at a wedding. Rebecca seemed fairly easy going I reasoned, so I couldn't see it would be a problem. I'd forgotten her reaction on learning that Katherine and I remained on good terms.

We talked more about the gym that was about to open in Chelmsford. It was approaching ten o'clock when Ingrid said, "I think I'll go and put my jim jams on."

"Yes of course go and help yourself," I said realising we hadn't had anything to eat. "Shall I get us a take away?" I said.

"No, don't bother for me," said Ingrid, shouting from the bathroom, "I had something earlier, some crisps would be fine if you have any."

"Sorry, I didn't quite catch that," I said, wandering half way up the stairs to see Ingrid padding out of the bathroom completely naked and into my bedroom!

'Oh God,' I thought, 'I should have changed the sheets!'

She was heading for the airing cupboard and when she emerged I was outside the bedroom. She had a towel turban on her head and a bath sheet wrapped around her. "The bedroom's looking good, I like your furniture, where did you get it?" Before I could answer she said, "Could you bring my things up please Simon?"

I picked up her expensive, heavy overnight bag and hauled it up the stairs. Ingrid was back in my bedroom, seated on the bed and rubbing her hair with a towel. "You know I was thinking Simon, maybe we should get married."

I stopped in my tracks. "Where's this come from?" I said, thrown.

"Well, you know we get on really well, we're really comfortable with each other, we don't have sex very often but when we do, it's okay."

"Oh thanks," I said, "just okay?"

Ingrid was evidently completely at home, she unzipped her weekend bag, found her hairdryer, plugged it in and started drying her hair.

She was speaking but I couldn't hear her. I just left her to get dressed. I didn't have to wait long.

In an attempt to sober up I made some coffee. When I went back into the lounge, she was already lounging on the sofa. She looked very sweet. She had on a pyjama shorts with a long sleeved tee shirt with flowers embroidered round the bottom. She'd brought down some nail polish and was painting her nails on the sofa, fingernails and her toenails. She had foam separator things between her toes and layers of tissue spread beneath her feet.

The evening passed pleasantly. We chatted, watched TV, drank some more wine, I found chocolates in the fridge which we gorged on, then we drank tea and at about 1 o'clock we snacked on cheese and biscuits. I'd caught up with everything and everybody in Ingrid's life and heading upstairs to bed, unsteadily, it seemed the most natural thing in the world to get into bed with Ingrid. A part of me, and you can guess which part, was actually hoping she didn't want to have sex because I was sore and I could barely walk because my hips were now burning so much, but of course we ended up having sex. Lots of sex.

Ingrid kept saying, "Ooh, if we were married, we could do this every night." In fact even during sex she was talking, the only break I got was when she had my cock in her mouth. We eventually fell asleep at about 3.00am.

Monday morning and Ingrid was up early, trying to find her work suit in her bag and still talking. I wouldn't say she was irritating but I'm not really a morning person and I realized that I now didn't like having my established routines interrupted. When watching breakfast news I like to skip through the channels, munching on my toast and coffee. This morning even helping Ingrid choose her underwear for the day (her request) was an unwelcome distraction from what I wanted to do.

"Stockings or tights?" Ingrid said.

"Well I don't really need to answer that one do I?"

"Not really," she said pulling on her stockings. "I don't know why I'm bothering really," she said, "I mean it's not like I'm your wife!" She spat the words at me. "I'm not coming home to you tonight. And I'm going to be sitting in my office all day with this suspender belt cutting into me just because you like watching me get dressed."

"True," I said, eating a bit of toast and enjoying the view.

I helped Ingrid down to the car park with her bags. As she jumped in her black BMW Z4, flashing the tops of her stockings quite deliberately, she blew a kiss and said, "Thanks for having me, Simon, say hi to Rebecca for me!" and roared off, waving a hand with exquisitely painted fingernails out of the window.

I got back into the flat, put my shoulders against the door and let out another very long sigh. I was exhausted. I pulled on my gym clothes but I wasn't sure I could make it onto the equipment, perhaps I'd have a warm up or maybe just a coffee. I pulled on my tracksuit top, zipped it up and headed slowly and painfully towards the gym.

Once there I knew a workout was impossible so I sat in the restaurant, ordered coffee and looked at my mobile phone. There were lots of messages.

I'd sent Rick the "Tsunami" text after Judy and he'd eventually replied saying "I thought she was away?" Then another one saying "Not the Indian woman again?" and then another one saying "You're not still shagging are you?"

I decided not to reply to any of them. It was far too complicated.

Then I heard: "Hi, Simon."

I turned round in my chair to see Shilpa.

"I'm just doing a step class – see you later, you okay?" she yelled, as she just scooted off to the upstairs gym.

"I'm fine," I replied, "enjoy."

Ian came over. "You okay, Simon? You're not going upstairs for a while?"

"Err, no," I said, "I'm feeling a bit rough."

And I was. God knows how many workouts I'd had over the last few days. As I sat I tried to square my conscience with what had happened.

I couldn't of course and resigned myself to the fact that whilst Rebecca may not be that pleased, at least I was getting things sorted out. My conscience would be completely clear-ish when I saw her next week. But it wasn't next week now. She was going to be back at the end of *this* week.

Decluttering – Part 2

"Hello Simon." I looked up. "I'm Kirsty. Ian told you about me? I'm writing a book about fashion and as I mentioned in my email, I thought you might be able to offer me some advice. May I join you?"

"Yes of course," I said. I stood up and pulled out a chair for Kirsty to sit down.

She wasn't wearing gym gear, she had that "Yummy Mummy" look about her, was much younger than me, probably about 30 at the most. She was slightly shorter and slender and wore a cream polo neck, a short black skirt and opaque tights and tan suede Ugg boots. She had short very dark hair cut in a bob style.

She talked easily, told me about herself and gave me a CV. She'd worked in fashion all her life, which wasn't that long, looking at her. She was now writing a simple guide to dressing elegantly. She had a publisher and seemed to have all the bases covered, so I said. "Looks like you're well on your way to publishing your book, you don't really need my help, I've an agent, but I write about cars, so I'm not sure what I can do to help."

I was trying not to be distracted by how she looked. My cock was very sore and very asleep and didn't murmur at all during this conversation, even when Kirsty crossed her legs, her dark opaque tights not giving away anything. In fact I'm not sure they were tights; they were probably leggings. I doubted if a woman in her 30s would be remotely interested in me and I was perfectly contented with that thought. I was trying to place her face though because she looked familiar. Who did she look like?

Then it came to me; the similarity was so apparent once I'd made the connection. The razor cut bob, tall slim physique, the slightly pouty expression; it was "Posh Spice" Victoria Beckham. She even had cheekbones like her, the turned up nose and she was wearing that pale lipstick that "Posh" often wears. She has apparently been criticized for this (according to my daughter, who is a fan).

Talking of criticism, I know there will be a number of people reading this book who will slam it shut at this point – probably all the women. For some reason, if you mention "Posh Spice" or Victoria Beckham to a group of women they all go "Ugh, she's horrible!" Teenage girls react differently but "Posh" seems to occupy one of those "all women hate her slots" along with Heather McCartney and Sarah Brightman.

I've always liked Victoria Beckham and okay, I don't know much about fashion, but the fashion she's designed, I like that, especially the military look; wide belt, lots of buttons, etc. She doesn't often smile, but then nor do I. Maybe she doesn't like having her photo taken after all or hates her teeth and okay, she can't sing, but I still don't know why she is so universally disliked by women. Is it because she married David Beckham?

While this was running through my head, Kirsty was still talking. She'd done a lot of research and knew of my articles because her father was in the motor trade and she'd read a couple of my pieces. She thought my style of writing was "conversational" and that this would suit her book, but she didn't have a developed conversational style. She had been experimenting with narrative for her book and knowing that I was local, wondered if I'd read what she'd produced. She reached into a deep bag and produced a bulky manuscript which she handed to me.

"I'd be pleased to," I said, "but don't expect much. I'm really not sure I can help."

She smiled, something that her namesake would never do, at least knowingly on camera. "I've jotted my mobile number on the manuscript Simon and I've a meeting with my publisher Friday in London, so if you could look at it before then, I'd really appreciate it."

"I'll see what I can do Kirsty," I said.

She flashed her leggings again as she got up.

"Gosh," I wanted to say to her, "Don't you look like Victoria Beckham?" I'm sure she heard it a thousand times before and anyway, her interest in me was purely professional. As I got up, the searing pain in my hips reminded me that I didn't need any more bedroom encounters, even if one was offered, which it wouldn't be.

When I got back to the flat, I reminded myself that apart from romantic ties, I had to sort out other stuff. I decided to schedule in a meeting with my agent to see what work was coming up and also to have a good look at my finances. I'd paid scant attention to these lately. Not sensible given that my background following my career in the RAF had been as a financial adviser; I was like a plumber with a leaky tap.

As I sat on the mezzanine floor, replying to my emails and sending a few messages I was hoping for contact from Rebecca. But there was nothing in my inbox.

I kept Sky News on all day, low in the background and from up in the mezzanine floor, I could hear that a story was unfolding. It was about

Northern Rock, the building society, being in a state of near collapse. It seemed hard to believe. I knew about *Northern Rock*. The company I worked for in the mid-80s had an agency with them. We could take deposits on behalf of clients, they even sponsored a sign to for installation above the office, commercially helpful for us except for the fact that when the builders came to put the sign up, they dropped and damaged the part of the sign that said "Rock", so for ages we just had "Northern" outside, which was a bit daft for a stockbrokers in Essex.

And bizarrely, instead of referring to them as *Northern Rock,* we called them the "Rock" because whenever their representative turned up to tell us as about a new product he always referred to them as being "solid as a rock". Looking at the queues of people on Sky News waiting to get their money out, I wondered how he was feeling now. Little did I realise that this financial hiccup would drag down most of Europe and signal the beginning of the worst recession this country had seen for decades.

Turning my attention from the news I scanned Kirsty's CV which was pinned to her manuscript.

I was surprised to note that her status was given as "divorced". I don't know why I felt this, as it goes without saying that there are more divorced people (myself amongst their number) than "marrieds" currently. She seemed rather young to be divorced, and so, well, happy! Joanna Lumley interrupted my thoughts "You have e-mail". That sexy voice!

Hoping this was going to be from Rebecca, I dropped the CV on the coffee table and headed stiffly up the spiral staircase to the mezzanine floor; it was just junk from some hotel.

But wait, no, looking again, it wasn't only that – there was also an e-mail from Rebecca. It read: "Hi Simon, managed to find the free internet access at the hotel here, not sure if you are going to get this, 'cos I'm not very good at pressing buttons (!) Hope you are enjoying your week of peace, (twang of guilt) look forward to seeing you as soon as I get back. Love, Rebecca" and three kisses! "PS Don't reply to this e-mail, I'll give you a ring as soon as my phone works the other end." – and another three kisses.

I was so pleased. And I had pretty much enjoyed my week hadn't I? A week I vowed she would never know about.

The next morning, Thursday, I was sitting in the gym's coffee lounge with Kirsty, flicking through her manuscript.

"As far as I can see," I said, "it looks very good, you've done a compelling synopsis and I think the photography, sketches, layout and themed seasonal ideas are excellent. It's attractively presented and the quirky narrative is conversational and I think works well. I have made a couple of changes, but they are minor and only my humble opinion."

Today she wore a grey fine woollen dress with black panels down either side, a slim black belt round her waist with a gold clasp formed by the letter "G" (Gucci?), opaque tights and short, black suede ankle boots. She wore more make up than when I'd first met her and her eyes were outlined and shaded, sort of smoky black pools. I was again struck by her resemblance to "Posh Spice". All she needed was a trademark sulky look and pair of dark glasses. She could easily have earned money as a double for Victoria Beckham.

I was going to mention it but this would have involved me interrupting Kirsty who was talking animatedly about her meeting the following day; it was a conference type arrangement at which she would be meeting potential marketing and advertising agents along with her publisher. Her agent was sub-contracting publicity aspects of the book and had arranged the meeting. The agent was to have a follow up meeting with her on Monday.

"Look Simon, you've done all this sort of thing before haven't you and you've got an agent? I was just wondering – I know it's a bit of a cheek really and very late notice, but I wondered if you'd come with me, for the meeting with the marketing people. I know it's a lot to ask."

Before I had even given much thought of the practicalities involved, I heard myself saying, "Yes, of course, where is it?"

It was at the Intercontinental Hotel in London's Hyde Park and she explained that it would be a good idea if I could get there for 3 or 4 o'clock in the afternoon.

As Kirsty stood up and left quickly via the swing door of the gym (why do all the women I know do that?) I lunged for my phone and re-scheduled the meeting with my agent for tomorrow morning.

Why do I get myself into this sort of thing, I mean what use could I be? My agent and solicitors dealt with all that sort of stuff. Kirsty seemed amply organized, informed and competent. The truth was that she almost certainly didn't need me at all. The truth of course was that I felt flattered. Anyway, I reasoned, a meeting in London would at least get me out of fish and chip Friday and I wouldn't have to explain my debauched antics during the week to Rick and Barry.

"You want to do what?" Rick was saying.

"Well, I was wondering," I said, "I've got to go up to London instead of fish and chips tomorrow, would you like to join me at the RAF club or somewhere else in London tomorrow evening?" I've tried ringing Barry but he's not picking up."

"Well, I don't know really," he said, "Why don't we make it Saturday instead?"

"Well, okay," I said, "it's just that I've got this meeting with my agent."

Without thinking I rambled on and spoke about the meeting with Kirsty and her marketing people.

As usual Rick was eating. In between loud mouthfuls he managed, "Who's this then?

I explained about Kirsty and her book; that she was a Victoria Beckham look-alike from the gym that I was assisting in getting her book about fashion marketed. Even seeing the words in front of me doesn't make it more credible.

"A book about fashion," said Rick, half way through what sounded now like a Kit Kat. "How the fuck are you going to advise her about a fashion book being marketed?"

Before I could answer and come up with something vaguely noble about assisting a fellow writer in the most difficult art of getting a book marketed, Rick came back with, "I suppose you just want to shag her don't you?"

"No, I do not," I explained as indignantly as I could, "I have absolutely no interest in her whatsoever."

"You're lying aren't you," said Rick, "I can always tell when you're lying. You're sounding like Robin Gibb now."

"She wouldn't be remotely interested in me!" I protested, shrilly now.

"Aha," said Rick, "so there's the truth in it! If you thought you had half a chance you'd be in there like a rat up a drainpipe."

"Not everything revolves around sex, Rick."

"Well it does with you!" he retorted.

"I'll tell you all about it when I see you on Saturday night and if you speak to Barry, let him know the day's changed."

"Have fun with Posh then," said Rick.

I couldn't resist saying, "It's not fun, it's just work, we're both writers. The only difference is she happens to be a girl." Click.

There were no more e-mails or texts from Rebecca and there was now a little over 48 hours to go before her beautiful, dainty feet touched down in the UK.

I wondered where we'd live eventually. I'd thought about how I'd be quite content to live in King's Lynn. We could wander round the quayside arm in arm – Tuesday market place – maybe we could meet Uncle Colin for lunch. And if she sold her house and I put the proceeds of my divorce settlement towards a jointly purchased property maybe we could afford a farmhouse near, or even within the Sandringham estate. We might even wave to the Queen as she went past. It was going to be wonderful; all she had to do was get back. I felt giddy with excitement and plans.

Then I had a reality check. It doesn't often happen, but just occasionally, I stop, take stock and acknowledge what is going on around me.

I was seated on the high-speed train to Kings Cross. I had arranged to meet Kirsty at the Hotel on Park Lane at 3pm. I became aware of some of my fellow passengers sharing newspapers; others were looking at their phones, tutting. A couple opposite were discussing The Northern Rock crisis and how it was deepening and its wider implications. I wondered if I should be taking much notice of it. I didn't have any money deposited with Northern Rock; in fact, I didn't have much money at all, which was one of the reasons I needed to talk to my agent. I had to have more work. Perhaps even take a staff job somewhere though I've never been much use at 9 to 5 office work. In my former incarnation as a financial adviser, I had taken every opportunity to get out of the office and when the opportunity arose, even out of the country. Clients in Switzerland and the USA were particularly popular.

I had my phone setting on vibrate. My thigh shivered. It was a text from Kirsty.

"Hi Simon looking forward to seeing you at the Intercontinental. I will be on time – there by 3pm. See you at reception. Thanks for offering to help. Kirsty." No kiss, but then I didn't expect one, this was a business arrangement. I'd probably only be there half an hour.

The meeting with my agent Robin didn't go that well. I hadn't had many cars to write about recently, apparently BMW weren't that impressed with my lukewarm article on the 6 series. I hadn't kept as scrupulously up to date with returns as I should have done and several reviews and pieces of work had been late or half-finished. I thought at one stage Robin was going to get the cane out.

The meeting was over in a couple of hours. We went through my finances, how much I would earn, what was owed in back revenue. A considerable amount. There was a prospect I may be invited to submit copy for a travel magazine; we discussed how perhaps mainstream car titles weren't ideal for me and that I should write more about the "indie" motor market; or specifically about my favourite cars – Alfas – so I did leave on a reasonably positive note. I showed him Kirsty's manuscript.

"We don't handle fashion or photography publications," he said. "It's pretty Avant grade. I bet she looks like a vamp, or has wild hair on a nodding acquaintance with grooming products and dresses in clothes that deliberately clash in colour," he said as I was heading to the door.

"She's not actually, she looks remarkably like Victoria Beckham." I said.

I had some time to kill and with the lovely Rebecca in mind, I headed to my favourite women's underwear store, *Agent Provocateur*. It's in the Royal Exchange building opposite the Bank of England; it's a tiny shop, now rolled out in major cities throughout the UK. They sell the most wondrous underwear and better still, the assistants wear it. They normally have gowns over them, but these are very tastefully open exposing the undergarments...

"Can I help you?" asked one of the Assistants.

"Uh, yes," I said trying not to stare at her tight fitting pink outfit, unbuttoned to above her waist, revealing white stockings, and white suspenders and lacy white knickers. "Uh... " Nothing came out of my throat so I coughed. "I'm looking for something for my girlfriend. I'll just have a wander round."

It isn't a large shop to wander round in but the latest creations were to the left of where we were standing and on the wall. One set took my eye immediately; it was vintage white with white rosebuds on the straps of the suspenders, the rose buds were sewn in, it would be impossible to wear something over the top of it, apart from something loose, but I wasn't really thinking of Rebecca wearing something over it at all. I quickly settled on it, as she would look fantastic in it.

"Do you know her size?" said the scantily dressed assistant.

"Err yes, she's a 30FF."

"Goodness," said the assistant, "you're a lucky boy aren't you? I'm not sure we've got that size."

She then went on to give some complicated explanation as to why a different size would fit her, probably by having a larger back size and a smaller cup size. How this works exactly I don't know, if you're a girl reading this you probably do. If you're thinking about buying some underwear, *Agent Provocateur* is a real treat except for your bank balance.

"Would you like this gift wrapped sir?"

I decided against gift-wrapping because I would have to go to my next meeting with an *Agent Provocateur* box and everyone would know what it was. So the delightful assistant carefully wrapped it in tissue paper, sellotaped the ends together and I popped it in my laptop bag along with Kirsty's manuscript.

I headed off to the Intercontinental Hotel. It's one of those swish London hotels, all marble, glass and cool style and I was glad I'd worn a suit. I'd had a few texts from Kirsty directing me to reception; the next sending me to the main bar where she was chatting with a few people. The bar in the Intercontinental is modish, minimalist; with low seating and stylish glass tables. It was busy with a crowd of smartly dressed guests and visitors. I'd been before so I felt comfortable there.

Kirsty appeared in front of me, rising from one of the low seating areas. "Simon," she said, holding out her hand. "So pleased you could make it."

She had her hair tied back in a sort of French pleat arrangement, still smoky eyed, but this time her lips were very pale, almost sun-block-ski-lipstick pale. It sounds odd but it looked good on her. She was neatly dressed in a fitted grey top and a skirt which was loose and had an asymmetric hemline. She seemed taller than the last time I'd seen her, then I noticed her shoes, they were extremely high. They were black, double platform, the heels must have been nearly 6 inches tall. She didn't appear to have any stockings

Kirsty introduced me to several people, some with foreign names. We then engaged in a dialogue about marketing profiles and rights. It was fairly tedious and I couldn't actually make sense of all that was being proposed. I realised what my agent did now and that he probably worked hard for his contractual 20% fee.

My nerves returned and I realized that Rick was right, I'd agreed to this meeting because Kirsty was attractive, I was flattered and found it difficult to say no to attractive women. I soon felt side-lined in the meeting, I tried to be helpful, but really the marketing of coffee-table boho fashion books was something I hadn't paid a great deal of attention to.

The hours ground by. At 6 o'clock, I was still there. I'd had two cups of coffee, a glass of white wine, was desperately trying to recall people's names and wondering how quickly I could go. Kirsty made an excuse about wanting to talk to me about something and we walked from the bar back to the reception area and sat down on a small circular bench. As she sat down Kirsty's grey dress rode up to reveal a good deal of thigh.

"I really can't thank you enough Simon."

"I haven't really done anything useful," I said, "you seem to be handling everything very competently on your own; I don't think there's much I can do."

"Oh yes there is," Kirsty said. "Look, it's just about finishing up here, you've been so kind. Why don't I treat you to dinner, I'm staying here?"

"You're staying here?" I said.

I don't know what the room rate is at the Intercontinental is, but since it's one of the most expensive hotels in London, I imagine it's not modest. There was a small dining room near the bar. I was indeed hungry and of course, I agreed.

I quickly texted Rick, though I don't know why because I knew I'd get abuse. I just said, "I'm at the book thing, with Posh Kirsty, going to have dinner with her, what you up to? Simon."

In an instant a text came back, "I'm not surprised!"

Dinner with Kirsty was entertaining. I knew nothing about her apart from what I'd gleaned from her CV. Seeing her in action with the marketing agents and independent publicists was insightful. She was smart; articulate and determined. We soon moved from discussing her work to her private life; she'd been divorced about a year, unlike most divorcing couples experience of reduced financial resources after divorce, Kirsty had found herself very comfortably off.

Her husband was a banker, one of those that was receiving bad press currently for causing the worldwide economic meltdown. Not him personally of course, but he was an investment banker, specializing in mortgage debt securities. Writing with the benefit of hindsight we all know that means ninja mortgages, mortgages awarded to homebuyers in the United States with no income, job or assets, mortgages to those in the UK on the basis of "self-certified" accounts. No independent scrutiny or verification. Perhaps I'll write another book about how bizarre this scenario was, but here was Kirsty with very substantial property in Essex, a new Volvo 4x4, and two children at private school and about £10,000 a month to spend how she liked.

I admired the fact that she had no need to work, could enjoy hobbies, friendships and time doing exactly as she pleased. She was pleasing herself writing and producing her book of course but it was clear that this was a serious endeavour; she had a clear goal, an exacting work ethic and she knew her stuff. We hadn't drunk that much, a bottle of Chablis between us at the meal – there was absolutely no flirting. I mentioned how

299

much she looked like Victoria Beckham and she laughed, well smiled really.

"People have mentioned it," she said, "and even today somebody asked me in the lift if I was Posh Spice. I don't really mind," she said. Then she smiled again. "Probably just as well as there's nothing I can do about it." I talked about my divorce and how I was hoping to expand my writing; she nodded and tipped her head to one side, rather attractively. 'It's time to go,' I thought.

"Well," I said, standing up, "it's been a fabulous evening and thanks so much for dinner, are you sure I can't pay for it?"

Kirsty looked suddenly surprised. "Are you going?" she said.

"Err, well," I said in my best 'Hugh Grant' voice, "I thought I'd dash back. When are you heading back?"

"I'm not," she said, "Remember Simon, I'm staying here tonight."

There was a slightly awkward moment. I don't know why, because I was just someone she was talking to, we were just colleagues, not even that really. I sat down again. Neither of us spoke. I studied my shoes for a while, not knowing what to do. Then we both spoke together, I said or tried to say, "Well, I'll be off then."

She said, "You don't catch on very quickly do you?"

"Pardon?" I said.

"You don't catch on very quickly do you Simon?" She repeated. The same intonation exactly.

I was bewildered.

Fortunately, Kirsty took the initiative: "Look, there's a great cocktail bar on the top floor here."

"Yes I know," I said, "I've been here before."

"Why don't we grab a cocktail up there and talk about it, just one last drink?"

Was I imagining it or were things were beginning to develop? The express elevator to the top floor seemed to intensify an unfolding moment between us. Kirsty was undoubtedly attractive. I was willing myself to not think about how appealing she was. After all, I was clearing the decks. Rebecca would be arriving in a little over 24 hours.

It was early in the cocktail bar.

"What would you like to drink?"

"Champagne please," said Kirsty.

I nodded to the barman: "Two glasses of champagne please.

I know what you're thinking, you're probably racing pages ahead now aren't you? We didn't speak, we sat on the tall stools just looking at one another.

Kirsty stroked her hair; she got a small mirror out of her handbag, another one with a big G on it. I could understand how she could afford all the Gucci clothes now. She looked at herself in the mirror, at me and pouted then laughed and put the mirror away. She took another sip of champagne.

I'd gulped most of mine with sheer nerves, the champagne mixing with the Chablis.

What was going on here? She couldn't possibly be interested in me? 'I'm so much older than her,' I thought again, and I certainly don't look like David Beckham – I don't even look like his Dad. Maybe it was some elaborate scam, but what could she scam me for? My 3-year-old Alfa Romeo, the manuscript to my yet untitled new book on the history of Alfa's?

Kirsty was apparently feeling tense too. With one gulp, she swallowed her entire glass of champagne.

"Another one?" I enquired. She nodded her mouth still full of champagne. I nodded to the barmen. We were almost the only customers there. The glasses arrived instantaneously. Kirsty picked hers up and we clinked glasses, but she didn't drink.

"Shall we just finish these in my room?" she said.

"Err, well, I, um, I'm not, well..."

I didn't know what to say. I just nodded.

And barely a few short steps away from the cocktail bar was Kirsty's room, one of the best rooms in the hotel surely? It was a small suite with a panoramic view of Hyde Park and surrounding London. The lights were starting to illuminate the skyline. I'd gulped most of my champagne, I needed to know what was happening. I felt out of my depth. Was I in her room to share the view, watch TV, head off home after a couple more drinks?

Kirsty spoke. "Look Simon," she said, "I know this is a bit forward. I've seen you in the gym and I know you've been going out with Shilpa, haven't you?" I just nodded.

"Well, it's been difficult for me to meet people and I did want your help at the meetings today."

I still couldn't speak. I wanted to say, "Surely you can't be interested in me?"

She seemed able to read my thoughts and said, "I've always liked older men, which I suppose is a sort of backhanded compliment, but of course if you're not interested, if you've got a girlfriend, I understand, we can just finish our drinks and get back to the bar. Have you got a girlfriend Simon?"

I held my glass champagne in one hand and turned aside to look out of the window. 'Had I got a girlfriend,' I thought. "Well…" I said turning back towards her.

Kirsty looked at me sideways on, her little finger tapping against the bowl of her champagne glass, her eyes widened as if to say well, answer the question.

"Well," I said again, probably sounding like John Alderton, "I don't really have a girlfriend, but…"

Kirsty walked over to me smartly, champagne sloshing about in the glass, and just put one finger to my lips. "Won't be long," she said, "Enjoy the view," and disappeared.

I really do hate it when women do that, but over the years, I've got used to it. A psychiatrist would probably diagnose "abandonment issues". The view of the rapidly darkened London skyline was breathtaking.

The capital comes in for a lot of criticism – clogged streets, overcrowded and unfit for purpose underground, litter, vermin, vagrants, but for me it's still one of the finest cities in the world and here it was, laid out in front of me from this glorious vantage point, this was England.

If this were a film "Rule Britannia" would now be playing as the camera pans round taking in the London Eye now, there, a quick flash of the Houses of Parliament, on to Buckingham Palace, Trafalgar Square.

It's such a cliché that when CNN or NBC do a report from London they invariably feature a red bus, a Beefeater or the Houses of Parliament in the background. As if Americans were so stupid that they couldn't work out which "London" the news channels mean; surely not London Ontario, now that really *is* a dump. Then again, we suffer equally hackneyed shots of the White House, in Washington D.C., on our news channels unnecessarily and presumably in case we Brits confuse the American capital with its namesake on Tyne & Wear!

I felt like Bond again, pulled the cuffs of my shirt straight, fiddled with my RAF crest cufflinks, straightened my tie and for no reason at all, turned round to view an even greater sight.

Kirsty had changed out of her grey dress and had on a short, very short black nightie with cream edging lace; over it she had on a long, floor length, lace top and black slippers like mules, but with a small heel and a black fluffy pom pom on the front.

I later learned that they were from *Agent Provocateur* as well. Nothing more needed to be said, really.

Putting my champagne glass down, I took hold of my tie and wrenched it off, tossed my jacket aside and within seconds we were on the bed together. Within a moment I was inside her. My efforts at foreplay hadn't exactly been repelled but Kirsty had pushed me into position between her cream coloured thighs almost immediately.

I kissed and fondled I wanted to say, "Well, I can't believe this is happening!"

Kirsty was beautiful, despite being slight she had large, very firm breasts. The sex was wonderful. Afterwards in the early hours of the morning she explained that she had had a boob job. I'd pretty much guessed that really, because when she was lying flat on her back her boobs were pointing straight up and even for a woman of 31 years that's good going.

At about two o'clock in the morning, after we'd enjoyed a full repertoire of bedroom antics and I was in considerable pain, Kirsty decided that she was hungry, was I? Was I? I was ravenous! We had a moonlight feast.

A discreet waiter from room service brought in a tray of goodies, a variety of food including miniature bacon sandwiches and scrambled eggs on toast. We sat on the floor, eating, drinking tea and watching London by night, the cars below like model toys and laces of lights along the Mall and around Buckingham Palace.

We talked until the late-early hours and then fell asleep. I was exhausted and my hips ached horribly.

I thought morning might prove awkward. It wasn't. Neither of us mentioned seeing one another again, keeping in touch, any kind of future. My impression was that we weren't side stepping the issue rather that we mutually understood we'd shared a night together, just that and no more. It was a one-night stand.

I never saw Kirsty again. She didn't return to the gym. By the time you read this, her book on contemporary boho fashion will be in on sale.

As I stared out of the train window on the way back to Essex I thought of what an odd week it had been. Loose ends sorted? I'd created a Gordian knot!

Rebecca

I was in the "Quiet Zone" on the train from Liverpool St when my mobile, set to "vibrate" once more, shimmied across the table. I picked it up and opened my messages…

"Hi Simon, I'm back, will call you as soon as I get in. Love your Rebecca" and a kiss.

Having reached home, I was travelling down to see her. The drive from Essex to King's Lynn isn't straightforward as I've explained and once off the M11 if you find yourself stuck behind something, that's it.

I didn't really mind. In years gone by, I'd have been in a hurry to get to Mum and Dad's and cursing the traffic if forced to creep along behind a combine harvester or a tractor. I remember one year when going up to see my parents without the family I'd become particularly frustrated, sitting behind a farm vehicle for mile after country mile. I was tired, there was nowhere for him to pull over and when he finally did, a completely open dual carriageway opened up in front of me. At the time, I had a convertible Audi – I remember reading in the papers that Princess Diana had acquired one the same week.

I thundered past and kept going, my foot buried into the firewall – there was nothing ahead or behind me. I was determined to make up some time though illogically for no real reason. I was under no time pressure. Mum and Dad weren't even expecting me.

As the needle climbed past 100 miles an hour and kept going, I glanced briefly in the rear view mirror. Far in the distance, I could make out a car. About ten seconds later, I checked again and the car was directly behind me. I pulled over to the nearside lane and began to slow down and as I did so the Police car's "blues and twos" began to flash simultaneously.

The police officer came over to me. I buzzed the electric window down. I knew he was going to have a lot to say. In a soft Norfolk accent I heard, "Morning sir, how fast do you think you were going there then?"

I cleared my throat, and even in those days before I perfected "Hugh Grant" I could do a passable impression of him. "Well Officer, I think I was going a bit fast, maybe 80 miles an hour?"

"We clocked you at 119," said the officer.

"Ah…"

Then suddenly he said, "Nice car this.

"Thank you," I spluttered.

"Hasn't Princess Di got one of these?"

"Yes, I believe she has," I said, waiting for him to tell me my fate.

"You see anything over 100 miles an hour is an automatic ban." He continued.

My heart sank. Even worse, I could see the combine harvester catching up. All of a sudden the "blues and twos" lights that had been extinguished as I was stopped flashed on the police car, accompanied by a siren.

The officer ran back to his colleague, I could see in my rear view mirror some activity.

Then "my" officer walked swiftly back to me and said, "You're the luckiest man in Norfolk today – we've just got an emergency. Take it easy in future." He sped back to the police vehicle and it tore off leaving me on the hard shoulder.

Today I was driving moderately, enjoying the experience and luxuriating in the journey taking me to Rebecca. I had had an extraordinary week. But none of the girls, relationships or couplings had any future. Rebecca was the one for me. She was attractive, educated, charming, single and wanted a long term partner/marriage. We had a lot in common and I would be happy to move to Norfolk. Whilst I still hadn't met her daughter, who was almost twenty, close in age to Victoria.

I was on my way to her house for the weekend. We'd spoken on the phone incessantly since she had returned from her holiday. At night and into the early hours, during the daytime, first thing in the morning.

As the Norfolk countryside slipped by, I didn't know why I hadn't signed up for a personal introduction agency when I was first alone and single.

Not that I regretted meeting anyone, Niamh was lovely. Shilpa, beautiful, a lot of fun (with the cringing exception of the golf club outing), sexy and engaging though it was now blindingly apparent she'd had no interest at all in a serious relationship. Ingrid – quick-witted, savvy, (perhaps I should have made more of my relationship with Ingrid, after all we did get on very well). Sex with her was great, whether she brought a friend or not.

But I was looking to the future. Work was trickling in but for now on the back burner. I did need to look at all my options there but I'd received a sizeable cheque for historic payments and royalties since meeting up with my agent and I was feeling less anxious about finances.

Friday fish and chips was beginning to peter out as I moved on. The boys had been understanding. The change in routine was predictable in the circumstances. I was entering a new phase of my life and I couldn't have been happier.

Rebecca was phoning and as the Bluetooth connected I heard her voice. "Hi Simon, are you on your way?"

"Yes, I'm well on my way, should be with you in about twenty minutes," I replied.

"Great," said Rebecca, "I'll put the kettle on." I heard her blow a kiss down the phone line.

"I don't know about putting the kettle on," I said out loud, after the phone had gone dead, "you can slip your knickers off for me." I pulled into Rebecca's just as the sat nav noted, "You have arrived at your destination."

'Too true,' I thought.

The leafy suburb of King's Lynn North Wootton is characterized by tree-lined avenues leading to large, detached houses. Rebecca lived in one of these.

The house was modern, built in an L-shaped plot with a large drive, double garage, study and five bedrooms. Rebecca's Mercedes SLK was parked on the drive. I parked beside it.

When she opened the door I nearly gasped, she was even lovelier than I remembered. Her long, blonde curly hair fell to her shoulders, she had on a black stretchy cowl neck jumper, her shoulders were bare, a large black belt with a huge buckle tied at her hips and white trousers, black shoes. She hurried from the entrance out onto the driveway, arms outstretched.

"Hello you," she cooed, put her arms around me and we kissed.

She smelt of a perfume I recognized, Calvin Klein's *Euphoria* a distinctive fragrance, citrusy with floral top notes. It was Ingrid's favourite and one I'd bought her for a birthday present. Rebecca smelt so strongly of it I thought she must have bathed in it.

Playfully, I put my arms around her upper body and lifted her couple of inches off the ground and twirled her around. She squealed with what I hoped was pleasure not pain! Reluctantly disengaging from her I flipped open the boot of the Alfa and grabbed my things trying to ignore the ache in my hips.

The interior of Rebecca's house was light in colour, stylish and immaculately clean and tidy.

The large entrance hall had ceramic tiling which shone. Rebecca seemed slightly nervous but evidently pleased to see me. I followed her into the large kitchen.

Paul Fox

"Let's get you a cup of tea," she said. "All that driving."

I just couldn't wait to touch her. I wanted her there and then. I didn't want tea, anything to eat, I didn't want to talk.

As she clicked the kettle on, I moved behind her, wrapped my arms around her and started kissing her neck. She put her hand back and held my head onto her neck, then almost under her breath said the words I was praying I would hear from her at some stage, "I so want you, Simon." I hadn't presumed it would be at this stage!

I thought I was going to faint with delight and anticipation. I felt for the large belt around her waist and with both hands managed to unbuckle it; let it drop to the floor, then slipped my hands to the waistband of her white trousers and undid those. Rebecca obligingly wriggled her hips allowing me push them to her knees with ease.

At first I didn't think she was wearing knickers, but on closer inspection I saw she had on a tiny white lace G-string (possibly the one I'd seen her in when she was changing in the shop?). Soon this, now less lace than a sliver of rumpled string, was round her knees as well. Rebecca leant over her kitchen worktop inviting me to enter her from behind.

I was fully erect and penetrated her with such enthusiasm she crashed against the kitchen cupboards and let out a long moan. I was really worried I'd had hurt her. I was also worried that I was in such a high state of arousal that I was going to come immediately. I forced myself to concentrate intently on not doing this. I so wanted, so really wanted, to burst inside her.

Whilst still welded together, Rebecca said, "The chair, sit on the chair", and we waddled backward together and I sat on the chair whilst still inside her. Rebecca leant forward, grabbed her ankles and then partly stood up she rocked forwards and backwards on me. She took my hand and placed it over her clitoris and showed what she wanted me to do to please her, rubbing her as she moved up and down on my cock.

She was very vocal and kept saying, "Now, now, now, now, now," this being followed by a pause and then "NOW!" at the top of her voice. This was her signal that she was about to orgasm.

When I came inside her after she'd reached orgasm, I felt utterly flooded with intense pleasure, emotion, relief. Rebecca stood, grabbing her knickers and trousers and pulling them up, she turned, kissed me deeply and said, "Welcome to King's Lynn."

"I was going to make you wait for that," she said.

Sipping tea in the lounge it was as though the previous few minutes hadn't happened. Rebecca had gone into the downstairs cloakroom, reapplied her makeup, made the tea and brought it in on a tray. I spoke first. "You know I was really worried about the sex thing."

"Oh," said Rebecca, "Why's that?"

"Well since you're a primary school teacher I wondered if you might be rather prim and proper. I thought I'd have to watch my Ps and Qs, especially my Ps."

Rebecca laughed lustily. "Oh, you don't have to worry about that Simon, I doubt you're going to corrupt me."

The lounge was as tidy as the hall and kitchen. We sat on two full sized Chesterfield sofas with a coffee table in the middle.

'Still much grander than my flat,' I ruminated. I had been relieved when Rebecca suggested I should visit her, rather than arrange a visit to mine. We chatted about what we would be doing for the weekend.

I was to be introduced to her parents that evening and we were going to go to dinner with them. Rebecca had already told me that my visit coincided with her Father's birthday. I'd bought him a bottle of wine, a decent St. Emilion having established that he liked French Bordeaux wines. I had written and sealed a card. I mentioned this to Rebecca and she told me how thoughtful it was, and that he'd love it.

I asked about her holiday, she asked what I was working on and of course, about how I'd spent my week.

In answer to this latter enquiry I smiled weakly, feeling genuine guilt. I said, "Oh just quietly." I was conscious that I was focused intently on controlling my vocal chords… "just working…" I squeaked. I hadn't even confessed the extent of my sinful escapades to Rick, let alone Barry who I knew would have been disgusted. I'm sure you are too, but I was consoling myself with the thought that that was then, not now. Shilpa, Judy, Ingrid, Kirsty, boxed and put into storage – in that place called "the past."

Apart from that question, I answered her others as truthfully as I could. I had begun to notice that there was a familiar thread running through her questioning. Many concerned finance; the value of my home, pension, my income and outgoings, shareholdings, the type of holidays/hotels I had stayed in etc.

Looking out of the window of the lounge and sipping her tea she said, for a second time, "Like your car, how much would one of those be?"

I answered these enquiries and others fully though I was trying to make light of the seriousness with which they were asked and to suppress a degree of mild irritation. Was Rebecca going to interrogate me about my financial status each time we met? Perhaps I was just feeling sensitive. I

Paul Fox

concluded that her inquisitiveness about the extent of my share of the equity in my marital home was due to a practical analysis of how much we might ultimately spend on buying a home together.

I asked her about the school she taught at and how long she had worked there; whether she enjoyed her work, the age of the children and about the subject she principally taught. She was less forthcoming that I expected and some of my questions went unanswered, but looking at her, listening to her and in the post-coital glow cast by the wonderful welcome I'd received, she was perfect.

We had much in common, books, films, Elton, music apart from Elton, mutual holiday destinations, food, and this was simply the beginning.

I was enormously attracted to her. She was irresistible with those large blue eyes, fine creamy skin, small slightly turned up nose and full lips. Her long hair, naturally blonde framed her heart shaped face perfectly. When she smiled her mouth crimped at the corners. She was a heartbreaker.

'What a lucky sod,' I thought, for about the 1,000[th] time.

I rang Uncle Colin on my mobile phone.

"Hello, Idiot Nephew!" he said.

"Hello Unc Colin," I said, "Yes, your favourite nephew here. I'm at Rebecca's house in North Wootton," I said, "just wondered if we could meet up with you."

"Yeah, that would be great," he said casually. "Which one's this?" he said.

I was hoping Rebecca hadn't heard she was still smiling broadly, so clearly she hadn't.

"Rebecca," I said, "she's a teacher here."

"Oh yeah, right. Why don't we meet up at the *Lavender Fields* in about an hour? I'm doing a job up here."

"Great, see you in the *Lavender Fields Café* at 3.00pm."

"Great," he said.

I explained to Rebecca that my Uncle Colin worked as a plumber. "A plumber?" she said.

"Yes," I said, "a plumber."

"What, he works as a plumber?"

"Yes, a plumber." There was one of those gaps. It's not difficult is it? "My Uncle Colin is a plumber, it isn't difficult is it?" Rebecca wanted to know more.

"Is he a plumber, as in he works as a plumber... or does he have his own business that employs plumbers?"

310

"No," I said, "he's a plumber, he works as a plumber and he's working on a plumbing job as we speak near the Lavender Fields and we can meet him there in an hour, is that okay?"

Rebecca just smiled. I thought she was going to say something.

"Another cup of tea?" she asked.

"Oh, yes please," I said.

As her *Euphoria* perfume wafted towards me again on her approach, Rebecca's beautifully manicured hand took my cup from me. I had a sneaky glance at her bottom as she went into the kitchen.

'What a lucky sod,' I thought again.

On her return to the lounge, the conversation started again.

"So where are we meeting him?"

"At the small café at the Lavender Fields," I said, "is it still there?"

"Oh, yes, it is," she said. "Is that where we're meeting him?"

I repeated again that Uncle Colin was working on a plumbing job near the Lavender Fields and we would be meeting him in an hour. I wondered if she hadn't heard or was feeling distracted and not concentrating.

"Oh right," she said. She looked slightly confused, but I just sipped my tea.

Then all of a sudden, she stood, came over to my sofa, kissed me full on the lips and said, "Well, we've got an hour, do you want to help me choose an outfit?"

"Great," I said.

Her bedroom was huge. It had an enormous, cast iron bed in the centre lavishly decorated with sumptuous covers, lots of cushions. There was an elaborate dressing table to one side with a small chair with a padded seat and an hourglass back. Then to the left of where you entered the bedroom, there was another sort of annex lined with built in wardrobes. These were all Rebecca's clothes.

"Wow, what's your knicker drawer like?" I said.

"Well, to be honest Simon, I don't often wear knickers."

I didn't know whether to feel pleased or not.

"But I know you like pink ones so I went and bought some."

"Lovely," I said, "I've bought you some as well," suddenly remembering my purchase from *Agent Provocateur*.

"Oh, that's lovely."

I made my way back downstairs, wincing from the pain in my hips as I went and found the pink and black tissue paper, enclosing my purchases. When I returned to the bedroom I found her standing in her underwear. It was an arresting sight. I don't think I've ever seen a bra so full. One of the doors to the wardrobes was open and Rebecca was flicking through dresses.

"I got you this," I said, proffering the package.

"Oh lovely, Simon, you're so kind." She unwrapped the tissue on the bed and seemed pleased. Holding up the basque, she said, "I hope I can get my boobs in here." I explained that the girl in the shop had assured me that even though it wasn't her exact size she should be able to fit into it.

"Shall I put them on later when we go to dinner?"

"Oh yes, please," I said.

"They're lovely," she said and gave me a long kiss.

I wanted her again. But I was in considerable discomfort now and time was short. Rebecca led me to her wardrobe. This was just getting better and better.

"Now, choose something for me to meet your Uncle Colin in."

"Well you're fine as you are, you look fantastic," I said.

"What, just in my bra and knickers?"

"No, just put your trousers back on, you look great."

"No, no," said Rebecca, "it's the first time I'm meeting him, I want him to have a good impression of me."

"Rebecca you'll be fine as you are, believe me you don't have to work that hard to impress Uncle Colin."

Eventually she chose a short black woollen skirt, some flesh-coloured lace top hold-ups, and a fresh pair of white knickers, a white blouse and a rose coloured cardigan. She looked delicious.

I was so proud when I introduced her to my Uncle Colin. The Lavender Fields in King's Lynn are just along from the Sandringham Estate. The fields are spectacular and add a welcome dash of colour to the otherwise rather grey Norfolk countryside.

As we pulled into the car park, I noticed Colin's van parked up, gleaming, as he always looked after it so well. We walked into the café and there he was.

He stood immediately: "Hello Idiot Nephew," he said. "Gosh, you must be Rebecca? Bloody hell, Simon," he said, "you didn't tell me how gorgeous she was!" Then he got hold of Rebecca and kissed her; she was slightly stunned. "You and I are going to get on really well," he said.

"Oh, I hope so," said Rebecca.

"Well, we have so much in common already," he said.

Rebecca looked slightly puzzled.

"Well, we're both very good looking aren't we?" I said laughing.

Uncle Colin was really charming with her. It was good to see him again.

Rebecca didn't say much during our meeting but she nodded and took things in, then she asked a question. "So, what sort of a business have you got?"

Uncle Colin explained, "I'm a plumber, didn't you see my van as you came in?"

"Do you employ any other staff?" said Rebecca.

"Erm, well, no," said Uncle Colin, "just me.

I was becoming irritated. We'd already had this conversation at Rebecca's home.

"How long have you been a plumber?" said Rebecca, carrying on her inquisition.

"Since I was 17," he said.

"And in all that time," said Rebecca, "have you ever employed anyone?"

I thought Uncle Colin was becoming exasperated too but he sipped his tea and said, "From time to time." Then he turned to me and said "Still got the Alfa then? Thought you'd have got yourself a proper car by now."

Rebecca spoke again. "How old is your car Simon?"

"Just coming up for three years," I said. I started to explain to Uncle Colin that I'd test driven a few BMWs recently but wasn't that impressed with them. He knows how much I love my Alfa though he's not a fan.

"Well it does go," he admitted, "but they're just Italian rubbish."

Rebecca piped up again, "Yes, wouldn't you be better off with a Mercedes?"

"Well maybe," I said. "Maybe I'll change the Alfa for a Mercedes, would you like me to?"

"Well I do like Mercedes," she said, "that's why I've got one."

Uncle Colin's mobile phone went off. He grabbed it from the table and said, "Hello? No, I'm not at a job, I'm just having a cup of coffee with Simon and Rebecca."

Whoever it was at the end of the phone didn't say anything other than, "Whom?"

"Rebecca... Simon and Rebecca... Simon's come up to see her." Then Uncle Colin just said, "Oh okay, I'll be there in ten minutes." Without any further ceremony, Uncle Colin got up, shook my hand, gave Rebecca a kiss on the cheek and said, "Nice to meet you – and get a proper car, Simon!" he said, as he got to the door of the café.

Rebecca looked at me after he'd gone and just said, "Oh, he's nice."

"Yes," I said, "he's a great guy."

On the way back to North Wotton in her car, she said, "You'd think he'd have expanded his business though wouldn't you?"

I hadn't really thought about it before, I didn't really know what to say. I just said, "Well, I think he's really happy doing what he's doing."

As we got back to her house, I couldn't wait to get her into bed despite my aching hips. I mean, I know it's dreadful but we were meeting her parents a bit later and I just couldn't wait for the evening to have her again. I assumed we would be sleeping together.

Rebecca could read my mind. In the hallway she put her arms around my neck rather tightly and said, "Well I'm going to need to start getting ready shortly."

I looked at my watch, it was only half past four and we were picking her parents up at half past seven.

"What would you like to do now Simon?"

I just smiled.

Upstairs in the bedroom Rebecca did a slow striptease and soon we were in bed together. It was very physical sex. Unlike Niamh, Rebecca enjoyed me thrusting hard and deeply inside her and gave me clear instructions, "Harder, harder still."

Whatever position we had sex in, it had to be hard. Although she had fabulous boobs the odd thing was that they were totally off limits. I wasn't allowed to touch or play with them.

Odder still, during the entire course of our relationship I never actually saw them! I'd asked her to keep her stockings on in bed, but she kept her bra on as well. And she nearly always faced away from me. Experience has shown me that every woman is different in the bedroom department. She was a very enthusiastic lover but acutely self-conscious about her breasts.

At half past six, we were still in bed. Rebecca on realizing the time yelled, "Oh my God, look at the time!" She climbed out of bed, sprinted for her en suite bathroom, then opened the door and shouted, "Simon, there's another bathroom along the hall if you want to use that."

I showered and shaved, dabbed on aftershave, pulled on my grey Gucci suit, white shirt and favourite tie and waited downstairs. It was now twenty past seven.

"Simon!" shouted Rebecca from her bedroom, "Do you want to help me do up my dress?" When I got back to Rebecca's bedroom, she was wearing the *Agent Provocateur* basque and knickers. She was just attaching her stockings to the rose petal lined suspenders, I wanted to take a photograph, and I know it sounds disgusting but she looked amazing. I'm sure *Agent Provocateur* could have used the photo in their advertising.

"Wow," I said, "you look beautiful."

"Its lovely underwear Simon, thank you ever so much."

As Rebecca was fixing her stockings, sitting on the small hourglass backed chair, on the bed was laying a black pinafore dress.

I picked it up. The top was black satin and the skirt tiers of velvet with a satin bow around the waist. I helped Rebecca step into it and secure it, she couldn't have looked lovelier. Her blonde curly hair was swept over one shoulder, she wore red lipstick and dark eye makeup outlining her large blue eyes.

The stockings I'd bought her from *Agent Provocateur* were black and she had some scarlet patent, very high, Jimmy Choo shoes on. She looked sensational.

Soon we were scrambling to get into the car and pick her Mum and Dad up from the farm near Potts Row. It was hard to keep my eyes off Rebecca and on the road, but suddenly my nerves returned. What if her Mum and Dad didn't like me?

Rebecca clearly had a very close relationship with her Mum and Dad. After her divorce, she had lived with them for some time. She had a sister as well who lived in London that she didn't say much about. I just knew this meeting had to go well.

I looked in the rear view mirror and happened to notice a few beads of sweat on my brow. I didn't know whether that had to do with the afternoon's exertions or meeting her Mum and Dad. I needn't have worried, as I swung the car through a large gate and short driveway up to the farmhouse, the door opened and out spilled Rebecca's Mum and Dad, Richard and Delia. They couldn't have made me more welcome; they rushed over to the car and kissed Rebecca.

Richard, who was an amiable, round faced man, took a firm hold of my hand, then grabbed me by the shoulder and said "Welcome, we've heard so much about you Simon, very pleased to meet you," I was charmed.

"Happy Birthday!" I suddenly remembered. I grabbed the bottle of wine and card I'd brought and gave them to Richard.

"Oh, you shouldn't have done that!" He seemed genuinely surprised.

Delia then came over to me, kissed me and said, "Thank you for making our daughter so happy, we've heard nothing else except Simon, Simon, and Simon for weeks!"

I didn't know what to say. I guessed that Delia must be in her early 60s; she still looked stunning, had a good figure, her hair was swept back and she had hardly any lines at all. She looked like Helen Mirren.

'This all bodes well for the future,' I thought, they always say girls end up looking like their Mums and that would be fine with me.

"Have we got time for a drink?" Delia said, "or shall we go to the restaurant straight away?" Rebecca looked at her watch and said, "Well I think we are a bit late, shall we just get going?"

Delia looked at me and said, "I'd said to Richard you'll be late, I know what you two have been up to."

'Oh my God!' I thought, 'Rebecca's Mum knows I've been shagging her all afternoon!'

Rebecca gave me a slightly worried look as well. I didn't say anything.

I helped Richard get into the back of the car as he was slightly arthritic and not as nimble on his feet as I'm sure he once was. We drove to a lovely restaurant called *The Hoste* at Burnham Market.

Now if you think Norfolk is full of carrot crunchers and rural pubs selling warm beer to men with eyebrows on their cheeks, you're wrong. Burnham Market is living proof of the fact that Norfolk has come a long way.

Its short high street has some fabulous boutique shops, selling everything from designer dresses to expensive watches. There were established outlets: *Jack Wills*, *Hollister*, *Karen Millen*, *Gant*, not to mention the best hat shop in the country. This, a celebrity secret, called "The Hat Shop". I knew about Burnham Market from my historic visits but I didn't realize until I returned how upmarket it had become and *The Hoste* Restaurant and Hotel was its epicentre.

Parking the car, I helped Richard in and he spoke all the time. He seemed genuinely pleased to meet me, Delia and Rebecca were engrossed in conversation and Rebecca was whispering in her Mum's ear and she was roaring with laughter.

'Oh my God,' I thought, 'what on earth is she telling her?'

The front part of *The Hoste* is a pub and we were decidedly overdressed for this, but as we walked through the bar, I could see lots of men eyeing Rebecca. There were a few knowing looks and guys digging each other in the ribs and nodding.

I felt like saying "Yeah, she's fantastic, I've been shagging her all afternoon and I'm going to shag her all night as well!" Disgusting I know, but I did feel good.

We toasted Richard a "Happy Birthday" with champagne and the evening went by in a flash. It wasn't at all awkward; Richard and Delia avoided overly personal questioning. They were charming and relaxed and I felt comfortable with them.

On our way back, we stopped at their home, *The Farmhouse* in Potts Row for a drink. This was a large, detached place with a gravel drive, leaded light windows and a thatched roof. Within the house had a country kitchen arrangement and a comfortable lounge with four large sofas in it. Why was it that everyone I knew had enormous houses?

Richard decided to open a bottle of Champagne, and I ended up sitting with him and talking and Rebecca and her Mum were on another sofa talking. I felt very contented. Not only was Rebecca stunningly attractive and lovely, she had delightful parents and lived in a part of the world I knew.

How clever were the people at *Across the Room* to put me in touch with her? I just so wished I'd done it first off without faffing about with all the internet stuff.

Richard was telling me about farming and kept urging me to drink more champagne.

"I'm going to have to be careful," I said, "because I'm driving."

"Leave the car here," he said, "I'll get you a taxi. We're going to be seeing you tomorrow aren't we?"

I didn't know anything about arrangements for the next day but that was fine by me. Delia then piped up, "Yes, you're coming here for lunch, I'm cooking tomorrow."

Rebecca said "We can leave the car if you want to, Simon and get a taxi back? I've got my car for tomorrow."

I don't know how many bottles of champagne we got through that night. By the time we got back to Rebecca's, it was nearly 2am. We fell into bed. Rebecca just took her shoes and dress off and got into bed in the wonderful underwear I'd bought her. I couldn't be bothered hanging my suit up I just threw it on the back of the hourglass chair and dived under the covers with her.

In the morning we had breakfast in bed. Rebecca awoke before me, showered, made coffee and brought this back up to bed on a tray along with toast and marmalade. She even had trays with little legs on for the bed.

"Well," said Rebecca, "you got the seal of approval from my Mum and Dad, they thought you were wonderful."

"Great," I said. "I liked them very much too and I'm really pleased we're going back there for lunch today. Have we got time to go to Mass?" Rebecca was Catholic as well.

"Well, if we rush," she added, "we could just make it to St Peter & Paul's. Shall we?"

I said it would be great to do that as I used to go to that very same church with my Mum. We just made it.

I remember the inside of the church, the round structure, very modern interior, probably built around the 1970s.

I suddenly remembered a kneeler, a small narrow embroidered cushion that as the name implies, makes kneeling down during services manageable for many. Probably twenty years beforehand, the church had appealed for people to donate these and my mother had one made for me with the crest of the Royal Air Force embroidered on it. I don't know why I hadn't thought of it before. As we sat down and joined the members of the congregation, something made me look to my right.

Across the aisle and slightly in front of me, I saw it.

The kneeler embroidered by my mum with the Forces crest. It was an emotional moment and I suddenly felt very close to my Mum, as well as to tears.

I wanted to say, "Look Mum, isn't she lovely? I'm going to marry her and we're going to live near here and I'll get my life back together."

Coming across the kneeler seemed an omen. Was it a seal on our relationship?

I looked around at those present in Church didn't recognize anyone in the congregation. Not surprising of course. Over 20 years or so congregations change irrevocably.

When it was time to go up for Communion, Rebecca didn't move.

I whispered to her "Aren't you coming up for Communion?"

"No," she whispered.

"Why not?" I whispered back.

"I just don't want to. Especially after what we've been doing all weekend."

I reflected on this briefly. Maybe I shouldn't be going to Communion; confession would be the better place for me after the week I'd had.

Afterwards I told Rebecca about the kneeler and as the congregation slipped out of the church, I picked it up. I lit a couple of candles for my Mum and Dad whilst holding it.

Why hadn't my parents lived long enough to see me happy again? To see me with a new partner, yet on good terms with Katherine and their beloved grandchildren.

Rebecca spoke, "You're not going to cry are you?"

"No," I said quietly, "I'm just having a bit of a moment." I put the kneeler back in place and said, "Let's get going, don't want to be late for lunch as well."

The journey from South Wootton to Potts Row is straightforward but Rebecca insisted on stopping off at her house. She hurried up to the bedroom to change her skirt, she'd decided hers was too creased.

The replacement was white and close fitting, she had a black blouse on with another cowl type neck, her boobs straining at the black fabric and over the top of that she wore a black and cream Chanel type jacket, another pair of skyscraper shoes.

Now, I know what you're thinking, I'm making this up. I can assure you I'm not, but we were both dressed I thought quite formally for lunch in a Norfolk farmhouse with close relatives.

Rebecca had asked me to put my suit on again and fortunately, I had another formal shirt with me that I quickly ironed. I'd thought I'd wear casual clothing to Sunday lunch but clearly things were different and standards were higher in Rebecca's family than I had anticipated. When we arrived back at the farm, my car still sitting on their drive, she turned to me and said, "I hope you're hungry."

"Well after last night," I said, "yes I am."

We had made love twice during the night, I couldn't get enough of her. Rebecca let herself in the front door with a key. "Hi Mum, hi Dad," she shouted, "we're here." Richard and Delia greeted us warmly. Richard was reading the *Sunday Times*.

He kissed Rebecca and grabbed my hand greeting me heartily. "You okay Simon?" he said. "Good night last night!" and jabbed me in the ribs.

'Oh my God,' I thought, 'what can he mean?'

Before I could say anything I was relieved to hear him add, "the Food at *The Hoste* is really good isn't it? I had a good birthday."

Lunch was in a conservatory at the back of the house, which I hadn't noticed on my earlier visit.

The conservatory was nearly as big as the house, it had stylish black and white tiled flooring and though I say "conservatory" it was more like an orangery. Tall exotic plants stood in ceramic pots and an established vine trailed across one wall.

"Can I help, Mum?" asked Rebecca.

"No," she said, "you just entertain Simon and your father, I've got everything covered."

Paul Fox

Richard had opened yet another bottle of champagne and whilst he carried on reading his newspaper in the lounge, Rebecca and I stood looking out of the back of the conservatory onto the farm.

There were outbuildings and tractors, the usual farm paraphernalia. Richard had explained to me the previous evening that it was arable farming and that mostly he grew rape for rapeseed oil, which had been very lucrative but was less so now due to the economic climate.

Rebecca held me close to her, looked deep into my eyes, kissed me, held her champagne glass up and said, "Welcome back to Norfolk Simon, are you having a good time?"

A good time? I was having the time of my life!

"Dinner is served," called Delia. "Come on you two lovers, sit down, I expect you're hungry Simon," giving me that knowing look again.

"As a matter of fact," I said, "I am, it must be the air."

The afternoon passed gloriously but it was time for me to go. I had to get back to Essex on the Sunday evening as I'd got another appointment with my agent in London on Monday morning and I knew that Rebecca had marking to do. After saying our goodbyes I followed Rebecca in the Alfa back to her house.

It was now approaching 5 o'clock. Lunch had sprawled into the late afternoon. I didn't want to leave Rebecca or for this idyllic weekend to end.

I started to pack one or two things from the spare bathroom and decided to change into something more comfortable for the long drive back to Essex. I put my suit in its suit hanger, pulled on jeans and a rugby shirt and brought everything downstairs from the bedroom.

I went out to the car and loaded the boot. Rebecca had moved to the study on the right of the hallway. "This is what I've got to get through," she said. There were piles of folders, books, each one of them had to be read, marked and assessed.

"Goodness," I said, "how long is this going to take you?"

"Oh, it will probably take me to the early hours."

"The early hours?" I said, "All this work? I hope they pay you well!"

"Hardly," she said, "I'm a school teacher, Simon. I've made you a cup of tea. Have it before you go," she said.

We sat in the study with our tea and I just poured my heart out to Rebecca, telling her how I couldn't believe my good fortune at meeting her, how lovely she was, how much I'd liked her parents and how they'd made me feel so welcome.

Rebecca gave me a hug and said she felt very happy that we'd met. She spoke very deliberately and I had noticed this on a couple of occasions. There were times when she didn't answer my questions or I needed to repeatedly explain something I'd just said. Sometimes she didn't seem to follow the sequence of conversation. I had wondered if she perhaps daydreamed or became easily distracted. The previous evening she had got all flustered because of a joke she'd obviously misheard or didn't understand.

Richard and I had been talking about old farm sayings and he'd started with the line, "Oh yes, red sky at night," and I'd chipped in with, "Barn on fire."

He'd roared with laughter and so did Delia, Rebecca had just looked horrified.

"The barn's on fire?" she said, "Why you didn't tell me? When did this happen Dad?"

"Don't be daft," he said, "Simon's just telling a joke."

I'd just put it down to the alcohol and the noise of the evening. It was of no consequence.

"Do I really have to go?" I said.

"I'm afraid you do, Simon, or I'll never get my work done."

I desperately wanted to make sure when I was seeing her again.

"Why don't I come to you next weekend?" she said. "Well that would be fantastic," I told her, "but I'm not sure I can wait a week until I see you again."

"Well, I've got evening classes Monday and Tuesday."

"What about Wednesday?"

"Yes that would be okay after school."

"Okay Rebecca, that would be lovely."

"But I will have to do some work," she said. I got in the car and as I drove off, Rebecca stood blowing kisses in the doorway.

As I drove away I just couldn't help feeling my life was now perfect. What could possibly go wrong?

Six of the Best

A month had gone by. I was driving back to Rebecca's in my new Mercedes. I'd decided to change the Alfa, well it was three years old now.

I had the impression Rebecca didn't really like it that much. She didn't really seem to "get" the Alfa thing at all and what did I need a saloon for? I'd dug deep into my savings, part-exchanged the car for a new, well nearly new 300 SL Mercedes, black, AMG wheels, cream leather upholstery.

What a month it had been! We'd established a routine of Rebecca coming to the flat one weekend, me dashing to meet her on a Wednesday evening, picking her up from school then spending the following weekend at hers. We'd already fitted in three lovely dinners and a trip to the theatre to see *Les Misérables*. I didn't think the RAF club was really Rebecca, so had decided to book us in somewhere a bit glitzier during our theatre trip. I chose the Savoy, it was just before they started renovation work.

I remember Rebecca being impressed as we drove up, on the wrong side of the road. Why is it that the Savoy entrance is the only part of the UK, as far as I know, that it is legal to drive on the wrong side of the road?

I'd booked a standard room, but they upgraded us to a superior. It was fabulous. Inside apart from the sumptuous bedroom, there was a small lounge complete with library. We had a bathroom each.

Rebecca grabbed hold of me and said, "I can't believe you booked this, thanks so much." I remember scooting down to reception to check we'd been upgraded and I wouldn't have to pay this. The charming lady on reception confirmed that our room was being decorated and as the superior was empty and they'd upgraded us.

I'd moved on from fish and chips with the lads, to theatre breaks at the Savoy, to driving a new Mercedes sports car and being totally besotted with Rebecca.

I was paying for it all of course, I never expected Rebecca to pay for anything. She never offered and never did. But I could afford it so why not?

As the Norfolk countryside sped past again on the umpteenth trip to Rebecca's, I decided not to play as much Elton John music. Rebecca liked the late, great, Michael Jackson and poor old Michael was now singing "Man in the Mirror" (great video).

I'd spoken to the lads on the phone quite a bit and seen Rick briefly when he'd popped into the flat.

In fairness to Rick, he was pleased and his parting shot was, "She sounds really nice, Simon, but don't go overboard will you?"

I hadn't told him about the new car or the Savoy trip, I'm sure he just assumed it was a car to write about. 'I'll tell him later,' I thought.

Barry said pretty much the same thing on the phone anyway, that she sounded everything I could have wanted. It obviously wasn't going anywhere with Shilpa or Niamh and this introduction agency really did seem to have got it right.

Rebecca's voice cut into Michael's.

"Hi Hun, are you on your way?"

"Yes darling," I said, "I'm just on the M11."

"Where are you?"

"Just on the M11?"

"Oh you're off the M11?"

"No, I'm still on the M11 so it'll be about forty minutes."

"What presents?" said Rebecca. "Sorry, I missed that. You said you'd brought me presents?"

I started to panic. Well I'd bought a nice bottle of wine for us to have. I said, "No I said I'll be about 40 minutes."

There was a long pause…

"Oh that's so lovely, you shouldn't keep buying me presents. I'll put the kettle on. Bye." Click.

I did consider switching on to the A11 and stopping to buy her something, but what could I buy her at a motorway service station? I decided against.

I must get this phone fixed because, like the phone in the flat, Rebecca often struggled to hear me.

I'd got a few important things to think about. It was coming up to half term and I wanted to dash away on holiday with her. I'd a few ideas, maybe a nice city break somewhere back to Italy perhaps, but it seemed to be that there was no point in talking to her on the phone because like the recent "present" issue, she often seemed to misunderstand me.

Michael was still singing away and we were now on to one of my favourites – "Thriller".

"Darkness falls across the land, the midnight hours close at hand…"

Apart from making plans for a holiday, Rebecca had been most anxious to talk to me about something "important" as she put it.

This weekend I was due to meet her sister and I was looking forward to it. Rebecca had been odd about her sister.

Every time I asked a question about her – normal stuff like: "Where does she live, is she married, has she any children?" – Rebecca gave me a blank look and she changed the subject or just didn't reply.

On three occasions during the week she had mentioned about sitting down and having a talk about her sister. All I knew was she was married, had two small children and lived somewhere in South London. She and her husband were coming up for the weekend, staying at the farm with her Mum and Dad and we were invited round for dinner on the Saturday night. That was all I knew. I'm sure that her sister, if she was anything like Rebecca, would be perfectly charming.

But she seemed to be hinting at something dark, something "I should know". I tried to work out what it could be, but had given up trying to hazard a guess.

As I negotiated the final roundabout before King's Lynn itself, I felt elated. I'd even rung Eleanor at *Across the Room* to thank her for introducing me to Rebecca. She was charming.

"I'm so pleased you're happy Simon. Do you remember the first time you came to see us and we did that dreadful speed dating event?" We both laughed. Eleanor left me with, "Please do invite me to the wedding, but give me plenty of notice so I can buy a big hat!" I told her about "The Hat Shop".

It seemed appropriate now that as my thoughts turned to love, Michael was singing, "I just can't stop loving you". I'm conscious that I'm well into this book and this is the first time I've really spoken of love, did I love Niamh and Shilpa? Had I ever been in love with Ingrid?

The answer has got to be "yes".

And had I been in love with my first wife? The answer to that is a definite, unqualified yes.

I'd been happy in the main being with Niamh and Shilpa too, but Rebecca was completely different. Was I in love with her? I was. Hook, line and sinker. I was totally and utterly besotted with her and there were so many bonuses.

Having lost my Mum and Dad, I'd gained her delightful parents and they treated me like a son. Richard would phone up during the week, letting me know how the farm was going, he would often end with a cheery, "Okay Simon, see you when you're up!"

I went to Mass with Delia, sometimes with Rebecca as well, but sometimes just the two of us and if I looked straight at the altar, out of the corner of my eye, I could just see the edge of Delia's immaculately coiffured hair, and just for a second I could imagine I was standing there with my Mum.

And the sex? Well Rebecca had an extensive underwear drawer, all of it beautiful and I'd bought her even more underwear, but gradually more of her personality was revealing itself. She had some very kinky underwear including crotch less knickers that she admitted to wearing to school. It hinted at a wild side that I was sure I was going to enjoy learning more about.

As I pulled onto Rebecca's drive, she was there already at the front door, looking gorgeous in a navy knee length pleated skirt, navy stockings, red shoes with ankle straps and a matching blue silk blouse.

"Hello gorgeous," I said, grabbing hold of her and kissing her in the hallway. I thrust a bottle of Chablis at her.

"I bought you this," I said, "I thought we could have it later."

Rebecca said, "I'll open it now, I've something to tell you."

"Err, yes, well, right."

She snatched the top of the wine bottle, twisted open the cap and poured two large glasses. It seemed churlish to say I preferred it chilled, but she was obviously a girl on a mission.

I sat down on one of the chairs at the kitchen table, expecting Rebecca to sit next to me as she normally did when we were together.

She remained standing, smoothed her skirt down continuously and took a large gulp of wine.

With her hands out in front of her like she was about to make a declaration she said with a deep breath, "You're going to meet my sister tomorrow."

"Yes, I know," I said, "I'm really looking forward to meeting her."

Rebecca kept one hand open, palm uppermost as if to say, "Shut up, I'm talking". She probably did that with the kids at school. "Let me finish," she said, rather snappily.

I felt as if I was back at school myself. I was hoping Rebecca was wearing the pink frilly knickers I'd bought her under that blue skirt, but anyway enough of that, this was serious, clearly serious by the look on Rebecca's face.

"I've got to tell you about my sister." Rebecca took another huge gulp of wine.

I just nodded. After what seemed ages, she took another deep breath and said, "I can't hide it from you any longer, you're going to meet her tomorrow, and I don't know how to tell you Simon." She looked miserable.

I was wide eyed with anticipation, what on earth was she going to say? My mind raced through the possibilities: she was a mass murderer or at the very least a former convict of some sort? She was having an affair and Richard and Delia didn't/mustn't know? What could it possibly be that Rebecca was so worried about?

I stood up and clasped Rebecca's hands in mine. "Look darling, just tell me, whatever it is, just sit down and tell me what the problem is, I'm sure it can't be that bad."

I thought Rebecca was going to cry. Then she started to talk in a slow voice, staring at her shoes, she spoke. "She's brought shame on me and my family. I know it happens… " and after another gulp of wine said "… even to the best of families. But I've been wrestling with how to tell you and how you'll take the news."

I kept reassuring her that whatever she said about her sister it wasn't going to affect how I felt about her, how could it? In truth I was starting to get a bit irritated as well, I wanted to shout at her, "Just tell me what it is!"

Rebecca was – rather dramatically, I thought – trying to compose herself. She took another deep breath, drained the wine glass and said "You're meeting my sister… " She stopped. Not a pause but a definite stop.

"And her husband… " I wanted to say in an effort to move the conversation along.

"Her… partner," she said, "and their two children tomorrow at Mum and Dad's for dinner."

"Yes," I said, "I know that bit."

"And well Sasha is married," and Rebecca put her two index fingers in the air to indicate inverted commas, "to Lesley."

"Yes," I said, "I still know that bit."

"And they've two children, Grace and Billy."

"Yes," I said, "aged 5 and 3 is that right?"

"Yes," said Rebecca.

"And?"

"And what?" said Rebecca.

"And what's the problem?"

Rebecca stood up, sat down, walked smartly round the kitchen a few times, I was getting cross now, then suddenly, theatrically, she stopped in the middle of the kitchen and said, "Well, Lesley… Lesley is… Lesley's a girl!"

Paul Fox

"Lesley's a girl? So Sasha is married in inverted commas to Lesley who's a girl?" I repeated.

"Yes," said Rebecca, launching herself at the fridge and opening another bottle of Chablis.

'Was I missing something?' I thought.

I'd hardly touched my Chablis but Rebecca topped it up and said, "There, I've told you."

I looked at her and the glass, looked away again and said, "But what's the problem?"

"She's married to a girl, another girl, didn't you hear what I said, Simon?"

I still thought there must be something I was missing. I said, "Well, is that all the problem is? She's married to a girl, do you mean that all this time you've been worried about telling me your sister's gay?"

"I hate that word," said Rebecca.

"Is that all?" I started to laugh, "you needn't have worried about that, I like gay girls." I experienced a flashback to the threesome. "That's nothing to be ashamed of," I continued, "lots of people are gay, it's not abnormal you know and it certainly doesn't matter to me," I concluded emphatically.

Far from calming down, Rebecca seemed incensed that I wasn't upset. "Oh that's bloody typical," she wailed, "I might have known you'd be so casual about it."

"Rebecca, you're not making sense," I said. "Your sister's gay, so what? Lots of people are gay, just get over it."

"Oh I should have just expected that of you," she said angrily.

"Why?"

"Well I suppose… as you like Elton John and the Eurovision Song Contest, I should have guessed you… " I was astonished at her petulance.

"Look Rebecca," I managed. "I'm not upset your sister's gay, so that makes me a bad person does it? This is ludicrous." I got up and headed towards the door.

I was heading to the car to get the rest of my bags, but Rebecca must have imagined I was going to drive off because she came running after me into the hallway, "I'm sorry Simon, I'm so sorry you're right of course, it's me that's being stupid, please don't go."

I decided to rebuke her in my best John Alderton voice. "Rebecca you've nothing to worry about at all. I'm looking forward to meeting your sister and her partner. You've made a mountain out of a molehill, acting like a silly schoolgirl."

Rebecca smiled, the first time she'd smiled since I arrived. "A naughty schoolgirl?" she said.

"Yes, you've been a very naughty girl Rebecca and I don't want to hear any more of this nonsense." We drifted back into the kitchen, Rebecca drank more wine. It was clearly starting to have an effect on her.

"Well," she said deliberately, slowly, "seeing as I'm a naughty schoolgirl and you're very cross with me."

"I am," I said, playfully.

"Well what are you going to do about it?" she asked provocatively. I started to smile as well. I didn't know exactly where this was going, but it seemed to be heading in a promising direction. I decided not to say anything but take my cue from her. Rebecca grabbed the hem of her skirt and lifted it up, teasingly, waved it about and poked her tongue out.

"Well, what you going to do about it then," she repeated.

"Well," I said, "I think I should… "

She butted in and said, "Spank me on my bottom, oh Sir, really?"

"Yes, I think I will," I said, "You've caused a great deal of upset all week over nothing at all and what's more you have criticized Sir Elton John."

Rebecca beamed, in an instant she grasped one of the other chairs from the table, took a firm hold of me and moved me across to it, then threw herself across my lap with the palms of her hands on the kitchen floor.

I was presented with her shapely bottom encased in a navy skirt. Well, this is a situation I don't often find myself in I thought, but in for a penny. I lifted up her skirt, underneath her nylon stockings were held up with the white rosebud suspender belt I'd brought her and she had a plain pair of white knickers on. I started to smack her knicker-covered bottom and she made the appropriate noises.

"Ooh, Sir!"

After about three or four I stopped and said, "Let that be a lesson to you, now pour me some more wine."

"Finished already?" Rebecca said looking over one shoulder and up at me.

"Surely naughty girls have their bare bottoms spanked?" She clearly wanted me to continue, she even lifted herself up slightly so I could take her knickers down to her knees.

Her bare bottom was slightly pink, so I gave her a few more taps on her bottom and then went to help her up.

"Simon I don't think that's nearly hard enough. If you're going to spank me do it properly."

I raised my hand quite high and was just about to bring it down on her bottom cheeks when the doorbell went.

"Oh Lord," she said, "Mum and Dad, I'd forgotten I'd asked them round!" Rebecca leapt up, yanked up her knickers, smoothed her hair down and marched out of the kitchen to the front door.

I stood up and as she hurtled past me to answer the door, she'd managed to tuck her skirt in the back of her knickers.

"Rebecca! Rebecca!" I shouted.

"What," she said.

"Your skirt!"

"Oh my God!" she shrieked, reaching round untucking her skirt from her knickers.

Whilst she was smoothing her skirt down, the doorbell rang again. Rebecca grabbed the door handle and opened it wide. "Hi Mum, Hi Dad!"

Richard and Delia were on the doorstep, Delia looked at me and smiled, then looked back at Rebecca. We were both quite flushed, luckily they couldn't see Rebecca's bottom. That was very flushed.

Richard leapt in with both feet and said, "Oh, Simon when you didn't answer the door I said to Delia, 'well they must be at it'!"

Rebecca just came out with "Oh Dad, as if!"

Delia deftly changed the subject. "We've just popped a few veg round and wanted to check that you're coming to us tomorrow night? Sasha and Lesley have just arrived, they were going to pop round with us but they're a bit preoccupied with putting the kids to bed so they said they'd see you tomorrow."

Rebecca flashed me a nervous look. We made our way into the lounge. I poured out the rest of the Chablis and everything appeared normal. Richard and Delia stayed for a couple of hours then announced that they had to leave because they due at a friends for dinner. Rebecca immediately said, "Oh don't let us keep you."

Richard looked at his watch and said, "Come on Mother we'd better be going we don't want to keep Jim waiting."

Rebecca reacted oddly to this, standing stiffly and remarking in a surprised tone, "You're not going to dinner at Jim's are you?" I hadn't heard the name Jim before.

"Oh he's okay," said Richard, clearly aiming to placate his daughter. "He's got a new one as well."

'A "new one",' I thought, a new... what? Car, tractor, combine harvester?

Rebecca seemed to be able to read my mind, "Girlfriend," she said.

"Oh really, that must be nice," I offered. Rebecca glared at me. As Richard and Delia headed for their car, on the driveway Delia turned to her daughter and said, "You'd better fill Simon in."

On our own again in the lounge Rebecca told me about Jim. He was a family friend in his mid-60s. His wife had divorced him about ten years previously and since then he'd had a string of girlfriends, all Russian. Apparently Jim had had enough of English women and decided to join a Russian dating agency.

As I tucked into my Chablis, the story unfolded. Apparently he went on regular trips; beauty parades of Russian girls, and he would take his pick. And every so often an immaculately-dressed thirty something Russian lady would appear on the farm.

"Where is this farm?"

"Up by the Lavender Fields where we met your Uncle Colin."

"And he just goes for Russian girls?"

"Apparently, and from what Mum and Dad were saying he's got a new one."

"What does he do with them then, does he trade them in?" I asked.

"Oh no," said Rebecca. "He gets engaged to them then breaks it off and starts again."

"Presumably he doesn't know anything about them at all? Does he speak Russian?" I asked her. She snorted.

"No... apart from a few swear words," she said, adding, "And a couple of the girls have been really dubious and they're all much younger than him. None of them have been above 35. My Dad's been trying to have a word with him about how dangerous it is."

"Dangerous?" I said.

"Yes, they could be anyone. His farm's isolated, he's conspicuously wealthy, drives a Bentley GT, got a yacht moored on the South Coast somewhere. His family doesn't bother with him; anything could happen at that farmhouse."

"When you say anything Rebecca, what do you mean? Do you mean, shagging?"

"Well apparently he's popped so many Viagra pills he's starting to turn blue."

We both roared with laughter. "Talking of Viagra," I said, Rebecca's eyes widened. "I believe we were in the middle of something weren't we?"

Paul Fox

Rebecca got up, reached under her skirt, pulled her knickers down and then off. She came over to my sofa, unzipped my trousers and as I put my cock into her mouth she said, "You're a horny bastard aren't you?"

Now where had I heard that before?

It was Saturday morning and I was at the farm with Richard. I had stayed at Rebecca's several times now, over two weekends and a couple of times during the weeks. I was enjoying getting to know about the farm. Richard was instructive and entertaining.

We got along well. I think he enjoyed showing a "townie" around and having another man to talk to. He had shown me how to drive a tractor, and I 'd had a fair crack at the baling machine, I was taking more than a professional interest in *Farmers Weekly* and to my surprise enjoyed reading it, especially browsing through the classified ads for wide track John Deere tractors to show Richard. Although I wasn't playing much Elton John at this time, I wasn't listening to Seasick Steve's hubcap music or The Wurzels either, (though I did like their hit "I've got a brand new combine harvester" circa 1972.)

Richard was keen to show me a new visitor to the farm. There were several large outbuildings which at different times during the farm's 50-year existence had served different purposes.

"Look at this, Simon, just come in here a minute." He motioned towards one of the outbuildings. As we approached a barn on the periphery of the farmyard, a little used and ramshackle unit, I followed Richard through a door with a missing panel. Inside were old tractors, rusting farm equipment from a bygone age and as my eyes adjusted to the light Richard was pointing high up towards one corner.

It took a while, but after a moment or so I could see what he was pointing at. It was an enormous beautiful owl. A barn owl with a pure white face and huge dark sorrowful eyes. These are nocturnal creatures and Richard was delighting in telling me about the creature. I'd never realized before how large barn owls were and he pointed out this one in his experience was an unusually large specimen.

Richard was explaining in a low voice that we had to keep quiet in order not to frighten it away when my mobile went off. Blast . In the silence and darkness of the barn it was an unwelcome and jarring intrusion. I hurried back through the barn door and answered it. It was Rebecca.

"Hello," she cooed. She really did coo.

I'm just with your Dad," I whispered. "We're down at the farm. He's showing me the owl."

" Has he shown you the pellets yet?" she asked.

"Pellets, I said? No, what are they?"

"Oh never mind, I just wondered when you'd be back?"

"Well your Dad's invited us round for a cup of coffee back at the house, he was hoping I could meet Sasha and Lesley." There was a gasp.

"But we're meeting them tonight," Rebecca sounded cross.

"Okay, okay," I said.

"Well, if you don't want me to call back at the farmhouse I won't." "No I don't," she said in her prim schoolmistress voice. "I wouldn't mind doing some shopping actually. I thought we could go over to Burnham Market, dinners not till 7.00."

"Okay," I said, "well I'll be back as quick as I can, I've just got to put the tractor away."

I was slightly annoyed at Rebecca's attitude but reasoned that perhaps she merely wanted to do the introductions herself. Why didn't she get in the car and come over to the farmhouse anyway?

But I made my excuses to Richard, reversed the tractor into the working barn and headed back to North Wootton to find Rebecca clearly out of sorts. I tried to explain what was going on at the farm, what her Dad and I had been doing and I also tried to get her to sit down. She was distracted and kept wandering in and out of the lounge, going up and down the stairs, not concentrating on what I was saying. I decided to put a stop to it, as she came downstairs for the umpteenth time I took hold of her round the waist, kissed her and said firmly.

"Rebecca what is the matter? Why are you so edgy?"

"Why am I what?"

"Why are you so EDGY!" I spoke loudly, precisely. I had been doing this for a while now. Emphasising words, speaking in a deliberate manner. Rebecca increasingly seemed to have difficulty understanding me. I had put it down to my Essex accent.

"Oh it's just tonight," she said, "I'm still worried about tonight." "Why? We've been through this haven't we? I'm looking forward to it," I said. "Please don't be worried."

She smiled and hugged me back. "Thanks Simon, for trying to make it easy. Did Dad say anything about Jim's Russian lady?"

"Not much really," I said "Apparently her name's Anastasia."

"Hmm," she remarked.

"She was the one who allegedly got away wasn't she?" I said.

Rebecca hadn't stopped darting about. "Got away from where?"

"Well the Royal family."

"Whose Royal family?"

"The Russian Royal family, you know they were all killed by the Bolsheviks? 1917 I think. Anyway years later it was alleged that Princess Anastasia had escaped the assassination and survived."

I doubted Rebecca was getting any of this, she wasn't even in the room when I was speaking. Suddenly there was a "thump, thump, thump" as she came down the stairs and into the lounge. She stood in the middle of the lounge and said.

"Who's being bolshy? I'm just getting ready to go out, I'm not being bolshy and who's Anita?"

I opened my mouth to explain again and decided against it. Rebecca's mood didn't improve much as we wandered round the shops in Burnham Market. She was looking for something to wear that evening.

Now you're probably thinking that a family dinner in rural Norfolk isn't an occasion for haute couture dresses. I didn't. But Rebecca had other ideas.

The novelty of watching Rebecca going in and out of the changing rooms hadn't worn off and though I knew what underwear she had on, I got a thrill at getting a flash of her black bra and knickers as she tried on different dresses.

She finally settled on a black bandage dress, very close fitting. It had a round collar, short sleeves and was made from stretchy material that hugged her every curve.

I wondered if her sister was attractive because Rebecca was going to considerable lengths to look so glamorous. Was this to do with sibling rivalry? I'd been given instructions to wear a formal grey suit and navy tie. I didn't argue with her although I felt we were going to be completely overdressed for the evening I anticipated we'd be having at her parents..

On the way back to King's Lynn we stopped off at Sandringham, the Queen's home in Norfolk of course. The estate, open to the public is a lovely place with attractive gardens. We had a coffee in the restaurant close to the car park and drifted around the gift shop.

"Shall I get something for Sasha and Lesley?" I asked.

"Oh that's nice of you," said Rebecca, "but it's not necessary."

"Well I want to take a bottle anyway so why don't I get some of the Sandringham wine, a couple of reds and whites to take perhaps?"

"Hmm. That's not a bad idea," she conceded.

I rang Uncle Colin from my mobile phone to see if he wanted to join us at the estate. Though it was Saturday again he was working.

I mentioned this to Rebecca and she said, "You'd think he'd get some other guys to work for him and then he could take Saturdays off."

"Yes, but then he'd have to pay them," I said. "He'd rather do the job himself and keep the money."

Glancing at my watch I could see it was approaching 5 o'clock and knowing Rebecca's extensive beauty regime, I suggested we head back. We drained our coffee cups and headed for the car.

Rebecca seemed tense again and was quiet as we drove back to her house. I decided I'd better ensure my shirt was ironed and not too creased; it was, so I decided to iron it. As I plugged the iron in and got the ironing board from the utility room, Rebecca announced that she was going to get ready.

Midway through ironing my shirt, she came thundering down the stairs and blurted... unnecessarily loudly.

"Haveiexplainedabouttheirchildren?"

"What children?" I said, taken aback and trying not to burn myself on the iron.

"Sasha and Lesley's children."

"Well, you've explained they've got two, what else is there to explain?"

"They're not adopted. Lesley had them naturally."

"Oh good," I said, "they no doubt employed the services of a turkey baster?"

I was hoping she might laugh, but she didn't, she just looked cross. "This is serious Simon," she grumbled.

That was it. I blew my top. I was thoroughly exasperated and ranted at her – said that it made no difference to me whether her sister was married to a woman, a man or her work, whether her children were adopted, natural or otherwise, I didn't care what creed or colour they were, I was looking forward to meeting them and if her sister was remotely as charming as her parents, I was sure we'd get on fine.

Rebecca's bottom lip wobbled.

"I have been rather silly haven't I?" she murmured, defensively.

"Well, I'm sure the evening will be a success particularly if you relax, so finish getting ready. I'll get my suit on and we'll get going so we can be early for once." We were normally at least half an hour late for social engagements and I hate being late.

I showered and shaved quickly, dressed in my suit and freshly-ironed shirt, gave my shoes a quick rub over and flicked through the channels of Sky TV whilst waiting for Rebecca to emerge. I had to wait a long time.

On one of our earliest dates Rebecca had told me that her husband would become so infuriated at the time she would take to get ready to go out, he would sit in their car, start the engine, sound the horn and rev the engine loudly.

I remembered saying "how rude" at the time, but now I felt a degree of empathy with him. It was now five to seven. We weren't going to be early, we were going to be late. I called up the stairs, "Rebecca it's nearly seven, we need to get going."

To my surprise she appeared at the top of the stairs, she wasn't dressed though she had done her hair and makeup. Trade mark scarlet lips. She was wearing a gold coloured bra and matching knickers edged with lace, black hold up stockings, and stilt like black Christian Louboutin shoes that I had bought her. She had on a midnight blue satin dressing gown which she held open with one hand held at the hip, revealing her underwear.

"Why aren't you dressed?" I said.

She took a step and started to descend the staircase, slowly, deliberately placing one foot on each stair. She was holding onto the rail with her right hand, her left hand behind her back.

As she reached the last step, standing above me she said. "I've been very naughty haven't I?"

"Yes you have," I said.

"But it's seven o'clock now."

She fixed me with a long look, smiled slowly… a wide smile. She tilted her head.

"I was wondering if you could do something for me?" she spoke softly, provocatively.

Then she revealed what she had been holding in her left hand, till then concealed. It was a riding crop. The genuine article. It had a leather looped handle and the switch was at least two feet in length. I thought for one horrible moment she wanted to hit me with it. I didn't know what to say. She did look amazing. Sexy, pouting, statuesque. I didn't say a word.

Rebecca took hold of the end of my tie and led me into the dining room through double doors. Unusually, the dining room table was set permanently for a meal, although we never ate in there. Taking hold of the back of one of the dining room table chairs she turned it round with one movement, removed a dinner plate from the table setting in front of it and placed it in the centre of the table. She stepped neatly out of her knickers, knelt on the chair and handed me the riding crop.

"Well," I said, in my best Simon Templar accent, "This is an interesting situation. What exactly would you like me to do now?"

Rebecca looked over her left shoulder at me. "Well, you need to teach me some manners, Mr Taylor."

She took hold of the hem of her dressing gown, lifted revealing her shapely bare bottom. The contrast between her pale bottom and the black stockings was striking. The red soles of her shoes lent a delicious, decadent frisson to the scene. She leant forwards until she was bent flat on the table, I still didn't know what to do. Rebecca did.

By way of encouragement, instruction, she said simply, "I think six of the best is traditional."

I put the looped handle of the riding crop around my wrist and took hold of its black patent top, rested the crop against Rebecca's bottom and said sternly, "Well, hopefully this will improve your manners, Miss."

I moved the crop back about six inches and whacked it against her bottom. Then I did it again. And again.

Rebecca looked over her shoulder again and said, "You're going to have to do it harder than that Simon."

So I moved the crop back about a foot from her bottom and struck again.

Rebecca raised herself from the table, grabbed the crop off me and said, "You've got to do it properly, do it harder."

By way of demonstration, she lifted the crop up then brought it down swiftly, slicing through the still dining room air, making a noise like a ferociously fast tennis serve. The air quivered palpably.

Handing the crop to me she resumed her position on the chair and over the table. This time I lifted up her dressing gown myself, took a step back and flicked the riding crop against her bottom. An angry red line appeared instantly. I thought I'd gone too far and stopped, shocked.

Rebecca said one word: "Harder."

I took two steps away from her and launched the crop at her bottom again.

Rebecca let out a long, "Aaah, that's better." Then "Five more of those."

I obliged, delivering five more whippings as hard as I dared, and when I had finished her bottom was criss-crossed with red welts, her eyes liquid with tears.

She rubbed her bottom and said matter-of-factly, "Right, I'm going to get dressed now."

I decided to follow her up the stairs, I felt conflicted and was worried I had injured her. She shrugged off the dressing gown, her white back and calves contrasting now with her blazing, inflamed bottom. Rebecca simply pulled on her new dress, reapplied her makeup and we headed downstairs and out to the car without discussing what had happened.

I opened the passenger door for her as I normally did, she lowered herself gingerly onto the car seat wincing as she sat down. I was in turmoil. I couldn't believe what I'd just done to her. But Rebecca wasn't simply blasé; she seemed energized, upbeat, and happy. She was also rampant for sex and kept rubbing my cock.

"Have we got time to stop so I can give you a blow job?" she said breathlessly. What a question.

"There's always time for that."

I pulled into a layby just before the farm and hoped her parents weren't looking out the window to see if we were arriving given the time.

Minutes later Rebecca was reapplying her lipstick as we entered the farm gates. I checked that my trouser zip was done up when I got out the car.

Richard and Delia greeted us warmly at the door as they always did. They were casually dressed and relaxed.

"Oh, you look lovely darling," said Delia, to Rebecca.

"Divine dress, my lovely," said Richard.

"Yes," said Rebecca. "Simon bought it for me today in Burnham Market."

Richard shook me by the hand as heartily as he had done that morning. "Come on in Simon, let's get you a drink."

I handed over the bottles of wine purchased that morning.

"Oh you shouldn't have done that Simon, especially after buying dresses for Madam and all," he said generously.

Within a few moments we were joined by Rebecca's sister Sasha and her partner Lesley.

Sasha wasn't the "stunner" I had imagined but she was a delightful woman, smart, warm and entertaining with a dry sense of humour. She bore no resemblance to Rebecca. She was shorter in stature and significantly larger, had short brown straight hair cut in a neat bob and wore jeans and a black tee shirt. She wore "flats" ballet-style shoes. Rebecca had on her sky-high platforms.

Lesley, welcoming and instantly likeable with a very pretty open face was slightly taller than Sasha. She too wore jeans, teamed with mauve Doc Marten style boots decorated with small flowers. I felt ridiculously overdressed.

I'm told that gay and lesbian couples sometimes adopt male/female roles in relationships. Elton and David Furniss? David's obviously the "girl". Or maybe I'm just stereotyping.

Here were two lovely women who both looked, being honest slightly masculine. They both kissed Rebecca and we headed into the lounge for a drink. Richard was pouring out some Champagne. Every time I went to the farmhouse there seemed to be a bottle opened and tonight was no exception.

"Champagne again Richard," I observed.

"Well," he said "all my favourite people together at once."

We stood and toasted one another and then headed into the conservatory where the dinner table was laid for our meal. Once seated, I enquired about the children.

"Oh they're asleep upstairs, hopefully you'll meet them tomorrow at Mass, Simon," said Sasha

The only person who hadn't sat down was Rebecca and looking at the hard chairs, I realized why. I pulled out a chair for Rebecca to sit next to me and she looked at me rather nervously. Without anyone noticing I found a cushion from a nearby armchair and placed it on the seat before she sat down. Gingerly.

She turned to me and whispered, "Thank you."

The evening was very pleasant. Rebecca's sister and Lesley were good company, attentive and amusing; there was no tension between Sasha, Lesley and Rebecca who chatted together with ease and there was much laughter. There was also a lot of wine drunk and I enjoyed listening to Sasha and Lesley recount stories of their children's antics, hobbies and friendships.

At one point during the evening Rebecca asked her Mother how their meal with Jim and Anastasia had been. Richard and Delia looked at one another and Delia said.

"Well... we've been dying to tell you. This one's different."

" Really?" said Rebecca, rather sarcastically, I thought.

"Yes. She's slightly older than the others, very glamorous, of course and Jim, well, he's different with her. She speaks impeccable English. "

"Better than I," Richard piped up and laughed at his own joke.

"I told them all about you and Simon and how happy you are together and how pleased we were you'd met one another."

"Thank you," I said.

"And they've invited us to dinner at theirs, all of us, next weekend."

"Great," I said. But too soon…

"Simon!" Rebecca admonished.

"Well, that'll be okay, wont it?" I was faltering.

"Well I'm not sure I want to go," Rebecca declared obstinately.

"Course you do," said Richard.

"Course you do darling," I added through gritted teeth. With my left hand held beneath the tablecloth I tapped the side of her left buttock and she yelped.

Rebecca Revealed

I didn't have any preconceived ideas about Russian women. All I knew was what little I had gleaned from my early experimental research on the internet when I had begun to check out dating sites. There, I'd come across the sites that promoted profiles of Russian girls keen to meet western men and husbands.

Many of the girls on the formal looking sites had detailed biographies that identified them as educated, often highly educated with more than one degree and several languages, some with professional qualifications, refined and confident. Many were also heart-stoppingly attractive.

This didn't surprise me. Why shouldn't they be? Economics came into the equation for these girls too. There was no reason why they shouldn't strive to improve their circumstances and lives. There were adverts from older women who had travelled and were looking for men to correspond with. They weren't necessarily contemplating a one-way migration but were interested in meeting European, often British men for exchange visits.

My experience as an Ian Fleming fan and keen filmgoer in his 40s obviously includes the "Russian" Bond girls – Olga Bisera in *The Spy Who Loved Me*, Tatiana Romanova (yes, the actress was Italian), Pola Ivanova (Fiona Fullerton) and Elektra King (Sophie Moreau). These admittedly were boy – fantasy "Russian" women. Then there had been Tatiana… wobbly screen moment and fade to grey here…

Almost a decade ago I attended a conference at The Dorchester Hotel on Park Lane, London. It was to do with the financial service industry. Not thrilling I recall. Martin and I were working together in those days. Martin of golf club "fame".

There was a platform of industry notables lecturing about the economy, financial service regulations, worthy but a bit dry. It wasn't dry in the evening though. Plenty of wine flowed and as I got up from our table at dinner and headed to the bar, I noticed a striking dark haired girl sitting on a barstool on her own. I soon engaged her in conversation.

She was charming, smart, quick witted and interesting. An effortless, natural conversationalist, she was brimming with cool confidence and had a tantalizing way of cupping her chin in her hand as she listened and laughed at my jokes about the conference and speeches I'd endured. She was dressed in a plain black fitted business suit with a short black skirt and white blouse with satin covered buttons. Barely black hosiery, black suede court shoes with a gold heel that complimented a gold clasp and chain on a Chanel handbag, sitting on the bar.

I couldn't believe that she had been at the conference, how had I missed her?

We were on our third drink when Martin materialized. In my slightly drunken state I put my arm round him and said, "Tatiana I'd like to introduce you to my best friend Martin, Martin this is Tatiana, Tatiana's from Moscow and she's working at the conference as a translator."

Martin just nodded. "Hello," he said, non-committally.

"Simon I need to have a chat with you," I remember him saying.

"Yes anything, what's up?"

"I need to have a chat with you over here," he hissed, getting hold of my elbow and pulling it sharply.

I nearly lost my footing and tumbled off the barstool. 'How rude,' I thought. I excused myself from Tatiana's gracious company and feeling irritated followed Martin out into the foyer.

"What? " I said, "I think I'm in there."

"Simon, you haven't got the brains you were born with, of course you're in there."

"Really? I said happily.

"Yes, I can guarantee Simon, you're in there."

"Great," I said.

"No, not great."

"Why?" I was having difficulty making sense of this. I was having difficulty standing, if the truth be told.

"She's on the game," he said.

"What game?" I replied.

"Simon, listen to me I've just spoken to one of the guys at concierge, she's nothing to do with the conference. She's well known to the hotel."

I stood open mouthed. "So you mean she's err…"

"Yes, she's a hooker," Martin had said.

I didn't believe him. "What? I said, "Looking like that?"

"Yes," he said. "And if you take her back to your room it's probably going to cost you a couple of grand."

"Don't be daft." But he was insistent.

"Simon you're going to get into all sorts of trouble, make your excuses and leave, she'll soon latch on to some other mug."

"Two grand," I said pensively, "couldn't be that much surely?" I wondered if she took American Express, then I got slightly anxious thinking about where she might have swiped the card.

I got back to the bar, Tatiana gave me a knowing look, and she was already engaged in lively conversation with another guy. The look said, "You can't afford me can you? But thanks for the Champagne!"

Back at the dinner table, a debate was raging about what this Russian woman was doing with Jim.

Richard and Delia were remarkably open about discussing sex and Delia was saying, "Well perhaps he's a bit kinky in bed and she does all the kinky stuff for him?"

Rebecca and I looked at each other slightly nervously, bearing in mind what I'd just done to her.

"Maybe she's genuinely in love with him," I said. They all laughed.

"Come off it, Simon," said Rebecca. "You are a hopeless romantic. She's obviously just after a passport."

"Well," I said defensively. "I probably am more romantic than you, but after all, we met through a dating agency."

There was silence. Complete silence at the table. And tumbleweed blew through the conservatory.

Rebecca's eyes widened, the unspoken message they sent was, "What HAVE you just said?"

In that instant I realized that Rebecca hadn't told her parents, least of all her sister and Lesley that we'd met through a dating agency.

Sasha smiled, "Really Simon? We were given to understand that you were introduced by friends."

Rebecca answered, "Well, yes through friends that run an agency."

There was another awkward moment.

I wondered why Rebecca hadn't told her family that we'd met through an agency, after all it was a respectable and perfectly legitimate one, lots of people use them.

Sasha wouldn't leave it alone. "So," pause, "this friend who runs an agency lives near you does she Simon? "

I cleared my throat and mumbled, "Yes." This was frankly bizarre. It was becoming a farce. Worse. Kafkaesque.

Fortunately Richard spoke. "Right," he said. "Enough of this Simon, I've got some lovely port for you to try, you being an ex-Air Force chap. Let's crack it open and leave the ladies to talk."

I was deeply grateful for the opportunity to escape from the conservatory and head back into the lounge. Richard didn't mention anything about how I had become acquainted with Rebecca and I was pathetically indebted to him for that.

Hours later we phoned for a cab. Rebecca gingerly lowered herself again into the taxi and we headed for her home.

I didn't know whether to be cross with her or not. I found it difficult to because I was so totally besotted with her. But I was curious.

"Why didn't you tell your Mum and Dad we met via an agency?" I asked casually.

"We'll talk about it at home," she said, nodding towards the driver. When we got back, a furious row ensued. She was incandescent.

I threatened to leave, I didn't know where I was going to go, I couldn't drive as I was well over the limit. The nearest hotel was about five miles away.

Rebecca eventually calmed down and attempted to explain, saying that she didn't think her parents would like anyone from a dating agency which of course only made it worse.

"You can't be serious," I said.

"I didn't tell them about the agency either because, well, I was embarrassed."

"Embarrassed?" I exploded.

"Well, they'd be bound to wonder why I can't meet someone without going to all that trouble and expense."

I tried to remain cross with her, but I couldn't. Not for long.

She cried and I found her distress unbearable. It was enough for me to forgive her. I held her in my arms and stroked her hair. We kissed and headed for bed.

After changing out of my evening wear, I brushed my teeth and when I walked into Rebecca's bedroom, she was lying face down on the sensual bed.

She had a white nightie on, which she'd pulled up round her waist, her bottom was as red and striped as I remembered it. Rebecca had opened a small jar of moisturizing cream.

"Could you do the honours," she asked, pointing to the cream and over her shoulder to her bottom. I scooped up a large dollop of the stuff with my finger, then more and layered it thickly along the stripes on her bottom. I was expecting to hear a "hsssss". I felt genuine remorse at having inflicted this on her.

"I went too far didn't I?"

"Not at all, it's just what I deserved," she said simply.

I wouldn't want you get the impression that I hadn't been a willing participant in the whipping that had taken place. But whilst a decent spanking was one thing, this was surely different?

I felt uncomfortable at inflicting such pain and what had taken place seemed to me to be more than just a bit of fun. There's a line and this was probably over the limit for me.

A Friend in Need

Monday morning. The phone rang. It was my bank manager Julian.

"I think we'd better have a chat Simon," he was saying. "You've been spending quite a bit lately haven't you?"

I bristled slightly. It wasn't that bad. I was overdrawn, but I was still within my overdraft limit. I'd spent a lot of my savings for a deposit on the SL and the £600 a month hire purchase charge was probably a little steep.

The marital home hadn't sold despite having been on the market for many months and I was still paying the mortgage on it. Receipts from royalties weren't as significant as I had been used to achieving. Julian was suggesting that I should reign myself in.

By chance that morning I'd opened my credit card statement. Rebecca's bandage dress had cost £220, there was £185 for shoes and I'd managed to spend £100 in Ann Summers. Then there were numerous dinners out at moderately priced to expensive restaurants, The Savoy, perfume and wine. I was spending a lot on fuel travelling backwards and forwards to King's Lynn.

Rebecca was worth it though and I was having fun.

I'd also paid a deposit on a holiday, I ended the call with a cheery "Well, I've still got plenty of money in my savings account haven't I? I'll chase my agent up about the aged debt and I've plenty of work in the pipeline so don't worry Julian."

"Okay," said Julian.

"Well, let's catch you in a month or so. Where are you off on holiday?"

"Rome," I said.

I was still attending the gym, though not as enthusiastically or as often as I had been. I'd had emails from Niamh, updating me on life in Ireland and from Kirsty letting me know that her book was due to be launched in the coming January. Perhaps we could get together again at the book launch she'd suggested. Shilpa always chatted when I saw her and Ingrid would text from time to time.

So although I was head over heels in love with Rebecca and faithful to her, I remained in touch with my other women friends; emailed and texted them; enjoyed an occasional coffee with Shilpa. That wasn't being unfaithful? I didn't think so.

Paul Fox

I was beginning to live a double life. During the week I stayed at the flat and at the weekends I travelled to King's Lynn to stay with Rebecca and spend time on the farm with her parents. In the coming months this division began to bother me.

Rebecca did visit the flat, though infrequently. I had the impression, though she wouldn't say so directly that she didn't like my admittedly quirky place and it was simply a launch pad to nights out in London, dining or seeing a show.

I was easily persuaded to spend the weekends at hers. I enjoyed seeing more of Uncle Colin in King's Lynn and my surrogate "parents" Richard and Delia.

Rebecca continued to surprise me, not always pleasantly. She could be irrationally jealous. One Sunday when I was driving back to the flat, I came off the M11 at Birchhanger services and travelled down the A130.

As I approached the new interchange I spotted a familiar car, it was Shilpa's unmistakable Amazon. Its hazard warning lights were on and the bonnet was lifted.

I instinctively indicated, depressed my own hazard lights and pulled up behind it.

A distressed Shilpa emerged from the other side of the Armco barrier. "Simon," she said plaintively.

"Shilpa, what's going on?"

"I don't know, my stupid car just stopped," she said forlornly.

I climbed over the barrier to her, she had on a light jacket over a dress and she was shivering. I offered her my jacket.

She took it gratefully and explained that she'd been out for the afternoon and was returning home when something went "bang" and she'd ended up at the side of the road.

Above the roar of the traffic she let me know the AA were on their way and indeed as she told me this, a yellow AA Recovery van pulled up behind us, its amber warning lights flashing in a row. I've always found the AA reliable and responsive and their engineers courteous. The AA engineer shook his head after a cursory inspection.

"It's going to have to go to a garage I'm afraid," he said, "I can't do anything here with it." He said he'd call for a tow truck.

"Don't worry Shilpa," I said. "I'll run you home."

She was relieved I had stopped, thanked me and sat in the passenger seat of the Mercedes. I put the electric seat on for her, she smiled and said, "Oh does this one vibrate as well?" It didn't.

348

I dropped her back at her home, declined her offer of coffee, she thanked me again, gave me a peck on the cheek and I had a text from her later saying, "Thanks for being my knight in shining armour."

All of this made me late arriving back at the flat and as I was just inside the door after trudging up the stairs, the lift having broken again, when the phone rang. It was Rebecca.

"Simon? Are you okay? You normally phone me."

I told her what had happened. Why shouldn't I tell her what had happened? I was just helping out a friend.

Rebecca was less than pleased. Her voice was clipped when she spoke. "Oh." Pause. "So you've been round to Shilpa's have you?"

"Yes," I explained "I've just dropped her off. I didn't go in," I added.

"Did she invite you in?" she asked.

"Well, yes."

"Oh I see." Pause again. Rebecca spoke sharply now. "I bet she planned it," she said to my surprise. I thought she was joking. She sounded serious though.

"Don't be silly. Her car broke down at the side of the road, I was passing and I just gave her a lift home," I explained again patiently.

There followed a barrage of questions; did I still find Shilpa attractive? What was she wearing? Has she got a new boyfriend? Did she call me after? Was I planning on seeing her? It went on and on.

In the end I had to get cross, I shouted down the phone, "Look Rebecca. Will you please get this in perspective: I just gave her a lift home, I'm sure any of your former boyfriends would have done the same if you were stuck by the side of the road."

What she said next shook me to the core. "My former ex's?" She spat, "My ex's! I wouldn't piss on any of them if they were on fire, least of all get in a car with them."

I was truly shocked, "Why would you feel so violently opposed to your ex's? I mean, obviously things didn't work out with them, but surely that doesn't mean you hate them."

Looking back, I should have asked a lot more questions. But I was in love and I didn't want to challenge the lovely Rebecca.

Roman Games

As is apparent, despite formerly being in the RAF and enjoying flying, I experience a lot of anxiety at airports until I complete the fandango of checking in, arriving at the Gate long before I need to etc.

Rebecca and I were off to Rome: the Eternal City. Being Catholic and well into my 40s you might have thought I'd already made it to Rome, but I hadn't. My Mum went on a coach trip there in the early 1950s when she was a schoolgirl. It left a lasting impression on her and after she died, some of the most poignant photographs I found of her were some taken when she was a teenager in the City; at the Spanish Steps; in dappled Piazzas; in front of the Vatican and outside the coliseum in the spring of 1955.

The other thing I like about air travel is that people tend to dress up – at least, if flying First or business class. Rebecca shared my passion for dressing up, in fact she always dressed smartly. Expensively. Sunday lunch in a Norfolk farmhouse with her parents; wandering round Cambridge; even at the local pub near her home; she looked as though she'd just stepped off a catwalk.

Today, as we sat in the airport lounge, courtesy of my American Express credit card, booked in business class, courtesy of Air miles I'd accumulated plus a bit extra, I felt proud to be with Rebecca. Her long blonde hair tumbled loosely around her shoulders. She wore a scarlet coloured denim-type skirt with stitched pockets, a red dotted white blouse that complimented the skirt and a white blazer. The outfit was teamed with red leather platform shoes and heel and nude coloured stockings.

She was flicking through the pages of *Harpers and Queen*. I'll let you into a secret, I like women's magazines as well. This might at first sound odd, but if you don't like football, or cricket or golf or rugby, but you do like shopping and pictures of girls in nice dresses, you can surely appreciate why H&Q is one of my favourites.

But it's not only me that enjoys reading or even just flicking through these publications. There are plenty of men, straight men who like looking at women's magazines. I know this because friends who know I like reading these have often confessed themselves to finding them entertaining. They wouldn't want me to name them in print perhaps, but if you're are a bloke, reading this and you enjoy the odd flick through *Hello* or whatever, don't feel uncomfortable. Women in glamorous settings wearing expensive clothes, shots of them in their scanties. What's not to like? Come on guys, loosen up.

Whilst waiting for our departure gate to flash onto the screens in the Club Class lounge, we toasted one another with complimentary Prosecco.

Rebecca cooed, "I'm so looking forward to this holiday, Simon, we can finally spend some quality time together rather than have all that dashing to and fro. Wouldn't it be wonderful to spend every day with one another?"

'Gosh,' I thought, 'this is going really well.'

The previous few weeks had been particularly hectic for Rebecca as the school had undergone an Ofsted inspection. That she had found it "stressful" was an understatement.

I'd heard of teachers complaining about workloads at dinner parties, but I'd really had no idea of how much they had to do and the amount of time it can take to prepare lessons, mark work, assess individual pupils, analyse targets etc. Arriving at Rebecca's one Saturday, I let myself in (I'd my own key) and found her slumped in the lounge surrounded by books, charts and her laptop whirring away. I rushed over to her, I thought she'd fainted or something, but she hadn't. She'd been up all night and had fallen asleep exhausted at about five o'clock in the morning. She had spent the following afternoon and evening working too.

So she was tired and in need of the holiday. I was looking forward to the trip and eager to spend time alone with her. Sex with Rebecca continued to be wonderful. She was highly sexed and had a huge appetite for encounters and when I recall I'd wondered initially whether she might be prim or reserved given her vocation as a rural primary school teacher, I have to laugh.

In fact Rebecca was becoming increasingly uninhibited. Well, what's wrong with that?

Nothing, I'm not a prude, but I'll give you an example: Sex toys. Vibrators in particular. They're normally between 10 inches and 2 foot long? (Sorry no, I made that last measurement up!). They're normally of large proportions, well compared to me they're very large, and they're often an odd colour, bright pink, green or blue. Some have coloured balls or glitter inside them. When switched on they can vibrate; jump up and down; spin around in a circle; light up; pulsate to music.

Now I'm only speaking for myself, not other men, but I can't get mine to whizz round in a circle. I pulsate to music but only when dancing.

Every woman I know has at least one sex toy. Rebecca had five. Different shapes and sizes, including a thin, poker shaped one. And she used to use them not simply when she was alone, but seated companionably beside me watching TV when we weren't, as well of course as when we were having sex.

Don't get me wrong, I am broad-minded but it was becoming a little off putting. Her favourite sexual encounter involved me taking her from behind while she put the largest of her dildos in her mouth.

She had another with a sucker on the end... no pun intended, not that end, the other end. She used to weld the wetted rubber sucker onto one of the dining room chairs and jiggle up and down on it whilst giving me a blowjob. She always said that she wanted to use it whilst she was having a dinner party. Bearing in mind she rarely wore knickers, if she had worn a wide skirt she could just about get away with it.

There had been more spanking sessions and I'd told Rebecca that I was anxious about using the riding crop on her forcefully. She was understanding. On yet another trip to *Ann Summers* with my credit card for company, she brought home a black leather paddle with a heart on it, and I used that on her bottom instead. That was fine. I used as much force as I felt comfortable with.

She often asked for me to use more though. Rebecca used to hide her sex toys down the back of her sofa in her lounge. She was particularly fond of one male TV presenter and a TV cook who hosts a show on a Saturday.

On occasions I'd come back from seeing her Father at the farm, let myself in with my key and hear a moaning sound from the lounge. Rebecca would be on the sofa, skirt up round her waist, knickers round her knees.

She would be masturbating with her rabbit whilst watching the television as her favourite presenter was on screen. She wouldn't stop simply because I had arrived on the scene. Occasionally though she would gasp, "Cup of tea please," and wave her free hand.

Is this normal? I confess thatit made me feel inadequate, like a spare part. When she'd finished, she'd just wipe her "pet" with a tissue, pull her knickers up, brush her skirt down, and drink her tea as if nothing had happened. As if I'd come in and she was reading the paper.

She even took her toys away for weekends. I knew she'd brought two with her in her bag on our trip to Rome. Other girlfriends have told me that their sex toys were used more or less as a joke or to get them in the mood or if they were alone, let's face it we all do it. But Rebecca and I we were having lots of sex. She just couldn't get enough.

As we were going through security at Heathrow Rebecca walked through the screening metal arch before me. We'd taken our shoes off and had been asked the several usual questions – what we had in our bags, what liquids, etc. Rebecca walked through the standard loop sensor and the alarm went off.

A female security officer approached with an electric paddle, not like the one we had got from Ann Summers but not dissimilar. Rebecca looked back at me and giggled. The paddle went off as well. The security officer was asking if she had any metal in her pockets, any coins, "No," she was saying, were her bracelets setting it off?

She took her bracelets off, watch off, went back through the hoop again and it still went off.

Other passengers were starting to murmur and fidget as we were bolding up the queue.

"Sorry madam, you'll have to come with us."

'Oh my God,' I thought, 'were are they taking her?'

"What about my boyfriend?" said Rebecca. A second security guard motioned me forward; I didn't set the alarm off. We were taken over to the edge of the security area. Two female security guards were there.

'Oh my God,' I thought, 'this is going to be a rubber glove moment.' But then, Rebecca might enjoy that! They were very friendly.

"What underwear have you got on?" Said one of the guards.

"Just my bra, knickers and a suspender belt," Rebecca replied.

"Has the suspender belt got metal clasps on the end?" said the other one.

"I can't remember," said Rebecca, "it might have."

"We're going to need to have a look," they said.

"You can come with us or we can have a look here."

"Here?" said Rebecca looking round at the packed terminal.

"Don't worry we'll put some screens round."

A triangular shaped screen appeared. It was free standing and covered the area between Rebecca's shoulders and knees. Rebecca took off her jacket and handed it to the assistant and they peered over the top of the screen whilst Rebecca undid her skirt and stepped out of it. There were a few wolf whistles as her skirt came out of the cubicle. They asked Rebecca to turn round and she did, then they gave her back her clothes and removed the screen. I thought she'd be furious, but she wasn't. It was the metal clasp of her suspenders that had set the machine off. So there's a warning girls, if you're going on holiday and want to get dressed up, you might want to make it a hold ups day.

What can I say about Rome? When in Rome, an ideal place to stay is in the vicinity of the Spanish Steps. When I'd booked our hotel I'd understood it was going to be closer to the Steps and Trevi Fountain than it turned out to It was nevertheless in a reasonable location, not far from the main Piazzas and within staggering distance of the Steps, an intimate boutique – type hotel, light and airy with a fashionable art deco interior. Italian hotels are not renowned for being opulent and spacious unless they are in the 5-star, Prestige bracket. Whilst I couldn't have afforded this given my bank balance, I didn't want opulent luxury anyway, I felt that what I had booked was ideal. Our room on the top floor afforded us a sideways view of the City and distant Tiber and to my great delight we could just see the Vatican.

We arrived about lunchtime, undid our cases, hung up our clothes and prepared to explore the city on foot. Rebecca was fully made up all the time and perhaps inadvisedly insisted on wearing her cork platform shoes to go out in. We made our way to the Vatican and were able to join a tour pretty quickly only waiting in line for about 40 minutes.

The American guide was knowledgeable and enthusiastic about the Vatican City, the smallest country in the World, but with a fascinating history. If you go make sure you join a tour because there is an abundance to see. The statistics are mind boggling. If you took just twenty seconds to stop at every painting, sculpture or relic at the museum; you'd be there for two years.

Moving into St. Peters itself, there was only one place I wanted to linger in, a place I'd heard about since I was a small boy growing up, from my Mum. It was on my "bucket list", so why had it taken me so long to see the ceiling of the Sistine Chapel?

You may have seen the photographs and possibly been there but if you haven't witnessed it for yourself, nothing can adequately prepare you for the sheer beauty of the ceiling. It was a special moment for me. I'd taken a photo of Mum along with me and it was in my wallet. I took it out and held it in my hand, so she was with me.

As I gazed up at God reaching out to David, their fingertips almost touching in that iconic pose, I became overwhelmed. It all got too much and I started to cry. I couldn't stop. The years of wanting to go to Rome, hearing my Mum's voice and now looking at the crumpled black and white photograph I had of her, I just felt incredibly sad that I hadn't made it there with her. I was aware then how I missed her.

Rebecca was very sweet and comforted me and even gave me her handkerchief. No one seemed at all phased at my emotional response.

When the tour was over we found a small café near the Parthenon and toasted my Mum. Rebecca was intent on cheering me up and how could anyone be sad for long in such an astonishingly beautiful place? Around every corner there's a relic, statue or church, I don't know how many churches there are in Rome, but there must be hundreds.

I've worked out that the Italians seem to have the best of everything, the best food, cars, clothes, architecture, and art. They're not however known for their financial acumen. That said as the Euro was heading for its biggest crisis since its inception, neither was any other European country looking well managed, with the exception of Germany of course. Back inside our hotel room, after having a whistle stop tour and seeing albeit briefly the Vatican, the Parthenon, Spanish Steps and Trevi Fountain, the Coliseum – only the outside – we were exhausted, at least I was.

There was a small restaurant in the shady street next to our hotel and we decided that we'd eat there that evening. It was too warm to waste an evening eating indoors. We couldn't face walking any distance and were too tired to bother exploring further by taxi. I tried calling reception to ask them to book it, but the phone just rang and rang. I couldn't remember the name of the restaurant so I told Rebecca I would just run down the road to the restaurant and book it myself.

"That's sounds fantastic," said Rebecca. "I'm going to grab a shower."

To reach reception guests on our floor had to take two lifts, one was a chicken wire and cage type arrangement that went down the stairwell, then on the third floor guests changed into a more conventional modern style lift. It was a lot of hassle so I just scooted down the stairs, out of the front doors of the hotel and across the road at least that was my intention. Have you ever tried crossing the road in Rome? They don't have zebra crossings, no one takes any notice of traffic lights and cars and motorcycles ignore pedestrians. Without exaggeration it took me at least five attempts to cross the street. I booked the table for 8pm and as I came out again to do battle with the Rome traffic all over again, this time in the other direction, my mobile went off. It was Rick.

"Hello old boy," he said.

"Are you there ?"

"Yes," I said raising my voice above the roar of the Rome traffic.

"Have you had a Cornetto yet?"

I laughed. "No, but we've been to the Sistine Chapel."

"What's that?" he said.

"Rick, even you know what the Sistine Chapel is. It's Michaelangelo's most famous work, well apart from the Last Supper I suppose, but that's in Turin."

"Oh right," said Rick, sounding bored.

"Anyway you got there okay did you?"

"Yes," I said. "Very pleasant flight." I explained that Rebecca had caused a bit of a stir at the airport with her suspender belt.

"Okay, well I hope you have a good time, haven't seen much of you lately, catch up when you get back. Oh, Barry says hi as well."

"Enjoy your fish and chips, I'm hoping I'll be tucking into my favourite pasta dish tonight.

As I hung up I felt rather sad. I missed the guys. I hadn't seen much of Rick or Barry lately. But that was understandable wasn't it? I mean Rebecca was the future wasn't she? And it was all going really well wasn't it? She was perfect wasn't she?

When I eventually made it back to the hotel after negotiating the hazardous traffic, and this time the two lifts, paying particular attention to the rickety chicken wire one, Rebecca had showered, changed and was lying on the bed. She'd got on a black Karen Millen dress, flesh coloured stockings, strappy cream shoes with a long cream silk scarf, woven and in folds around her neck. The dress had a deep "V" front and Rebecca's enormous boobs were no doubt being reined in place by acres of tit tape.

"Gosh."

I said, suddenly turning into Hugh Grant, wishing I wasn't so sweaty from my exertions.

"You look rather ravishing, dressed already?"

" Mmmmm," said Rebecca.

"Well it's been a rather fraught and emotional day and so I thought I'd make a special effort."

I didn't know what to say, apart from what Hugh Grant would have said, "Well, you always look lovely." And she did.

I leant over and kissed her, she kissed me back and then said, "Fuck me."

Now Rebecca didn't often use such graphic language but I was always happy to oblige, and as I pushed her dress up her thighs and put my fingers round a pair of frilly knickers – pink. "Aaah..."

She lifted up her bottom and said, "I've got a treat for you."

"Oh really?" I said thinking that I had already seen this, and it was the pink knickers.

Manoeuvring myself into position and as I began to enter her she took a deep breath and said, "I want to do something different."

She started to unravel the scarf from around her neck. I knelt up and moved across her in order to push her onto her tummy and take her from behind. That was what I thought she wanted.

"Ah, no," she said, "I want you to do something with this," and she handed me the ends of the unfurled scarf. I didn't know what she meant.

"Go on," said Rebecca.

"What?" I said, "What do you want me to do?

When she told me I nearly stopped breathing. I couldn't believe what I'd heard.

"Strangle me," she said. Her perfectly made up face and large blue eyes were staring up at me. By now I was standing by the bed.

"What!" I said.

"Strangle me."

"Rebecca what are you talking about strangle you? Why would I want to do that?"

"While you are fucking me," she said. I couldn't believe it. I'd lost my erection and sat down on the bed. Rebecca smoothed down her dress, sat up with her head against the headboard with her knees up. Her knickers were still around her calves. She peeled out a length of the scarf, one loop of which remained around her neck, then she tied it in front again and said.

"Look it's quite easy, while you're riding me just grab hold of this end and pull it tight."

"Rebecca," I said, not comprehending. "Why would you want me to do that to you?"

"You must have heard about it Simon?" she said in a mocking tone.

"It's called auto-eroticism. It heightens my orgasm to a point where I almost pass out. It's an incredible feeling..."

I wanted to buy myself some thinking time. Trying to sound normal I said, "I thought that that meant enjoying watching *Top Gear* and being interested in cars, like Alfas." But I knew it wasn't. She didn't laugh.

Having since done some research on this practice, I have learned that it has claimed many lives, amongst them well known signer Michael Hutchence and MP Stephen Milligan. News archives are testament to many losses caused by it. Rebecca wanted me to strangle her during normal intercourse with me. You may be reading this and thinking 'well what's wrong with that?' It can be done carefully, so it's safe.

Rebecca was annoyed with me and said crossly, "Oh I didn't realize you'd be scared Simon, it's perfectly safe," when I told her I just couldn't do it.

Over dinner at the restaurant opposite that night, I tried to explain to Rebecca that I felt it was too dangerous. Surely putting any sort of ligature round a neck was a highly risky thing to do? And if I was doing it to her, how would I know when enough was enough? When she turned blue? When there was a cracking sound? When she stopped breathing? She brushed all my worries aside.

"People do it all the time," she said airily making me feel inadequate and unsophisticated.

When I asked her about those who had died doing it her response was that they hadn't done it properly!! She knew how to do it and it couldn't go wrong if done properly.

I asked her whether she did when she was alone.

Taking a mouthful of ravioli she just nodded, "Yes, of course, often when I'm using my toys." This said as if it was perfectly natural.

At the time I thought that it had to just be me being inhibited and prudish, but I later discussed it with friends and all of them were equally horrified.

The issue didn't cloud our holiday and we spent the rest of the days sightseeing; enjoying meals in the sunshine, eating ice cream, taking photos, visiting exhibitions and relaxing in our hotel. Rome is stuffed with treasures.

Between the Old City and Coliseum, on every street corner there's something to marvel at. We took an open top bus tour around the City. This has to be one of the best ways of getting a birds' eye view of any city. Rebecca ushered me to the back seat, we both put our sunglasses on and listened to the commentary, I was fascinated and soon lost in a world of gladiators and Nero and Caesar and the Popes.

As the bus turned to cross the Pont D'i Angelo, Rebecca took my hand and pushed it up her skirt. She wasn't wearing any knickers and as the bus came into St Peter's Square, so did she, disguising her orgasm with a loud cough and a small "thank you".

I'd taken lots of photographs but Rebecca was reluctant to have her picture taken. I couldn't reconcile this with her lack of inhibition about sex or that fact that she'd had those professional photos taken to produce a profile picture for the Introduction Agency.

At the Spanish Steps I insisted on taking at least one photograph of her sitting on the fountain's low wall. The Steps are in an odd location, tucked down a side street off an unassuming Piazza. I have some wonderful photographs of Rebecca there. I persuaded her to allow a local to take a photograph of us together on my camera. I was slightly worried he might run off with it, but of course, he didn't. We threw a handful of Euros into the water.

I couldn't have been happier.

It was our final day. I wanted to organize a special dinner for our last night. The hotel had recommended the restaurant of the *Imperial Hotel* to us on arrival and on our second night we'd dropped in and had drunk Bellinis there. It was very luxurious. The bar was high-ceilinged, mirrors everywhere, columned. I'd caught Rebecca looking at herself several times in the many mirrors. We'd noticed the restaurant in passing.

The dining area was classic, intimate, and quietly opulent. Rebecca had been impressed and I knew she would enjoy eating there. It was mind-bogglingly expensive, but this was a special occasion. I didn't tell Rebecca where we were going, but in the small hotel room I indicated to her that it was going to be special.

"Ooh, not the fabulous hotel we had the cocktails in?" She'd guessed already.

"Yes," I said.

"Oh Simon you are wonderful," she had responded, throwing her arms around me.

"What's the time?" she said, looking at her watch. "Oh five o'clock. I must start getting ready," and she threw off her clothes and swept into the bathroom.

I knew she'd be hours so I settled down to watch TV. Italian TV is stuck in the 1970s; there's no political correctness at all, which is great!

I was trying to make sense of what looked like an Italian version of *Countdown*, but with a raft of contestants made up purely of super models. It was intriguing but baffling. The girls looked good though. I was flicking through the channels looking for the TV show where everyone had to strip naked, but maybe it was too early for that.

It was warm in the room so I leant over and opened one of the windows, it opened on a spindle. After spending a further 20 minutes channel surfing, checking my mobile and answering a few texts from Rick, Barry and my children, (all along the lines of "how are you?" "Are you having a nice and time?" "And when are you coming back?") I decided to start getting ready.

To my surprise, Rebecca was getting quicker at doing so and she was currently blow-drying her long blonde hair and applying make-up at the same time. She was completely naked.

As I headed for the shower and for a reason I still can't fathom, I asked Rebecca if she had picked up my camera. It occurred to me that I hadn't seen it for a while.

"No," Rebecca indicated, shaking her head having failed to make herself heard over the noise of the hair dryer.

It was only a small hotel room, but I started to panic. It was an expensive camera and the last time I remembered having it was at the Trevi Fountain. Like most couples on holiday, Rebecca's handbag had become a repository for my stuff as well.

"Is it in your bag?" I mouthed, holding this up and pointing at it.

"Have a look," she motioned back, hair dryer on blast furnace mode and this time with a hair grip in her mouth. I opened up the top of her brown soft leather bag, delved around a bit... no... it wasn't there. I moved over to my side of the bed, checked my things, mobile phone, wallet, reading glasses – no camera.

"Is it under the bed?" Yelled Rebecca. Now, quite why the camera would be under the bed, I don't know, but I bent down to have a look anyway.

"No," I said and straightened up.

Therein lay my mistake. I felt an agonizing pain to the crown of my head, a "crump "sound, felt something sharp, then all the lights went out. Not the lights in the room, my lights. I know people describe seeing stars. I experienced instant night.

When I came round I was aware of something warm and sticky all over my face, running in my eyes and Rebecca was screaming, "Oh my God, Simon, oh my God!"

As I had straightened up, a sharp corner of the open window had wedged itself in my head. I hadn't noticed that as the window opened outwards, a small portion of it remained, poking into the room. That was all for later, for now, I fell back on the bed and put my hands over the top of my head.

The blood spurted through my fingers, it was everywhere. Over me, all over the bed, a pool on the carpet. As my heart was beating faster so the blood was pumping faster, it was like a scene from *Carrie*. Rebecca grabbed the phone in the room and jabbed away at the buttons.

"Reception, reception!" she was screaming. "They're not answering, they're not answering, I'll run down to reception," I heard her say.

I couldn't reply, moving into and out of consciousness. Rebecca still naked headed for the door and then snatched the Burberry mac she'd brought and threw it on.

I don't know how long she was gone but I was next aware of the small hotel room being full of people wearing fluorescent jackets and a Policeman!

A medic examined me, gabbled away in Italian to his colleagues and then said to Rebecca in perfect English, "It's a deep cut, he'll need to go to hospital for some stitches, and we can't get a stretcher up here."

In my groggy state, three ambulance men helped me down the stairs and soon Rebecca and I were in the back of an ambulance hurtling towards the nearest A&E. The paramedics had tied a bandage around my head, but it hadn't stemmed the blood flow completely. The attendant with me was trying to help me to mop up some of the blood in my eyes. I had managed to pull on a white shirt and the grey trousers of my suit, the white shirt was sodden with blood. I imagined later I looked like a Christian victim of a Roman encounter with a lion at the Coliseum, though my throbbing head was still attached to the rest of me. Rebecca had phoned Katherine to tell her what had happened.

I understand she was sympathetic but also said matter-of-factly, "He's always doing things like that," which in fairness, being clumsy, I was.

The A&E department of the hospital I was taken to was pretty much like an English counterpart – distressed looking people, waiting areas littered with tired and bored looking relatives, fractious kids, the odd scream from a distant corridor. It didn't take that long to be seen by a charming Australian doctor. Rebecca explained what had happened, he said the wound would have to be sterilized and I'd need a few stitches, they'd have to shave some of my hair away.

'Oh God,' I thought, 'I'll look like a monk.'

On closer acquaintance however there one evident difference between this A&E and any other emergency department I'd been to in England (and I'd been in a few!). This one was filthy. I had to keep my head down and look at the floor whilst the doctor was examining my head then stitching the wound, and was thus in pole position to see used dressings on the floor, bits of bandage, grey puffballs of dust, clots of dried blood.

As he shaved away at my head, it added to the general mess. There was so much spilt, dried blood. It had the appearance of a field hospital in a forward position in Afghanistan, or how I imagined that would be, rather than a modern European city emergency unit. The Australian doctor mercifully injected my head with anaesthetic, which stung and was briefly painful but within a short time it was completely numb.

As he stapled my head with what sounded like a regular staple gun. *"Ddung… ddung… "* I felt pressure, no pain.

Inside an hour we were back on the street, I looked like the victim of a road accident, and even the taxi driver taking us back to the hotel seemed concerned about my appearance and no doubt his upholstery.

Rebecca still had her Burberry coat on buttoned through to her neck. Beneath this she was of course completely naked. No wonder the paramedics seemed to be giving her as much attention as me. Knowing how careful Rebecca was at getting in and out of vehicles, I'm sure they saw everything.

The management at the hotel were attentive and kind. Several of the staff came to help me in the door, the manager came up to see us and explained the bleeding obvious, pardon the pun, that yes, part of the window does jut into the room when it's opened fully.

Rebecca spoke up, indicating that this warning was slightly too late but she stopped short of threatening legal action.

The manager was keen to offer us a complimentary dinner in the hotel. I did half-heartedly say to Rebecca I was still happy to go to the Imperial, but she'd said "no, of course not" and "let's just pop downstairs and have something to eat". Then she unbuttoned her Burberry raincoat and added, "Give me a few minutes whilst I put on some clothes."

The next day we flew back to England. Me with a large plaster and dressing over the bald patch on my head and the mother of all headaches.

Arrivederci Rome. I'd had a fabulous time notwithstanding the trip to A&E.

From Russia with Love?

Rick was waving his fork about. We were back in the 'FishnChickn', the three of us. It had won a prestigious award in my absence and this had generated more local business. We were lucky to keep our old table.

As the fork moved, Rick spoke "We've not done this for ages have we Simon? Well Barry and I have, but you've been too busy with Rebecca, shagging in Norfolk and cutting your head open in Rome."

I gave him a sarcastic smile.

Barry, the voice of reason, chipped in and said, "So how's it going with Rebecca then, Simon, you've met her Mum and Dad and her daughter?"

I had. We got along well and I liked her very much. I thought she would get on well with Victoria and Daniel when they met.

He continued. "Here we are early November and what plans for Christmas? Take it you won't be going to Venice again?"

"No, not at all," I said. "It's all sorted, we're having a family Christmas in Norfolk with Rebecca's parents."

"Very nice, very sensible Simon," said Barry approvingly.

"They really are great people, her parents," I said. "I've taken to farming well."

Rick was now waving more forked food at me, "You a farmer? Never. You seem to be happy, though, I'll give you that. How's work going? I've not heard much about that lately. Had you had any posh cars to test, or now you've got your own posh car, are you not interested in cars?"

I'd had to admit the Mercedes SL was mine. I was slightly embarrassed that I'd spent so much money on it.

"Oh yeah what did you get that for? Just to impress Rebecca?" Rick had said.

"No," I tried. Well, it wasn't actually "no" it was more of a squeak.

"You're lying aren't you?" said Rick.

I didn't try to deny it, I had bought it to impress Rebecca.

"What was wrong with the Alfa?" asked Barry.

"Well it was coming up for three years old," I said, "and I don't need a big motor any more, the kids have their own cars, I just fancied something a bit sporty. You know wind in my hair whilst I've still got some."

"It's grown back now," said Rick.

"You don't look as much like Friar Tuck as you did. "

"But you love Alfas," said Barry.

"Well, I wouldn't say that," I said.

Rick coughed and banged his chest. "This is Rebecca's influence isn't it?" he spluttered. "How many times have you sat here and banged on about how wonderful Alfas are and how boring Mercs are. And another thing," Rick was waving a now empty fork. "Am I right in saying this is the first year you haven't been to see Elton John live somewhere?

"And it's nearly November," added Barry.

"Well," I said, "I've seen him a lot and anyway, Rebecca..."

"Doesn't like him," said Rick triumphantly, finishing my sentence.

There was no point in denying it, Rebecca didn't like him, though when we met she'd said she did. I think the truth was she didn't like him as much as me and given that I own every album, CD and DVD he's ever made and am a paid up member of his fan club "The Rocket Club" – that's a lot.

"Well, there's still time," I said, "maybe he'll do a Christmas concert and I'll take her to that and she'll change her mind."

I decided to tuck into my meal before the next volley of abuse.

As I attacked my cod and chips Barry said, "It's not that we don't like Rebecca, Simon, I mean we haven't met her yet of course, but you seem to be changing. I just hope she doesn't think that you're so besotted with her, you'll do anything she says."

"Well, I love her," I said, "and I want to be with her and it's all about give and take isn't it?"

Head down in his plate almost Rick mumbled, "There doesn't seem to be much take from what I can see."

My children had come round to see me as I was at the flat. They were grown up and sensible. Obviously they take after their mother. Both Dan and Victoria had coincidentally voiced their concerns that I appeared to be giving up some of the things I'd loved. I'd pointed out to them they were essentially trivial things and Rebecca had introduced me to other things that were important and special. Some, admittedly I could well have done without. But I didn't mention any of that stuff to my children obviously. I spoke instead about the farm.

I pointed out to the guys in the fish and chip shop that this weekend I was going up to Rebecca's and we were meeting her Mum and Dad's friends Jim and Anastasia and going to their farm for a meal. This meal had been arranged, cancelled and rearranged more than once and was finally destined to take place tomorrow.

"Good luck," they both said, as we said goodbye in the car park.

I realized that it had been months since we'd met up on a regular basis and I thought again ruefully how things had changed. I couldn't commit to another meal in the near future either. It was a shame.

The next morning I found myself back on the familiar two-hour drive up to Rebecca's. I knew the road so well M11, A10, I'd even got to grips with the new flyover at the Hardwick roundabout that goes in the wrong direction! King's Lynn Highway Department please take note.

Rebecca's voice cut into Michael Jackson again. I think it was "Smooth Criminal" this time. "Hi hun, where are you?" that trademark "cooh."

"Just pulled onto the A10," I said.

"Where?"

"Just pulled on to the A10.

"A11?"

" No, A10."

"Oh, how long will you be then if you're still on the M11?"

I muttered under my breath "for fuck's sake."

"What was that?"

"Nothing," I lied, "I'll be with you in about forty minutes, get the kettle on. I'll get cracking."

"Yes, okay. Bye then, see you soon."

The line disconnected and Michael Jackson's voice boomed through the car speakers again.

I'd given up trying to adjust telephone settings or trying to speak to Rebecca sensibly in noisy restaurants or shopping centres and always made sure that if I had something important to say, she was seated squarely in front of me.

And as I'm sure you've worked out, Rebecca was deaf. Not profoundly so but sufficiently impaired to warrant the use of two hearing aids, which of course she was always too vain or shy to wear, at least in my company.

If I picked her up from school I was now aware that she would dash straight into the bathroom when we reached hers. She rarely wore her hair back in a ponytail in front of me but loose. I'd realized that she wore hearing aids when I noticed that apart from frequently not hearing what I said, the insides of her ears were reddened sometimes.

On a trip out to Cambridge, delving into her handbag (with her permission of course) I found them.

"It's nothing to be ashamed of," my Mum used to say when talking about my Dad, who was profoundly deaf as a result of working in noisy factories without ear protection throughout his life. If alive today, he would receive compensation for such an avoidable affliction. Mum also said that it was dreadful but true that if you lost your sight you had everyone's sympathy but if you became deaf people found it amusing or a source of irritation.

It wouldn't have mattered remotely to me whether Rebecca wore her hearing aids when I was with her, whether they were visible or not. It would certainly have made life a lot easier. I never got to the bottom of how or why she was deaf and though I tried to talk to her about it she adamantly refused to discuss it. It was a "no go" area I couldn't negotiate a route through. It had become something about her that her that I'd got used to.

Then she rang back, "Hiya, where are you now?"

"Only about five miles from where I was when you last phoned," I said sarcastically.

"I forgot to say," she said, "I love you and I'm looking forward to seeing you, I haven't seen you for a whole week because I've been such a naughty girl and been studying so much."

She was studying for qualifications that would allow her to apply for senior management posts at school. She wanted to become a Head teacher. Rebecca finished with, "Well I'm looking forward to seeing you so be here as quick as I can. I'll be in the lounge waiting."

Now "being in the lounge waiting" had become shorthand for my being treated to something sexually and when Rebecca referred to herself being "naughty" this normally meant that she wanted me to spank her. I was getting quite good at it and her bottom was becoming as recognizable to me as her face. As I floored the accelerator I mused on what my special treat was. About twenty minutes later I pulled onto her drive.

It was dark and as the headlights of the Mercedes caught the window of her lounge I could see that it was lit but only dimly. I pulled my overnight bag out of the small boot and let myself in with my key.

"Hi Rebecca, it's me."

'Now, maybe I'm going deaf,' I thought when I heard Rebecca say something inaudible, and then like, "Hi. I'm in the lounge."

At least that was what I thought I heard, because her voice sounded faded, muffled. This was definitely a special night though because on the parquet flooring of the hallway she'd carefully placed a dozen or so tea light candles leading to the lounge door. The hall was in darkness and the lounge door was slightly open.

I sprinted towards the lounge door expecting to find Rebecca in one of her sexy uniforms. So far there'd been Rebecca dressed as an airhostess, a French maid, a school girl and a nurse greeting me. Conventional as dressing-up goes, but a lot of fun all the same.

As I flung the door open, I was wholly unprepared for what I saw. I stood, rooted to the spot, staring in her direction.

Rebecca had indeed chosen a new outfit to dress up in and greet me with and it was little wonder she couldn't speak intelligibly. She was wearing a black shiny rubber skin-tight suit.

Around her waist she had a large leather belt with inset punk rock style studs, the suit covered her from head to toe, the back of the head part of the suit was cut away and her blond hair was pulled through the opening. There were leather clasps all the way down her hair. She had on black gauntlet gloves with huge studs across the knuckles, thigh length leather boots with precipitous six inch stiletto heels, four inch platforms. In her mouth was what I later found out is a "ball gag". This was like a huge gobstopper or snooker ball, pink in colour and attached to leather straps. Her mouth was forced open and the ball was jammed in her open mouth attached to the leather straps which fastened in a large buckle at the back of her head. Over her eyes she had a cat woman style mask and in her hands she held her familiar riding crop.

When I did speak I just said, "Oh my God!" I just didn't know what to do.

Rebecca tried to speak but I couldn't understand what she was saying. I'd loved all her other outfits, but this one not only looked bizarre, it was alarming. I wondered how long it had taken for her to get into it all. I didn't find it remotely erotic. It looked ridiculous and painful.

I found it frankly a complete turn-off. I'm sure some guys will be reading this and thinking "you lucky sod, wish my missus would do that for me". I undid the ball gag in her mouth and the first thing she said was.

"You're supposed to keep that on. You don't like it do you? Oh that's typical," Rebecca said.

"Do you know how long it's taken me to get dressed up like this?"

"Hours?" I suggested.

"All for you because I wanted us to have a nice time together."

I was determined not to argue with her. "But you did mention about being naughty," so I grabbed the riding crop.

Rebecca demurred, smiled and let me lead her into the dining room. Why she always wanted me to use the riding crop on her in the dining room, I don't know. She could just as easily have bent over the back of the sofa. She leant flat on the dining room table and I brought the riding crop down on her latex covered bottom six times.

I then helped her out of her suit. We had sex in the hall with the rubber suit dangling round her ankles and her large breasts swaying from side to side, I hoped the doorbell didn't ring as we'd struggle to explain this to her Mum and Dad. Rebecca headed upstairs and showered, came down in her dressing gown and explained this evening's itinerary.

"We're heading round to Jim and Anastasia's. Mum and Dad are going to pick us up as we won't all get in your car and it would be too much of a squash in mine for dad."

"Great," I nodded.

Rebecca handed me a glass of wine, we'd started buying it in bulk from the local wine merchant now. She had kindly opened an account for me. And even more thoughtfully, she'd ordered a couple of bottles of Champagne to take round for Jim and Anastasia.

She'd also bought a new dress from "Goddards" in King's Lynn along with a new shirt and tie for me to wear that evening. I'd opened an account there at her suggestion. Though an expensive shop it was handy as they did sell lovely clothes and as Rebecca had pointed out, you normally get what you pay for.

I was relieved that we weren't going out for another expensive meal at *The Hoste* in Burnham Market – our favourite local restaurant as I was now speaking to Julian, my bank manager on a regular basis about my overdraft. Two bottles of champagne at £35 each were a lot less than a meal there.

I still felt wholly committed and attached to Rebecca, but something Rick and Barry had said in the fish shop, was bothering me. Apart from my children and my Uncle Colin, Rebecca hadn't met any other members of my family or friends. Was it my imagination, or was she avoiding doing so? Invitations to meet up with my friends were regularly side-lined and I sensed that she wasn't that bothered about meeting them or even Vicky and Dan, my children. I put it down to her busy work/study commitments; having a family nearby she saw regularly and little opportunity for trips to mine.

Now with Christmas coming, spending time in King's Lynn again, and my other friends making plans for Christmas, it didn't seem as if there'd be many opportunities to arrange for her to meet them any time soon.

'Ah well,' I thought, 'such is life.'

Richard and Delia arrived on cue at 7 o'clock. They always made a joke about ringing the doorbell now and I was glad, bearing in mind we seemed to have more sex in the dining room and lounge than we did in the bedroom.

Rebecca opened one of the bottles of Champagne and we all had a glass. Richard and I were soon once again engaged in conversation about the farm, what was growing, what was planted for next year, I even knew a bit about wholesale prices now and irrigation.

Delia complimented Rebecca on her new peach coloured dress and soon it was time to head off to Jim and Anastasias.

Jim's "farm" wasn't actually a farm at all. It was a property on a far grander scale than Richard's and his "farmhouse" was a detached honey coloured stone built Hall. This and the estate surrounding it were enclosed by a lengthy stone perimeter wall. There was a large circular gravelled driveway with a fountain. Rebecca had been right when she'd described it as remote.

I estimated the nearest house we'd passed along the quiet public road that then became Jim's private road was at least a couple of miles away. I had a quick look in the window of Jim's Bentley GT parked on the drive. I'd been fortunate enough to drive and write about one for a motoring magazine. I had been impressed by the car and written a positive piece. I was glad I wouldn't have to defend a poor review to my host.

Jim greeted us in the hallway. Now those of you "of a certain age" may recall the TV series *On the Buses* with Reg Varney as the driver? Well the conductor "Jack" played by actor Bob Grant had long teeth, a horse-like face and long scraggly hair. Reg Varney was "Stan" – Jim was the image of the conductor. But Jim was better dressed.

The hallway was lined with paintings of what I assumed were ancestors, there were mounted stag horns from some unfortunate deer that had ventured onto Jim's farm. I wondered if he had souvenirs of his ex-girlfriends as well. Jim greeted Delia and Richard, then got hold of Rebecca by both her arms, pinned them by her sides and gave her a long, maybe too long, kiss on the lips.

"You must be Simon," he said, thrusting his hand at me."

"Err, yes," I said.

"You lucky fellow," he said, nudging me in the ribs with his elbow.

"Rebecca's gorgeous isn't she?"

"Yes, she is rather," I said sounding like Hugh Grant.

Rebecca was straightening up her peach dress.

I did smile to myself and thought, 'Hmmm.'

I knew Rebecca had a strapless bra on, flesh coloured hold up stockings and nothing else underneath that dress. But anyway, enough of being smug.

"Welcome, welcome," he said.

"Come on in, Anastasia is still getting ready. I've some Champagne Richard, I know you love a bit of shampoo."

I was glad I wasn't driving. Looking round at this sumptuous house, I couldn't help thinking that Jim must be making an awful lot of money out of not farming.

"How are you getting on with your Bentley? " I asked.

"Oh that, I love the speed," said Jim. "I've just ordered another one," he said.

"How many have you had?" I said.

"Oh, this will be my fourth," he replied.

"Goodness," I said. "I hope they give you a discount."

Then everyone stopped talking and looked towards the lounge door. Anastasia had arrived.

She was probably in her early 40s but looked younger. She was indeed striking, with a statuesque hourglass figure and mid length jet-black hair. She was wearing an exotic green satin floor length dress. I gazed at her, probably for too long.

Jim threw his arms up and said, "Everyone I'd like you to meet the lovely Anastasia." She smiled and took a step forward. The green dress was slashed almost to her waist and a long black-stockinged leg appeared. I gulped. Rebecca looked at me and narrowed her eyes.

"Wow," I said involuntarily. Rebecca kicked me.

Before anyone could respond, a dapper portly red-faced fellow with long whiskered cheeks appeared, "Dinner is served," he announced.

"Thank you, shall we go in everyone, cook says she's done us proud," Jim said.

Anastasia still hadn't spoken. We crossed the hall into the mirror-lined dining room. Jim not only had staff but a butler as well. He hadn't been introduced but was clearly orchestrating the evening's events. Rebecca and I looked at one another.

"Wow?" said Rebecca sarcastically. I ignored her mimicry of me and simply said.

"This is nice," I leant towards her, "have you been here before?"

"It was a while ago," she replied. "All of it is new though, the furniture is different and I don't remember this room being here."

Richard and Delia were regular visitors to Jim's place and were clearly at home amongst the gilt and glamour. Still Anastasia hadn't spoken.

I whispered to Rebecca, "Does she speak any English?" Forgetting for a moment that she couldn't hear me.

"What?" she said loudly.

I coughed in an attempt to brush this aside.

Jim's butler was topping up our glasses and asking if we'd like red or white with the meal. I never did catch his name, so I shall call him "Mellors".

The dining table was interesting. It was completely transparent formed from a single sheet of glass. There was no tablecloth. We had individual "testers" upon decorated silver placemats. The table was probably a nightmare to clean, I considered. I was sure that that didn't bother Jim or Anastasia.

Our hosts sat at opposite ends of the table and Rebecca and I were seated opposite her Mum and Dad. Through the glass of the table I could see Anastasia had crossed her legs and I could just see an expanse of black-stockinged thigh. Richard looked at me and smiled.

'Oh my God' I thought, 'I hope he didn't catch me looking,' but he almost certainly had.

Jim was playing his part as host. "Another toast," he said, "to all my friends here at once." I raised my glass, assuming I was included in that. "And nice to see you as well, Simon," he said.

Finally, Anastasia spoke, "I understand you live in Surrey?" She said in a thick Russian accent. This was a lie Rebecca had told her parents when she had first introduced me to them, telling me it was because she thought they might not be impressed that I was from Essex! I had of course protested and said she couldn't be serious and that they would need to know the truth. The issue simply hadn't arisen for discussion since however though I wasn't prepared to leave it and Surrey would have to be explained eventually.

Clearly this misinformation had reached Jim and Anastasia.

Rebecca chipped in, "nearby don't you?" nodding at me furiously.

"Yes I said, nearby."

"Vot brings you to Norvok?" asked Anastasia politely.

"Well, err, this lovely lady," I said aware that I sounded like Hugh Grant again.

Rebecca nodded accepting my compliment though I doubt she even heard what I said.

Then Delia piped up, "Yes, Simon and our daughter, Rebecca," said Delia very clearly and slowly.

"Have been seeing one another for a few months now," Anastasia looked confused.

"They are an item," said Delia.

"Item?" repeated Anastasia even more confused now. "Vot is this item?"

Jim roared then spoke. " 'Item', you know like you and me are an 'item', we are together."

Anastasia remained perplexed.

Jim stood up, swigged some champagne and said, "You know, like you and me," pointing to her and then to him and thrusting his hips back and forwards.

Delia and Rebecca lowered their eyes. "Yes, I think we get the picture," said Delia.

Underneath her hand Rebecca said to me, "Oh my God, he's completely pissed, I think they spend all day drinking and shagging."

I decided to ask Anastasia a question and as the conversation died down I looked at her and asked her where she came from in Russia?

Anastasia took a while to process my question and then said, "Volgograd."

"Ah," said Rebecca. For one awful moment in time I thought she was going to say "is that where they make Volvos?" For a teacher her grasp of geography as well as history left a lot to be desired.

"Oh, how interesting," I said, "formerly Stalingrad, is that right?"

Anastasia smiled and seemed to warm to me. "You know your Russian history Simon?

"Oh, not really," I grinned and smiled. Rebecca looked at me and rolled her eyes.

Richard entered the conversation and said, "What's the main industry in Volgograd then, Anastasia?"

Anastasia glanced at Jim for a translation. "Industry, what do they make in Volgograd?" he said. Anastasia still looked blank.

I decided to try and help her out. "Tractors I believe, Richard," I offered. Anastasia leapt on that word and said, "Yes, tractors, we make tractors," and acted as though she was steering a wheel in front of her.

Jim got up again, "And lots of nice Russian ladies, hey?"

I thought for one dreadful moment he was going to start the humping thing again, but he sat down as our starter arrived, prawns and avocado.

The conversation seemed to start and then stop again.

I suspected Anastasia was having difficulty understanding us, she didn't join in and when asked a question she responded with a one word answer. I asked if she had children, she said "yes" and left it at that. She didn't ask if I had any.

She completely ignored Rebecca, which was probably just as well because the combination of Anastasia's broken English and Rebecca's deafness would have made a conversation between them farcical.

"Mellors" darted round the table, topping up our wine. Though Richard was driving he didn't stint on the wine.

I didn't realize quite how plastered Jim was. Every so often there was a toast to " absent friends". Then as we finished our main course, roast meats and turkey, with an enormous platter of vegetables, choices of potatoes, gravies and condiments, he spun in an odd arc out of the room, returned with a small gong, placed it on the table and struck it with his fork.

"Ladies and gentlemen, I have an announcement to make. I want my dear friends and Simon to be the first to know that Anastasia and I are engaged."

We all cheered and clapped.

"Not again," said Rebecca whilst we were clapping. "This must be the third one at least."

"That's wonderful, many congratulations," I said and offered a toast to the happy couple. I got slightly withering looks from Richard and Delia.

Jim now joined Anastasia at her end of the table.

"Did anyone bring their camera?" asked Richard. No one had.

"Well, I've got a camera on my phone," I offered.

"Good, let's have a photo then," Rebecca being camera-phobic was of course reluctant.

I still have the photo and I'm looking at it now. Richard and Delia, beaming away, Jim looking dishevelled and pissed, Anastasia looks serene and Rebecca, caught when she wasn't aware, angelic – almost. What a photo. What a story.

I wish I could tell you more about Anastasia but she kept herself very much to herself. Looking back now, I realize that Jim had had a succession of fiancés that he probably knew very little about. I still don't know if the girls became disenchanted or whether he got cold feet.

There was obviously more to Anastasia: Jim didn't speak Russian as Rebecca had said, he'd been to Volgograd once since he had met Anastasia. On that occasion he met her fifteen-year-old son who wasn't joining her in her new life in England and an ancient relative that Jim joked insensitively he was too pissed to remember.

He'd described the flat where her son lived and presumably Anastasia had before she met Jim, as a "shithole".

It would be easy to dismiss her as a fortune huntress but she was providing companionship and presumably affection and sex to Jim and they appeared, superficially at least, content with the arrangement. What price security, comfort, remittances to needy loved ones in their homeland? Maybe this relationship was going to succeed and perhaps for some men, like Jim, Russian male order brides make the perfect second wife.

I was relieved I'd met Rebecca and blessed that my internet search had only gone as far as King's Lynn and not as far as Volgograd.

After dessert, a stack of profiteroles and an apricot tart with cream, the ladies retired to the living room leaving myself, Jim and Richard to drink a glass of port. It was like a scene from *Downton Abbey*.

I didn't want port. I would have preferred to join the girls as I was more interested in learning about Anastasia than Jim.

I didn't dislike him. Not at this stage anyway.

He was a generous host, friendly and welcoming towards me but there was something about his treatment of Anastasia that I felt uneasy about. He was evidently very pleased with himself.

Understandably so. He was a successful wealthy guy, he'd got a youthful attractive girlfriend, an impressive home and a conspicuously luxurious lifestyle.

As he poured out drinks, without a hint of embarrassment Jim began extolling the virtues of Viagra. I thought it was a joke, but I was wrong. He was telling Richard, who looked increasingly aghast, that if he took two 50mg tablets, which he said he did all the time, he could stay hard all night and most of the morning. I could see Richard didn't know what to say, I didn't know what to say, I know lots of people do use them, but do they use them routinely?

"Do you get them from your Doctor?" asked Richard eventually.

"No, I get them off the internet."

"Have you ever tried them Simon?" asked Jim.

"Err, well, no I haven't," I said.

"Oh I'll get you some," he said blithely.

"Oh, no, but thanks anyway," I protested.

"Go on give Rebecca a real good time," he insisted.

It was my turn to be shocked. Suggesting that I should take the stuff was bad enough but doing so in front of her father! Then Richard asked him a profound question.

"Why do you have to go to Russia to get your girlfriends, Jim? There's plenty of girls round here and they're all made the same."

Jim attempted to pour more port for himself, missing his glass and slopping most of it over the glass table.

"Bugger that," he said. "I've had it with English birds, all they want is money, they're far too spoilt, most of them have got kids they want you to parent. No, these Russian birds are fantastic, and they f..."

Fortunately the door opened, it was Rebecca. I was the only one who stood up. "Hello darling," I said.

"I don't want to be a spoilsport, but I think it's probably time we were going," she said.

Jim answered for me, "We're only having a drink, don't bother us just now," he said rudely.

I felt offended on her account. Jim evidently had a jaundiced view of women. Apart from the house and the Bentley it's difficult to see what Anastasia saw in him. I'd love to know what she really thought and what her motives for being with him were. It had to be the money or lifestyle.

Out in the hallway Rebecca hissed at me, "It's bloody agonizing in here – she hasn't said a word... Mum and I are talking for the sake of it and she's just sitting there. It's really embarrassing! I want to go Simon. Jim's drunk and being disgusting."

I couldn't argue with that.

"Okay," I said, "I'll wrap it up as quickly as I can."

As I returned to the dining room Jim was recounting tales of Viagra fuelled sex sessions and describing how Anastasia could get her ankles right past her ears. I could tell that Richard didn't want to know.

Catching my eye Richard interjected and said that we really ought to be going.

"Jim thanks for a lovely evening." I held out my hand.

"Got to go already," he said.

"Oh well more time for "rumpy-pumpy". Anastasia!" He roared. Within a second she was standing next to him. "Our guests and Simon are going now."

Jim stayed where he was, Anastasia led us out into the hall, shook hands with Richard and Delia and Rebecca and then suddenly kissed me on both cheeks and said, "Goodbye Simon, nice to meet you."

In the car Rebecca was furious. We should all have been concentrating really hard because Richard had consumed at least one and a half bottles of wine and a lot of Champagne and I was worried he was going to take a side swipe at one of Jim's gate posts.

"Goodbye Simon, kiss, kiss," mocked Rebecca. "I don't know why you had to flirt with her all evening."

"I didn't flirt with her," I protested.

"Tractors! Former Stalingrad!" She minced.

"Well, I was just making conversation, that's more than you did," I retorted.

"Well, I've decided she's horrible," said Rebecca childishly.

"Well she's not that bad," I said, "think of it from her point of view."

"Oh I might have known you'd take her side, you could barely take your eyes off her legs!"

I was probably slightly guilty of that.

There are lots of Russian brides in the UK along with Thai and Filipino wives and there is a popular presumption that many aren't proper love matches? I wondered if statistically they might have the same measure of success as arranged marriages. Whether marriages of convenience involving Russian brides might with luck and in time result in them becoming loving married partners to cash-rich British men? Or is that a hopelessly romantic idea? Was what these women were seeking so different to the security and affection that Rebecca and I hoped to find and why did their aims seem so calculated when I'd gone to a dating agency to meet Rebecca?

In the town where I lived there was a Thai bride coffee morning group, there were so many Thai women living locally and there are many mixed couples from Eastern Europe in King's Lynn and Cambridgeshire.

What had shocked me most about the evening though was Jim's chauvinist attitude. Anastasia might as well have been his new Bentley or a piece of furniture.

As he'd so charmlessly put it when speaking to Richard, "Wives are like gadgets that you screw to the bed who do your housework."

'Good luck Anastasia,' I thought. 'You're going to need it.'

Rock & Dole

The Northern Rock crisis had rumbled on and with the financial climate in Europe deteriorating and our own economy struggling, things were clearly going downhill fast.

Multi-national corporations as well as High Street banks were in crisis, unemployment was rife, familiar high street businesses were careering into liquidation, house sales had stagnated.

Katherine and the children were still in the former marital home. It hadn't sold though it had been on the market for well over a year. She hadn't had anyone view it for months.

It was the first weekend in December and unusually Rebecca had stayed in the flat with me as she was due to attend a teaching training day and conference in London the following Monday. We'd been to a show at the Cliffs Pavilion in Southend-on-Sea.

It was 8.30am on the Monday when the landline rang. I was due to drive Rebecca to the train station to get her train for 9 o'clock so she was busy getting ready, clambering into tights and long boots.

It was my publisher's assistant Adrian. I couldn't understand why he was ringing so early. "Simon, sorry to ring so early," he said. "I just wondered what you were doing today."

"Err, well, I'm just running Rebecca to the station and then I've just got a few things to finish, I'm sorry I'm a bit behind."

Adrian said, "I think you should come up to our offices, there's a bit of a crisis going on."

"What sort of a crisis?" I said.

"Well, I can't say much over the phone, do you think you could get here for 10.30?" He sounded concerned.

I agreed, dressed hastily and joined Rebecca on the train into London. I was worried.

"Why does your publisher want to see you at such short notice?"

I decided to play it down, "Oh, I don't know, I'm normally behind with stuff."

She didn't delve further.

We arranged to keep in touch during the day and perhaps get something to eat in London before I returned home. Rebecca was due to travel back to King's Lynn via Liverpool Street as she had school the next day.

I got to my publishers office on Fenchurch Street in the City and could tell that something was wrong as soon as I stepped inside the book lined hallway.

Adrian looked ashen faced. "Simon thanks for coming. The partners are in a meeting at the moment."

He ushered me into a small side office. "Coffee?" he asked.

I nodded.

He returned with two cups, sat down opposite me and put his head in his hands. "I don't know what to say Simon, but I think we're going bust."

I'd suspected as much. Looking back my royalty cheques had stalled and I wasn't being prompted for outstanding work. It was still a shock though – hearing his words made my stomach flip. "Oh my God," I said. "Really?"

"I just wanted you to know," he said. The rest of the conversation between us was fragmentary and anxious. There wasn't much to say. Eventually one of the senior partners appeared and without any preamble simply said to the fifty or so staff now assembled that no decision as to the Publishing House's future was yet known. We would all be notified officially of what was happening within the next 48 hours.

I left the office feeling numb and wandered about in a daze watching everyone go about their business in the city. The *Evening News* headline summed it up: "Worst financial crisis in a generation," it read. I'd been so wrapped up in Rebecca I hadn't paid proper attention to the worsening financial climate and its impact on my work. I decided to ring Rick.

"Hello old boy," he said. "Where are you shagging at the moment?"

"Shut up," I said, "this is serious. I'm in London, looks like my publisher is going to go bust."

"What?" said Rick. "Oh my God, Simon how awful. Do they owe you a lot of money?"

"Enough," I said.

"What can I do to help?" For all of Rick's annoying habits and constant criticism of everything I do and worse, *Sir* Elton John, I know he's got my best interests at heart and would help in any crisis if he could. I felt a rush of gratitude.

"Thanks," I said, "I don't really know what's going to happen yet. Anyway, how's things in IT?"

"Pretty rough really, I've had a couple of customers go bust."

We agreed that Rick would come over that night so we could talk about things further, maybe even have an early fish and chip night. "I'll see if Barry's free," he said.

As soon as I'd ended the call, my mobile rang immediately. It was the bank. "Hi Simon, its Julian. I thought I'd give you a call about your overdraft." I'd been fobbing off Julian with tales of unfinished work and cheques for royalties on their way. "Have you chased up those unpaid fees and royalty cheques yet, or do you want me to do it for you?"

I felt very cold. I mumbled something unconvincing like, "I've not had a chance yet, I'll call you back," trying to get him off the phone. Being a friend as well as a Bank Manager, Julian had cut me some slack, but he was firm on this occasion and wouldn't be fobbed off. "You're way over your agreed overdraft limit Simon, you don't have anything left in your savings account."

I did a quick calculation in my head. Surely I was within my overdraft limit, still? There must be some mistake. I felt indignant.

"I'll just read you out the last few transactions on your account," Julian said, sensing my mood change. "You've been buying a lot of wine recently haven't you? There's a direct debit here going out to Clarkes of King's Lynn for £550, Goddard's Taylors £1650, two to *The Hoste* of over £250 each, and another direct debit to a gym in King's Lynn, you're nearly £5,000 over your overdraft limit, I'm getting some heat from upstairs Simon, you need to bring it down."

Rebecca's conference was being held at St. Pancras. The delegates were having a break for lunch and we met up in the Landmark Hotel. I'd been to the hotel before for a conference with Martin years earlier. It's an impressive building, originally two separate units they've built a domed glass roof over these flooding areas of the dining and public bar with light. It's a famous hotel and the developers in restoring original Victorian features have succeeded in creating a vibrant venue popular with European and International travellers. It is also expensive.

Rebecca came rushing in as always pleased to see me. "Hi Hun," she said breezily, "had a great morning, got on really well." She rattled on about some new-fangled teaching system that she'd been learning about. For once I wasn't hanging on her every word, I was completely distracted.

"How did you get on?" she said.

I wanted to tell her, after all we were a couple, a proper couple and hopefully we were going to spend the rest of our lives together. I needed to tell her what was going on in my life. But I didn't. I felt sick to my core but I was sure something would turn up. Once the house sold I could sort my debts out. Then I realized the payment on the SL Mercedes was due the next day. That was over £600.

I noticed that Rebecca had a large Karen Millen bag with her. "Hope you don't mind darling," she said following my gaze. "I bought the most divine coat from Karen Millen."

I'd given her my credit card a few weeks before. She got her purchase out to show me. I tried to be interested, as I normally was with any clothes she bought because she always looked so wonderful in them. It had cost over £400. £400 that I didn't have!

Rebecca had to return to her conference after our light lunch and I paid the bill – £65 for two glasses of wine, a couple of sandwiches and two coffees. Rebecca sensed something was wrong.

As we walked down the carpeted stairs to the exit doors of the hotel, she grabbed hold of me tightly and said, "Everything is okay Simon isn't it, you seem rather remote, is there anything I can do? I won't see you till Wednesday."

"No, I'm fine," I lied.

She whispered in my ear, "Would you like me to suck your cock for you?"

'I did,' I thought. But I was so anxious I didn't think it would stiffen up even under Rebecca's expert touch. I decided to head back to the flat straight away to gather my thoughts and think about what I was going to do.

Once there I found a sheet of paper and totted up my assets and debts. I knew I was spending heavily and had done for some months, but hadn't appreciated that my income had virtually dried up.

The rent on the flat was nearly £800 a month alone. Then there was food at Rebecca's and mine. I realized I'd been paying for practically all Rebecca's outgoings, including fuel, her dentist, clothes, her gym membership. I just couldn't afford it. I had to tell her that I was going to have to draw my horns in, crack on with work and find a new publisher. Or a regular job.

Barry rang as well and so did Martin that afternoon. I arranged to meet the boys at six o'clock at the FishnChickn. A crisis meeting.

Seated round our restaurant table, like we had done for so long, so regularly before I broke with tradition on meeting Rebecca, I poured out the whole sorry story; the fact that the bank were on my tail; what was happening with my publishers; the drop off in work commissions; the scale of my debts.

Barry as always gave me some sound advice. "Well, clearly you need to wait and see what happens with the publishers, start looking around now. There's no point hiding from the bank, make an appointment to see Julian and lay your cards on the table. Can you get out of the lease on that car?"

"I doubt it," I said, "I've only had it a few months."

"Well, ring Mercedes up and see what the deal is to take it back."

"But I need a car," I said. "I have to be able to get up to Rebecca's at least."

They both looked at one another.

"What's Rebecca's take on all this?" Rick asked.

"What do you mean?" I said.

"Well, a great deal of this money has been spent on her hasn't it? You need to tell her that things have got to change, have you spoken about living together?"

"Yes, of course," I said, shrilly.

Barry continued "Well, now would be the ideal time, it would save you all that money from living in the flat, you're only in it three or four nights a week now. If you're going to move in with her, move in. Start writing. If she really loves you and wants you to move in, that would be a way of halving your outgoings at least."

It made complete sense. We'd spoken about living together when the time was right and about getting married too. I loved her and King's Lynn and I'd be able to see more of my Uncle Colin. The kids could visit. There was space. Maybe this was the silver lining.

Saying goodbye to the guys in the car park that night, I felt heavy with anxiety. I knew that my personal financial crisis was embarrassing but all around me Companies were going bust. Lehman Brothers had failed spectacularly putting hundreds of highly paid merchant bankers out of work; factories and high street shops and businesses were closing on a daily basis.

Once inside the flat I decided to make the best of things, take a deep breath, phone Rebecca and tell her exactly what was going on.

'I couldn't do that without a drink,' I thought, reaching inside the fridge and grabbing a bottle of Chablis.

As I poured my first glass the phone rang. It was Ingrid.

"Hi Simon, haven't heard from you for ages so I thought I'd give you a ring. How's tricks? You still in lurve with Rebecca?"

It was so good to hear her voice, her deep voice. I poured out all my troubles to her.

"I'm so sorry to hear that, Simon," she said. "It's been a really tough time financially for me too actually, but I've got some money put by, if you need any help, let me know."

"That's so kind Ingrid," I said. I meant it. "But don't worry, I don't think things are that bad."

I rehearsed my plan of speaking to Rebecca, telling her all about it and in my script she agreed that it made no sense living where I did anymore. My life was destined to be in King's Lynn with her and we should live together.

"Just ring her up and tell her," Ingrid had said when I discussed my plan with her.

I laughed, "Well it's not all that easy," I said explaining about the difficulty we had in communicating by phone. "I find going to see Rebecca easier because she doesn't hear all that well."

"Get it sorted out," Ingrid had said. "Let me know what happens and I'll come and see you and Rebecca in sunny King's Lynn."

She really cheered me up. She often e-mailed and sent texts now, seeing how I was getting on, caring about me. I'd hear about her boyfriends (and girlfriends) from time to time.

I decided to plan what I was going to do, it was now late Monday evening and whilst I'd been at the fish and chip shop and on the phone to Ingrid, Rebecca had sent some texts along the lines of: "Hope you're having a really good time with the boys, I'm exhausted after my trip to London and I'm off to bed." And "Thanks for my lovely coat, I'll ring you from school tomorrow, look forward to seeing you on Wednesday. All my love, Rebecca xxx".

I had managed to fend off two further calls from Julian I had just said firmly, "Look, I've made quite a lot of money so can you just calm down."

"Well, I will do Simon, but we need some money paid in soon otherwise we're going to have to start returning cheques," he'd said finally.

I remembered I had a small amount of money in a building society, only about £1,000. It was rainy day money and at the moment it was pouring. It took me a while to find the debit card for the account. Then I felt worried. It was a building society and a small one at that. What if they'd gone bust? Fortunately they hadn't.

I found a hole in the wall machine that accepted their card and drew out £300, stuffed it into my wallet, filled the Mercedes up at Asdas, (£75), and spent Tuesday scouring the internet for a new publisher.

I completed all of my outstanding work and editing and ironically did the best days work in probably a year. I still couldn't bring myself to speak to Rebecca. I'd managed to do an online transfer to pay for another month's rental of the Mercedes.

As I pressed "confirm" I closed my eyes. Had Julian already placed a bar on my current account? But the transfer went through. I fell into bed exhausted. I hardly slept.

I was anxious to get up to Rebecca's as soon as possible the following day. I was tired and couldn't face the journey late in the day when traffic would be heavy.

I decided to surprise her by meeting her from school at 3.30pm. I could leave at noon and have a stop en route. Driving up to Rebecca's this time I didn't play any music. I was deep in thought. I wasn't used to being hard up and was trying to come to terms with the fact that my financial future was in total disarray.

It was now official: my publishers were going into administration and the liquidators would be in touch shortly. Since I was an unsecured creditor and well down a long list of these the likelihood was that I would receive nothing. I calculated I had lost about £82,000.

I decided to take my time with the drive and reflect on my situation. It had been a turbulent couple of years, from the decline of my marriage and separation, those early beginnings in the flat, meeting Niamh on the singles holiday in Venice last Christmas, the saga that was Shilpa, Ingrid. It had taken me so long to find Rebecca, but did I want a future with her? Yes I did.

I had a few reservations about some of the sexual stuff and her jealous nature would prove difficult, but I was getting used to her ways. I loved her and I thought her Mum and Dad were great. I got on well with her daughter. I felt Richard and Delia would understand. Richard was constantly thanking me for making his daughter happy and I genuinely enjoyed his company and spending time with him on the farm. I believed this was mutual and that he liked me too.

"It really is a pleasure," I said. "She makes me really happy."

So even though things were tough financially, suddenly and unusually fate was pushing me against the open door of where I wanted to be. Living with Rebecca.

Outside the village of Sketchley there is a small lay-by on the exit from the roundabout and it's the first mile marker to King's Lynn on the A10. "King's Lynn 31 miles" it reads.

Paul Fox

I decided to stop and stretch my legs. I was too early.

I pulled my coat round me and wandered along looking at the December skyline. It was a cold grey afternoon. I could make out Christmas tree lights in some nearby homes.

'Marriage' I thought, 'that's it.'

I'd spoken to Rebecca about being married one day, but hadn't of course formally proposed to her. I'd had an idea I'd take her somewhere exotic, Paris, Venice, New York and pop the question. But it seemed so right now.

I didn't want to just move in, I wanted us to be married. We were both free to marry, my divorce had come through months ago and she'd been divorced for over two years. We needn't have a big "do", not until I'd got myself back on my feet anyway. We could even have it at the Conservative Club at King's Lynn. It was Christmas, I'd almost forgotten, it was Christmas. In just two weeks' time.

Marching back to the car briskly, throwing my coat onto the passenger seat, I flipped through my selection of Elton CDs and found one from the 1980s that seemed to say it all. As I wheel-spun away from the lay-by Elton belted out "Are you ready for love".

There's a small florists on the corner of the Wootton Road where I'd bought Rebecca flowers a few times.

'You can't really ask someone to marry you without a bunch of flowers," I thought. Looking at the dwindling cash in my wallet though, instead of a dozen red roses I settled on a classic – a single red rose.

The sales assistant Sarah, said, "Oh, Rebecca's a lucky girl."

I very nearly said, "Yes, I'm going to ask her to marry me," but resisted the temptation. It was still too early to drive to Rebecca's school so I decided to see if my Uncle Colin was about.

His van was outside his flat and I rang the bell. "Bloody hell," he said. "Come on in Simon. You're all in a rush. What's occurring?"

I blurted out, "Publishers gone bust, but I'm going to ask Rebecca to marry me."

Uncle Colin advised caution. "Do you think that's wise Simon? I mean isn't it worth at least putting all your cards on the table first?"

"Well, I'm going to, I've no intention of deceiving her, it's only a temporary blip, I'll be back on my feet in no time."

"Well, I'm sure you will," said wise Uncle Colin. "But just see how the land lies. I mean are you sure she's that keen on you moving in?"

386

"Keen?" I said, "She's practically begged me to move in in the last couple of months."

"Really!" said Uncle Colin. I decided that I would take his advice though and not overwhelm Rebecca with everything at once. It was nearly 3.15pm. I said goodbye and as I parted he counselled, "Just take it easy and let me know what happens."

"I will do," I said.

I waited outside the school gates clutching my red rose. Several pupils walked past nudging one another and giggling. I heard one of them say, "that's Miss's boyfriend, he's ever so rich."

'Huh,' I thought, 'if you only knew!'

And there she was. She was surprised to see me but seemed delighted, quickly released her hair from its ponytail and pulled her loosened tresses around her ears.

"Simon," said Rebecca. "You're early. What a lovely rose, thank you."

"Well I've got so much to tell you," I said.

"Oh really? Well, I'll just get my car and..."

"Don't worry about your car," I said, "just jump in." I didn't want to go to her home, so we drove to the *Rose and Crown* at Snettisham. It's a comfortable friendly old-fashioned pub.

Long before I had met Rebecca me, Katherine and the kids in company with my parents had enjoyed many family meals there. I felt a close affinity to it – my local in Norfolk. It represented security – a port in a storm I suppose.

I ordered two glasses of the house Champagne (£14!), turning round to look at Rebecca I couldn't stop myself from smiling. She was so lovely. I did wonder whether she had her crotchless knickers on underneath her school skirt, but quickly checked myself, I had serious business to discuss with her.

"Oooh," Rebecca cooed, "cheers, are we celebrating?"

"Hmm, well, sort of," I said, "could be. So much has happened and I just wanted to tell you about it."

"Hmm," said Rebecca. "Tell me about it then." She had developed a habit of repeating the last words I'd said, maybe it was a way of checking she'd heard properly.

Suddenly I didn't know how to say what I had to say. I took a couple of deep breaths but still nothing. Rebecca was smiling and tilting her head to one side.

"Go on Simon what did you want to tell me?"

It spilled out. All at once. I told her everything, the publishers going bust, how hard up I was, how I felt about her, how much I loved her, and it would make sense for me to move in if she'd have me.

It was going really well, Rebecca was just nodding and smiling, moving her head from side to side. I thought I'd go for it. "Then maybe Rebecca, we could well, you know..."

"You know what?" said Rebecca immediately.

"Well, maybe we could get married. After all we've spoken about it enough haven't we? I could help your dad out on the farm, I can drive a tractor," I said jokingly.

"Hmmm," said Rebecca clasping both my hands in hers. "So let's just get this right. The publishers have gone bust and they owe you a lot of money?"

"Yes, "I said.

"And your lovely car's going to have to go back?"

"Well, yes," I said, "but it's only a car, ha ha."

"And you think we should get married?"

"Well, in time maybe. I will get back on my feet."

I'd been sitting talking to Rebecca for more than an hour and a half now. She stood up, "I'm just going to the ladies," she announced. She was gone a long time. I looked round the small bar, its whitewashed walls and plain wooden tables seemed to be closing in on me.

A few locals were coming into the bar some dressed in farm gear, others in suits probably just off the train from London. I decided to go and find Rebecca. When I did, she wasn't in the toilet.

She was in the car park on her mobile phone. "No, really," she was saying.

I didn't know who she was talking to. I leant out to touch her to let her know I was there, that I wasn't creeping up on her. She pulled away,

"Oh, I've… I've got to go now," she said, stuttering into her phone.

"Darling, I said. Are you okay?" I was worried.

"I need to go home, Simon," said Rebecca shortly. "You'd better take me to my car."

I drove to the school car park. Rebecca got out and without a word marched to her car. I followed her the short distance to her home and parked my car next to hers in its usual place on the driveway.

I thought that all I'd said was bound to have come as a shock, as it had to me. Maybe I'd said too much. That was it, she'd had a long day at school, and the last thing she'd want to hear was my problems, why had I been so insensitive? I had wanted to reach out and touch her, I wanted some reassurance that everything was going to be okay, but I knew instinctively it wasn't. It was far from okay. Instead of ripping her clothes off and having sex on the kitchen floor, or advising me how naughty she'd been that day and taking her across my lap, we tiptoed around one another.

Every time I tried to get close to Rebecca, she moved away. She half-heartedly put the kettle on and then went upstairs for ages.

I drifted into the lounge. She had started putting Christmas decorations up. Should I wait in the lounge? Should I go upstairs and talk to her? Should I just go? I felt dreadful. Tears were welling up in my eyes as I realized I'd made a big mistake. I reached into my pocket for a handkerchief just as I heard Rebecca coming down the stairs slowly.

She normally ran up and down the stairs, but this time she was taking one step at a time. When she reached the foot of the stairs I realized why. She was carrying my clothes.

Over the months I'd left suits and shirts and jeans, pants and socks, various after shaves, cufflinks. I'd even had a section in one of her wardrobes. That was what she'd been doing, clearing out my section of the wardrobe. I just looked at her and she dropped my clothes. She'd also been crying. We stood looking at one another for what seemed like ages. One of us had to speak.

It was me. "Why Rebecca?"

"Why?" She rounded on me. "What do you mean why? You're broke and you think you can just move in here, just like that? Do you take me for some kind of fool Simon?" Her words stung me.

"No of course not," I said, "I thought we were going to get married anyway? I love you Rebecca, I thought you loved me?"

"I don't know what my Mum and Dad are going to say," she said, "they really liked you."

"And I really like them," I said. "In case you haven't noticed Rebecca, there's a lot of financial hardship about – I'll find another publisher or a job."

I felt a powerful urge to get away, quickly. I felt as though I could throw up.

I'd spent so much time in this house with her. We'd enjoyed many happy times together in it, relaxing, sharing meals, having sex, listening to music, talking and drinking wine in the lounge in the summer with the doors and windows open wide, entertaining her parents on the lawn; mornings we'd laid in bed till lunchtime. I realized it was all over.

"I suppose I'd better go then," I said.

"Yes, you better had," said Rebecca who turned and ran upstairs crying.

In a daze I began to pick my things up, I made two trips to the car. Rebecca was still upstairs. I couldn't just leave like this, surely she wouldn't want that, surely she'd come to her senses? I'd been good to her, I'd been kind to her, I'd given her everything I could, more than I could.

I went upstairs. Rebecca was lying sobbing on her bed, the large bed I was so familiar with. She dabbed her eyes as I stood at the bedroom door.

"Do you really want me to go?" I said.

"No," said Rebecca.

"Thank God for that," I said. "I'll stay then. I'll stay forever if you like."

My heart leapt. It had been an awful shock for her. A few more tears and we'd sit, talk calmly, drink some wine and make plans.

Rebecca rose. Walking past me she made her way down the stairs. I followed her. I was confused. I'd left the front door open and chill air was filling the hallway.

"Of course I don't want you to go," she spat, "but I can't have a broke boyfriend!" Her face was twisted with fury.

I thought I was going to faint. I wanted to scream but couldn't even speak.

I summoned all the dignity I could and while she had her face buried in her hands, I kissed the back of her head and said, "Goodbye Rebecca."

I started the car and drove to the end of the road. I couldn't see as the tears in my eyes were obscuring my vision. There was only one place I could go in such a state. I drove to Uncle Colin's.

As he opened the door I just stood on the doorstep and sobbed. He put his arm round me. "I take it she didn't take the news too well then?"

I tried to laugh. "No," I said unnecessarily. "Not all that well."

The End of the Beginning

I stayed with Uncle Colin that night and he did his best to console me. As I drove back to Essex the following morning, I knew I wouldn't see Rebecca again. I'd had a text from her that evening saying that she was sorry and that maybe we should talk in a week or so, that she'd get the remaining few bits I'd left at hers together and maybe I could do the same with her things that were at mine when I got back to the flat.

I'd phoned Rick the night before and his reaction wasn't typical. I expected him to say something like "fucking bitch" or whatever but he just said, "Aah, that's a shame, I know you were really keen on her mate, give me a ring when you're back and I'll pop round."

Getting back to the flat was dispiriting. To make it worse, wherever I looked I saw traces of Rebecca. I'd encouraged her to leave things at the flat.

When there alone I used to enjoy going into the bathroom and seeing her toothbrush, perfume and make up lying around. It was confirmation that I was in a relationship and even though she rarely visited, there'd been a gradual build up over the months of clothes perfume, scarves, bits and pieces that were hers.

I decided to gather them up quickly, I had a spare box from moving in and put them in that and then ceremoniously put them in the spare room. I phoned the children and they came round to see me. It was difficult telling them everything. I kept the financial issues confidential but decided they were old enough to know about what had happened so I brought them up to date with how things had fallen apart and how the relationship with Rebecca had ended.

I was dreading Christmas.

I felt numb. Everyone rallied around and I was fortunate enough to spend the day with friends.

The previous year my fears of being the spare singleton had led me to Venice. This year I was grateful for the fact that I could spend Christmas, Boxing Day and "Twixtmas" with old friends.

I'd had an email from Niamh telling me of her plans for a singles holiday in Prague and wishing me a "first wonderful Christmas" with Rebecca.

Paul Fox

I couldn't bring myself to email her about what had happened so simply sent her a message wishing her a lovely time in Wenceslas Square.

Ingrid phoned from Barbados and tried to get me on a plane to go out and see her. I didn't tell her that I couldn't afford to buy the kids presents, let alone the return airfare to visit her. If I had she would have insisted on paying for me to go. I didn't want that.

It's not easy being alone at Christmas even amongst friends.

When I turned on the radio, Mud's "Lonely this Christmas" seemed to be on a loop playing on every channel and when I put random-play on my CD collection, there was Elton singing "Cold as Christmas in the Middle of the Year". At midnight Mass I was pleased to see Judy who was accompanied by a tall, tanned good-looking guy. I assumed correctly he was her husband. I thought she might ignore me but she didn't. She nodded and smiled.

I returned to my old routine of going to the gym, meeting the guys on a Friday night for fish and chips, seeing my children, emailing friends I'd lost touch with, listening to Elton on my sound system. I looked on the internet at dating sites again, but my heart wasn't in it.

I did manage to find a job, selling cars for a local BMW dealership. I was lucky to get this and did so only because I knew the manager there and he knew of my work as a motoring journalist. I had to work long hours and earned little, but it was a job, I could pay my rent, start sorting out my debts and I was grateful for it.

Since writing this I've realized several things.

Firstly, I don't regret anything that happened to me. I had some entertaining experiences when dating. I'd made new friends and had enjoyed exchanging emails with women I'd been introduced to. It had helped me cope in the early months of being newly single.

Dating had served to confirm what I already knew and to appreciate what I had. I don't think many of the women I'd met through the internet were truly interested in finding someone to settle down with. Like me most had or were developing settled lives and routines. They wanted an occasional companion, the confidence of being found desirable, sex, someone to take to formal dinners possibly, but not more. Well, perhaps a kitchen fitter! There's nothing wrong with that obviously, if it's understood by both parties. I know many women feel this about men they meet online.

I had believed Rebecca was different and I suppose that was what hurt most. We'd met through an introduction service and while it gave us an opportunity to meet it obviously wasn't a guarantee of an enduring relationship, let alone marriage however compatible we might appear.

I'd been hopelessly blind and naïve. In the cold light of day I think what Rebecca wanted was a man comfortably off with cast iron financial security, to dine and have sex with, accompany her on holidays and pick up a lot of her bills. I was okay with that up to a point but I thought that we were in a loving relationship and a "couple" at a stage where, if we encountered a problem, we'd work at resolving it. That we would get through tough times as well as enjoying good ones. I thought she loved me as I did her. I had genuinely believed that we were destined to marry one day.

I was hoping to see her when we did the exchange of one another's stuff, maybe sit down and talk. Not persuade her to take me back or anything like that. Just talk. I missed her.

I borrowed one of the demonstrators from the BMW garage I worked at and drove up one weekend to King's Lynn, the cardboard box of her personal possessions in the boot. I'd sent a text to say I would deliver her things. On the way my phone message signal sounded It was a text from Rebecca. I pulled into the layby, the same one that I'd pulled into on the fateful day before Christmas, when I was going to ask her to marry me. How different this journey was.

I looked at my phone and her text simply read, "Your things are in the garage, take them and leave mine please. Rebecca." No "x".

And that's what I did. On arriving at her house I pulled up the door of the unlocked garage and there were a few clothes, a couple of suits, toothbrush, after shave, a couple of pairs of socks and pants I'd left along with a book I'd bought at the King's Lynn market I'd been half way through.

I left her box in the same place, pulled the garage doors shut and took one last look at the house. I knew she was inside watching me and I wanted to knock on the door and maybe I should have done. She was definitely inside. Her car was on the drive, but I just got in mine and drove away.

A harder decision was to decide whether to see her parents or not. I wanted to, but I was certain Rebecca would be against it and I didn't want to embarrass them. The reality was that I'd not only formed a relationship with Rebecca but had enjoyed a bond with her parents as well. As I drove along the Wootton bypass I decided not to call in and see Richard and Delia.

The envelopes from *Across the Room* kept coming, the personal introduction service spitting out "suitable dates". When every so often one of the Agency's expensive looking envelopes arrived they remained unopened on the desk on the mezzanine floor.

Then one morning an envelope arrived and I did open it. It contained a profile and a series of professionally taken photographs. Rebecca's details again! She'd renewed her registration. Those large blue eyes gazing at me were all the confirmation I needed. It was over and I needed to move on.

That Friday at the 'FishnChickn' I spoke to Rick and Barry about what I felt.

Barry was the first to give advice. "Well, Simon, you've tried pretty much everything, speed dating, internet dating, singles holidays, personal introduction agencies and blind dates with friends... and you're still on your own."

"Yes," said Rick, "but look on the bright side, you've done loads of shagging!"

Barry ignored him and continued. "So why don't you do what I suggested a year and a half ago, calm down, relax, meet someone in your own good time and just let it happen. Don't say 'no' to anything; accept all invitations you receive and don't rush in thinking it's going to be wedding bells after the first date."

Rick with a forkful of chip pointed at me had the final say: "Steer clear of nutters, gold diggers, lesbians and kinky sex merchants and you'll be fine."

As I walked back to the flat I decided that that was exactly what I was going to do. I was not going to take part in any more internet dating, I was just going to live my life and see what happened. After trudging up the stairs and letting myself into the flat the phone rang.

It was Rick. "Oh I forgot to ask you something earlier," he said.

"What's that then?" I asked.

"Yeah, look old boy. Do you fancy going to a football game?"

"Rick, you know I hate football," I said.

"Well, I know that but it's just a game and it'll give you something to do and stop you moping about the flat won't it. And you have just told Barry you won't say 'no' to any invitations... "

"Yeah, okay then, when is it?" I sighed, defeated.

"Tomorrow," he said.

"I'll pick you up at 7.30am."

"7.30!?!" I said, "Where is this game?"

"We're off to Stockport."

"Stockport!" I said. "Where on this God forsaken earth is Stockport? Are you seriously asking me to go with you to Stockport and to a football match? It's a stupid idea. You know how much I loathe the game. And it'll be freezing. In fact, now I come to think about it, wasn't Stockport the place where they made hats using mercury a couple of centuries ago? The poison caused the poor sods who worked with the stuff to go insane. That's where the phrase 'mad as a hatter originates! Victoria did a project on it years ago." I took a breath.

Rick spoke. "Anyway, back on planet earth, I'll pick you up at half-seven," he stated.

I was stuck and obviously going to Stockport. Prawn sandwiches for afternoon tea!

"Rick I am never going to meet anyone in Stockport."

But do you know something? It turns out that Stockport is the most romantic location in the UK. That's a fact. Well it is for me.

At a football match in a far-flung Northern Town and with Rick and Beryl in tow I met someone truly special. She was at the game for prawn sandwiches too. And she owns and drives a Lexus.

And on a more intimate acquaintance they aren't that bad after all.

www.ingramcontent.com/pod-product-compliance
Lightning Source LLC
LaVergne TN
LVHW021121080426
835509LV00011B/1365